FREE Study Skills Videos/DVD Offer

Dear Customer,

Thank you for your purchase from Mometrix! We consider it an honor and a privilege that you have purchased our product and we want to ensure your satisfaction.

As part of our ongoing effort to meet the needs of test takers, we have developed a set of Study Skills Videos that we would like to give you for FREE. These videos cover our *best practices* for getting ready for your exam, from how to use our study materials to how to best prepare for the day of the test.

All that we ask is that you email us with feedback that would describe your experience so far with our product. Good, bad, or indifferent, we want to know what you think!

To get your FREE Study Skills Videos, you can use the **QR code** below, or send us an **email** at studyvideos@mometrix.com with *FREE VIDEOS* in the subject line and the following information in the body of the email:

- The name of the product you purchased.
- Your product rating on a scale of 1-5, with 5 being the highest rating.
- Your feedback. It can be long, short, or anything in between. We just want to know your impressions and experience so far with our product. (Good feedback might include how our study material met your needs and ways we might be able to make it even better. You could highlight features that you found helpful or features that you think we should add.)

If you have any questions or concerns, please don't hesitate to contact me directly.

Thanks again!

Sincerely,

Jay Willis
Vice President
jay.willis@mometrix.com
1-800-673-8175

SCAN HERE

Texas Property and Casualty Insurance License Exam Prep 2025-2026

3 Full-Length Practice Tests

Secrets Study Guide and Review

Detailed Answer Explanations

Written and edited by Matthew Bowling

Printed in the United States of America

This paper meets the requirements of ANSI/NISO Z39.48-1992 (Permanence of Paper).

Mometrix offers volume discount pricing to institutions. For more information or a price quote, please contact our sales department at sales@mometrix.com or 888-248-1219.

Mometrix Media LLC is not affiliated with or endorsed by any official testing organization. All organizational and test names are trademarks of their respective owners.

Paperback
ISBN 13: 978-1-5167-2770-4
ISBN 10: 1-5167-2770-3

DEAR FUTURE EXAM SUCCESS STORY

First of all, **THANK YOU** for purchasing Mometrix study materials!

Second, congratulations! You are one of the few determined test-takers who are committed to doing whatever it takes to excel on your exam. **You have come to the right place.** We developed these study materials with one goal in mind: to deliver you the information you need in a format that's concise and easy to use.

In addition to optimizing your guide for the content of the test, we've outlined our recommended steps for breaking down the preparation process into small, attainable goals so you can make sure you stay on track.

We've also analyzed the entire test-taking process, identifying the most common pitfalls and showing how you can overcome them and be ready for any curveball the test throws you.

Standardized testing is one of the biggest obstacles on your road to success, which only increases the importance of doing well in the high-pressure, high-stakes environment of test day. Your results on this test could have a significant impact on your future, and this guide provides the information and practical advice to help you achieve your full potential on test day.

Your success is our success

We would love to hear from you! If you would like to share the story of your exam success or if you have any questions or comments in regard to our products, please contact us at **800-673-8175** or **support@mometrix.com**.

Thanks again for your business and we wish you continued success!

Sincerely,
The Mometrix Test Preparation Team

TABLE OF CONTENTS

Introduction

Thank you for purchasing this resource! You have made the choice to prepare yourself for a test that could have a huge impact on your future, and this guide is designed to help you be fully ready for test day. Obviously, it's important to have a solid understanding of the test material, but you also need to be prepared for the unique environment and stressors of the test, so that you can perform to the best of your abilities.

For this purpose, the first section that appears in this guide is the **Secret Keys**. We've devoted countless hours to meticulously researching what works and what doesn't, and we've boiled down our findings to the five most impactful steps you can take to improve your performance on the test. We start at the beginning with study planning and move through the preparation process, all the way to the testing strategies that will help you get the most out of what you know when you're finally sitting in front of the test.

We recommend that you start preparing for your test as far in advance as possible. However, if you've bought this guide as a last-minute study resource and only have a few days before your test, we recommend that you skip over the first two Secret Keys since they address a long-term study plan.

If you struggle with **test anxiety**, we strongly encourage you to check out our recommendations for how you can overcome it. Test anxiety is a formidable foe, but it can be beaten, and we want to make sure you have the tools you need to defeat it.

1

Secret Key #1 – Plan Big, Study Small

There's a lot riding on your performance. If you want to ace this test, you're going to need to keep your skills sharp and the material fresh in your mind. You need a plan that lets you review everything you need to know while still fitting in your schedule. We'll break this strategy down into three categories.

Information Organization

Start with the information you already have: the official test outline. From this, you can make a complete list of all the concepts you need to cover before the test. Organize these concepts into groups that can be studied together, and create a list of any related vocabulary you need to learn so you can brush up on any difficult terms. You'll want to keep this vocabulary list handy once you actually start studying since you may need to add to it along the way.

Time Management

Once you have your set of study concepts, decide how to spread them out over the time you have left before the test. Break your study plan into small, clear goals so you have a manageable task for each day and know exactly what you're doing. Then just focus on one small step at a time. When you manage your time this way, you don't need to spend hours at a time studying. Studying a small block of content for a short period each day helps you retain information better and avoid stressing over how much you have left to do. You can relax knowing that you have a plan to cover everything in time. In order for this strategy to be effective though, you have to start studying early and stick to your schedule. Avoid the exhaustion and futility that comes from last-minute cramming!

Study Environment

The environment you study in has a big impact on your learning. Studying in a coffee shop, while probably more enjoyable, is not likely to be as fruitful as studying in a quiet room. It's important to keep distractions to a minimum. You're only planning to study for a short block of time, so make the most of it. Don't pause to check your phone or get up to find a snack. It's also important to **avoid multitasking**. Research has consistently shown that multitasking will make your studying dramatically less effective. Your study area should also be comfortable and well-lit so you don't have the distraction of straining your eyes or sitting on an uncomfortable chair.

 The time of day you study is also important. You want to be rested and alert. Don't wait until just before bedtime. Study when you'll be most likely to comprehend and remember. Even better, if you know what time of day your test will be, set that time aside for study. That way your brain will be used to working on that subject at that specific time and you'll have a better chance of recalling information.

Finally, it can be helpful to team up with others who are studying for the same test. Your actual studying should be done in as isolated an environment as possible, but the work of organizing the information and setting up the study plan can be divided up. In between study sessions, you can discuss with your teammates the concepts that you're all studying and quiz each other on the details. Just be sure that your teammates are as serious about the test as you are. If you find that your study time is being replaced with social time, you might need to find a new team.

2

Secret Key #2 – Make Your Studying Count

You're devoting a lot of time and effort to preparing for this test, so you want to be absolutely certain it will pay off. This means doing more than just reading the content and hoping you can remember it on test day. It's important to make every minute of study count. There are two main areas you can focus on to make your studying count.

Retention

It doesn't matter how much time you study if you can't remember the material. You need to make sure you are retaining the concepts. To check your retention of the information you're learning, try recalling it at later times with minimal prompting. Try carrying around flashcards and glance at one or two from time to time or ask a friend who's also studying for the test to quiz you.

To enhance your retention, look for ways to put the information into practice so that you can apply it rather than simply recalling it. If you're using the information in practical ways, it will be much easier to remember. Similarly, it helps to solidify a concept in your mind if you're not only reading it to yourself but also explaining it to someone else. Ask a friend to let you teach them about a concept you're a little shaky on (or speak aloud to an imaginary audience if necessary). As you try to summarize, define, give examples, and answer your friend's questions, you'll understand the concepts better and they will stay with you longer. Finally, step back for a big picture view and ask yourself how each piece of information fits with the whole subject. When you link the different concepts together and see them working together as a whole, it's easier to remember the individual components.

Finally, practice showing your work on any multi-step problems, even if you're just studying. Writing out each step you take to solve a problem will help solidify the process in your mind, and you'll be more likely to remember it during the test.

Modality

Modality simply refers to the means or method by which you study. Choosing a study modality that fits your own individual learning style is crucial. No two people learn best in exactly the same way, so it's important to know your strengths and use them to your advantage.

For example, if you learn best by visualization, focus on visualizing a concept in your mind and draw an image or a diagram. Try color-coding your notes, illustrating them, or creating symbols that will trigger your mind to recall a learned concept. If you learn best by hearing or discussing information, find a study partner who learns the same way or read aloud to yourself. Think about how to put the information in your own words. Imagine that you are giving a lecture on the topic and record yourself so you can listen to it later.

For any learning style, flashcards can be helpful. Organize the information so you can take advantage of spare moments to review. Underline key words or phrases. Use different colors for different categories. Mnemonic devices (such as creating a short list in which every item starts with the same letter) can also help with retention. Find what works best for you and use it to store the information in your mind most effectively and easily.

3

Secret Key #3 – Practice the Right Way

Your success on test day depends not only on how many hours you put into preparing, but also on whether you prepared the right way. It's good to check along the way to see if your studying is paying off. One of the most effective ways to do this is by taking practice tests to evaluate your progress. Practice tests are useful because they show exactly where you need to improve. Every time you take a practice test, pay special attention to these three groups of questions:

- The questions you got wrong
- The questions you had to guess on, even if you guessed right
- The questions you found difficult or slow to work through

This will show you exactly what your weak areas are, and where you need to devote more study time. Ask yourself why each of these questions gave you trouble. Was it because you didn't understand the material? Was it because you didn't remember the vocabulary? Do you need more repetitions on this type of question to build speed and confidence? Dig into those questions and figure out how you can strengthen your weak areas as you go back to review the material.

 Additionally, many practice tests have a section explaining the answer choices. It can be tempting to read the explanation and think that you now have a good understanding of the concept. However, an explanation likely only covers part of the question's broader context. Even if the explanation makes perfect sense, **go back and investigate** every concept related to the question until you're positive you have a thorough understanding.

As you go along, keep in mind that the practice test is just that: practice. Memorizing these questions and answers will not be very helpful on the actual test because it is unlikely to have any of the same exact questions. If you only know the right answers to the sample questions, you won't be prepared for the real thing. **Study the concepts** until you understand them fully, and then you'll be able to answer any question that shows up on the test.

It's important to wait on the practice tests until you're ready. If you take a test on your first day of study, you may be overwhelmed by the amount of material covered and how much you need to learn. Work up to it gradually.

On test day, you'll need to be prepared for answering questions, managing your time, and using the test-taking strategies you've learned. It's a lot to balance, like a mental marathon that will have a big impact on your future. Like training for a marathon, you'll need to start slowly and work your way up. When test day arrives, you'll be ready.

Start with the strategies you've read in the first two Secret Keys—plan your course and study in the way that works best for you. If you have time, consider using multiple study resources to get different approaches to the same concepts. It can be helpful to see difficult concepts from more than one angle. Then find a good source for practice tests. Many times, the test website will suggest potential study resources or provide sample tests.

Practice Test Strategy

If you're able to find at least three practice tests, we recommend this strategy:

UNTIMED AND OPEN-BOOK PRACTICE

Take the first test with no time constraints and with your notes and study guide handy. Take your time and focus on applying the strategies you've learned.

TIMED AND OPEN-BOOK PRACTICE

Take the second practice test open-book as well, but set a timer and practice pacing yourself to finish in time.

TIMED AND CLOSED-BOOK PRACTICE

Take any other practice tests as if it were test day. Set a timer and put away your study materials. Sit at a table or desk in a quiet room, imagine yourself at the testing center, and answer questions as quickly and accurately as possible.

Keep repeating timed and closed-book tests on a regular basis until you run out of practice tests or it's time for the actual test. Your mind will be ready for the schedule and stress of test day, and you'll be able to focus on recalling the material you've learned.

5

Secret Key #4 – Pace Yourself

Once you're fully prepared for the material on the test, your biggest challenge on test day will be managing your time. Just knowing that the clock is ticking can make you panic even if you have plenty of time left. Work on pacing yourself so you can build confidence against the time constraints of the exam. Pacing is a difficult skill to master, especially in a high-pressure environment, so **practice is vital**.

Set time expectations for your pace based on how much time is available. For example, if a section has 60 questions and the time limit is 30 minutes, you know you have to average 30 seconds or less per question in order to answer them all. Although 30 seconds is the hard limit, set 25 seconds per question as your goal, so you reserve extra time to spend on harder questions. When you budget extra time for the harder questions, you no longer have any reason to stress when those questions take longer to answer.

Don't let this time expectation distract you from working through the test at a calm, steady pace, but keep it in mind so you don't spend too much time on any one question. Recognize that taking extra time on one question you don't understand may keep you from answering two that you do understand later in the test. If your time limit for a question is up and you're still not sure of the answer, mark it and move on, and come back to it later if the time and the test format allow. If the testing format doesn't allow you to return to earlier questions, just make an educated guess; then put it out of your mind and move on.

On the easier questions, be careful not to rush. It may seem wise to hurry through them so you have more time for the challenging ones, but it's not worth missing one if you know the concept and just didn't take the time to read the question fully. Work efficiently but make sure you understand the question and have looked at all of the answer choices, since more than one may seem right at first.

Even if you're paying attention to the time, you may find yourself a little behind at some point. You should speed up to get back on track, but do so wisely. Don't panic; just take a few seconds less on each question until you're caught up. Don't guess without thinking, but do look through the answer choices and eliminate any you know are wrong. If you can get down to two choices, it is often worthwhile to guess from those. Once you've chosen an answer, move on and don't dwell on any that you skipped or had to hurry through. If a question was taking too long, chances are it was one of the harder ones, so you weren't as likely to get it right anyway.

On the other hand, if you find yourself getting ahead of schedule, it may be beneficial to slow down a little. The more quickly you work, the more likely you are to make a careless mistake that will affect your score. You've budgeted time for each question, so don't be afraid to spend that time. Practice an efficient but careful pace to get the most out of the time you have.

Secret Key #5 – Have a Plan for Guessing

When you're taking the test, you may find yourself stuck on a question. Some of the answer choices seem better than others, but you don't see the one answer choice that is obviously correct. What do you do?

The scenario described above is very common, yet most test takers have not effectively prepared for it. Developing and practicing a plan for guessing may be one of the single most effective uses of your time as you get ready for the exam.

In developing your plan for guessing, there are three questions to address:

- When should you start the guessing process?
- How should you narrow down the choices?
- Which answer should you choose?

When to Start the Guessing Process

Unless your plan for guessing is to select C every time (which, despite its merits, is not what we recommend), you need to leave yourself enough time to apply your answer elimination strategies. Since you have a limited amount of time for each question, that means that if you're going to give yourself the best shot at guessing correctly, you have to decide quickly whether or not you will guess.

Of course, the best-case scenario is that you don't have to guess at all, so first, see if you can answer the question based on your knowledge of the subject and basic reasoning skills. Focus on the key words in the question and try to jog your memory of related topics. Give yourself a chance to bring the knowledge to mind, but once you realize that you don't have (or you can't access) the knowledge you need to answer the question, it's time to start the guessing process.

It's almost always better to start the guessing process too early than too late. It only takes a few seconds to remember something and answer the question from knowledge. Carefully eliminating wrong answer choices takes longer. Plus, going through the process of eliminating answer choices can actually help jog your memory.

Summary: Start the guessing process as soon as you decide that you can't answer the question based on your knowledge.

7

How to Narrow Down the Choices

The next chapter in this book (**Test-Taking Strategies**) includes a wide range of strategies for how to approach questions and how to look for answer choices to eliminate. You will definitely want to read those carefully, practice them, and figure out which ones work best for you. Here though, we're going to address a mindset rather than a particular strategy.

Your odds of guessing an answer correctly depend on how many options you are choosing from.

Number of options left	5	4	3	2	1
Odds of guessing correctly	20%	25%	33%	50%	100%

You can see from this chart just how valuable it is to be able to eliminate incorrect answers and make an educated guess, but there are two things that many test takers do that cause them to miss out on the benefits of guessing:

- Accidentally eliminating the correct answer
- Selecting an answer based on an impression

We'll look at the first one here, and the second one in the next section.

To avoid accidentally eliminating the correct answer, we recommend a thought exercise called **the $5 challenge**. In this challenge, you only eliminate an answer choice from contention if you are willing to bet $5 on it being wrong. Why $5? Five dollars is a small but not insignificant amount of money. It's an amount you could afford to lose but wouldn't want to throw away. And while losing

$5 once might not hurt too much, doing it twenty times will set you back $100. In the same way, each small decision you make—eliminating a choice here, guessing on a question there—won't by itself impact your score very much, but when you put them all together, they can make a big difference. By holding each answer choice elimination decision to a higher standard, you can reduce the risk of accidentally eliminating the correct answer.

The $5 challenge can also be applied in a positive sense: If you are willing to bet $5 that an answer choice *is* correct, go ahead and mark it as correct.

Summary: Only eliminate an answer choice if you are willing to bet $5 that it is wrong.

8

Which Answer to Choose

You're taking the test. You've run into a hard question and decided you'll have to guess. You've eliminated all the answer choices you're willing to bet $5 on. Now you have to pick an answer. Why do we even need to talk about this? Why can't you just pick whichever one you feel like when the time comes?

The answer to these questions is that if you don't come into the test with a plan, you'll rely on your impression to select an answer choice, and if you do that, you risk falling into a trap. The test writers know that everyone who takes their test will be guessing on some of the questions, so they intentionally write wrong answer choices to seem plausible. You still have to pick an answer though, and if the wrong answer choices are designed to look right, how can you ever be sure that you're not falling for their trap? The best solution we've found to this dilemma is to take the decision out of your hands entirely. Here is the process we recommend:

Once you've eliminated any choices that you are confident (willing to bet $5) are wrong, select the first remaining choice as your answer.

Whether you choose to select the first remaining choice, the second, or the last, the important thing is that you use some preselected standard. Using this approach guarantees that you will not be enticed into selecting an answer choice that looks right, because you are not basing your decision on how the answer choices look.

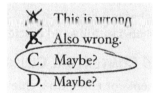

This is not meant to make you question your knowledge. Instead, it is to help you recognize the difference between your knowledge and your impressions. There's a huge difference between thinking an answer is right because of what you know, and thinking an answer is right because it looks or sounds like it should be right.

Summary: To ensure that your selection is appropriately random, make a predetermined selection from among all answer choices you have not eliminated.

Test-Taking Strategies

This section contains a list of test-taking strategies that you may find helpful as you work through the test. By taking what you know and applying logical thought, you can maximize your chances of answering any question correctly!

It is very important to realize that every question is different and every person is different: no single strategy will work on every question, and no single strategy will work for every person. That's why we've included all of them here, so you can try them out and determine which ones work best for different types of questions and which ones work best for you.

Question Strategies

☑ READ CAREFULLY

Read the question and the answer choices carefully. Don't miss the question because you misread the terms. You have plenty of time to read each question thoroughly and make sure you understand what is being asked. Yet a happy medium must be attained, so don't waste too much time. You must read carefully and efficiently.

☑ CONTEXTUAL CLUES

Look for contextual clues. If the question includes a word you are not familiar with, look at the immediate context for some indication of what the word might mean. Contextual clues can often give you all the information you need to decipher the meaning of an unfamiliar word. Even if you can't determine the meaning, you may be able to narrow down the possibilities enough to make a solid guess at the answer to the question.

☑ PREFIXES

If you're having trouble with a word in the question or answer choices, try dissecting it. Take advantage of every clue that the word might include. Prefixes can be a huge help. Usually, they allow you to determine a basic meaning. *Pre-* means before, *post-* means after, *pro-* is positive, *de-* is negative. From prefixes, you can get an idea of the general meaning of the word and try to put it into context.

☑ HEDGE WORDS

Watch out for critical hedge words, such as *likely, may, can, sometimes, often, almost, mostly, usually, generally, rarely,* and *sometimes.* Question writers insert these hedge phrases to cover every possibility. Often an answer choice will be wrong simply because it leaves no room for exception. Be on guard for answer choices that have definitive words such as *exactly* and *always.*

☑ SWITCHBACK WORDS

Stay alert for *switchbacks.* These are the words and phrases frequently used to alert you to shifts in thought. The most common switchback words are *but, although,* and *however.* Others include *nevertheless, on the other hand, even though, while, in spite of, despite,* and *regardless of.* Switchback words are important to catch because they can change the direction of the question or an answer choice.

✓ FACE VALUE

When in doubt, use common sense. Accept the situation in the problem at face value. Don't read too much into it. These problems will not require you to make wild assumptions. If you have to go beyond creativity and warp time or space in order to have an answer choice fit the question, then you should move on and consider the other answer choices. These are normal problems rooted in reality. The applicable relationship or explanation may not be readily apparent, but it is there for you to figure out. Use your common sense to interpret anything that isn't clear.

Answer Choice Strategies

✓ ANSWER SELECTION

The most thorough way to pick an answer choice is to identify and eliminate wrong answers until only one is left, then confirm it is the correct answer. Sometimes an answer choice may immediately seem right, but be careful. The test writers will usually put more than one reasonable answer choice on each question, so take a second to read all of them and make sure that the other choices are not equally obvious. As long as you have time left, it is better to read every answer choice than to pick the first one that looks right without checking the others.

✓ ANSWER CHOICE FAMILIES

An answer choice family consists of two (in rare cases, three) answer choices that are very similar in construction and cannot all be true at the same time. If you see two answer choices that are direct opposites or parallels, one of them is usually the correct answer. For instance, if one answer choice says that quantity x increases and another either says that quantity x decreases (opposite) or says that quantity y increases (parallel), then those answer choices would fall into the same family. An answer choice that doesn't match the construction of the answer choice family is more likely to be incorrect. Most questions will not have answer choice families, but when they do appear, you should be prepared to recognize them.

✓ ELIMINATE ANSWERS

Eliminate answer choices as soon as you realize they are wrong, but make sure you consider all possibilities. If you are eliminating answer choices and realize that the last one you are left with is also wrong, don't panic. Start over and consider each choice again. There may be something you missed the first time that you will realize on the second pass.

✓ AVOID FACT TRAPS

Don't be distracted by an answer choice that is factually true but doesn't answer the question. You are looking for the choice that answers the question. Stay focused on what the question is asking for so you don't accidentally pick an answer that is true but incorrect. Always go back to the question and make sure the answer choice you've selected actually answers the question and is not merely a true statement.

✓ EXTREME STATEMENTS

In general, you should avoid answers that put forth extreme actions as standard practice or proclaim controversial ideas as established fact. An answer choice that states the "process should be used in certain situations, if..." is much more likely to be correct than one that states the "process should be discontinued completely." The first is a calm rational statement and doesn't even make a definitive, uncompromising stance, using a hedge word *if* to provide wiggle room, whereas the second choice is far more extreme.

⊘ BENCHMARK

As you read through the answer choices and you come across one that seems to answer the question well, mentally select that answer choice. This is not your final answer, but it's the one that will help you evaluate the other answer choices. The one that you selected is your benchmark or standard for judging each of the other answer choices. Every other answer choice must be compared to your benchmark. That choice is correct until proven otherwise by another answer choice beating it. If you find a better answer, then that one becomes your new benchmark. Once you've decided that no other choice answers the question as well as your benchmark, you have your final answer.

⊘ PREDICT THE ANSWER

Before you even start looking at the answer choices, it is often best to try to predict the answer. When you come up with the answer on your own, it is easier to avoid distractions and traps because you will know exactly what to look for. The right answer choice is unlikely to be word-for-word what you came up with, but it should be a close match. Even if you are confident that you have the right answer, you should still take the time to read each option before moving on.

General Strategies

⊘ TOUGH QUESTIONS

If you are stumped on a problem or it appears too hard or too difficult, don't waste time. Move on! Remember though, if you can quickly check for obviously incorrect answer choices, your chances of guessing correctly are greatly improved. Before you completely give up, at least try to knock out a couple of possible answers. Eliminate what you can and then guess at the remaining answer choices before moving on.

⊘ CHECK YOUR WORK

Since you will probably not know every term listed and the answer to every question, it is important that you get credit for the ones that you do know. Don't miss any questions through careless mistakes. If at all possible, try to take a second to look back over your answer selection and make sure you've selected the correct answer choice and haven't made a costly careless mistake (such as marking an answer choice that you didn't mean to mark). This quick double check should more than pay for itself in caught mistakes for the time it costs.

⊘ PACE YOURSELF

It's easy to be overwhelmed when you're looking at a page full of questions; your mind is confused and full of random thoughts, and the clock is ticking down faster than you would like. Calm down and maintain the pace that you have set for yourself. Especially as you get down to the last few minutes of the test, don't let the small numbers on the clock make you panic. As long as you are on track by monitoring your pace, you are guaranteed to have time for each question.

⊘ DON'T RUSH

It is very easy to make errors when you are in a hurry. Maintaining a fast pace in answering questions is pointless if it makes you miss questions that you would have gotten right otherwise. Test writers like to include distracting information and wrong answers that seem right. Taking a little extra time to avoid careless mistakes can make all the difference in your test score. Find a pace that allows you to be confident in the answers that you select.

⊘ Keep Moving

Panicking will not help you pass the test, so do your best to stay calm and keep moving. Taking deep breaths and going through the answer elimination steps you practiced can help to break through a stress barrier and keep your pace.

Final Notes

The combination of a solid foundation of content knowledge and the confidence that comes from practicing your plan for applying that knowledge is the key to maximizing your performance on test day. As your foundation of content knowledge is built up and strengthened, you'll find that the strategies included in this chapter become more and more effective in helping you quickly sift through the distractions and traps of the test to isolate the correct answer.

Now that you're preparing to move forward into the test content chapters of this book, be sure to keep your goal in mind. As you read, think about how you will be able to apply this information on the test. If you've already seen sample questions for the test and you have an idea of the question format and style, try to come up with questions of your own that you can answer based on what you're reading. This will give you valuable practice applying your knowledge in the same ways you can expect to on test day.

Good luck and good studying!

General Insurance Terms and Concepts

INSURANCE OVERVIEW AND RELATED CONCEPTS

Insurance is a method of transferring risk. Organizations purchase insurance contracts from third parties, who in turn assume responsibility for any loss or liability associated with a particular risk event if it occurs. Fire insurance, for example, covers any losses caused by fire damage. In most cases, an insurance company charges a premium for its services and distributes damage payments from the combined premiums collected from all organizations. To calculate premiums, loss ratios, and other insurance information for a specific policy, the insurance company must collect risk data from a group of similar items. For instance, when determining the theft insurance premium for a particular home, an insurance company calculates the total number of thefts in a population of similar homes. According to the **law of large numbers**, larger populations allow for more accurate calculations, while smaller populations result in less accurate calculations. Using statistics, one can make assumptions about what an average value will be based on the information known. The basic principle of the law of large numbers is that the larger a statistical sample gets, the closer the average of the sample gets to the expected value, so long as the expected value was accurate. If a large sample does not align with the expected value, that is an indication that the expectation was inaccurate.

RISK

Risk is the likelihood that an organization will incur some type of loss. It only applies to uncertain and unpredictable events, such as theft, accidental damage, or weather damage. Organizations can handle risk using a variety of strategies:

- **Avoidance**—The risk is avoided. For instance, an organization can avoid earthquake damage simply by not building near fault lines.
- **Reduction**—The loss associated with the risk is reduced. A possible reduction strategy would be installing a security fence in an effort to reduce the number of burglary attempts.
- **Transference**—The responsibility for a risk is transferred to a third party, usually in exchange for financial compensation. The most common method of transferring risk is through acquiring an insurance policy that covers the specific types of risk a person or organization has. Another transference strategy is using a **hold harmless agreement**, in which a contractor agrees to accept responsibility and liability if a particular event should occur.
- **Retention (or acceptance)**—An organization does nothing to mitigate the risk. It simply accepts any consequences, losses, or liabilities associated with a particular risk event.
- **Sharing**—The risk is shared across a number of people or organizations, as with group health insurance.

Not all risks are insurable. In most cases, a person or organization cannot acquire insurance for a risk unless the following criteria are present:

- The person or organization must have an **insurable interest** in the risk.
- The risk must be **pure**, not **speculative**.
- The risk must be accidental and unexpected.
- For the purpose of setting a policy period, the risk must be constrained to a definite place and time.

15

- The risk must involve substantial loss for the insured with the likelihood of financial hardship for the person or organization.
- The insurance company must be able to calculate any loss incurred as a result of the risk event.
- The person or organization must be able to afford the insurance premiums.
- The law of large numbers must apply to determine the predictability of loss due to a certain risk. Otherwise, the insurance company will not be able to calculate premiums due to a lack of cases.

An **insurable interest** must be present before insurance can be acquired. A person or organization only possesses an insurable interest if they stand to suffer a financial loss when the insured item is damaged or destroyed. Insurable interest is not limited solely to property. In the context of insurance, a person can have an insurable interest in another person, especially for the purposes of life insurance. A married couple may purchase life insurance policies for each other because each party would be negatively affected financially if the other passed away suddenly.

A **speculative risk** is any risk that offers an opportunity for both gain and loss. Speculative risks are **not coverable** by insurance. An example of a speculative risk is a stock market investment.

A **pure risk** is any risk that presents only the opportunity for loss and is the only type of risk covered by insurance. Examples of pure risks include theft and fire.

PERILS AND HAZARDS

The intention of insurance is to provide a protection against the harm that would be caused by a specific peril. **Perils** are the actual events that create loss, such as adverse weather, natural disasters, theft, industrial accidents, and fires. A peril is different from a risk in that the risk refers to the likelihood that a particular loss will occur.

A **hazard** is a factor that increases the chance of loss. For the purposes of insurance, there are three main types of hazards to consider:

- **Physical hazard**—This applies to the usage, occupancy, and state of the actual property. Flammable construction material is an example of a physical hazard.
- **Moral hazard**—This describes a person's inclination for dishonest or illegal behavior so that they may receive a financial benefit. For example, people may damage their own property or mislead the insurance company in the hopes of getting money. Fraud is a common moral hazard in the insurance domain.
- **Morale hazard**—This applies to losses resulting from the careless or irresponsible behavior of a person. In terms of insurance, a morale hazard may be present when a person behaves in a manner more reckless than they typically would due to the knowledge that insurance is available to cover losses that may occur.

OBLIGATIONS AND DUTIES OF AN INSURER

Insurance companies have special duties and obligations to their customers due to the nature of the insurance business. The insurance industry is highly regulated to ensure that insurers fulfill their duties and obligations when conducting business. These include:

- **Performing the duties outlined** in the applicable insurance policy
- **Fair dealing and good faith**—An insurance company must always treat their customers' best interests with the same consideration as their own. Insurance companies who act in bad faith are at risk for lawsuits, regulatory penalties, and even license revocation.

- **Claims duties**—Insurers are legally obligated to adequately investigate claims, issue claim payments promptly, and ensure that policyholders have the information necessary to make decisions regarding claims.
- **Duty to defend**—If provided for in the policy purchased, the insurance company must provide a defense for matters covered under the policy. This is usually fulfilled by paying for legal counsel to handle any lawsuit brought against an insured.
- **Duty to indemnify**—This goes hand in hand with the duty to defend. This requires the insurer to pay any settlements or judgments on behalf of the insured when there is a covered loss.

CONTRACTS

A **contract** is an agreement between two or more parties, all of whom are competent to represent themselves, to exchange things of value or refrain from doing a particular thing. The **offeror** is the party who initiates the contract process by making an offer to another party. The **offeree** is the party to which the offer to enter into a contract is made. A contract is not considered valid if it requires one of the parties to do something that is either legally or actually impossible. A contract must have several important characteristics to be legally enforceable. There must be:

- An offer and acceptance of the offer
- Consideration
- Mutual assent
- **Capacity** and **competency** of all parties involved
- Legal purpose

OFFERS

In order for a **contract offer** to be considered valid, it must meet three requirements:

- It must have **serious intent** to assure the offeree that the offeror is intending to enter into a binding agreement.
- It must be **expressed clearly** and in **reasonably definite** terms to eliminate any doubt regarding the intentions of the offeror.
- It must be **communicated** to the offeree through whatever means are desirable and convenient. The communication of a contract offer may be **expressed** or **implied**.

When the offeree **accepts** a contract offer, he or she agrees to be bound by the terms established by the offeror. No one other than the offeree may accept the offer. By accepting the offer, the offeree is indicating that he or she accepts all of the terms stated in the offer. This is known as the **mirror image rule**, meaning that the terms expressed in the acceptance are an exact duplicate of the terms expressed in the offer. In some cases, the offeree does not need to make a verbal or written acceptance in order for his or her agreement to be established. Under these circumstances, an **implied acceptance** is sufficient.

CONSIDERATION

A contract is not rendered valid solely by the acceptance of an offer. It must also entail an exchange of either **benefits** or **sacrifices** by the parties. The exchange of things of value is known as **consideration**. When one of the parties to a contract does not receive consideration, the contract cannot be considered binding. Consideration must involve a **mutual exchange** of gains and losses by the parties to the contract. When the contract requires a party to refrain from exercising a legal right, this is called **forbearance**. For the consideration outlined in a contract to be legitimate, it must meet three criteria:

- It must be **bargained for**, meaning that one promise is made in exchange for another promise, act, or forbearance.
- It must be **adequate**, meaning that the consideration offered is something of value.
- It cannot require any party to perform an **illegal act** or involve **illegal goods**.

MUTUAL ASSENT

For a contract to be valid, there must be **mutual assent**. All involved parties must agree to all the terms of the contract. Mutual assent can only exist when all parties understand all the terms of the contract and willingly agree to abide by them.

CAPACITY AND COMPETENCY

In order for a contract to be considered valid, all parties must have **capacity,** meaning they must have the legal ability to enter into a contract. A person is considered to have such ability if he or she is **well-informed** about the contract and possesses **free will**. A person's capacity may be challenged if he or she is a minor. All parties must also conform to the legal definition of **competency**. The agreements entered into by a mentally impaired person or a severely intoxicated person may be rendered invalid if such parties are deemed to not be mentally competent to agree to the terms of the contract.

LEGAL PURPOSE

Finally, a contract must serve a **legal purpose** to be binding under the law. A contract will not be considered valid if it requires one or more parties to perform **illegal acts**. The court system will not enforce any contract that requires the performance of an unlawful act or involves use or handling of illegal items. Furthermore, agreements that run contrary to **public policy** are unenforceable. For example, agreements to obstruct justice, interfere with public service, or defraud creditors will all be rendered invalid.

TYPES OF CONTRACTS

Adhesion contracts involve situations where one party has more power in drafting the contract than the other party. Insurance contracts are considered contracts of adhesion because the insurance provider writes contractual provisions with little or no input from the insured party, who simply agrees to the terms. Unfortunately, adhesive contracts often use ambiguous language. This can leave the insured party confused about the exact terms and conditions of the contract. In cases where ambiguity creates confusion, courts normally rule in favor of the insured.

Aleatory contracts are those in which the exchange of value between the two parties may be unequal. Insurance contracts are aleatory because their payout is based on the occurrence of an uncertain event. If the event never occurs, the insured party never receives any financial benefits in exchange for their premium payments. If the event does occur, the insurance company may pay out more than it has received in premiums.

Conditional contracts include provisions that both parties must fulfill. In the case of insurance contracts, the first condition the policyholder must fulfill is paying the premiums for the policy. In the event of a loss, the insured party must alert the insurance provider. Then, the insurance provider must assess the damage and determine a value amount according to the methods set forth in the contract.

Personal contracts are those that only apply to the specific party that enters into the contract. These contracts usually involve conditions that can only be performed by that particular party.

Unilateral contracts are those in which the offeree is not explicitly named. Only one party promises to do something in return for the performance of a particular act, and the contract is considered accepted when the action is performed.

Bilateral contracts are those in which both the offeror and offeree make promises within the contract. For a bilateral contract to have been satisfied, both parties must have performed their duties in accordance with the terms of the contract.

INSURANCE CONTRACTS

An **insurance contract** is a legally binding agreement between an insurance provider and a party seeking insurance coverage. It obligates the provider to protect the insured against any losses associated with a certain risk event, such as theft or fire.

Insurance contracts are divided into the following sections:

- **Declaration page**— This lists the identity of the insured, his or her address, the cost of the policy, a general description of the items being insured, and the coverage amounts.
- **Insuring agreement**—This specifies the property being covered, its type, the perils against which it is protected, and the exact loss amount the insured will recover (indemnity).
- **Conditions**—This explains the responsibilities of both parties and the provisions they must fulfill.
- **Exclusions**—This identifies any losses or perils that are not covered (indemnified) by the contract.
- **Definitions**—This section defines and clarifies the terms found in the policy. These terms are often specific to the type of policy being issued.

PARTIES TO AN INSURANCE CONTRACT

Multiple parties are involved in an insurance contract. Knowing which category a person or entity falls into is key to properly interpreting the language contained in an insurance policy.

- **Named insured**—The insured parties listed on the declarations page. The policy language may also extend named insured status to certain parties not listed on the declarations page, such as spouses, executives, partners, and members. The named insured is usually referred to in the policy as "you."
- **First named insured**—The primary named insured listed first on the policy declarations. This is the party that will be the point of contact for any communications from the insurer, as well as the only party who may make changes to the policy.
- **Insured**—Any party that meets the definition of an insured as described in the policy.
- **Additional insured**—A party who is added to the policy as an insured by endorsement, usually due to a contractual obligation of the named insured.
- **Insurer**—The insurance company providing the coverage promised in the insurance policy. The policy usually refers to the insurer as "we" or "us."

Copyright © Mometrix Media. You have been licensed one copy of this document for personal use only. Any other reproduction or redistribution is strictly prohibited. All rights reserved. This content is provided for test preparation purposes only and does not imply an endorsement by Mometrix of any particular political, scientific, or religious point of view.

Certain parties only come into play when there is a claim made against the policy. It is important to distinguish between these parties because the obligations of the insurer are determined by which party is making the claim.

- **First-party claimant**—Anyone making a claim under the policy as an insured. The duties the insurer owes to a first-party claimant are based on both the insurance policy and the laws of the applicable jurisdiction.
- **Third-party claimant**—Anyone making a claim against an insurer asserting liability for damages. The obligations of the insurer to a third-party claimant are based upon the jurisdictional laws that apply to the loss.

UTMOST GOOD FAITH AND REASONS FOR VOIDING A POLICY

Insurance contracts must be entered into with **utmost good faith,** meaning both parties involved in the contract are relying on their mutual integrity. For instance, an insurance contract is issued under the following assumptions: the insurance provider will fulfill its obligation to cover any losses, and the insured will be honest regarding any losses incurred.

Insurance companies have the right to void a policy if any of the following activities are discovered:

- **Misrepresentation**—This can be either intentional or unintentional, and involves an applicant misstating a fact, either verbally or in writing. The policy can only be voided if the misrepresentation involves a **material fact**, which is any factor that would influence the company to reject an application or alter or raise the policy's premium.
- **Concealment**—This occurs when an applicant withholds material facts.
- **Fraud**—This is always intentional because it involves a deliberate deception that is harmful to the company. For an action to be considered fraud, the following elements must be present: an individual must intentionally lie in order to alter someone's decision; the individual's lie must result in the decision being altered; and the lie must result in damage.

WAIVER AND ESTOPPEL

A **waiver** occurs whenever a person or organization intentionally gives up an established right. For instance, an insurance producer may waive some of the conditions of a policy in order to secure the agreement of the customer. The waived terms are no longer applicable to the policy. In some cases, companies may waive these rights even when they have the option to exercise them. Ideally, a waiver should be executed in writing to avoid any misunderstanding of the waiving party's intent. An insured may be determined to have implicitly waived his or her rights if he or she engages in acts that violate the terms of an insurance contract. Not all rights can be waived, including facts and certain requirements for insurance, such as an insurable interest.

Estoppel is a legal doctrine that prevents a party from making assertions that are in conflict with a past act or statement. With regard to contracts, estoppel generally applies by preventing one party from denying the existence of an agreement. Estoppel is applied to prevent unjust actions from taking place. For example, if a representative of an insurer represents to the insured that there is comprehensive coverage on an auto policy when there is no such coverage on that policy, the insurer may be estopped from denying coverage for a claim that arises. So long as the insured accepted that representation in good faith, the insurance company would not be allowed to decline coverage for a comprehensive auto loss. Because of this doctrine, it is extremely important to confirm that the coverage communicated to the policyholder is accurate and, in the event of a claim, notify the insured of any potential coverage issue in writing as soon as it is identified. This is usually accomplished by sending a **reservation of rights** letter that outlines the reason coverage is in question, including any relevant policy language.

PRINCIPLE OF INDEMNITY

The **principle of indemnity** applies when the insurance contract begins issuing payments following a loss. It dictates that the insured must be returned to his or her approximate financial state before the loss occurred. Generally, indemnification means the insured does not gain or profit from a loss; however, indemnity does not always cover the actual loss amount. For instance, valued or stated amount policies may issue payments totaling more than the actual loss amount, while deductible or coinsurance policies may pay out less than the total loss.

DIRECT LOSS AND INDIRECT LOSS

The insuring agreements section specifies the type of loss covered by a property insurance policy. **Direct loss** is the result of physical damage, loss, or destruction to property; and it can be caused by theft, fire, weather, and other similar perils. **Indirect loss**, also known as **consequential loss**, includes any financial hardships incurred as a by-product of the direct loss. For instance, when a car is stolen, a person not only loses the value of his or her car but may also incur additional expenses if he or she is forced to rent a car. The cost of automobile rental is an example of indirect loss. Another example would be the cost of renting a hotel room when a home is destroyed. Policies can extend their coverage to include indirect costs. In some instances, indirect coverage is a basic component of the policy.

NEGLIGENCE AND DAMAGES

Negligence is an **unintentional tort** and is caused by the insured's accidental failure to exercise reasonable care to prevent injury or damages. In most cases, casualty insurance does not cover **intentional torts**. The insured cannot be held liable for damages unless the accuser can prove negligence, which requires establishing the presence of four factors:

- A legal duty must be owed. The insured is legally obligated to act in a **reasonable** and **prudent** manner to protect the safety and property of another person.
- The legal duty owed must have been breached. The insured may owe different levels of protection to different people. These different levels are known as a **degree** or **standard of care**.
- The insured's failure to act must have been the **proximate cause** of the act.
- There must be an actual injury or property damage.

According to the principle of **contributory negligence**, if a person has sustained damages or injury through some fault of their own, they cannot hold another party liable, even if they share responsibility for those damages.

According to the principle of **pure comparative negligence**, if a person has sustained damages or injury due to both their own fault and the fault of a separate party, the court will assess liability on both parties and award damages based on the level of responsibility held by each party. Consider, for instance, a person who is injured while shopping at a store. The court may rule that the person is 20% responsible for their injuries and the store is 80% responsible. Consequently, the person would receive 80% of the possible damage settlement.

Many states have adopted a **modified comparative negligence** standard. Under this doctrine, a party is barred from being compensated for their own injuries if their own negligence is in excess of the established percentage for that venue. The standards used for this form of negligence are 51/49 and 50/50. The former requires that an injured party be less than 51% liable for their own damages

21

to collect from another party. The latter requires that the injured party be less than 50% liable to pursue compensation.

People and organizations can use the following defenses against accusations of negligence:

- **Assumption of risk**—The injured party has no right to collect damages if they knew the risks beforehand and still placed themselves in the situation.
- **Intervening cause**—The accused is not liable if the damage or injury was caused by an intervening cause beyond their control.
- **Last clear chance defense**—The injured party has no right to collect damages if they had the **last clear chance** to circumvent the loss and ignored it.
- **Contributory negligence**—The injured party cannot hold another party liable if their injuries were partly their own fault.
- **Comparative negligence**—The injured party is only entitled to part of the damages if they were partly responsible for their injuries.

If a party is found liable for another's losses, they will be required to pay that party for one or more types of damages. The four types of damages that a plaintiff can seek are as follows:

1. **Compensatory damages** include any legal remedy in which an individual is compensated for the amount of money that he or she actually lost or the physical or mental harm that occurred as a result of a civil offense. Compensatory damages can be one of two types:
   a. **Special damages** are awarded to the plaintiff for the exact amount of financial loss caused by the civil offense. Most commonly, special damages include the cost to repair or replace damaged property, medical expenses, and reimbursement for lost wages. They can also be for any quantifiable expense that was incurred due to the loss, such as transportation expenses, room and board, or necessary services. Special damages need to be supported by written documentation such as receipts or invoices.
   b. **General damages** are awarded to the plaintiff for the physical or mental harm that any individual affected by that specific civil offense would sustain. General damages are non-quantifiable and are usually based on the court's reasonable estimate of value.
2. **Liquidated damages** include any legal remedy in which an individual receives the amount that a contract says the individual will receive from the other parties involved in the agreement if the contract is breached.
3. **Nominal damages** include any legal remedy in which an individual receives a small amount of money to make it clear that a civil offense was committed against the individual even though no actual financial harm was done.
4. **Punitive damages** include any legal remedy in which the court orders an individual who committed a civil offense to pay a certain amount of money to punish that individual for committing that offense. Punitive damages are used to indicate that the at-fault party acted in a way that was exceptionally dangerous or performed in a wanton or willful manner.

Bodily injury losses can also lead to secondary or consequential losses that may be compensable depending on the jurisdiction in which the accident occurs. These losses are not suffered directly by the injured party but rather by members of their family such as children or spouses.

The first type is **loss of consortium**. This loss is usually claimed by the spouse or partner of the injured person and entails impairment or inability to engage in companionship, affection, intimacy, or comfort with the injured party in the same way as prior to the accident. Loss of consortium damages are considered as part of general damages.

The second type is **loss of services**, sometimes called **loss of household services**. These damages can be claimed by a spouse, partner, or any other family member who is deprived of the injured party's services. For example, the injured party is a grandmother who enjoys caring for her two grandchildren while her son works. She does not charge for her services. After she is injured, she is unable to care for the children and her son must pay for day care until she recovers. The cost of the day care would be considered under a loss of services claim. Loss of services damages fall into the compensatory damages category.

PROXIMATE CAUSE

A **proximate cause** is an occurrence or action that initiates an unbroken chain of events resulting in damage or injury. Proving proximate cause is essential to establish liability against another party to collect damages. An action cannot be considered a proximate cause unless **both** the following criteria are met:

- The subsequent series of events occur in an uninterrupted and continuous manner.
- The loss would not have occurred if the action had been absent.

Assume, for instance, that a fire occurs at a department store. While firefighters are attempting to control the fire, the digital security cameras at the front of the building get wet and are damaged beyond repair. The fire would be considered the proximate cause of the damage to the cameras because it set off an unbroken chain of events that led to the damage, and the cameras would not have sustained water damage had there not been a fire that needed to be extinguished. In contrast, if the cameras were stolen off the building while it was unoccupied following the fire, the fire would not be the proximate cause of the loss. The theft would be an **intervening cause** that could have occurred in absence of the fire.

TYPES OF INSURANCE
PROPERTY INSURANCE AND CASUALTY INSURANCE

Insurance providers are often classified according to the insurance line (or type) they write. One such line is **property insurance**, which covers damage to physical property and any income it produces. **Casualty insurance** provides non-property coverage, such as liability, workers' compensation, crime, fidelity, and surety. People and businesses purchase casualty insurance to protect themselves against liabilities and to reimburse the cost of paying legal settlements. Specifically, casualty insurance protects against **civil wrongs**, also known as **torts**, which involve the private (non-contractual) relationships between parties. There are three types of torts coverable by casualty insurance:

- Bodily injury to another person that results from the insured's alleged failure to take proper care
- Damage to another person's personal property that results from the insured's alleged failure to take proper care
- Personal injury caused by acts of the insured, including any consequential bodily injury

Casualty insurance does not protect against **criminal acts**, which are prosecuted by authorities at the state and federal level. A person or business convicted of a criminal act may pay fines that are not covered by insurance.

An insurance provider can be further classified as either **monoline**, meaning it handles only one line of insurance, or **multi-line**, meaning it handles multiple lines. Lines can also be categorized as personal or commercial. **Personal lines** include property and casualty policies intended for persons and families. **Commercial lines** protect businesses and organizations. By analyzing statistical data on each line and gathering premium information, companies can determine the most profitable and least profitable insurance types.

Specific Insurance, Blanket Insurance, and Endorsements

Specific insurance establishes limits on the items being insured. Despite being designated as "specific," the policy does not have to list each item. However, every insured item must be part of the overall property. Consider, for instance, a homeowners insurance policy. Even though the policy may not list any furniture or appliances, they are still covered. **Blanket insurance** can cover multiple properties at different locations. For example, a person who owns several buildings might purchase a blanket policy, thereby covering every building under the same policy.

Endorsements are forms added to policies to amend the coverage or provisions of a policy. This is done for a number of reasons, including adding specialized coverage, compliance with insurance regulations, and eliminating coverage an insured may not need. Endorsements generally fall into one of three categories:

- **Restrictive endorsements** modify coverage by limiting, eliminating, or reducing the coverage under the policy. These can be used when an insured does not need a specific coverage that is included in a standard policy, or when there is a high risk associated with an insured that an insurance company does not have the appetite to take on.
- **Additive endorsements** increase or add coverage to the standard policy. They are used when an insured wishes to purchase an optional coverage, or if there is a need to increase the coverage available for certain losses.
- **Administrative endorsements** are used when information associated with the policy is changed, such as updating an address or removing a listed driver. These endorsements prevent the insurer from needing to issue a new policy for minor changes.

The policy declarations page includes a list of endorsements that apply to the policy, and these endorsements are treated as part of the policy in question. Agents and underwriters must review endorsements to make sure there aren't any unexpected restrictions or exclusions and to confirm coverage for any items that may have been accidentally omitted.

Liability Insurance

Parties often find themselves liable when another person suffers bodily injury or property damage. Consequently, many parties purchase **liability insurance**, which covers any legal defense costs or damages resulting from such injuries. Different types of liability insurance cover different categories of liability exposure. These categories include the following:

- **General liability**—Covers the usage and maintenance of a property and the operation of a business.
- **Personal liability**—Covers the activities of a person and his or her family when those activities are not business related. It may also cover damages resulting from the use of the residence property, as well as damages caused by animals owned by the insured.
- **Professional liability**—Covers the liabilities associated with a particular profession.
- **Business liability**—Covers business conduct.

- **Personal and advertising injury liability**—Covers personal injuries resulting from the violation of a party or entity's rights, such as libel, slander, copyright infringement, and privacy violations. Advertising injury entails these same injuries, but only when they occur due to some form of advertisement, such as a defamatory television commercial or printed advertisement.

There are other types of liability that may fall within the scope of the aforementioned policy types, but generally there are not policies written just for these types of liability. These are:

- **Vicarious liability**—Liability for damages incurred as a result of one person's legal responsibility for another person or animal. For instance, parents can be held liable if their children vandalize another person's property.
- **Strict (absolute) liability**—Liability resulting from dangerous practices and defective products. Negligence is not a consideration with this type of liability.

INSURANCE PROVIDERS AND PERSONNEL
TYPES OF INSURANCE PROVIDERS

Stock companies and mutual companies are the most common types of insurance providers. The main goal of a stock company is to generate a profit for the stockholders or shareholders. Stock companies operate by using money generated from the sale of stock. If a stock company needs additional funds for growth or operations, those funds may be acquired by selling additional stock in the company. Stockholders are not required to purchase insurance from their company and can acquire insurance from any provider without affecting their ownership rights or the dividends they receive. There is no direct sharing of profits or losses with the policyholders.

Mutual companies are owned by the policyholders themselves, who vote on management decisions and receive dividends like stockholders. The primary goal of a mutual company is to provide at-cost or nearly at-cost insurance products to the policyholders. While many consider the focus on the benefits to the policyholders to be a desirable aspect of a mutual company, the potential downside of a mutual company is the inability to raise any needed additional funds via the equity market. Mutual company profits get returned to the policyholders via dividend payments or a decrease in premiums. Mutual companies take one of two possible forms:

- **Advance premium**—This is the most common form because it charges non-assessable premiums, meaning policyholders are never assessed any fees other than their premium payments, regardless of whether a loss occurs. Expenses in excess of those projected are paid out of the company's surplus and are not directly charged against the policyholders. Excess expenses or losses may result in an increase in premium at renewal.
- **Assessment**—This is much less common because policyholders may be charged a pro rata share to cover losses. Assessment companies have highly variable costs of coverage, and primarily offer fire and windstorm protection for properties in rural areas.

Fraternal benefit societies are incorporated but offer no stock and do not operate for profit. In most cases, they offer only health and life insurance. They typically function under a lodge system, whereby they only offer coverage and benefits to members of the society. Fraternals often use **open contracts**, which incorporate the society's charters, bylaws, and any amendments to the charter. Although the contract can change if the charter is amended, a fraternal can never take away benefits.

A **Lloyd's association** is not a company; rather, it is a group of people, or **syndicate**, who voluntarily pool their resources to insure contracts. A syndicate is personally responsible for the insurance amount that is drafted. Lloyd's associations are named for **Lloyd's of London**.

A **risk retention group** (RRG) consists of multiple product manufacturers who want to insure themselves against product liability. RRGs are a type of mutual insurance company. These groups were established under the Product Liability Risk Retention Act of 1981 and include **self-insurance programs** and **captive insurance companies**. Risk retention groups are regulated in their states of origin and require valid licensing in a minimum of one state in which they conduct business. Unlike other insurance providers, risk retention groups are not subject to state insurance regulations and are not required to be licensed in every state in which they conduct business.

A **purchasing group**, which was also established under the Product Liability Risk Retention Act of 1981, is a group of businesses operating within the same industry or trade. These businesses purchase liability insurance collectively. Purchasing groups are regulated in their states of origin, but they need not be licensed since they are only insurance purchasers. Both purchasing groups and risk retention groups are allowed to conduct business in multiple states.

A **reciprocal insurer**, also known as an **exchange**, is an unincorporated group of people who insure each other. Members of a reciprocal group or exchange are referred to as subscribers. The group shares insurance costs, as well as any losses incurred by its members. An **attorney-in-fact** is responsible for managing the reciprocal and all its business.

Self-insured organizations and individuals have chosen not to acquire protection from an insurance provider and simply cover any losses with their own resources. Such organizations will typically set aside an amount of funds intended to pay for losses. Self-insured organizations and individuals tend to be quite wealthy.

Government insurance is provided by state or federal governments rather than private insurers. State governments often insure people who are too high-risk for private insurers against unemployment, worker injury, disability, medical malpractice, and property damage. The federal government may provide insurance against catastrophic loss (floods, weather, etc.) or **residual market insurance** to subsidize private carriers.

INSURANCE SALES SYSTEMS

An **exclusive** (or **captive**) **agency system** is a system in which the insurance company contracts agents from independent agencies. The agents work on commission; they represent and sell insurance for only one contracting company.

A **direct writer system** is a system in which agents are employed by the insurance company directly, not by a separate agency. The agents can work for commission, a salary, or a combination of the two.

Independent agency systems rely on **independent** or **nonexclusive agents**, who represent and sell insurance for more than one provider. The agency contracts independently with multiple providers, and the agents work entirely on commission.

Direct response systems do not use agents. Instead, the provider uses media such as the internet, the telephone, and mail to sell insurance directly to the client.

INSURANCE COMPANY DEPARTMENTS

Policy issue and administration reviews new applications after they have been approved by the underwriting department and creates a policy form for the applicant. **Policy analysts**, also known as **screeners**, verify the accuracy and completeness of information included in the policy. **Raters** calculate the premium amount at which the policy should be assessed.

The **actuarial and statistical department** is filled with **actuaries** who establish separate rates for each insurance type by analyzing computer data and statistics gathered from other insurance providers.

The **investment department** invests company funds with the goal of not only earning enough money to pay claims and future obligations, but also generating a high rate of return for the company. Part of the investment must be easily liquefiable.

Miscellaneous support departments, which include general administration, assistance, training, management information systems, and maintenance, assist other departments in their operations.

The **claims department** is responsible for indemnifying (paying) insured parties after a loss occurs. This department includes **claims adjusters**, also known as **representatives**, who inspect the damage and determine if the loss is covered by the policy. They may even distribute payments. Depending on the company's size, claims adjusters can be employees or contract workers.

The **accounting department** issues the appropriate compensation (commissions, salaries, or a combination of the two) to agents, credits premiums to the correct accounts, and keeps up reserve accounts.

The **agency department** recruits, trains, selects, and directs agents. It is also responsible for tracking agent sales and matching agents with their most appropriate market.

The **marketing department** directs the marketing strategy of the company. It creates advertisements and often works collaboratively with the advertising department.

The **audit department** handles policies for which premiums are not established until after the policy term has commenced. The audit department sets these premiums by examining the company's payroll, receipts, and number of employees, and the accounting records of the insured.

The **loss control department**, sometimes called the **risk engineering department**, helps insured individuals reduce risk and avoid loss by recommending preventative measures.

The **legal department** ensures that the company is following all applicable laws and regulations. It interprets these laws and handles any legal issues or court cases that arise in connection with the company. The legal department is also responsible for establishing the payout for policies.

The **reinsurance department** acquires insurance for the insurance provider. This process is known as reinsurance, and it protects the provider against losses resulting from unfavorable underwriting results.

INSURANCE PROFESSIONALS

Insurance agents represent the insurance provider to their clients and potential customers.

Consultants charge a fee in exchange for insurance advice, such as explaining which policies are the most beneficial.

Solicitors have many of the same duties that agents have. They can represent the company, sell insurance, and receive premiums. However, they do not issue or countersign policies. Solicitors may work for agents.

Brokers are employed by the party seeking insurance. They represent the insured and may speak with several different insurance companies to find the best offer. Brokers cannot bind or legally represent an insurance provider.

Excess or **surplus lines agents** sell **surplus lines of insurance**, which cover unique or high-risk situations. Very old homes, professional athletes looking to insure their bodies, tuition refunds, and medical malpractice are some examples of things that might be covered by surplus lines of insurance. These agents can handle surplus lines even in states where such insurance is not authorized.

Producers include all sellers of insurance, which includes agents and all the professionals described above.

Claims adjusters handle the investigation and resolution of claims that are made against insurance policies. Adjusters can be retained under a contract with an insured or an insurance company, or may be employed by an insurer directly.

AGENCY RELATIONSHIP

Agency relationships are present wherever a principal (such as an insurance company) has empowered agents to act on its behalf. Insurance companies generally grant their agents the power to write contracts and receive payments. Because agents represent principals, any information presented to an insurance agent is simultaneously presented to the insurance company.

Many states mandate that agents undergo continuous education to improve their skills and keep up with the latest knowledge, trends, and developments. To better their reputation and increase their desirability, many agents earn professional accreditations and designations. Commonly sought designations for insurance agents include:

- Issued by the National Alliance for Insurance Education and Research:
  - Certified Insurance Counselor (CIC)
  - Certified Risk Manager (CRM)
  - Certified Insurance Service Representative (CISR)
- Issued by the Institutes Knowledge Group (formerly the Institutes)
  - Associate in Insurance (AINS)
  - Associate in Insurance Services (AIS)
  - Accredited Adviser in Insurance (AAI)
  - Chartered Property Casualty Underwriter (CPCU)

DUTIES OF AN INSURANCE AGENT

An insurance agent has several duties:

- **Selling insurance**—This generates commissions for the agent and revenue for the organization.
- **Countersigning**—This authenticates the contract. Agents must review and sign each new policy.

- **Providing quotations**—This informs potential clients of the premiums on a proposed contract. The agent is also responsible for acquiring information on clients, determining their needs, recommending coverage types, and assisting them in completing applications.
- **Field underwriting**—This involves determining the risk level of a particular business by using a set of established criteria.
- **Meeting service needs**—This refers to any assistance the insured may require after the policy has been signed. Agents must help the insured with any policy changes, name changes, or claim filing. Agents should keep current records of these changes. They should reassess the sufficiency of the client's coverage on an annual basis.

AUTHORITY HELD BY INSURANCE AGENTS

Express authority includes any powers formally granted to the agent, such as the power to write specific insurance lines, countersign, issue policies, deliver policies, bind coverage, accept premiums, and settle claims. Because express authority is laid out in writing or verbally, the powers associated with this level are the most clearly defined.

Implied authority includes any powers that have not been formally granted, but that are necessary for the agent to fulfill his or her duties. An example is the agent's ability to recommend and describe coverage options for the client.

Apparent authority is based on the assumptions of a "reasonable person" about the powers an agent should have. For instance, a reasonable person might assume that an agent represents the insurance company to the general public.

OBTAINING INSURANCE AND UNDERWRITING—GENERAL CONCEPTS
APPLICATION PROCESS FOR ACQUIRING INSURANCE AND BINDERS

Before insurance can be acquired, the person seeking insurance and the agent must complete an **application** and submit it to the insurance company. The application contains vital information about the client's risk level and is the primary factor in the company's decision about whether to insure the client. Because of this, the agent must make sure that all information on the application is complete and accurate. If the agent neglects these duties, he or she may face lawsuits from the agency, the insurance company, and the client. The information needed on an application may vary by line of business or insurance company, but the application form will generally include:

- The name, address, and contact information of the applicant
- The type of insurance the applicant is seeking
- The amount of coverage desired
- Details about the specific risk(s) being insured, such as construction type, schedule of locations, list of drivers, or specific liability exposures
- Any relevant claims or loss history
- Information on the prior insurer, if applicable
- Names of any additional parties who have insurable interest, such as a mortgage holder or additional insured
- Any optional coverages the applicant wants to include on the policy

It is also important that the applicant makes truthful **representations** because representations make up most of the information on an application. Insurance companies cannot void an application based on inaccurate representations only. When the prospective insured provides details on the application, he or she is making a **warranty** that the information provided is factual and agreeing that specific conditions will be met. Warranties are considered part of the insurance policy. If a warranty is violated, whether purposefully or accidentally, the entire policy can be voided.

After the application has been submitted, the agent may be empowered to issue a **binder**, which is a verbal or written agreement providing immediate insurance coverage to the client. Verbal binders must be transferred to a written document in a timely manner. Binders do not guarantee the application will be accepted and can be canceled via formal notice or when the new policy takes effect. Once coverage is bound, the agent may need to issue a **certificate of insurance**. This document indicates that a policy has been written and issued. It can serve as evidence of coverage when various legal and financial issues arise. If the insurance covers a group of people, one person will be designated as the **certificate holder**.

DEPOSIT PREMIUM AND PREMIUM AUDIT

If an insurance company is willing to provide insurance for an applicant, the company will determine the amount of **premium** that will need to be paid in exchange for insurance coverage. A premium is a monetary amount that is determined by the insurer's evaluation of the insured's risk profile. For commercial policies, it is not uncommon for the insurance company to charge a **deposit premium**. The premium amount is not always fixed and may change based on what occurs during the applicable policy period. A deposit premium is the insurer's estimate of the minimum amount the insured entity needs to pay to secure the coverage being offered.

When policies require a deposit premium, the final premium is not determined until the conclusion of the policy period. A **premium audit** is completed to calculate the final premium. It entails the insurance company reviewing a variety of factors to establish the insured's true risk exposure. This can include examining payroll records, employee classification documents, general ledgers, tax forms, and claims made during the policy period. A premium audit may result in a balance due to the insurance company that the policyholder is responsible for paying, and timely payment is essential to make certain that needed coverage remains in force. If the audit finds that the policyholder has overpaid, then either the difference will be refunded, or a credit will be applied to the next policy period's premium.

UNDERWRITING DEPARTMENT

The goal of **underwriting** is to insure only those risks likely to fulfill the insurance provider's economic goals. The underwriting department evaluates the risk level of each application against a set standard. The personal judgment of the members of the underwriting department is also considered. Applications are normally rejected if their potential for loss outweighs their potential for gain. When making these decisions, underwriters consider the **loss ratio, expense ratio,** and **combined ratio.** These terms are defined in the following section.

The underwriting department also has the following responsibilities: identifying which policy forms are necessary to provide the coverage an applicant is seeking, evaluating loss experience, and offering judgment rates.

INSURANCE FINANCIAL TERMINOLOGY

Combined ratio is a measure of an insurer's profitability. When the combined ratio exceeds 100%, the company has suffered a loss. When the combined ratio is less than 100%, the company has earned a profit. The formula for the combined ratio is:

$$\frac{\text{Incurred Losses} + \text{Expenses}}{\text{Earned Premium}}$$

Earned premium is the portion of advance paid premiums for which the policy period has passed. For example, if the policy period is one year long, the premium is only fully earned when that year has elapsed. In cases where the full policy period has not passed, earned premium is based on the proportion of the time that has passed in relation to the length of the policy period. Premiums paid in advance cannot be considered in an insurance company's revenue until they have been earned.

Expense ratio is an indicator of the insurer's profitability from underwriting operations. The lower the expense ratio, the more profitable the insurer is. There are two methods of determining the expense ratio: the trade method and the statutory method. Insurance companies tend to use the statutory method, as it is a more conservative measure of underwriting profitability. The formula for this method is:

$$\frac{\text{Underwriting Expenses}}{\text{Earned Premium}}$$

Incurred loss includes all corporate expenditures for handling or covering losses on claims.

Loss ratio is an indicator of an insurance company's handling of claims and their associated expenses. A lower loss ratio is desirable, as it indicates the insurer is taking in more earned premium than it is spending on claims. The formula for the loss ratio is:

$$\frac{\text{Claims Payments} + \text{Adjustment Expenses}}{\text{Earned Premium}}$$

Underwriting expenses include salaries, commissions, administrative costs, regulatory costs, and advertising.

Written premiums include all premium income, such as earned premiums, unearned premiums, renewals, policy endorsements, and new business.

RATING A POLICY

In most industries, determining a price is done with a fairly simple equation: Costs + Profit = Price. Determining the price of insurance is more complicated because it involves costs that are not entirely predictable, since most claims involve unexpected or accidental events. Because of this, the rate-making process is essential to ensuring a company's profitability. Premium rating is also regulated to ensure that certain conditions are met:

- The amount charged must be **reasonable and fair** in comparison to the risk being assumed.
- The amount charged needs to be **adequate** to preserve the financial health and solvency of the insurance company.
- The determination of the premium **cannot be unfairly discriminatory**, and insureds in the same class with comparable risk levels are charged comparable premiums.

After a company decides to insure an applicant, it must determine a premium amount for the policy, which can be highly individualized depending on the risk the policyholder presents. Premium rates are calculated using one of three possible methods: judgment rating, manual rating, and merit rating.

Manual rating, also known as **class rating**, is the most common method and is used when an insured's risk level is quantifiable or when there is sufficient statistical data available for the risk category in question. It is referred to as a manual rating because information is typically pulled from a premium rating manual or guide. In these manuals, premium rates are organized by category and listed on a table. An underwriter analyzes the characteristics of the risk, and then classifies the risk according to the categories on the table. A premium is selected based on the corresponding category. The total premium is calculated by multiplying the rate by the number of insurance units. Consider, for instance, a person who purchases $500,000 of insurance at a listed rate of $5 per $2,500. The total premium would be $5 \times \frac{\$500,000}{\$2,500} = \$1,000$.

Judgment rating is the oldest method, relying solely on expert judgment rather than tables. Underwriters simply assess the policy's risk level and determine a premium. Judgment rating is subjective and is used in cases where the risk is not easily quantifiable.

Merit rating is used when a risk has unusual or unique characteristics; the underwriter or agent determines a manual rating and then adjusts it based on the unusual qualities of the risk. Common types of merit rating include:

- **Experience rating** examines the **loss experience** of the insured. In most cases, loss experience is the three-year difference between the premiums collected from the insured and the amount the insured has received in claims. If the insured's loss experience is worse than the average loss experience, the premium will be higher than the manual rate. If the insured's loss experience is better than the average loss experience, the premium will be lower than the manual rate.
- **Schedule rating** assesses a system of debits and credits according to the insured's characteristics.
- **Retrospective rating** considers any losses incurred by the insured over the policy period once that policy period has expired. The adjustments to the premiums are applied retroactively.

UNDERWRITING RESOURCES

When determining whether an applicant should be insured, underwriters assess the applicant's risk level by examining the following sources: the application, the company's claim files, industry bureaus, government agencies, inspections services, other insurers, and financial information services. Because many of these sources provide highly personal information, underwriters must abide by the **Fair Credit Reporting Act**. Underwriters must be wary of **adverse selection**, which applies to applicants who are especially susceptible to a certain kind of loss. A person living in Kansas, for instance, might face a high risk of storm damage. Consequently, an insurance company could face substantial losses if it provided storm insurance for a large number of individuals living in Kansas. Insurers will usually combat adverse selection by diversifying the portfolio of products offered, as well as the locations the company decides to serve.

Insurance Regulation

STATE REGULATION OF INSURANCE COMPANIES

Insurance companies are mainly regulated at the state level. Laws vary from state to state, but all states appoint a **commissioner**, also known as a **director** or **superintendent**, who oversees an **insurance department** responsible for regulating insurance activities. State insurance departments enforce laws and regulate the conduct of agents and companies, as well as the sale of various insurance types. When violations are reported, the department must investigate and levy penalties whenever necessary. Penalties include fines, the revocation or suspension of a company's license or its right to conduct business in a certain state, and even incarceration.

NATIONAL ASSOCIATION OF INSURANCE COMMISSIONERS

The **National Association of Insurance Commissioners (NAIC)** consists of commissioners from every state who meet periodically to coordinate activities, share knowledge, and make recommendations. There are no laws requiring states to implement NAIC recommendations, but most states do adopt them in some form. NAIC oversight is not limited to property and casualty insurance; health and life insurance are also addressed by the NAIC. One of the biggest functions of the NAIC is providing a framework for insurance legislation in the form of **model laws, model regulations,** and **model acts.** These models serve as archetypes for state regulators to communicate expectations and standards for insurance companies. They were developed to improve consistency in insurance regulation between states. Some of the topics addressed in NAIC models include unfair claims settlement practices, producer licensing, rating law, and financial reporting requirements.

STATE-MANDATED REGULATIONS

State insurance departments impose financial regulations on insurance companies. According to these regulations, companies must maintain certain capital and surplus requirements, distribute yearly financial statements, and disclose a certain level of financial data, depending on whether they are classified as a domestic, foreign, or alien company. By monitoring these disclosures, the insurance department can assess the financial health of a company to identify problems as early as possible, maintain solvency, and protect insured persons in the event of insolvency. Several states have **insurance guaranty associations**, which pay claims when an insurance provider suffers insolvency. States will also inspect insurance providers on an intermittent basis, assist the provider if it falls into financial trouble, and manage liquidations if the provider goes under. Independent organizations, such as S&P and Moody's, often rank insurance companies according to their financial strength. These rankings are based on factors such as investment performance and claims experience.

State insurance departments require that agents fulfill the following regulations:

- **Licensing**—Agents can only sell insurance in states in which they are properly licensed to do so. To receive a license, agents must pass a state insurance exam.
- **Maintain fiduciary relationships with clients**—Agents are required to receive and handle premiums from clients.
- **Avoid twisting**—Twisting is an illegal activity in which agents mislead clients into canceling their current policies and purchasing new ones. This is done solely to benefit the agent.

33

- **Avoid false advertising**—Agents cannot misrepresent any part of the policy or the company's financial information. All information must be accurate.
- **Avoid rebating**—Rebating is the practice of offering money, gifts, kickbacks, or any other benefit to coerce clients into purchasing insurance. (Rebating is actually legal in California and Florida.)
- **Avoid unfair discrimination**—Agents must offer the same rate to all clients in identical situations and cannot take bribes.

STATE FILING OF NEW RATES AND FORMS

When an insurance company changes its rates or policy forms, it requires approval from the insurance department in its state of operation. Different states have unique ways of granting approval:

- **Prior approval states**—These must approve the new rate or form before the insurance company can use it. Some states allow insurers to assume approval has occurred after a specific period of time has passed without communication from the state insurance department.
- **File and use states**—These allow companies to use new rates and forms immediately after they have been filed. The insurance department will accept or reject the·changes at a later date.
- **Use and file states**—These allow insurers to use new rates and forms immediately, but they must be filed with the state within a specified time period after they are initially put into use. Acceptance or rejection will be communicated to the insurer after the filing is made.
- **Mandatory states**—These require companies to use forms and rates that are standard in that state.
- **Open competition states**—These permit companies to use the rates they select and compete with them. However, they still must abide by nondiscrimination and adequacy regulations. These are also referred to as no filing states.

RATE-MAKING

Rate-making is when an insurance provider sets their own rates and presents them to the state. Rate-making is necessary in non-mandatory states, and rates are based on comprehensive operational, premium, financial, and loss statistics. Non-mandatory states, sometimes referred to as no filing or open competition states, are those that do not require rates to be filed with the state for approval.

Loss costs are the most important determinant of an insurance rate because they indicate the amount necessary to cover the company's expected losses. Rating standards require that rates must be fairly allocated based on the risks each prospective insured carries; they must be sufficient to cover incurred losses without producing an unreasonable profit for the insurer; they should be reviewed and revised often to ensure they are in line with current costs; and they should be of an amount that compels insureds to make efforts to prevent losses.

Insurance companies often seek membership in **service bureaus**, such as the Insurance Services Office (ISO) or the National Council on Compensation Insurance (NCCI). Service bureaus assist in gathering loss statistics and other relevant information. Service bureaus collect and analyze statistics from every membership company and store them with their state insurance department. Companies can deviate from these rates within a certain range. When companies submit their rates to the state, they must identify where they obtained their loss data and any other determining

factors, by either listing their service bureau or explaining that they collect their data independently.

ADMITTED AND NON-ADMITTED COMPANIES AND DOMESTIC, FOREIGN, AND ALIEN COMPANIES

State insurance departments have certain responsibilities, such as determining whether insurance companies are conforming to state regulations and how the companies are licensed. Conforming companies are known as **admitted** or **authorized insurers** and are allowed to conduct business within the state. Non-conforming companies are known as **non-admitted** or **unauthorized insurers** and are only allowed to do business in specific situations. Insurance departments also classify companies according to their state of incorporation. Under law, companies can only be incorporated in their home state, but can operate in any number of states or countries. **Domestic companies** are insurance providers that operate in their home states. **Foreign companies** are providers that operate in states other than their states of incorporation. If a company is operating in the US, but has been incorporated in another country, it is classified as an **alien company**.

FEDERAL REGULATION OF INSURANCE COMPANIES

Little insurance regulation occurs at the federal level, but a few regulations and programs exist. Some of the most important federal insurance laws are under **United States Code Title 18 Sections 1033 and 1034** and the **McCarran-Ferguson Act**. Insurance-specific federal programs include the **National Flood Insurance Program (NFIP)** and the **Terrorism Risk Insurance Act (TRIA)**. The **Federal Emergency Management Agency (FEMA)** is also involved with some insurance matters. Other regulations, such as the **Fair Credit Reporting Act (FCRA)** and the **Gramm-Leach-Bliley Act**, apply to many different industries, but have an impact on insurance company policies and operations.

THE MCCARRAN-FERGUSON ACT AND USC TITLE 18 SECTIONS 1033 AND 1034

The McCarran-Ferguson Act was ratified by an act of Congress in 1945. The purpose of the act was to give state regulation precedence over federal regulation in most insurance matters. Further, it gave the individual states the authority to regulate insurance. It also granted insurance companies exemption from federal antitrust laws in most scenarios as a means to encourage collaboration between insurers and foster competition for the benefit of customers. Due to this act, federal regulation only supersedes state laws when the federal law explicitly states that it pertains to the "business of insurance" or when the alleged violation involves boycott, coercion, or intimidation.

Because there are some violations that can extend across more than one state, federal insurance laws are needed to handle situations that impact interstate commerce. The most important laws to be aware of are under United States Code Title 18 Sections 1033 and 1034. For the purposes of this law, interstate commerce is defined as commerce within Washington D.C. or any other US territory; any commerce conducted between states, territories, or possessions of the US; any commerce occurring within a single state if at any point the commerce must go to a place outside of that state; or any commerce within the jurisdiction of the US. Section 1033 states that if anyone who is engaged in the business of insurance in a way that affects interstate commerce commits certain dishonest actions, such parties will be subject to punishment under the law.

Subsection (a) outlines the law pertaining to dishonest actions intended to mislead or deceive any regulatory agency or official. To be guilty of such an offense, the party must have knowingly engaged in making materially false statements or reports or materially overvaluing any property, security, or land with the intention to deceive. These false or deceptive reports or statements must have been made in connection with financial documents presented to an insurance regulator intending to manipulate the actions of that official. Any person found to have committed such actions may be fined, imprisoned for up to ten years, or both. The maximum prison sentence is increased to fifteen years when false reporting endangered the financial fitness of an insurer to the extent that the insurer was placed under rehabilitation, conservation, or liquidation by a court holding proper jurisdiction. Subsection (b) states that any individual acting as a director, officer, employee, or agent of an insurer who fraudulently handles funds, premiums, credits, or property of an insured does so in violation of the law. This can be via embezzlement, abstraction, purloinment, or misappropriation. The penalties for such actions are the same as those for subsection (a) except for cases in which the amount involved is $5,000 or less. When this is the case, the punishment will be a fine, up to one year in prison, or both. Subsection (c) states that any person making false statements of material facts in any book, report, or statement intending to deceive any other person or party has committed a crime under this law. The penalties for subsection (c) are the same as those for subsection (a).

Subsection (d) declares that anyone in the business of insurance cannot coerce any other party to engage in actions that violate the law. This includes any attempts to corruptly influence, obstruct, or impede any pending legal or insurance regulatory action. Coercion also cannot be used to manipulate the behavior or actions of any insurance regulatory agency or official. Violators will be subject to up to ten years in jail, a fine, or both. Subsection (e) pertains to any person who has been previously convicted of a crime under 1033 or of any felony crime of dishonesty. If such a person is found to be knowingly engaging in interstate insurance business, the penalty may be up to five years in prison, a fine, or both. The same punishment applies to anyone who permits someone with such a criminal history to conduct insurance business.

Section 1034 describes the civil actions the Attorney General may take in response to violations of Section 1033. These civil remedies have no impact on any other civil or criminal actions that may be pending against the violating party. The Attorney General may file a civil complaint in a United States District Court against anyone who acts in violation of Section 1033. If the civil action results in that party being held responsible for such violations, a monetary civil penalty will be imposed. This penalty will be the greater of $50,000 per offense or the amount of money the defendant received or offered. The Attorney General is also entitled to file an injunction against anyone suspected of violating Section 1033 asking the court to prohibit that person from continuing to engage in such actions.

THE NATIONAL FLOOD INSURANCE PROGRAM (NFIP)

The National Flood Insurance Program was put into law in 1968. The NFIP is intended to provide subsidized flood insurance for homes and businesses in flood-prone areas and to place limitations on development in areas identified as floodplains. The program is administered by the Federal Emergency Management Agency (FEMA) through the **Federal Insurance and Mitigation Administration (FIMA)**. The specifics of the coverage provided under the NFIP will be discussed later in this guide.

Although federal law requires flood-prone communities to apply to the NFIP, many other communities apply voluntarily. When acquiring insurance, communities must complete and submit an NFIP application and pay the gross policy premium in full. Then, they must wait 30 days from the application date before coverage takes effect. This waiting period is waived in the following situations:

- Any waiting period is negated if the insurance is purchased in conjunction with a loan.
- If existing insurance covers property whose title is being transferred, the coverage takes effect on the day of title transference.

- For first-time participants in the program, coverage goes into effect at 12:01 a.m. on the day after the community mails the application and premium payment.
- Changes made to an existing policy go into effect at 12:01 a.m. on the fifth day after the changes and the premium payment have been mailed.

The **Write Your Own program** enables private insurers to sell NFIP policies. The FIMA determines coverage conditions, eligibility requirements, and rates, while the insurer handles premiums and loss reimbursements. Participating insurance companies are required to refund the United States Treasury for any surplus premium if the amount paid in losses is less than the amount of premiums collected. However, the FIMA covers any premium deficit when the funds collected are insufficient to cover all losses.

TERRORISM RISK INSURANCE ACT (TRIA)

Following the events of September 11, 2001, the president signed into law the **Terrorism Risk Insurance Act (TRIA)**. The purpose of the act was to share the responsibility for terrorism losses between insurers and the federal government. This voluntary addition to commercial insurance policies provides coverage for acts of terrorism. There is a limitation to this coverage: The occurrence must be certified by the United States government to have been an act of terrorism. These acts are otherwise excluded on all policies. TRIA coverage is offered on all commercial insurance policies and must be either elected or rejected in writing by the insured at the time of binding the policy. While intended to be a temporary measure, the act has already been reauthorized several times, with the current extension ending in 2027.

FEDERAL EMERGENCY MANAGEMENT AGENCY (FEMA)

The Federal Emergency Management Agency was created via executive order in 1979. The purpose of FEMA is to provide coordinated responses to disasters, natural or otherwise, to avoid exhaustion of resources at the local and state levels. FEMA also oversees programs dedicated to mitigating the impact of disasters and emergencies. To invoke FEMA assistance, the governor of the affected state must declare a state of emergency alongside a request for federal assistance. During an emergency, FEMA can deploy units focused on medical care, search-and-rescue efforts, and maintaining communication channels.

FAIR CREDIT REPORTING ACT (FCRA)

According to the Fair Credit Reporting Act, credit reporting agencies must maintain a consumer's right to privacy, exercise their duties impartially, alert the consumer under certain circumstances, and update information that is old or false. The act not only regulates agencies and entities that provide credit reporting information, but also regulates the parties who request and use that information. Consumer credit information may only be requested when it is needed for a **permissible** purpose, one of which is underwriting insurance.

Insurance companies frequently hire credit reporting agencies to prepare credit reports on applicants. Credit reports are classified as either **consumer** or **investigative consumer**. These differ only in that investigative consumer reports involve personal interviews with the consumer's associates. Neither type of report can include bankruptcy information older than ten years or legal actions older than seven years.

If an insurance company orders an investigative consumer report, it must send **initial written notice** to the applicant within three days of making the order. Consumers then have the right to request additional information, which must be sent in five days. They also have the right to challenge information included in the report. If a person finds errors or discrepancies on his or her credit report, the FCRA requires that each credit bureau have a process in place to dispute such issues. Any disputes must be investigated and resolved. Once it is determined that the credit report contained inaccurate information, the credit bureau must resolve the errors within 30 days. Additionally, if an insurance company raises rates or denies coverage, it must inform the applicant of the specific information that led to the decision.

THE GRAMM-LEACH-BLILEY ACT (GLBA)

Also referred to as the **Financial Services Modernization Act of 1999**, the Gramm-Leach-Bliley Act created standards for how financial institutions, including insurance companies, handle and use the non-public personal financial information of customers. Protected information includes that provided during the application process, claims records, income data, and credit history. Under the act, financial entities must inform customers of their privacy policies, as well as how and when non-public personal financial information may be provided to non-affiliated parties, and they must advise on how to "opt out" of sharing such information. Because insurance companies fall under the definition of financial institutions, insurers are bound to follow the policies mandated by the act when using non-public data about customers.

Property and Casualty Policies Overview

POLICY BASICS

NAMED INSURED, FIRST NAMED INSURED, ADDITIONAL INSUREDS, AND POLICY LIMIT

The following terms are included within the declaration section of an insurance policy:

- **Named insured**—This is the person or business that has been issued the policy.
- **First named insured**—This is the person or business on the policy with the most rights or duties. This designation is used when a policy insures more than one entity.
- **Additional insureds**—These are any other entities covered by the policy and are usually listed in the declaration or endorsement section. It should be noted that a policy may cover insureds that are not listed in either the declaration or endorsement sections.
- **Policy limit**—This is the maximum amount a policy will indemnify the insured in the event of a loss, and is also known as a **limit of insurance**, **limit of coverage**, or **limit of liability**. The policy limits will be shown on the policy declarations page for any purchased coverage. This limit may involve a **value** (or **agreed**) **amount contract** if the coverage item is especially difficult to value. The insurer and the insured simply agree to pay out a certain amount if a total loss occurs. If there are other coverages on the policy, such as liability or medical payments coverages, the policy limits will also be defined on the declarations page.

POLICY LIMITS OF LIABILITY INSURANCE

A **policy limit** is the maximum amount an insurance policy will pay for any one loss, and it is listed in the declarations section. Policy limits can be applied using a variety of methods:

- **Per occurrence**—The loss occurs in a particular place at a specific time or over a period of time. This method will cover losses caused by repeated exposure to a harmful condition over a long period of time.
- **Per accident**—The loss occurs in a specific place over a set period of time. This method is not used to cover losses caused by repeated and lengthy exposure to harmful conditions.
- **Per person**—There is a maximum reimbursement limit for any single person for a particular injury.

After a loss has been reimbursed, the full policy limit is restored and available for the next loss. However, the policy may also have an **aggregate limit**, which places a limit on the amount a policy can pay out per year. This limit is restored on an annual basis based on the policy term. Aggregate limits are used mostly with commercial liability policies and are very rarely seen in personal lines policies.

POLICY PERIOD AND NONRENEWAL

The **policy period**, also known as the **policy term**, is the time between a policy's effective date and its expiration date. Essentially, it is the length of time for which insurance is provided. Most policy terms are six months, one year, or three years, provided they are not canceled. According to most state laws, if a policy is not renewed, its coverage ends at 12:01 a.m. on the expiration date. Therefore, to maintain continuous coverage, the effective date of the new policy should fall on the same day as the expiration date of the old policy.

Nonrenewal options are normally given at the end of the policy period. Policy coverage is discontinued if the insured or the insurance provider chooses not to renew the policy after its

expiration date. In most cases, insured individuals can exercise their nonrenewal options without having to fulfill any requirements. Insurance companies, however, may require a valid reason to decline renewal, and may need to provide notification.

CONDITIONAL RENEWAL

In some cases, the insurance company may need to modify a policy when it renews. This can be due to eligibility changes, premium increases unrelated to loss experience, or exclusion of losses that were previously covered under the policy, among other reasons. While not outlined in the conditions of most policies, this situation results in the carrier issuing a **conditional renewal**. A conditional renewal essentially tells the insured that the policy will be renewed, but only if the policy is modified to meet the new requirements or conditions. For example, if a homeowners policy is due for renewal and the insurance company updates the policy to exclude losses stemming from home-sharing activities, the policy will only be renewed with that modification in place. If the policyholder declines to accept the change in coverage, the policy will not be renewed. In most states, the insurance company is required to send a written notice to the first named insured advising of the change in advance. The advance notice requirement ranges from 10 days to 120 days depending on the state and line of business involved. This is necessary so that the insured has the opportunity to look into other coverage options before agreeing to renew the policy with the modified terms in place.

CANCELING A POLICY

Nearly all insurance policies are required to contain a clause explaining how and when the policy can be canceled. Policies can be canceled in several different ways. If the insured wishes to cancel their policy, they can relinquish it or write a letter to the insurance provider. They then receive **unearned premiums**, which include any premiums the policy has not yet used. Unearned premiums are often repaid on a **short-rate basis**, which means that the company will keep a portion of the unused premiums to cover expenses.

Insurance providers seldom have the same right to arbitrary cancellation that insureds have. The most common reason an insurance company will cancel a policy is non-payment of premiums by the insured. Other reasons include the policyholder violating policy terms, a significant change in the insured's risk, and fraud or misrepresentation committed by the insured. Furthermore, companies must provide the insured with written notification of cancellation and must repay premiums on a **pro rata basis**, which means the insured is refunded for the portion of the premium proportional to the time remaining on the policy period. For example, if an insured purchases a 12-month policy for $240 and the insurer cancels the policy after 4 months, the insured would be refunded $160. The premium divided by the number of months in the policy period works out to $20 per month, so the insured would be refunded $20 for each month remaining in the policy period at the time the insurance company cancels the policy. When the insurer initiates the cancellation, the company is not allowed to keep any unused premiums for expenses. Another cancellation method is known as **flat cancellation**, which involves canceling the policy on its effective date. Under this method, the policy period never began, so if the premium was paid in advance, the insurance company would need to refund the entire premium because none of it was earned. In most cases of flat cancellation, the insured did not pay the renewal premium, so there would be no refund due at cancellation.

If a policyholder is discovered to have knowingly provided false information on the policy application or made a material misrepresentation, the insurance company may **rescind** the policy. When this occurs, the insurer retroactively cancels the policy going back to the initiation of the policy that was issued based on the fraudulent or misleading information. The insured will usually

be refunded for any premiums that have been paid. When a rescission occurs, the insurance company essentially negates the policy, and any claims that would have been covered by the policy will be denied.

Personal Lines Residential Insurance

INTRODUCTION

Insurance for private residential properties is available via a **dwelling insurance** policy, sometimes called a **dwelling fire insurance** policy, or through a **homeowners insurance** policy. Both of these are designed to provide some degree of property coverage for the residential structures and the personal property contained within them. Depending on the policy purchased, there may also be coverage for other costs, such as additional living expenses or medical payments. Many residential insurance policies also provide some degree of personal liability coverage for the policyholder and other eligible insureds.

CONDITIONS COMMON TO RESIDENTIAL INSURANCE POLICIES

The conditions section of an insurance policy outlines various duties and obligations for both the insured and the insurance company. It can also outline how a claim will be valued and paid, how the insurer will respond to certain losses, and administrative protocols. There are 26 conditions that are found in both dwelling and homeowners policies.

- **Policy period**—States that the policy only applies to losses that occur during the policy period
- **Deductible**—States that the insurance company will only pay for losses in excess of the applicable deductible and that in cases where more than one deductible may apply, only the highest will be used
- **Insurable interest and limit of liability**—States that no matter how many people hold an interest in insured property, the insurance company will not pay more than the insured's interest in such property or the applicable policy limit for any single loss
- **Death**—States that upon the **death** of the insured, the insurance company will provide coverage to the legal representatives of the insured to the extent that party represents the insured, and that any party with temporary custody of the deceased's property will be covered until a legal representative can be appointed
- **Assignment**—States that **assignments** of policyholder's rights under the insurance policy will not be considered valid unless they come with the written consent of the insurance company
- **Waiver or change of policy provisions**—States that any waivers or modifications of any policy provision must be confirmed in writing by the insurer to be valid, and the insurer's rights are not waived by a request for appraisal or examination
- **Nonrenewal**—States that the insurance company has the right to not renew the policy when it expires so long as written notice is provided at least 30 days before the policy expiration date
- **Cancellation**—Outlines the protocol for cancellation for when the policyholder cancels the policy and for when the insurance company cancels the policy
  - The insured may cancel a policy at any time by sending written notice to the insurer or sending the policy back to the insurer; such correspondence must include the specific date upon which the insured wants the policy to terminate.
  - The insurance company may cancel a policy for any reason within the 60 days following the policy inception and must provide at least ten days' prior written notice to the insured.
  - After 60 days, the insurer may only cancel for unpaid premiums, material misrepresentation by the insured, or a significant change in the insured's risk.

42

- o For nonpayment of premiums, written notice must be sent to the first named insured at least ten days before the cancellation date.
- o For any other reason, written notice must be sent by the insurance company at least 30 days in advance.
- o Any premium refund will be prorated based on the time between the cancellation date and the original policy expiration date, and the balance will be issued to the first named insured within a reasonable time.

- **Liberalization**—States that when the insurance company makes a change to the policy that broadens coverage without increasing the premium, the change applies to the existing policy automatically when the change goes into effect in the policy's jurisdiction, as long as the effective date is either within the policy period or within the 60 days immediately following the beginning of the policy period; this clause is not applicable to modifications to general program revisions that both expand and restrict coverage
- **Subrogation**—States that prior to a loss, the insured may waive his or her recovery rights against any party, but if a waiver is not executed, the insurer can require the insured to assign his or her right to recovery to the insurance company for the amount the company pays; this condition also requires the insured to cooperate with the company to recover from a third party
- **Duties after loss**—States that the insured party has certain duties immediately after a loss, including:
  - o Providing **prompt notice** either to the insurance company or to an agent of the insurance company
  - o Making any reasonable and required repairs to avoid any **further damage** to the covered property
  - o Maintaining an accurate set of **records** for such repair expenses
  - o **Cooperating** with any investigation the insurer takes on in relation to the claim
  - o Compiling an **inventory** of all the property that has been damaged
  - o Showing the property to the insurer, providing requested records and documentation, and submitting to an examination under oath as often as the insurer reasonably requires
  - o Providing a signed, sworn **proof of loss** to the insurance company within 60 days of the insurance company's request
- **Appraisal**—States that when the insurance company and the insured party disagree about the amount of loss, either side may request an appraisal; the process is as follows:
  - o Each side selects an impartial and qualified appraiser within 20 days; each side pays for their own appraiser.
  - o The two chosen appraisers agree on an umpire to whom that matter will be presented should the appraisers be unable to agree on the loss amount; the sides split the cost of the umpire equally.
  - o Each appraiser submits their assessment of the loss amount.
  - o If they agree, that amount will be paid.
  - o If they do not agree, the umpire will complete their assessment.
  - o If the umpire agrees with either of the appraisers, this will be the amount paid.
- **Our option**—States that the insurer has the option to repair or replace damaged property with that of like kind and quality, so long as written notice is sent to the policyholder within 30 days following the submission of the signed, sworn proof of loss

- **Loss settlement**—Outlines the valuation protocol for covered property, including how losses are handled when the property is underinsured (insured for an amount that is less than 80% of the actual value of the property); this can vary from policy to policy, but losses are typically valued using one of the following:
  - **Replacement cost value**—The cost to replace destroyed or damaged property with new property of the same or a similar type
  - **Actual cash value (ACV)**—Replacement value less deductions for depreciation; sometimes referred to as the market value
  - **Stated value**—An amount usually provided by the policyholder to the insurance company that is the maximum amount the company will pay for a loss to that property
  - **Agreed value**—A value specified in the insurance contract for how much will be paid out in the event of a total loss that is agreed upon by the policyholder and the insurer
- **Loss to a pair or set**—States that if the property lost is part of a pair or set, the insurance company may decide either to repair or replace the necessary part to restore the pair or set to its pre-loss value, or simply to pay the difference between the ACV of the property pre-loss and post-loss
- **Loss payment**—States that the insurance company will handle all losses directly with the named insured and that any payment made will be issued to the insured, unless another party is listed as a payee on the policy or is legally entitled to receive payment; payment will be issued within 60 days of:
  - Reaching an agreement with the named insured
  - A final judgment being entered with the court
  - An appraisal award being filed
- **Loss payable**—States that for certain types of property, if there is a loss payee shown on the declarations page, the loss payee is considered an insured under the policy; such a loss payee is entitled to notification of cancellation or nonrenewal
- **Abandonment of property**—States that the insurance company has no obligation to take ownership of any property abandoned by the insured
- **Recovered property**—States that if property is recovered subsequent to payment under the policy, the recovering party must notify the other party; if the policyholder chooses, the property will be returned to him or her and the loss payment will be adjusted accordingly; if not, the insurance company will assume ownership
- **Mortgage**—Outlines the protocol for dwelling and other structure claims when there is a mortgageholder listed on the policy:
  - Payments for these losses will be apportioned between the policyholder and mortgageholder as appropriate.
  - If there are multiple mortgageholders, payments will be prioritized based on the order they are named in the policy.
  - Denial of an insured's claim does not constitute denial of the mortgageholder's claim so long as the mortgagee has met certain conditions: namely, the mortgagee must have notified the insurance company of any changes in ownership, occupancy, or risk; must have paid any outstanding premiums; and must have submitted a signed, sworn statement of loss within 60 days of receiving a demand for this statement.
  - A mortgageholder is entitled to at least ten days' advance written notice when the policy is not renewed or is canceled.
  - Subrogation will not impair the mortgageholder from recovering the full amount of their claim.

- **No benefit to bailee**—States that the insurance company will not recognize any assignment or grant any coverage benefiting a person or organization that is handling or storing property for a fee
- **Suit against us**—States that any legal action against the insurance company must be brought within two years of the date of loss and that no such action may be brought unless the insured has fully complied with the terms described in the policy
- **Concealment or fraud**—States that if the insured commits fraud related to the policy at any time, the policy is void, including any misrepresentation or intentional concealment of material facts related to the policy, the covered property, or a claim made under the policy
- **Other insurance and service agreement**—States that when a claim is covered by another policy of a similar type, the insurance company will only pay its fair share of the loss (usually determined by a pro rata share calculated as the percentage of coverage under this policy in relation to the sum of all coverage available); if the property is covered by any sort of warranty or service agreement, this policy will pay only on an excess basis
- **Nuclear hazard**—States that losses resulting from a nuclear hazard will not be covered for explosion, fire, or smoke, even when such perils are named in the policy; the policy will not cover direct or indirect losses caused by a nuclear hazard except for direct loss due to fire
- **Volcanic eruption period**—States that all volcanic activity occurring within a period of 72 consecutive hours will be treated as a single occurrence

Homeowners Insurance

Homeowners insurance is a personal lines package policy designed to provide the property and liability coverage most commonly needed by homeowners. There are two revisions of the homeowners coverage forms currently in use, one from 2011 and one from 2022. Key differences between the forms will be highlighted during the discussion.

COVERAGE FORMS

HO-1, also known as the **homeowners basic form,** is the most restrictive when it comes to covered perils. This form covers only named perils listed in the policy, which consist of **fire or smoke, explosions, lightning, hail or windstorms, theft, vandalism or malicious mischief, damage caused by aircraft or vehicles, riot or civil commotion,** and **volcanic eruption.** The unendorsed HO-1 policy does not provide coverage for personal property or personal liability. It should be noted that due to the barebones nature of this form, most states no longer allow HO-1 policies to be used. Due to this, the nuances of the HO-1 policy will not be discussed in the remainder of this section.

HO-2, also known as the **homeowners broad form**, protects against all the perils covered by the basic form plus the additional perils of **falling objects;** damage from the **weight of ice, snow, or sleet;** damage from the **overflow of water or steam; sudden and accidental cracking, tearing, or burning of a water heater or sprinkler system;** damage caused by **artificial electrical current;** and **frozen pipes.** HO-2 policies typically offer some coverage for personal property damaged by a named peril and may provide personal liability insurance.

HO-3, also known as the **homeowners special form**, covers losses to dwellings and structures on an open perils basis, providing coverage for any loss type that is not explicitly excluded by the policy. Home contents are insured on a named peril basis for the same perils listed in the HO-2 policy. Personal liability coverage is generally included in the HO-3 policy. The open peril protection also covers loss of use of real property such as the dwelling and other structures. The HO-3 is the most commonly written homeowners policy.

45

HO-4, also known as the **renters' contents broad form**, the **tenant's form**, or the **renter's form**, provides named peril protection for the personal property of tenants—those who rent apartments, mobile homes, condominiums, and single-family homes. This form covers personal property on a named perils basis and covers the same perils as the HO-2 form but does not cover dwellings or structures. Personal property losses are paid at ACV. HO-4 also provides limited insurance coverage for improvements and additions if the policyholder has paid for their installation.

HO-5, also known as the **homeowners comprehensive form**, extends open peril protection to personal property. It also protects the dwelling and other structures and covers loss of use. This policy is intended for individuals who own and occupy one-, two-, three-, and four-family homes.

HO-6, also known as **the condominium unit-owner's form**, extends named peril protection to the personal property of condominium or cooperative owners. HO-6 provides a level of personal property insurance that is similar to HO-2, HO-3, and HO-4. Loss assessments are covered up to a limit of $1,000.

HO-7, also known as the **mobile home broad form,** mirrors the coverage under the HO-3 form, including the perils covered, but is tailored to the specific needs of the owner of a mobile or manufactured home. Mobile home insurance can be acquired as a **separate package policy**, an endorsement on dwelling policies, or an endorsement on homeowners policy forms HO-2 or HO-3. The HO-7 form has largely been replaced by policies amended with the mobile home endorsement.

HO-8, also known as the **homeowners modified coverage form**, is intended for uniquely constructed properties and older properties whose replacement costs are substantially higher than their market values. This form extends basic named peril protection to dwellings and personal property, and it offers extended coverage for certain perils, including vandalism and malicious mischief (V&MM). Loss settlements are paid on an ACV basis.

HO-14, also known as the **contents comprehensive form**, is a newer form that was introduced in 2022. It provides coverage similar to that provided by an HO-4, but coverage is provided on an open perils basis as opposed to being limited to the perils named in the policy. As with the HO-3 form, any peril that is not specifically excluded by the policy is covered. Additionally, losses to personal property are paid at replacement cost value.

ELIGIBILITY

The primary use of homeowners policies is when the policyholder owns and occupies the location listed on the policy; however, the eligibility requirements are rather broad and vary based on the coverage form. The eligibility requirements are as follows:

Type of Policyholder	Eligible Homeowners Coverage Forms
Owner-occupant: The policyholder owns and occupies the insured property.	HO-1, HO-2, HO-3, HO-5, HO-8
Purchasers under contract: The policyholder is purchasing the insured property under a contract, usually a mortgage.	HO-1, HO-2, HO-3, HO-5, HO-8
Tenant/rental occupants: The policyholder rents the dwelling he or she occupies from the owner of the property.	HO-4, HO-14

Type of Policyholder	Eligible Homeowners Coverage Forms
Owner-occupant with tenants: The policyholder owns and occupies the insured property with up to two boarders. No more than two families may live in each unit of a two-, three-, or four-family dwelling. Each unit may have a maximum of two boarders.	HO-1, HO-2, HO-3, HO-5, HO-8
Occupant under a life estate arrangement: The policyholder does not own the insured property but has full usage and possession of the property for his or her natural lifetime.	HO-1, HO-2, HO-3, HO-5, HO-8
Occupant under a trust agreement: The policyholder occupies the covered premises under the terms of a trust agreement.	HO-1, HO-2, HO-3, HO-5, HO-8 (Requires a trust endorsement to be attached to the policy.)
Dwelling under construction: The policyholder is having a dwelling built with the intention of being the owner-occupant upon completion.	HO-1, HO-2, HO-3, HO-5, HO-8
Joint owner non-occupants: The property is owned by more than one party, of which none reside in the covered property.	HO-1, HO-2, HO-3, HO-5, HO-8
Co-owner occupants: Ownership of a two-, three-, or four-family dwelling is shared among the occupants, who live in separate units within the dwelling.	HO-1, HO-2, HO-3, HO-5, HO-8 (Only one of these may be purchased per property. Any other occupants would need to be covered by a HO-4 or HO-14 policy.)
Seasonal occupancies: The policyholder only uses the dwelling seasonally, and it is a secondary residence. This situation requires a separate policy from the one written for the primary dwelling.	HO-1, HO-2, HO-3, HO-5, HO-8
Condominium or cooperative unit-owner: The policyholder owns and occupies a unit in a condominium building or cooperative residence.	HO-6

SECTION I—PROPERTY COVERAGES

Coverage A—dwelling insures the dwelling listed on the policy declarations page and any attached structures. It also covers any fixtures or materials used to maintain the dwelling, as long as they are attached to or located on the premises. Coverage A also applies to any materials and supplies on or adjacent to the residence premises that are used to construct, alter, or repair the dwelling or other structures on the residence premises. There is no Coverage A on HO-4 and HO-14 forms. On HO-6 forms, Coverage A has a standard limit of $1,000 per occurrence.

Coverage B—other structures insures other buildings that are located on the same premises but are separate from the dwelling, though they may be connected by a utility line or fence. The maximum coverage amount is 10% of Coverage A's limit for one- and two-family dwellings. It is 5% of the Coverage A limit for three- to four-family dwellings. Coverage B does not cover structures used for business-related purposes, nor does it cover structures rented to others, unless the renter is a tenant of the dwelling. An exception is made for private garages rented to non-insureds.

Coverage C—personal property provides worldwide coverage to personal property owned or used by an insured. The policy will also cover, at the request of the insured, any personal property owned by others while it is on the residence premises of the insured, or any personal property of a guest or residence employee while on the insured premises. If property owned by the insured is usually kept at another residence owned by the insured that is not listed on the policy, coverage is limited to $1,000 or 10% of Coverage C's limit, whichever is greater. This limitation does not apply when such property has been removed from the insured location because it is not safely habitable and is undergoing repairs, rebuilding, or renovations. If the insured is moving to a new principal residence, his or her personal property is fully covered for a maximum of 30 days from when it is moved to the new location. For personal property that is located in a self-storage facility, coverage is limited to 10% of the Coverage C limit or $1,000, whichever is greater.

On homeowners insurance policies, Coverage C imposes **special limits**, also known as **sublimits**, which provide less coverage than the policy limit for certain categories of property. Many of these special limits were increased in the 2022 update to the homeowners policy forms. The updated amounts are in parentheses.

Special limits applicable to HO-2, HO-3, HO-4, HO-5, and HO-6:

- $200 ($300) on money, coins, precious metals (not including goldware, silverware, or platinumware), bullion, smart cards, medals, and stored value cards
- $1,500 ($2,000) on securities, accounts, deeds, evidences of debt, letters of credit, notes other than bank notes, manuscripts, personal records, passports, tickets, and stamps (the limit applies regardless of what media are used for these items and includes research, restoration, and repair costs)
- $1,500 on business-related property kept off the residential premises
- $2,500 ($3,000) on business-related property kept on the residential premises
- $1,500 ($2,000) on electronic accessories that are powered by either a car or a motor vehicle while they are in or on the car/motor vehicle
- $1,500 ($2,000) on watercraft and all related trailers and equipment
- $1,500 ($2,000) on trailers not associated with watercraft
- $1,500 ($2,000) on stolen jewelry, precious stones, watches, and furs *(the HO-5 form also covers loss or misplacement of these items)*
- $2,500 ($3,000) on stolen firearms *(the HO-5 form also covers loss or misplacement of these items)*
- $2,500 ($3,000) on stolen silverware, platinumware, pewterware, and goldware *(the HO-5 form also covers loss or misplacement of these items)*
- $2,000 on model or hobby aircraft or watercraft *(new for 2022)*

For the HO-14 form, many items do not have a specific dollar amount as the sublimit but are instead limited to 10% of the Coverage C limit in total for a single loss. Losses subject to this sublimit include:

- Money, coins, bank notes, precious metals (not including goldware, silverware, or platinumware), bullion, smart cards, medals, and stored value cards
- Securities, accounts, deeds, evidences of debt, letters of credit, notes other than bank notes, manuscripts, personal records, passports, tickets, and stamps (the limit applies regardless of what media are used for these items and includes research, restoration, and repair costs)
- Theft of watches, jewelry, furs, precious stones, and semiprecious stones
- Theft of firearms and related equipment

- Theft of silverware, goldware, platinumware, and pewterware
- Property used for business
- Antiques, fine art, paintings, and similar articles

Coverage D—loss of use reimburses the insured if a dwelling is rendered uninhabitable by a covered loss. There are two possible methods of reimbursement:

- **Additional living expense**—If the dwelling is the insured's residence, the policy allows the insured to preserve his or her typical standard of living.
- **Fair rental value**—If the insured is renting out the dwelling to another person, the policy repays any lost rent payments.

These expenses are also payable if a civil authority prohibits use of the residence premises due to a loss at an adjacent property. The loss must be from a peril that would be covered under the homeowners policy, and coverage is limited to two weeks.

BASIC PERILS

All homeowners insurance policies cover the following basic perils:

- **Fire or smoke,** except for smoke from industrial operations or agricultural smudging
- **Explosions**
- **Lightning**
- **Hail or windstorms,** but interior damage is only covered if the exterior of the building is breached; provides coverage for damage to watercraft and related equipment when located in a fully enclosed structure
- **Vandalism or malicious mischief** as long as the property has not been vacant for 60 or more consecutive days immediately preceding the loss
- **Theft,** excluding theft of materials at a dwelling under construction; property within any portion of the residence the insured rents to a non-insured; off-premises theft of trailers, semitrailers, campers, watercraft, and related equipment; property at any other location owned, rented, or occupied by an insured that is not a listed location on the policy unless being used as a temporary dwelling
- **Damage caused by aircraft**
- **Damage caused by motor vehicles** unless the vehicle is owned or operated by a resident of the insured premises and damage is to a fence, driveway, or walk
- **Riot or civil commotion**
- **Volcanic eruption,** excluding damage caused by earthquake, tremors, or land shock waves

PERILS COVERED ON BROAD FORM (HO-2)

The broad form, or HO-2, covers all the basic perils, as well as some expanded perils. These perils are also included on HO-4 and HO-6 forms, and are as follows:

- **Falling objects,** but interior damage is only covered if the exterior of the building is breached
- **Weight of ice, snow, or sleet,** excluding damage to awnings, fences, patios, swimming pools, foundations, pavement, retaining walls, piers, wharves, docks, or bulkheads
- **Overflow of water or steam** from plumbing, HVAC systems, household appliances, or automatic sprinkler systems
- **Sudden and accidental cracking, tearing, bulging, or burning** of plumbing, HVAC systems, household appliances, or automatic sprinkler systems

- **Artificial electrical current,** excluding damage to transistors, tubes, household appliance electrical components, computers, fixtures, and home entertainment systems
- **Freezing** of plumbing, HVAC systems, household appliances, or automatic sprinkler systems, but only when the insured has taken reasonable measures to prevent freezing, such as ensuring heat is maintained in the building or shutting off water supply when the heat cannot be maintained

EXCLUSIONS COMMON TO ALL HOMEOWNERS FORMS

Homeowners policies generally exclude coverage for losses resulting from the following:

- **Earth movement,** including tremors and land shock waves from volcanic eruption, earthquakes, landslides, sinkholes, subsidence of earth, mudslides, and mudflows
- **Water damage** caused by flood, overflow of a nearby body of water, tidal water, water blown by wind, or waves, as well as water that is backed up in sewers or drains, or which is overflowing from a sump; damages caused by waterborne materials are also excluded from coverage
- **War,** including any military action
- **Nuclear hazard,** including contamination and radiation
- Enforcement of **ordinance or law** relating to the construction, demolition, or alteration of property, including any consequential loss of property value and any expenses related to pollutant assessment or cleanup
- **Power failure** originating at a location off of the insured premises
- **Governmental action,** including government seizure or demolition of property
- **Intentional loss** caused by the insured or at the direction of the insured
- **Neglect** by the insured's failing to take appropriate action to protect covered property, especially after a loss occurs

Under Coverage C—personal property, certain types of property are generally excluded from coverage:

- Property covered under other insurance
- Animals, fish, and birds
- Motor vehicles legally required to carry insurance and to be registered in the state of principal garaging, as well as any related equipment; exception is made for portable electronic devices that do not require the vehicle's power to function
- Aircraft, including related parts and equipment; exception is made for hobby or model aircraft
- Hovercraft, including related parts and equipment
- Property of anyone occupying the insured dwelling as a part of any "home-sharing host activities"
- Property located in areas rented to or held for rental to a "home-sharing occupant"
- Property mainly used for "home-sharing host activities"
- Property of roomers or boarders who are not related to the insured
- Property contained within an area the policyholder rents to others or holds for rental to others; there is a limited coverage for landlord's furnishing under Additional Coverages
- Off-premises property rented to or held for rental to others
- Business data regardless of medium
- Credit and debit cards or other fund transfer devices except for limited coverage provided under Additional Coverages

- Virtual currency in any form
- Cannabis and other controlled substances except for those possessed with a valid prescription or products derived from hemp

HOMEOWNERS SPECIAL FORM (HO-3) AND HOMEOWNERS COMPREHENSIVE FORM (HO-5) EXCLUSIONS

The HO-3 form provides open peril protections for Coverages A and B and named peril coverage for Coverage C. The form covers any direct physical loss to covered buildings or structures unless the cause of loss is specifically excluded under the policy, while coverage for personal property is limited to the loss causes outlined in the policy. The HO-5 form also covers personal property on an open peril basis under Coverage C. The exclusions under these forms are more expansive than they are for named peril policies. In addition to the common exclusions, HO-3 also excludes many perils for Coverages A and B. For Coverage C under HO-3, personal property is covered for the same named perils that are listed in the HO-2 form. The HO-5 form excludes many perils for Coverages A, B, and C. These exclusions include:

- **Weather conditions**, but only those that result in a loss of the type listed in the common exclusions
- **Acts or decisions** of any entity, including the failure to act or decide
- Losses resulting from **faulty, defective, or inadequate** *(does not apply to Coverage C on the HO-5 form)*:
  - Planning, development, surveying, or zoning
  - Design, workmanship, repair, specifications, grading, remodeling, compaction, or construction
  - Materials used in repair, construction, remodeling, or renovation
  - Maintenance
- **Collapse**, except for the limited coverage described in the "other coverages" clause *(does not apply to Coverage C on the HO-5 form)*
- **Freezing, leaking,** or **discharge** of a plumbing, HVAC, or fire suppressing sprinkler system unless the insured party has taken reasonable steps to shut off the water supply, drain the appliances, and maintain heat in the building
- **Freezing, thawing,** or **pressure of water or ice** damage to walls, bulkheads, fences, pavement, foundations, footings, swimming pools, patios, retaining walls, wharves, piers, or docks
- **Theft** resulting from "home-sharing host activities" *(does not apply to Coverage C on the HO-5 form)*
- **V&MM** resulting from "home-sharing host activities"
- **Theft** from a building or structure that is under construction, including theft of materials or supplies
- **Theft** and **V&MM** to buildings that have been vacant for more than 60 consecutive days prior to the loss; a dwelling under construction is not deemed to be vacant
- **Repeated or continuous leaking or seepage of water or steam** coming from household appliances, plumbing, sprinkler systems, heating systems, or air conditioning systems when it occurs over a period of weeks, months, or years
- Damage to trees, shrubs, plants, lawns, and outdoor antenna equipment caused by **wind, hail, ice, sleet,** or **snow**
- **Wear and tear, deterioration,** or **marring**
- **Mechanical breakdown, hidden or latent defect,** or **inherent vice** of property that causes it to damage itself

51

- **Rust or corrosion**
- **Smog**
- **Mold, wet rot,** or **dry rot,** except for hidden damage that results from the accidental discharge of water or steam from plumbing, HVAC systems, automatic fire sprinkler systems, and household appliances on the residence premises, or off-premises storm drains, sewer pipes, water pipes, or steam pipes
- Release or seepage of **pollutants**
- **Cracking, settling, shrinking, expansion,** or **bulging** of pavement, patios, bulkheads, foundations, walls, roofs, floors, and ceilings
- Damage from **domestic animals, birds, vermin,** and **insects**
- **Smoke** from agricultural smudging or industrial operations

There are some additional exclusions for Coverage C under HO-5 that are not included in HO-3. These exclusions are:

- **Atmospheric dampness**
- **Sudden changes in temperature** unless directly caused by snow, rain, hail, or sleet
- Damage sustained during **renovating, repairing,** or **refinishing** property, except for jewelry, watches, and furs
- **Collision, sinking, stranding,** or **swamping** of watercraft, including any related trailers or equipment; exception is made for collisions with land vehicles

Certain articles that are highly susceptible to breakage are only covered when the damage is the result of specified causes. These items include glassware, eyeglasses, bric-a-brac, porcelain, statues, and other highly fragile personal articles. This limitation does not apply to watches, jewelry, bronze, photographic lenses, or cameras. For such property, HO-5 insures against all the Basic perils, except for volcanic eruption. It will also provide coverage for the following additional perils:

- **Sudden and accidental cracking, tearing, bulging, or burning** of plumbing, HVAC systems, household appliances, or automatic sprinkler systems
- **Water,** unless the result of an otherwise excluded cause
- **Sudden collapse** of all or part of a covered building
- **Theft,** including attempted theft

ADDITIONAL PROPERTY COVERAGES

Additional coverages are supplemental coverages that are automatically provided to the policyholder with the homeowners policy. The coverages in this section apply to expenses and losses that may not fit cleanly into one of the other coverages on the policy or losses for which the insurer only wants to provide limited coverage. Any changes to coverage limits made in the 2022 policy revision are indicated in parentheses.

Debris removal coverage reimburses the cost of removing debris if the damage was caused by a covered peril. The insurance company will also pay for any ash, dust, or particles resulting from a volcanic eruption. This coverage does not include tree removal. It is subject to the applicable property policy limit. Most policies increase the maximum available coverage by 5% when the combined cost of property damage and debris removal is greater than the policy limit.

Tree debris removal coverage covers the expenses of removing the insured's tree if it is knocked down by wind, hail, or weight of ice, sleet, or snow. It will also pay for removal of a neighbor's tree if it is knocked down by any peril included under Coverage C, but only if the tree is blocking entry to the insured's property or is blocking a fixture designed for handicapped assistance. Coverage is limited to $1,000 ($3,000) per occurrence and $500 ($1,500) per tree. Tree removal costs are payable in addition to the applicable limit of liability. The HO-14 form does not include this additional coverage.

Trees, shrubs, and other plants coverage insures trees, shrubs, and other plants if they are damaged or lost due to fire, explosion, lightning, riot, theft, V&MM, or aircraft that is not operated by an insured. There is no coverage for vegetation that is grown for business purposes. The 2022 form adds an exclusion for cannabis plants regardless of the intended use. On most policies, coverage cannot exceed 5% of Coverage A's limit, and there is a maximum payment of $500 ($1,500) per tree, shrub, or plant. On HO-4 and HO-6 policies, coverage cannot exceed 10% of Coverage C's limit, with a maximum payment of $500 ($1,500) for any single tree, shrub, or plant. This coverage is provided on top of the applicable policy limit. The HO-14 form does not include this additional coverage.

Reasonable repairs coverage reimburses the insured for any reasonable costs that he or she must pay in order to repair damage caused by a covered peril. These repairs must be necessary to protect the property against additional damage and loss. This coverage is subject to the applicable property limit of insurance shown on the declarations page.

Property removed coverage insures property as it is being moved from a location that is threatened by a covered peril. It will also cover the property while it is at its temporary location for a maximum of 30 days. Amounts paid under this coverage count against the applicable property policy limit.

Loss assessment coverage reimburses a maximum of $1,000 ($2,000) for loss assessments required by a corporation or property owners' association. The loss assessment must be necessitated by a covered peril that causes a direct loss to property owned collectively by all members in the association, such as a stairwell in a condominium building. The stairwell is owned collectively by each condominium owner in the building. The stairwell is damaged by a covered peril causing the condominium owners' association to conduct a loss assessment. Each owner in the building is required to pay a portion of the assessment. If an owner has homeowners insurance, the loss assessment coverage would pay his or her part of the assessment. Losses caused by earthquakes, land shock waves, or tremors are not covered. Loss assessment losses are paid in addition to the policy limits. There is also no coverage for any assessments charged by a governmental entity. The HO-14 form does not include this additional coverage.

Fire department service charge coverage provides a maximum of $500 to pay the fire department when it must save or protect covered property. This additional coverage does not carry a deductible and does not count against the policy limits. It is not covered when the loss is inside city limits where fire department services are provided. The HO-14 form does not include this additional coverage.

Credit card, electronic fund transfer card or access device, forgery, and counterfeit money coverage provides a maximum of $500 when the insured is legally obligated to pay losses caused by the following:

- Stealing or illegally using the insured's cards
- Accepting counterfeit money in good faith
- Forging or altering the insured's checks

This coverage does not include a deductible and does not cover losses caused by the insured's own business operations or dishonesty. When losses under this section lead to legal action against an insured, the insurer may provide a defense for such legal action. The 2022 coverage forms eliminate this coverage entirely; however, the insured may purchase an endorsement for this coverage, if desired.

Collapse coverage insures property against physical loss resulting from building collapse, provided it is caused by a covered or additional peril. This coverage is available on HO-2, HO-3, HO-4, HO-5, and HO-6. This coverage does not increase the applicable property limit of insurance.

Landlord's furnishings coverage insures appliances, carpeting, and various household items within apartments that are located on residence premises and are being rented or held for rent by the insured. Only losses resulting from the perils named in the HO-2 form are covered, excluding losses due to theft. This coverage provides a maximum limit of $2,500 ($3,000) and is only available on HO-2, HO-3, and HO-5. This coverage is subject to the applicable property policy limit.

Grave markers coverage insures grave markers and mausoleums against perils included under Coverage C for the HO-3 policy and for any insured peril under the other eligible policy forms. The coverage limit is $5,000 and is available on HO-2, HO-3, HO-4, HO-5, and HO-6.

Glass or safety glazing material coverage insures against glass breakage in a building and covers property like windows and storm doors. It also covers damage caused by flying glass shards. If covered glass breaks at a location that has been vacant for the 60 or more consecutive days preceding the loss, there is only coverage for breakage caused by earth movement. Payments under this coverage are included in the applicable policy limit. The HO-14 form does not include this additional coverage.

Building additions and alterations coverage insures installations, fixtures, and improvements if the insured has paid for their construction. This coverage has a maximum limit of 10% of Coverage C's amount and is only available for HO-4. Payments under this coverage are in addition to the policy limit.

Ordinance or law coverage provides a maximum of 10% of Coverage A's limit when the insured must rebuild or repair structures to conform to new building laws or land use codes. It does not reimburse for any loss of property value, or any costs associated with pollutants. This coverage is available on HO-2, HO-3, HO-4, HO-5, and HO-6. Payments under this coverage are in addition to the policy limit.

There are two Additional Coverages that are unique to the HO-14 form. These are:

- **Hard drive data recovery** coverage will reimburse up to $300 per policy period for expenses related to diagnosis and recovery of electronic data that has been lost due to deletion, corruption, or viruses. There is no deductible for this coverage, and it applies in addition to the policy limit.
- **Bed bug remediation** coverage will pay up to $500 per policy period for treatment of bed bug infestations at the residence premises. The need for treatment must be determined by someone licensed to make such a determination. Covered treatments include fumigation, heat, and spraying of pesticides. It does not cover the cost to replace damaged or infested property or for the cost of establishing whether an infestation exists. There is no deductible for this coverage, and it applies in addition to the policy limit.

PROPERTY CONDITIONS

Homeowners insurance policies contain similar policy conditions for property across the board. The property conditions common to the homeowners policies are as follows:

- Insurable interest and limit of liability
- Deductible
- Duties after loss
- Loss settlement
- Loss to a pair or set
- Appraisal
- Other insurance and service agreement
- Suit against us
- Our option
- Loss payment
- Abandonment of property
- Mortgage clause *(not on HO-4 or HO-14)*
- No benefit to bailee
- Nuclear hazard
- Recovered property
- Volcanic eruption period
- Policy period *(not on HO-14)*
- Concealment or fraud
- Loss payable

LOSS SETTLEMENTS

How a property claim is paid under a homeowners policy depends on the policy form being used. The **loss settlement** condition of the homeowners forms outlines specific methods of reimbursement for different types of loss.

HO-2, HO-3, and HO-5:

- Coverages A and B—Paid at the lower of the cost to repair or replacement cost
- Coverage C—Paid at the lower of repair/replacement cost or ACV

These forms also specify that carpeting, awnings, household appliances, outdoor antennas, outdoor equipment, grave markers, mausoleums, and structures that are not buildings are paid the lower of repair/replacement cost or ACV.

HO-4:

- Coverages A and B—N/A
- Coverage C—Paid at the lower of repair/replacement cost or ACV

HO-6:

- Coverage A—Paid at the actual cost to repair or replace the property when repaired or replaced within a reasonable time; if not repaired or replaced within a reasonable time, the lower of repair/replacement cost or ACV
- Coverage B—Not applicable
- Coverage C—Paid at the lower of repair/replacement cost or ACV

This form also specifies that grave markers and mausoleums are paid at the lower of repair/replacement cost or ACV.

HO-8:

- Coverages A and B—When repaired or replaced within 180 days, paid at the lower of the applicable policy limit or actual repair/replacement cost; if not repaired or replaced within 180 days or if the insured opts to not repair or replace the property, paid at the lowest of the applicable policy limit, the market value not including the value of the land, or repair/replacement cost less a reduction for depreciation
- Coverage C—Paid at the lower of repair/replacement cost or ACV

This form also specifies that carpeting, awnings, household appliances, outdoor antennas, outdoor equipment, and structures that are not buildings are paid at the lower of repair/replacement cost or ACV.

HO-14:

- Coverages A and B—Not applicable
- Coverage C—Paid at the least of replacement cost, the full cost of repair, the policy limit, or, if applicable, the special limit listed in the policy; this includes carpeting, household appliances, awnings, outdoor antennas, and outdoor equipment

This form also outlines certain property types that are not eligible for payment at replacement cost. For these items, the loss will be paid at the lower of repair/replacement cost or ACV. Such property includes:

- Jewelry
- Golf clubs, equipment, and clothing
- Furs and garments made with fur
- Cameras, projectors, films, and similar equipment
- Musical equipment
- Memorabilia, collectibles, souvenirs, and similar items
- Goldware, silverware, platinumware, and pewterware except for pencils, pens, smoking implements, and flasks
- Antiques, fine art, paintings, and similar articles
- Property that has not been maintained or is not in working condition
- Obsolete or outdated property held in storage and not used

Under the HO-2, HO-3, and HO-5 forms, payment for a dwelling or other structure is paid at the **replacement cost value** so long as the policyholder purchases coverage with a limit of at least 80% of the property's actual value. If a dwelling or structure is not sufficiently insured, payment will be made based on the ACV or the replacement or repair cost less a **coinsurance** penalty against the property's value, whichever is greater. The loss payment in these circumstances is calculated as follows:

Step 1:

$$\text{Replacement Cost of Property} \times 80\% = \text{Amount of Coverage Needed}$$

Step 2:

$$\frac{\text{Amount of Coverage Carried}}{\text{Amount of Coverage Needed}} = \text{Coinsurance Percentage}$$

Step 3:

$$\text{Loss Amount} \times \text{Coinsurance Percentage} = \text{Proportional Loss Amount}$$

Step 4:

$$\text{Proportional Loss Amount} - \text{Applicable Deductible} = \text{Claim Payment}$$

Assume, for example, that a person owns a house with a $100,000 replacement value, but only purchases $40,000 worth of insurance and has a $500 per loss deductible. If a $20,000 loss occurs, the proportional replacement cost would be calculated as follows:

- Step 1:

$$\$100,000 \times 80\% = \$80,000$$

- Step 2:

$$\frac{\$40,000}{\$80,000} = 50\%$$

- Step 3:

$$\$20,000 \times 50\% = \$10,000$$

- Step 4:

$$\$10,000 - \$500 = \$9,500$$

The amount payable to the insured in this situation is $9,500.

The HO-2, HO-3, and HO-5 policies continue by stating that the policy will only pay the ACV of the property until the repair or replacement is completed. Once this occurs, the balance of the replacement cost will be paid. In scenarios where the repair or replacement cost is less than $2,500 ($5,000 in the 2022 update) and also less than 5% of the insurance carried, the repair or replacement need not be completed for those amounts to be paid. The policyholder may opt to accept the ACV as payment and not complete the repair or replacement. If this option is exercised, the insured has until 180 days from the date of loss to notify the insurance company that he or she would like to pursue the balance of the cost.

SECTION II—LIABILITY COVERAGES
COVERAGES

Coverage E—personal liability is a type of liability coverage available on all homeowners policies except HO-1. It covers the insured when he or she is found liable for another person's **bodily injury** or **property damage**. The policy limit for Coverage E starts at $100,000 in damages per occurrence. In addition to this limit, the insurer agrees to pay court costs and post-judgment interest. However, the insurer will not cover any additional costs once it has paid the full policy limit in damages.

Coverage E protection applies in all the following locations:

- Anywhere the insured is found liable for bodily injury or property damage resulting from actions that have no business relation
- Residences acquired after the commencement of the policy period
- Property listed in the declarations section
- Property rented by the insured for non-business uses
- Temporary residences acquired by the insured
- Land on which the insured is building a new residence
- Vacant land in the insured's possession that is owned or rented by the insured
- Burial vaults/cemetery plots

Coverage F—medical payments to others is a type of liability coverage available on all homeowners policies. It covers **bodily injuries** sustained in the following situations:

- The injured party is staying at an insured location with permission from the insured.
- The injured party is not staying at an insured location, but the injury is caused by one of the following: an accident on insured property, a residence employee, or an animal in the insured's care or possession.
- The injury occurs on a property adjacent to the insured property.

Coverage F reimburses any necessary medical expenses up to three years after the injury has occurred. There is a minimum policy limit of $1,000 per person. This coverage is applicable regardless of the insured's liability for the injuries. Coverage F does not cover injuries to any insured or to those who are regular residents of the property except for residence employees.

EXCLUSIONS

Coverages E and F exclude damages and injuries from liability coverage if they result from or involve any of the following:

- Property damage or bodily injury that is **expected or intended** by the insured, except when using reasonable force to protect persons or property
- Losses resulting from the insured's **business activities,** except if the insured is less than 21 years old and self-employed on an occasional or part-time basis and has no employees
- Damage or injury arising out of the **rental** of any part of the property by the insured; exception is made for:
  - Property used for rental only on occasion and only for residential purposes
  - In a single-family residence, rental to no more than two boarders
  - Property used as an office, private garage, school, or studio
- Losses resulting from "home-sharing host activities" *(new for 2022)*
- Losses related to the provision of **professional services**
- Injuries or damages arising from a location owned, rented by, or rented out by an insured that is not an **insured location**
- Losses involving the ownership, maintenance, use, or transport of **motor vehicles;** exception is made for:
  - Vehicles in dead storage at the insured location
  - Vehicles used solely to service the residence
  - Vehicles used to assist the handicapped
  - Vehicles designed for use off public roads

58

- o Unmodified golf carts capable of a speed of 25 miles per hour or less when used in places it is legal to do so
- o A riding lawnmower being used as intended *(new for 2022)*
- Injury or damage related to the ownership, maintenance, use, or transport of a **watercraft**
- Aircraft or hovercraft liability
- Injury or damage caused directly or indirectly by **war** or other military action
- Transmission of a **communicable disease** by the insured
- Losses related to physical abuse, mental abuse, sexual molestation, or corporal punishment
- Damages or injury related to the use, sale, production, possession, or transfer of a **controlled substance** *(the 2022 version specifies that losses related to cannabis are excluded regardless of whether it is considered a controlled substance in the jurisdiction where the loss occurs)*

Under certain circumstances, Coverages E and F will extend liability protection to losses involving watercraft. These circumstances include the following:

- Watercraft in storage
- A sailing vessel that is less than 26 feet long
- A sailing vessel that is more than 26 feet long and is not owned or rented by the insured
- A non-sailing vessel that is powered by an inboard or inboard-outdrive engine or motor with power of no more than 50 horsepower that is not owned by the insured
- A non-sailing vessel that is powered by an inboard or inboard-outdrive engine or motor with power of more than 50 horsepower that is not owned or rented by the insured
- A non-sailing vessel that is powered by one or more outboard engines with power totaling more than 25 horsepower
- A non-sailing vessel that is powered by one or more outboard engines with power totaling more than 25 horsepower and the engine is not owned by the insured
- A non-sailing vessel that is powered by one or more outboard engines with power totaling more than 25 horsepower and the engine was acquired by the insured during the policy period
- A non-sailing vessel that is powered by one or more outboard engines with power totaling more than 25 horsepower and the engine was acquired before the policy period, and the insured must have declared them at the beginning of the policy or send written request for insurance within 45 days of acquiring them

The 2022 revision of the homeowners coverage forms simplified the exceptions relating to watercraft. The updated criteria are:

- Watercraft in storage
- A sailing vessel that is less than 26 feet long
- A sailing vessel that is more than 26 feet long and is not owned by the insured
- A non-sailing vessel that is powered by one or more engines with power totaling no more than 25 horsepower that is not owned by the insured
- A non-sailing vessel that is powered by one or more outboard engines with power totaling more than 25 horsepower and the engine was acquired before the policy period, and the insured must have declared them at the beginning of the policy or send written request for insurance within 45 days of acquiring them

Coverage E excludes the following from coverage:

- **Loss assessments** charged against the insured party as a member of a community, association, or corporation of property owners. It also does not apply to any liability taken on by the insured under any **contract or agreement**, except for written contracts that relate directly to the ownership, use, or maintenance of an insured location, or in which the insured party assumes liability for others before a particular event occurs.
- Property damage to property **owned** by the insured or property **occupied by, rented to,** or **used** by the insured.
- Bodily injury suffered by a person who is eligible to receive **mandatory or voluntary benefits** from the insured based on occupational disease law, non-occupational disability law, or workers' compensation law.
- Bodily injury or property damage when the injury or damage is also covered by a **nuclear energy liability policy**, or when the injury or damage would also be covered by a nuclear energy liability policy were the limit of liability not exhausted for the policy.

Coverage F excludes the following from coverage:

- Bodily injury suffered by a residence employee when injured **away from the insured location** and the injury does not arise out of the course of the employee's normal employment
- Injuries to any person who is eligible to receive **mandatory or voluntary benefits** under an occupational disease law, workers' compensation law, or non-occupational disability law
- Injuries resulting from radioactive contamination, nuclear radiation, or nuclear reaction
- Injury suffered by a person who **regularly resides on the insured location** but is not a residence employee

ADDITIONAL LIABILITY COVERAGES

All additional coverages for liability are paid in addition to the limit of insurance indicated on the policy declarations page.

Claim expenses coverage pays back defense costs, post-judgment interest, lost bond premiums, and any other reasonable expenses the insured may incur at the insurer's request.

First aid expenses coverage pays back any costs the insured may have incurred when rendering first aid during an accident.

Damage to property of others coverage provides a maximum of $1,000 (increased to $5,000 in the 2022 forms) per occurrence when the insured damages or destroys property, even if he or she is not legally liable. This coverage applies to property rented or borrowed by the insured, but not property owned by the insured. This coverage only applies if the property is not covered by the property coverages in Section I.

Loss assessment coverage provides a maximum of $1,000 (increased to $2,000 in the 2022 forms) so the insured can pay his or her portion of any loss assessment required by a property owners' association or corporation during the policy period. This coverage does not apply unless the loss occurrence is included under the liability section of the policy or the liability is incurred by a director, officer, or trustee of the insured.

SELECTED DEFINITIONS

There are some specific terms defined within a homeowners policy that are vital to correctly understanding and interpreting the coverage contained within. For the homeowners policy forms, the definitions are typically found at the beginning of the policy. This section highlights some of the important terms defined in the policies.

Bodily injury—Sickness, harm, or disease to a person's body, including necessary care, loss of services, and death that results from such injury.

Business—An occupation, trade, or profession performed full-time, part-time, or occasionally, including activities for which an insured receives more than $2,000 ($5,000 in the 2022 form) in compensation during the 12 months immediately preceding the policy period. Business does not include volunteering activities, unpaid home day care services, or home day care provided to a relative.

Cannabis *(new for 2022)*—Any product that contains any tetrahydrocannabinol (THC) or any other cannabinoid, including but not limited to marijuana.

Home-sharing host activities *(new for 2022)*—The rental or holding for rental or a mutual exchange of services of any part of the insured location by the insured to a "home-sharing occupant" through a "home-sharing network platform" including any related property or services offered by an insured in relation to the use of a "home-sharing network platform."

Home-sharing network platform *(new for 2022)*—An online application, digital network, or website that is used to arrange, for payment or other compensation, the rental of all or part of the residence premises that allows the agreement and compensation to occur via the internet.

Home-sharing occupant *(new for 2022)*—Anyone other than an insured that enters into an agreement or arranges payment with an insured using a "home-sharing network platform" for "home-sharing host activities" including anyone accompanying the "home-sharing occupant" under a home-sharing arrangement.

Insured—The policyholder and/or named insured and relatives residing with them are considered insureds under the policy. The following parties also meet the policy definition of insured:

- Anyone under the age of 21 and under the care of the policyholder or a resident relative.
- Students living away from home to attend school full-time if under age 24 and a relative of the policyholder OR under age 21 and in the care of the named insured or a resident relative.
- Any person or organization for which the policyholder or other insured is legally culpable is also considered an insured with respect to covered losses involving animals or watercraft.
- Anyone using a motor vehicle covered by the policy while working as an employee of any previously described insured or while using the vehicle on the insured location with appropriate consent of an insured.

Insured location—The "residence premises" listed on the policy is considered an insured location. The following locations also qualify as insured locations under the policy:

- The portion of any other premises, grounds, or other structures used by the policyholder as a residence so long as it is listed on the declarations page or was acquired during the active policy period

- Any premises used in connection with any of the above-described locations
- Any portion of a premises being used by an insured as a temporary residence that the insured does not own
- Vacant land owned or rented by the insured and not used for farming
- Grounds owned or rented by the insured upon which a dwelling of up to four units is being built intended for use as the insured's residence
- Cemetery plots or burial vaults owned by an insured
- Premises that are rented to the insured on occasion for non-business usage

Occurrence—An accident occurring during the policy period that causes "bodily injury" or "property damage" inclusive of repeated or continuous exposure to a harmful condition

Property damage—Damage or destruction of tangible property or the inability to use tangible property

Residence premises—The single-family dwelling in which the insured resides, a multi-family dwelling with up to four units in which at least one is occupied by the insured, or a portion of any other building in which the insured resides that is listed in the policy declarations, including any other structures or grounds at such a location

OPTIONAL ENDORSEMENTS

There are cases where the policyholder's insurance needs are not adequately met by the standard homeowners insurance policy. Property endorsements offer increased or broadened coverage in exchange for an additional premium. Liability endorsements are used to add coverage for liabilities that are excluded under the standard policy.

Under the **scheduled personal property** endorsement, the insured can schedule a separate insurance amount for certain property types. This endorsement provides open peril protection, carries no deductible, and reimburses losses at ACV, market value, repair or replacement cost, or stated value.

This endorsement can be used for the following types of property:

- Cameras, film, and various projection equipment
- Golf equipment
- Postage stamps
- Coins
- Fine art
- Jewelry
- Furs and similar clothing
- Silverware, goldware, and platinumware

The **personal property replacement cost** endorsement reimburses losses at replacement cost rather than at ACV. Consequently, certain items are excluded from this endorsement, such as antiques and rare paintings.

The **permitted incidental occupancies** endorsement eliminates many of the exclusions that deny or limit property insurance to residence-based businesses. When the incidental activities are done in a structure other than the main dwelling, this endorsement extends property coverage to that structure. It also removes the Coverage C special limit for business personal property so that the entire Coverage C limit is available for such losses.

Other property endorsements can be used to expand the perils for which the policy provides coverage. The **earthquake** endorsement covers earthquake damage to dwellings, structures, and personal property. This endorsement considers all earthquake activity occurring within 72 consecutive hours to be a single occurrence. The **sinkhole collapse** endorsement eliminates the policy exclusion for earth movement with respect to sinkhole collapse.

The **home day care coverage** endorsement provides both property and liability coverage for losses related to home day care businesses. This endorsement applies to both child day care and adult day care. This endorsement is subject to an aggregate limit of liability, meaning that there is a cap on how much will be paid for losses that occur within the same policy period.

The watercraft endorsement broadens the liability coverage losses involving watercraft. Rather than the limited coverage provided in the standard policy, coverage extends to losses involving the following:

- Watercraft equal to or less than 26 feet in length with outboard engines/motors outputting greater than 25 horsepower
- Watercraft with inboard or inboard-outboard engines/motors
- Sailboats longer than 26 feet in length

A **business pursuits** endorsement extends coverage for liability and medical payments to some business activities performed at the insured residence. The insured location must still be primarily used as a residence, and any business pursuits must be incidental for coverage to apply under this endorsement.

A **personal injury** endorsement expands bodily injury liability coverage to include personal injury. Personal injury entails reputational or other nonphysical harm caused by:

- False arrest, detention, or imprisonment
- Malicious prosecution
- Libel or slander
- Defamation
- Violation of another's right to privacy
- Unlawful entry
- Wrongful eviction

A **limited fungi, wet or dry rot, or bacteria** endorsement is only available for HO-3 and HO-5 policies and is offered on both the property and liability sections of the homeowners insurance policy. As a property endorsement, it covers all losses caused by mold if the loss was a product of a covered peril. It also covers expenses related to removing mold and the removal and replacement of property if required to access damaged areas. As a liability endorsement, it covers damages sustained by non-insureds resulting from actual, alleged, or threatened mold contact.

The 2022 revision of the homeowners insurance program also added a number of endorsements related to **home-sharing host activities**. These endorsements remove many of the exclusions in the standard homeowners policy related to home-sharing. When added to a policy, these endorsements add coverage for property, liability, and loss of rental value.

Dwelling Insurance

ELIGIBILITY

Dwelling insurance is a personal package policy intended for residential risks that do not meet the eligibility requirements for a homeowners insurance policy. Such criteria include:

- The owner is not an occupant of the dwelling.
- The dwelling is used as a rental property.
- The insured desires coverage that is less than the minimum requirement for a homeowners policy.
- The property is of low value.
- The dwelling is newly constructed, vacant, and pending sale.

The most common use of dwelling insurance is when the owner of the property does not live there and rents it as a residence to others. There is some overlap between the parties who are eligible for dwelling insurance and those who are eligible for homeowners insurance. Dwelling policies may be written for:

- Purchasers under contract
- Tenant occupants
- Co-owner occupants
- Joint owner non-occupants
- Seasonal occupancies
- Occupants under a life estate agreement or arrangement
- Dwellings under construction

Dwelling insurance may only be purchased for residential buildings and structures. Dwelling insurance covers the following types of property:

- Dwellings housing no more than four families, or apartments housing no more than five boarders
- Private outbuildings that are part of an insured property
- Mobile homes at fixed locations on a permanent foundation (DP-1 only)
- Vacant dwellings (with the appropriate coverage endorsement)
- Personal property contained in eligible dwellings

COVERAGES

Dwelling insurance includes three different policy types: **basic form (DP-1)**, **broad form (DP-2)**, and **special form (DP-3)**. The insured is not required to purchase the below coverages, even though they are preprinted on the dwelling policy form. The coverages purchased will be reflected on the policy declarations page. Each form gives progressively more coverage than the last. Dwelling insurance policy forms include the following sections:

- **Coverage A—dwelling**: This insures the dwelling, all attached structures (such as an attached garage), fixtures, doors, windows, and all materials, supplies, or equipment used to build, maintain, or service the property.
- **Coverage B—other structures**: Also referred to as **appurtenant structures**, this insures all structures that are part of the property but detached from the dwelling. A structure is still considered detached even if it is connected to the main dwelling by only a utility line or fence so long as there is clear space between the dwelling and the structure.

- **Coverage C—personal property**: This covers the personal property of the insured and anyone else living in the dwelling, including family members. The property must be usually within the dwelling, and certain types of property are excluded, including animals, aircraft, motor vehicles, hovercraft, any boats other than rowboats and canoes, business equipment and records, manuscripts, and financial instruments such as money, coins, bank notes, deeds, evidence of debt, and letters of credit. It does not cover gold other than goldware, silver other than silverware, or platinum other than platinumware. It does not cover any data or records, regardless of whether they are stored in computers or on paper. It does not cover credit cards or electronic funds transfer cards. Property of guests and servants is subject to limited coverage while on the insured premises. Finally, it does not cover water, steam, or grave markers. Coverage C also includes an **automatic removal coverage** provision, which protects property as it is being moved to a newly acquired location. This coverage lasts for up to 30 days or to the policy expiration date, whichever is shorter.
- **Coverage D—fair rental value**: This is a **loss of use** coverage. It covers any losses in rent payments resulting from covered property damage. For example, Mike is renting a room from Joe. If the room is damaged and rendered uninhabitable, Joe can no longer collect rent from Mike, but Joe is reimbursed the rent payment under Coverage D. This coverage even applies when damage to a separate, adjacent property renders the insured property uninhabitable. Under this condition, the time period over which reimbursement payments are made cannot exceed two weeks.
- **Coverage E—other coverages** *(under DP-1 form only)*: This coverage part provides additional coverages not addressed elsewhere in the policy.
  - **Other structures**—This section specifies that the insured may use up to 10% of the Coverage A limit for losses that fall to appurtenant structures, but that payments will reduce the available Coverage A limit of liability. Any amount paid for other structures using this extension will no longer be available for other property that falls under Coverage A for the same loss.
  - **Debris removal**—The policy will also pay any reasonable expense for the removal of debris left over from a covered loss, including any ash, dust, or particles resulting from a volcanic eruption. Payments for debris removal will be applied to the policy limit under which the damaged property is covered.
  - **Improvements, alterations, and additions**—This section states that if the insured party is a tenant of the location described on the declarations page, he or she may use up to 10 percent of the Coverage C limit of liability for covered losses to upgrades or alterations the insured paid for. Payments for these items reduce the limits available under Coverage C for the same loss.
  - **Worldwide personal property**—This covers personal property no matter where in the world it is located. Items are covered up to a maximum of 10% of the Coverage C limit. Payments under this section reduce the amount available under Coverage C for the same loss.
  - **Rental value**—This section gives the insured party the option to use up to 20% of the limit of liability under Coverage A for loss of rental income when a covered loss renders the property uninhabitable. Although very similar to Coverage D, rental value is a completely separate coverage. These payments will reduce the limits available under Coverage A for the same loss.
  - **Reasonable repairs**—This covers expenses incurred because of necessary measures to prevent further damage, but this coverage does not increase the applicable policy limit.

- o **Property removed**—There is coverage for property that is damaged while being moved away from the premises to avoid covered peril. This coverage lasts a maximum of five days and does not change the policy limit applicable to that property.
  - o **Fire department service charge**—The policy will pay up to $500 of the costs incurred when the fire department must come to protect or save covered property. This is considered additional insurance and is not subject to a deductible. However, fire department service charges are not covered when the property is within the city or district limits of the fire department.
- **Coverage E—additional living expense *(included in the DP-2 and DP-3 policies, may be added to the DP-1 by endorsement)*:** This provides reimbursement for any increased living expenses resulting from a covered loss when such loss makes the property unsuitable for its normal use. This coverage applies to expenses such as dining, motel, laundry, and transportation expenses. These costs are reimbursed until the insured's property is repaired or he or she can relocate to a permanent dwelling. Coverage is provided for the shortest amount of time needed to make the damaged property habitable or for the insured to settle in at the new location. If use of the covered premises is prohibited by government or civil authority due to conditions at a neighboring property, coverage lasts for a maximum of two weeks.
- **Coverage F—other coverages *(under the DP-2 and DP-3 policies)*:** This provides many of the same coverages as listed in Coverage E under the DP-1 policy but with some changes to how the other coverage applies to the policy limits. The coverage for **debris removal** and **worldwide coverage of personal property** both still fall within the applicable coverage limit. **Reasonable repairs coverage** does not change the limit of liability applicable to the loss. The coverage for **fire department service charges** is the same as under the DP-1.
  - o **Other structures**—This is the same as the coverage under the DP-1 except it is considered additional insurance, meaning it can be paid in addition to the applicable policy limit. The sublimit for this coverage remains 10% of the Coverage A limit.
  - o **Improvements, alterations,** and **additions**—This is the same as the coverage under DP-1 except it is considered additional insurance. The sublimit for this coverage remains 10% of the Coverage C limit.
  - o **Property removed**—The coverage is the same as in the DP-1 policy except that the timeline for covering removed property is extended to 30 days under the DP-2 and DP-3 policies.

Section F of the DP-2 and DP-3 policies includes several other coverages that are not part of the standard DP-1 policy:

- **Rental value and additional living expense**—This provides coverage similar to the rental value coverage under the DP-1 form but expands coverage to include additional living expense. The insurance company will pay up to 20% of the Coverage A limit for these losses, and the coverage is additional insurance that does not reduce the policy limit.
- **Trees, shrubs, and other plants**—This coverage pays for losses to shrubs, trees, lawns, or plants at the insured premises. There is only coverage for damage caused by: fire, lightning, explosion, civil commotion, riot, aircraft, vehicles not owned or operated by an insured, vandalism, and malicious mischief. Payments for plants will not exceed 5% of the Coverage A limit, and no more than $500 will be paid for damage to any one plant, shrub, or tree. This coverage is additional insurance.

- **Collapse**—This provides limited coverage when the damage is the result of a sudden collapse. The collapse must have been caused by a covered peril or one of the following: hidden decay; hidden insect or vermin damage; the weight of possessions, equipment, animals, or people; the weight of rain; or the use of defective materials or methods during the construction or renovation process. This coverage does not increase the applicable limit of liability.
- **Glass or safety glazing material**—This section covers the breakage of glass or safety glazing that is part of a covered storm door, storm window, or building, including that caused by earth movement. It also provides coverage for other property that is damaged only by the pieces of broken glass from any of these items. If the covered dwelling has been unoccupied for at least 60 consecutive days preceding the loss, the loss will not be covered.
- **Ordinance or law (may be added to the DP-1 by endorsement)**—This coverage will pay any extra costs incurred by the insured party in order to comply with the enforcement of an ordinance or law while rebuilding, repairing, or replacing the damaged property damaged by a covered cause of loss. The maximum amount that will be paid is 10% of the Coverage A limit, or, if the policy does not have Coverage A, 10% of the Coverage B limit. This does not cover any expenses caused by or related to the discharge of pollutants.

DWELLING PROPERTY BASIC FORM (DP-1)

The **dwelling property basic form**, or **DP-1**, automatically protects against **fire, lightning,** and **internal explosions**. The policy does not cover steam explosions caused by equipment that is leased, operated, or owned by the insured. The insured can also purchase **extended coverage**, or **EC**, against the following perils:

- Windstorm or hail
- **Explosion,** including explosions that are external, internal, or occur at adjacent properties
- **Civil commotion and rioting**
- **Volcanic eruption,** excluding damage from tremors, land shock waves, or earthquakes
- **Aircraft** contact with the dwelling
- **Vehicle** contact with the dwelling, excluding damage to fences, driveways, or walkways or when the vehicle is owned or operated by an insured resident
- **Smoke,** except for damage caused by fireplaces, industrial operations, or agricultural smudging

DP-1 also offers coverage for **vandalism and malicious mischief (V&MM)**; however, it is optional, and the declarations page must show the coverage for it to apply. When V&MM coverage is purchased, there are limitations on it. It does not cover damage to glass or safety glazing material or any loss due to theft. If the insured location has been vacant for more than 60 consecutive days at the time of the loss, there will be no coverage for any V&MM damages.

DP-1 excludes coverage for any damage caused directly or indirectly by the following:

- The enforcement of any **ordinance or law** applicable to construction, repair, or renovation of property, including any resulting loss of property value or expenses related to pollutants
- **Water damage,** including that caused by flood, waves, tidal water, wind-driven spray, sewer backup, seepage, or leakage through the building or structure, including any damage attributable to waterborne materials; exception is made for fire or explosion caused by water
- **Earth movement,** including earthquake, landslide, mudslide, and sinkholes regardless of cause; exception is made if such movement results in a fire or explosion

- **Intentional loss or damage** caused by either the insured or a person acting under the direction of the insured
- **War** or any other military action
- **Nuclear hazard,** including radiation and contamination
- **Neglect** of the insured, particularly failure to mitigate further damage to property after a loss event
- **Power loss** if the loss occurred somewhere off of the insured's property; exception is made when the power loss results in a loss of a covered type
- Seizure or destruction of insured property due to **governmental action,** except when such action is taken to mitigate the spread of fire

DWELLING PROPERTY BROAD FORM (DP-2)

The **dwelling property broad form**, or **DP-2**, automatically covers the following perils:

- All regular and EC perils covered under DP-1
  - Coverage for smoke damage is extended to include that resulting from fireplaces
  - Coverage for damage caused by vehicles is extended to vehicles owned or operated by an insured so long as the damage is not to a fence, walkway, or driveway
- Weight of sleet, ice, or snow against the roof and exterior walls
- Physical damage caused by burglars, excluding theft
- Falling objects
- Sudden and accidental discharge or overflow of water or steam from plumbing, air conditioning, heating, or sprinkler systems or from appliances
- Sudden and accidental damage from artificial electrical current
- Sudden and accidental cracking, burning, or tearing apart of any water, steam, or air system
- Freezing of sprinkler systems, plumbing, heating, air conditioning, or other household appliances unless the insured has taken proper measures to protect these items from freezing

DP-2 forms automatically include Coverages A, B, C, D, E, and F. As stated earlier, Coverage E is for additional living expense, and Coverage F is other coverages for the DP-2 form. DP-2 provides all other coverages found in DP-1, as well as a few additional other coverages that will be discussed in more detail later in this section. The exclusions in the DP-2 form are the same as those in the DP-1 form.

DWELLING PROPERTY SPECIAL FORM (DP-3)

The **dwelling policy special form**, or **DP-3**, differs from the DP-1 and DP-2 forms, as it provides **open peril** protection on Coverages A and B and **named peril** protection on Coverage C. Open peril contracts cover any cause of physical loss unless the specific risk has been excluded in the contract.

DP-3 forms exclude the following risks:

- All exclusions listed in the DP-1 form
- Applicable to Coverages A and B only:
  - **Weather conditions**, but only those that result in a loss of the type excluded in the previous section
  - **Acts or decisions** of any entity, including the failure to act or decide
  - Losses resulting from **faulty, defective, or inadequate**:
    - ❖ **Planning, development, surveying,** or **zoning**

- ❖ **Design, workmanship, repair, specifications, grading, remodeling, compaction,** or **construction**
- ❖ **Materials used in repair, construction, remodeling,** or **renovation**
- ❖ **Maintenance**
  - ○ **Collapse,** aside from the limited coverage provided in the "Other Coverages" section
  - ○ **Freezing, leaking,** or **discharge** of a plumbing, heating, air conditioning, or fire-protective sprinkler system unless the insured party has taken reasonable steps to shut off the water supply and maintain heat in the building
  - ○ **Freezing, thawing,** or **pressure of water or ice** to a fence, pavement, swimming pool, patio, retaining wall, or dock
  - ○ **Theft** of property that is not part of a covered building or structure
  - ○ **Theft** from a building or structure that is under construction
  - ○ **Theft** and **V&MM** to buildings that have been vacant for more than 60 consecutive days prior to the loss
  - ○ **Repeated or continuous leaking or seepage of water or steam** coming from household appliances, plumbing, sprinkler systems, heating systems, or air conditioning systems when it occurs over a period of weeks, months, or years
  - ○ Damage to trees, shrubs, plants, lawns, and outdoor antenna equipment caused by **wind, hail, ice, sleet,** or **snow**
  - ○ **Wear and tear, deterioration,** or **marring**
  - ○ **Mechanical breakdown**
  - ○ **Any quality inherent to the property that causes it to damage itself, including hidden or latent defect**
  - ○ **Rust or other corrosion**
  - ○ **Smog**
  - ○ **Mold, wet rot,** or **dry rot**
  - ○ Seepage or discharge of **pollutants**
  - ○ **Cracking, settling, shrinking, expansion,** or **bulging** of pavement, patios, bulkheads, foundations, walls, roofs, floors, and ceilings
  - ○ Damage from **domestic animals, birds, vermin,** and **insects**

CONDITIONS

The dwelling policy carries all the common conditions explained earlier in this chapter; however, the **loss settlement** condition of the dwelling property forms outlines specific methods of reimbursement for different types of loss. Under a DP-1 form, damage to the dwelling or other structures is paid at the lesser of the cost to repair or replace the damaged property or the actual cash value (ACV). Under the DP-2 and DP-3 forms, payment for a dwelling or other structure is settled at replacement cost value as long as the property is insured for at least 80% of its actual value. If the property is not sufficiently insured, the loss will be paid at ACV or at repair/replacement cost subject to a coinsurance penalty. The method for calculating this penalty is identical to the method previously outlined in the homeowners insurance section. Under all DP forms, losses to personal property are paid at ACV.

Like the homeowners policies, the loss settlement condition states that only the ACV of the property will be paid until the repair or replacement is completed. After repair or replacement is completed, the balance of the replacement cost will be paid. If the repair or replacement cost is less than $2,500 and also less than 5% of the insurance carried, replacement cost will be paid regardless of whether the repair or replacement occurs. Should the insured decide not to repair or replace the damaged property, he or she is entitled to be paid up to the property's ACV. The insured has 180 days from the date of loss to make a claim for the difference between the replacement cost and ACV.

Dwelling Policy Optional Endorsements

Theft coverage can be added as an endorsement to dwelling policies. Coverage for theft of personal property is specifically excluded in all DP forms, so only an endorsed policy will cover stolen items. The policyholder may choose between the **limited theft coverage endorsement** or the **broad theft coverage endorsement.** Both endorsements exclude coverage for losses occurring at premises that have been vacant for more than 60 consecutive days immediately preceding the loss.

Limited theft coverage insures against theft, attempted theft, and V&MM. The limited theft endorsement provides coverage for personal property that is owned by an insured or a residence employee and is located at the insured premises. Coverage also extends to owned personal property that is at a bank, a safety deposit company, a public warehouse, or an occupied dwelling. If at an occupied dwelling, it cannot be owned, occupied, or rented by the policyholder. Limited theft coverage includes the following sublimits:

- $1,500 on watercraft, including equipment and trailers
- $1,500 on other types of trailers
- $2,500 on firearms and related equipment

This endorsement excludes the following kinds of property:

- Precious metals
- Money
- Securities
- Jewelry
- Silverware
- Watches
- Furs
- Animals, birds, and fish
- Motor vehicles requiring registration in the state where they are principally garaged
- Credit cards
- Property in the mail
- Property in the custody of a bailee
- An employee's business property
- Aircraft, including related parts and equipment
- Hovercraft, including related parts and equipment
- Property that is for sale or used as samples
- Property of tenants who are not relatives of the insured
- Property covered by other insurance

Broad theft coverage insures against theft of personal property and protects property both on and off the premises. The endorsement separates coverage for on-premises and off-premises losses, and each will have a limit indicated on the policy declarations when purchased. For on-premises coverage, the property must meet the same criteria outlined under the limited theft coverage endorsement. To qualify for off-premises coverage, the insured must have also purchased on-premises coverage, the property must not be on the insured location, and the property must be used or owned by an insured or owned by a residence employee. Off-premises coverage does not extend to property that has been relocated to a new permanent residence. This endorsement

70

Copyright © Mometrix Media. You have been licensed one copy of this document for personal use only. Any other reproduction or redistribution is strictly prohibited. All rights reserved. This content is provided for test preparation purposes only and does not imply an endorsement by Mometrix of any particular political, scientific, or religious point of view.

contains the same exclusions as the limited theft endorsement, with the exception of the property listed below, which are subject to the listed sublimits:

- $1,500 on watercraft, including equipment and trailers
- $1,500 on other types of trailers
- $2,500 on firearms and related equipment
- $2,500 on silverware, pewterware, and goldware
- $200 on money, precious metals, bank notes, bullion, and coins
- $1,500 on securities, accounts, letters of credit, debt instruments, and similar items
- $1,500 for jewelry, watches, precious stones, and furs

Coverage L—personal liability and **Coverage M—medical payments to others** can be acquired as an endorsement or as a standalone policy. Generally, the two coverages are provided together and are listed on the same endorsement form.

Coverage L—personal liability covers the insured against personal liability for bodily injury or property damage for which he or she is determined to be legally responsible. To be covered, the damage or injury must have been caused by an **occurrence** that the endorsement defines as an accident, including continuous or repeated exposure to the same harmful condition. In addition, the insurance company pays to defend the insured against lawsuits, including fraudulent ones. It provides coverage to the policyholder and resident relatives for losses that occur on the insured premises, such as a trip-and-fall, or losses that occur off the premises for which the insured is liable, such as the insured's dog biting another person. Personal liability coverage has a minimum limit of $100,000.

Coverage M—medical payments to others covers reasonable medical expenses incurred due to bodily injury arising from the following:

- A person is injured while staying on the insured's property with permission from the insured.
- A person is injured off the insured's property as a result of the insured's activities, a situation at the insured's property, or the insured's animal(s).

The Coverage M endorsement does not cover injuries to the insured or his or her family. However, it does apply to situations in which the insured is not liable. The minimum coverage limit is $1,000 per person. Coverages L and M include the following additional coverages: **damage to others' property, claims expenses,** and **others' first aid expenses**. When the insured damages the property of others, the insurer provides a maximum reimbursement of $1,000 per occurrence. First aid expenses are only covered when they involve a bodily injury covered under the policy.

The personal liability endorsement also reimburses the following covered claims expenses:

- The insured's court costs, if the suit is covered under the policy
- Defense costs
- Post-judgment interest on settlements
- Bond premiums if the bond is needed as part of the insured's legal defense and the premium does not surpass Coverage L's limit
- Expenses incurred by an insured due to requests by the insurer that are intended to facilitate claim investigation or defense; the daily limit for lost earnings is $250

Coverages L and M exclude coverage for losses resulting from the following:

- War
- Communicable diseases transmitted by the insured
- The insured's business activities and decisions
- Sexual, physical, and mental abuse, including corporal punishment
- Losses that the insured expects or intentionally causes
- Damage arising from premises that are owned by, rented by, or rented to others by an insured that is not an insured location under the policy
- Use of controlled substances, other than the legal use of prescription drugs
- Most damages caused by motor vehicles and watercraft
- All damages caused by aircraft or hovercraft

Coverage L does not provide reimbursement for the following losses:

- Losses already protected by laws such as workers' compensation
- Losses related to any contractual obligations assumed by the insured, except when the contract directly relates to the ownership or use of the insured premises or when the insured assumes the liability of another party prior to an occurrence
- Loss assessments charged against the insured by a homeowners association or other body made up of property owners
- Property damage if the property is owned by the insured
- Property damage if the insured is renting, occupying, or using the property
- Losses that are already covered by other insurance
- Injuries sustained by the insured or any family members or minors living in the insured's household
- Losses for which the policyholder is also an insured under a nuclear energy liability policy

Coverage M excludes the following injuries from coverage:

- Nuclear hazard-related injuries
- Injuries to people who reside in the insured dwelling but are not residence employees
- Injuries to residence employees if the injuries are sustained off the insured property and are not related to work performed on the insured property
- Injuries already covered by laws such as workers' compensation

Automatic increase in insurance endorsement provides annual increases to the property insurance coverage limit, typically 4%, 6%, or 8%. This endorsement is intended to offset higher costs due to inflation.

Dwelling under construction is also a dwelling policy endorsement. It covers a partially completed dwelling where the named insured is the intended occupant.

EARTHQUAKE INSURANCE

Earthquake insurance can be offered either as an endorsement on dwelling and homeowners policies or as a separate policy. It insures structures and their contents against damage caused by earthquakes and their aftershocks. According to the policy, a single earthquake occurrence includes the initial tremor and any aftershock for the next 72 hours. It does not extend coverage to damage from tidal waves or tsunamis. A special deductible applies to earthquake claims. It is calculated

based on a percentage indicated on the endorsement or coverage form. There is generally a minimum deductible of $500.

MOBILE HOME INSURANCE

Mobile home insurance is available as a standalone policy but is most commonly written by adding an endorsement to the HO-2 or HO-3 policy. It provides coverage quite similar to that provided under the homeowners policy. Coverage for collision damage sustained while transporting a mobile home is available through an optional endorsement. Mobile home insurance covers the following:

- The mobile home unit itself, including any built-in equipment
- Any equipment or structure that is attached but not originally built in, such as carports, water pumps, and shelters
- Loss of use in the form of additional living expenses
- Homeowners liability, much like Section II of the homeowners policy

WINDSTORM INSURANCE

If an insured lives in an area especially prone to serious storms, an insurance company may decline to write a homeowners or dwelling policy unless it is endorsed with a windstorm and hail exclusion. This is especially true for people living in coastal or plains areas. Endorsing the residential policy in that way will also exclude damages resulting from tornadoes and hurricanes. Because an insured in such an area still needs protection from those perils, there is the option to purchase a separate **windstorm insurance policy**. Obtaining one of these policies will typically require an inspection of the insured's residence to check for any pre-existing hail or storm damage or to ensure that any previous repairs were done correctly and in compliance with local building code.

PERSONAL UMBRELLA LIABILITY AND EXCESS LIABILITY INSURANCE

If a policyholder needs liability coverage beyond that provided in an auto or homeowners policy, he or she may purchase additional coverage under an **umbrella liability policy** or an **excess liability policy**. While these policies can serve similar functions, there are some very important differences. Excess liability policies provide coverage in instances where the **underlying liability coverage** is not sufficient to pay for a loss. For example, an insured carries $250,000 per person in auto bodily injury liability. The insured is involved in an at-fault accident that causes $500,000 in bodily injury damages. An excess policy would cover the amount in excess of the $250,000 provided by the auto policy. Excess policies require the insured to carry primary policies for all perils covered by the excess policy.

Umbrella policies will also cover the excess liability but may provide broad coverage for loss types that are not covered by the underlying policy. For example, the typical homeowners liability coverage will not cover personal injuries such as slander or libel. If the insured engages in activities that create a risk for such losses, he or she can purchase an umbrella policy that would provide that coverage. The umbrella policy will require underlying coverage for those losses for which a primary policy is available; however, for losses that are not usually insured by an underlying policy, such as personal injury in the above example, the umbrella will be the primary coverage. Typically, the exclusions for an umbrella policy are for intentional acts, events covered by workers' compensation, and events that occur while at work or in pursuit of business objectives.

Both policies mandate a minimum level of coverage on the applicable underlying policies. If this amount is not maintained or if a required underlying policy is allowed to lapse, the insured will need to pay out of pocket for the amount the underlying policy should have or would have covered. Some policies that cover such losses contain a **retention limit**, which is the loss amount the insured must pay out of pocket before coverage applies. These limits, ranging from $250 to $10,000, are chosen by the insured. A similar provision applies to commercial umbrella and excess policies, which will be discussed in more detail later in this guide.

Auto Insurance

Personal Auto Insurance

Personal auto insurance is a personal, multi-line policy that covers both property and casualty losses. Insurers can issue auto policies either on an individual basis or a joint basis to spouses living in the same household. In many states, the insured is legally required to have auto liability insurance. In every state, the insured must have a minimum coverage limit on certain types of liability if he or she has been in an accident, has been found guilty of a serious traffic offense, or was unable to pay a fine from a previous traffic offense. These limits vary from state to state.

The limit of liability on Part A is provided on either a **combined single limit basis (CSL)** or a **split limit basis**. Under a CSL, bodily injury and property damage are covered collectively with a single amount, such as $75,000 for all damages resulting from a single accident. Under a split limit, each type of liability has a separate limit. Split limits are expressed as a sequence of three numbers, such as 20/40/15:

- $20,000 for bodily injury per person
- $40,000 for bodily injury per accident
- $15,000 for property damage per accident

Personal auto policies also offer property insurance, which protects the insured against property damage resulting from collision and non-collision losses. These coverages are usually optional, and the limit of insurance is based on the ACV of the vehicle that is insured.

An **assigned risk plan**, also known as an **automobile insurance plan**, helps drivers who are especially risky to insure for auto insurance coverage sufficient to fulfill state law requirements, usually bodily injury and property damage liability. Under an assigned risk plan, multiple insurance companies in the same state voluntarily pool their resources, and each company is assigned high-risk drivers at random.

Personal auto policy (PAP) is a basic type of auto insurance containing a declarations section and a policy form. It includes four essential coverages, each of which has unique insuring agreements, conditions, and exclusions:

- **Part A**—liability coverage
- **Part B**—medical payments coverage
- **Part C**—uninsured motorists bodily injury coverage
- **Part D**—coverage for damage to your auto

The insured is not required to purchase all coverages. However, state laws may dictate which coverages he or she must have. For instance, Part A is always a requirement, while Part B is usually optional. A PAP covers **private passenger autos**, which include vehicles identified in the declarations section, as well as **newly acquired autos** obtained during the policy period, **non-owned autos** including **temporary substitute autos**, and **trailers**. Private passenger auto is not a defined term within the PAP. The definition of a private passenger auto may vary slightly from state to state, but it is generally described as a vehicle having four wheels that is designed for use on public roadways and is used for personal reasons such as commuting to school and work or running errands. A vehicle of this type that is used to transport passengers for pay is not considered a private passenger auto for insurance purposes, aside from some limited exceptions that are outlined within the policy language. Most states mandate registration and minimum insurance coverage for private passenger autos that are used on public roads. The PAP does provide definitions for "newly acquired auto," "non-owned auto," and "trailer," which are provided later in this section.

Regarding new vehicles acquired during the policy period, these vehicles are covered temporarily, but need to be listed on your policy as soon as possible. Each policy and insurer can have a different grace period, but most allow a new vehicle coverage for 14 days without being scheduled, though they prefer it to be added sooner.

SELECTED DEFINITIONS

Prior to discussing the details of the coverage provided by the policy, there is a section devoted to important policy definitions. There are also a few definitions in other sections of the policy. Key policy definitions include:

"You" and "Your"—The named insured listed in the policy declarations and his or her resident spouse. If the spouse should cease to reside with the named insured, the spouse will only be considered "you" under the policy until 90 days following the change in residency, the inception of another auto policy under which the spouse is a named insured, or the end of the active policy period, whichever is earliest.

"We," "Us," and "Our"—The insurance company writing the policy and furnishing coverage.

Bodily injury—Any sickness, injury, or disease suffered by a person, up to and including death.

Business—Any trade, profession, or occupation.

Collision—Impact with another auto or object or the upset of an auto.

Custom equipment—Any parts of an auto that were not from the original manufacturing of the auto or replaced with parts of similar like, kind, and quality to the manufacturer's original parts. It does not include electronics that reproduce, receive, or transmit audio, visual, or data signals.

Family member—Any resident of the named insured's household who is related to the insured via blood, marriage, or adoption, including foster children and wards.

Newly acquired auto—Any private passenger auto that the insured comes to own during the policy period. It includes pickups or vans so long as the following criteria are met:

- It is not covered by any other insurance.
- It has a gross weight of no more than 10,000 pounds.
- It is not used for delivering goods or materials, except when such use is incidental to the insured's business of installing, maintaining, or repairing furnishings or equipment or used in farming or ranching.

Non-owned auto—A private passenger auto, pickup, or van that is not owned by the insured or regularly available for any insured's use, that is being driven by the named insured or one of his or her family members. This includes any non-owned auto or trailer that is used temporarily as a substitute for a covered auto that is out of service due to breakdown, repair, service, loss, or destruction.

Occupying—In, upon, entering or exiting, or getting on or off.

Property damage—Damage to or loss of use of tangible property.

Trailer—Any vehicle designed to be towed by a private passenger auto, pickup, or van, including any farming trailers pulled by any of these.

Transportation network platform *(new to 2018 edition)*—An application or digital network that uses the internet to put drivers in contact with passengers to provide prearranged transportation services in exchange for money or other compensation.

Your covered auto—A vehicle listed in the policy declarations, a newly acquired auto, an insured-owned trailer, or any trailer or auto being used as a temporary substitute for any of the preceding vehicles out of service due to breakdown, repair, service, loss, or destruction. Temporary substitutes are not considered covered under Part D—Coverage for Damage to Your Auto.

COVERAGES

Part A—liability coverage insures the policyholder against bodily injury and property damage for which he or she is legally liable. This coverage does not apply unless the insured is legally responsible for injuring or damaging the property of another person, the injuries and damages are covered under the policy, and the loss is caused by an auto accident. Under most circumstances, Part A insures the following groups:

- The named insured and his or her family when they are operating any automobile
- Any person operating the insured's car if he or she has received permission from the insured
- Any other person or organization who shares liability with the insured
- Any other person or organization who incurs liability from operating an automobile or trailer owned by the insured and his or her family

The policy reimburses any damages or settlements up to the limit of liability. The policy also pays **supplementary payments,** which include defense costs, pre-judgment interest, and claims adjusting expenses. This section of the policy will also reimburse an insured up to $250 per day in lost wages if the insurer requires his or her attendance at trials or hearings related to a covered claim. Once the policy limit has been paid via settlement or judgment, however, the insurer is not obligated to pay any additional expenses.

The **out-of-state coverage** provision insures covered autos being driven through multiple states. It guarantees the PAP will fulfill the financial responsibility and legal requirements of any state through which the auto is driven so long as it is within the coverage territory described in the policy.

According to the **other insurance** clause, when a vehicle is covered by multiple insurers, the insurer is only obligated to pay its fair share of the loss. This fair share is the portion of the liability coverage's limit of liability in relation to the total of all applicable limits. This portion is determined by dividing the liability limit of the insurer's policy by the total liability limit of all policies. For instance, assume a single auto is covered by two policies: policy A and policy B. Policy A has a liability limit of $40,000, while policy B has a limit of $30,000. If an accident occurs, policy A will reimburse 57% ($40,000/$70,000) of the liability damages. This clause also notes that any insurance provided for a vehicle not owned by the insured party, including any vehicles being used as a temporary substitute for a listed vehicle, should be considered excess over any other collectible insurance. Further, coverage under this policy will be primary over any policy written as excess to this policy.

Part B—medical payments coverage reimburses any reasonable medical expenses incurred when the named insured, his or her family members, or passengers are injured in an auto accident. Part B is not liability coverage. Rather, it applies no matter who is at fault, and it covers medical and funeral costs for the following parties for a maximum of three years following the date of the accident:

- The named insured and his or her family members, whether they are occupants of autos and trailers intended for public road use or pedestrians hit by such vehicles
- Another person who is occupying the named insured's vehicle with the insured's permission

The insured cannot collect duplicate payments under Part B if a loss is already covered elsewhere in the policy. Also, the other insurance condition under Part B is identical to the other insurance condition under Part A. Part B provides coverage subject to a single limit of liability. This means that the coverage available is a flat amount that applies to each injured person eligible for coverage. The most commonly selected limits are $1,000 or $5,000.

Part C—uninsured motorists bodily injury coverage (UMBI) protects the insured when he or she is involved in an auto accident with an uninsured or underinsured person. It reimburses certain losses that would have been covered by the other person's insurance. Bodily injury is normally the only loss covered by Part C. Punitive damages are never covered. Part C insures the following persons: the named insured and his or her family; any person occupying the covered auto; or any person who has the right to recover bodily injury damages for the injured party when the injury is caused by an uninsured motorist (such as a parent who is reimbursed the medical expenses of a child involved in an accident). A loss must meet the following four conditions before Part C takes effect:

- There must be an auto accident resulting in bodily injury.
- The insured must incur a loss.
- The insured must have a legal entitlement to collect bodily injury damages.
- The other driver must fulfill the definition of an uninsured motor vehicle.

A motor vehicle is considered uninsured if it meets the following criteria:

- It is without liability coverage when the accident occurs.
- It has insufficient liability coverage according to state laws.
- Its liability coverage is invalid because the insurer has denied coverage or has suffered insolvency.
- Its driver is unidentified after committing a hit-and-run against the insured, his or her family members, the insured auto, or any motor vehicle occupied by the insured or his or her family.

A motor vehicle cannot be considered uninsured if any of the following criteria are present: the vehicle is owned by or regularly used by the insured or his or her family members; the vehicle is owned by the government; the vehicle is owned or used by a self-insured person or entity (unless they become insolvent); the vehicle is used as a residence; the vehicle is intended for off-road use; the vehicle is run on crawler treads or rails.

Part C's limit of liability is either a **single limit** (one limit covering every type of loss) or a **split limit** (a separate limit for each type of loss). Part C does not cover losses in the following situations:

- They have already been reimbursed on behalf of the responsible party (duplicate coverage).
- They are also covered by workers' compensation or disability benefits.

According to the **other insurance** clause, when multiple PAPs are covering the same person, the maximum insurance limit cannot exceed the Part C limit of the largest single policy. For instance, assume that a person is insured by three separate PAPs. Policy 1 has a Part C limit of $300,000, policy 2 has a Part C limit of $250,000, and policy 3 has a Part C limit of $100,000. In the event of an accident with an uninsured motorist, the insured cannot collect more than $300,000 because policy 1 has the largest single Part C limit.

Part D—coverage for damage to your auto insures against physical damage to vehicles owned or used by the insured. This coverage only applies when the loss is direct and accidental, and caused by the following:

- Collision
- Other than collision (OTC)

In essence, Part D provides open peril protection, but only covers the vehicle and its attached components. It does not apply to any personal property stored within the vehicle. Part D also offers **transportation expense coverage**, which pays the insured $30 per day (up to a $900 maximum total limit) when he or she incurs the following expenses:

- Transportation expenses due to physical damage or loss to the insured's auto if the damage is covered under collision and OTC
- Loss of use expenses resulting from any legal liability the insured may incur as a result of damage to a "non-owned auto" as defined in the policy
- Transportation expenses due to theft of the insured's auto (in this situation, there is a 48-hour waiting period before coverage is provided)

The collision and OTC coverages protect the insured against physical damage to his or her vehicle. Physical damage loss is reimbursed by paying the **ACV** or the **repair/replacement value**, whichever is lesser. **Collision** coverage applies when the insured's vehicle collides with another object or vehicle. **Other than collision (OTC)** coverage applies when the insured's vehicle sustains virtually any other type of direct and accidental loss not excluded under the policy. OTC coverage protects against the following kinds of perils: glass breakage; fire; water, flood, and hail; windstorm; theft or larceny; riot; bird or animal contact; explosion; earthquake; vandalism and malicious mischief; and falling objects such as missiles. The insured does not have to purchase both kinds of coverage and can even use different coverages for different cars. Part D also provides coverage for **temporary substitute autos** and **non-owned autos**, which are defined as any autos not owned by the insured. For each occurrence covered under collision coverage or OTC coverage, there is a separate deductible.

Part D excludes the following types of damages from coverage:

- Freezing, wear and tear, electrical/mechanical breakdown, and road wear on tires
- Nuclear or war-related activities
- Insurrection or rebellion

- Government destruction or confiscation of property (the interests of a loss payee are still covered)
- Participation in a prearranged speed or skills contest, such as a race
- Radar, laser, and other types of detection equipment
- Usage as public or livery transportation
- Usage for business-related activities (the named insured and his or her family members are covered as long as they are using private passenger autos or trailers)
- Usage as part of an auto business
- Usage of a non-owned auto by the named insured or his or her family if they lack permission or entitlement to do so

Part D excludes the following types of property from coverage:

- All visual, audio, and data electronic equipment, such as radios, CD players, tape players, PCs, phones, VCRs, and videos, including their parts, accessories, and media. (This type of equipment is not excluded if it is permanently installed in the auto or operated by the auto's electrical system via a detachable housing unit.)
- Trailers, campers, and motor homes, including their refrigeration, dining, cooking, and plumbing equipment, if they are not included in the declaration section. (If the trailer is not owned by the insured, it is not excluded from coverage.)
- Any type of equipment intended to expand living space, such as awnings and cabanas.
- Custom furnishings and similar equipment in pickups and vans. (Caps, bedliners, and covers are covered.)
- An auto that a named insured or his or her family member is renting, as long as state laws or the rental agreement prohibits the rental agency from collecting from the insured or his or her family member.

CONDITIONS

The **other sources of recovery** provision applies when there are multiple auto policies covering the same person. It is very similar to the other insurance condition under Parts A and B of auto policies; there is one major exception, which is that if a loss occurs, the insurer will factor in every source of recovery, including sources other than insurance, when determining what percentage of the loss it owes.

The **limit of liability** provision explains the limitation on coverage for damages to the insured party's automobile. Specifically, the limit of liability for loss will be either the **ACV** of the stolen or damaged property, or the amount required to **replace or repair** the property, whichever is smaller. It is noted that the insurance company will pay a maximum of $1,500 for damages to trailers that are not owned by the insured. Losses to permanently installed electronic equipment are insured to a maximum of $1,500. This condition also states that the insurer is entitled to make deductions for depreciation when valuing damaged property. Should a repair result in the property being in better condition than it was prior to the loss, the insurance company will not reimburse for this betterment.

According to the **no benefit to bailee** condition, if an insured auto is damaged while in the possession of a bailee, such as a repair shop or parking garage, the bailee cannot receive any insurance benefit.

The **appraisal** condition explains that if the insurance company and the insured party do not agree on the value of the loss, either side is entitled to request an appraisal. The protocol for appraisal is that both sides select an appraiser, and these two appraisers select an umpire. The two appraisers will submit independent estimates, and if they fail to agree, the difference will be mediated by the umpire. Any decision agreed upon by two of the three appraisers will be binding to all parties. Each side will pay for its own appraiser, and the cost of the umpire will be split equally. The insurer specifies that an agreement to appraisal does not constitute a waiver of any policy provisions.

According to **Part E—duties after an accident or loss**, the insured must perform the following duties after a loss:

- Notify the police as soon as possible if the loss involved a hit-and-run accident or theft.
- Notify the insurance company immediately of the location, time, and circumstances of the accident or loss.
- Provide the names and addresses of all injured persons and all available witnesses.
- Cooperate during the investigation, defense, or settlement of any claims or suits. The insured party should also.
- Deliver copies of any notices or legal papers associated with the loss or accident as soon as possible.
- If requested, submit to physical examination or examination under oath, the expense of which will be borne by the insurance company.
- Authorize the insurance company to obtain any medical reports or relevant records.

Part F—general provisions explains coverage conditions of the policy, including the duties and obligations of both the insured and the insurer. This section is similar in purpose to the Conditions section of a residential policy. These conditions, duties, and obligations include the following:

- **Policy period**—Losses are covered only when they occur during the policy period.
- **Coverage territory**—Losses are covered only when they occur within the coverage territory. This territory consists of the United States, its territories and possessions, and Canada.
- **Changes**—The policy represents all of the agreements made between the policyholder and the insurer. Any changes to the policy must be approved by the insurer and be confirmed by a written endorsement.
- **Legal action against us**—The insured can only take legal action against the insurer if all policy terms have been fulfilled, and he or she can never sue to determine liability for a loss.
- **Our right to recover payment (subrogation clause)**—Upon payment of a claim, an insured's recovery rights are granted to the insurer to the extent that the insured was paid. The insured is also obligated to assist the insurer in recovering funds from a third party if requested. The insurer will not pursue recovery against a person who is operating a covered auto with permission or entitlement to do so.
- **Termination**—This provision explains the cancellation and nonrenewal requirements for both the insured and the insurer. It also explains that if there is a premium refund owed due to the termination, the refund will be sent to the first named insured. The amount will be based upon the portion of the policy period remaining at the time of termination.
  - **Cancellation**—The insured can cancel on any date by providing written notice to the insurance company. When the insurer wants to cancel, it is bound by far more stringent cancellation rules. Within the first 60 days of a new policy, the insurer is subject to the following requirements:
    - It must provide 10 days' written notice if cancellation is because the insured is failing to pay premiums.
    - It must provide 20 days' written notice if cancellation is for some other reason.

After the first 60 days of a new policy or if the policy is a renewal of an existing policy, the insurer can only cancel under the following conditions:

- The insured is failing to pay premiums.
- The insured has misrepresented material facts within the policy.
- The license of the insured vehicle's driver has been revoked or suspended.
  - **Nonrenewal**—If the insurance company decides not to renew or continue the policy, it is required to mail notice to the named insured party at least 20 days before the end of the policy period. For policy periods other than one year, the insurance company may only decline to renew on the anniversary of the original effective date.
  - **Automatic termination**—The policy will automatically terminate if one of the following occurs:
    - ❖ The offer of renewal is not accepted by the named insured; this will terminate at the end of the policy period
    - ❖ The named insured fails to pay the renewal premium; this will terminate at the end of the policy period
    - ❖ The insured obtains comparable insurance on a covered auto from a different insurer; this will terminate the policy on the effective date of the replacement policy
- **Bankruptcy**—If the insured goes bankrupt or otherwise becomes insolvent, the insurance company is not relieved of any obligations under this policy.
- **Fraud**—There will be no coverage for any insured who makes knowingly fraudulent statements or commits fraud related to a loss under the policy.
- **Transfer of your interest in this policy**—The named insured cannot assign his or her interest in the policy to another party without the written permission of the insurance company. Should the insured listed in the policy declarations pass away, their interest in the insurance policy is transferred to either the resident surviving spouse or the appointed legal representative of the insured's estate. Coverage in this scenario will only persist until the end of the current policy period.
- **Two or more auto policies**—If a loss is covered by more than one auto policy, recovery will not exceed the maximum limit of liability under any single policy.

EXCLUSIONS

Part A excludes the following liabilities from coverage:

- Bodily injury or property damage that the insured has purposefully caused
- Bodily injury or property damage that is already covered by or should be covered by a Nuclear Energy Liability policy
- Bodily injury sustained by an employee of the insured while in the course of the insured's business—domestic workers are not subject to this exclusion unless the insured provides or is required to provide workers' compensation
- Damages arising from the insured's use of a vehicle as a public conveyance, including any time logged into a ride-sharing or transportation network platform
- Damage to property that is used by, rented to, or in the care of the insured, except for private dwellings and garages
- Damage to property the insured owns or is transporting
- Damage to off-road vehicles and vehicles with fewer than four wheels

- Liability incurred when the insured's auto is involved in an auto business such as repairing, servicing, selling, parking, or storing—exception is made for a covered auto being used by an insured, the insured's family member, or any partner, agent, or employee of either of these
- Liability incurred when a vehicle is being used without the insured's permission
- Damages arising from the insured's use of a vehicle while working or otherwise engaged in business—exception is made for private passenger autos, vans, or pickups, as well as any trailer being used with any of these
- Liability incurred when a vehicle is a contestant in a prearranged race or other driver skill or stunting contest
- Damages incurred while the auto is being used as part of a private vehicle-sharing program and driven by anyone other than the insured or his or her family members
- Accidents involving autos owned by or furnished for the regular use of the insured or his or her family members that are not listed on the auto policy—exception is made when the named insured or spouse is maintaining or occupying such a vehicle
- Damages caused by any vehicle designed for or capable of flight

Part B excludes injuries from coverage if they result from the following:

- Occupying a motor vehicle that has fewer than four wheels
- Participating in or preparing for a prearranged race or contest
- Using a covered auto as a means of public or livery transportation
- Using the vehicle as part of the insured's business except when the vehicle is a private passenger auto, van, pickup, or trailer used with any of these
- Occupying a vehicle that is also used as a residence
- Accidents involving autos owned by the insured or a family member or furnished for regular use by these parties that are not covered autos under the policy
- Occupying a vehicle that is uninsured, even when the insured owns it
- Another person occupying an uninsured vehicle that is owned or regularly used by the insured's family member
- An insured occupying a vehicle when he or she does not have permission or reasonable evidence of entitlement to do so
- War or nuclear hazards
- Accidents already covered by workers' compensation
- Injuries sustained when occupying or struck by any vehicle designed for or capable of flight

Part C excludes coverage in the following situations:

- The insured is occupying or struck by an auto that is owned by the insured but not covered under the policy's uninsured motorist coverage
- A family member of the insured that is occupying or struck by an auto that is owned by the insured and covered by another policy
- Settlements made without permission from the insurance company if that settlement compromises the company's ability to recover payment
- Injuries sustained while an auto is being used for livery or public transportation including when logged into a transportation network platform
- Accidents involving an auto that the insured is using without entitlement or permission to do so

- Injuries sustained while the auto is being used as part of a private vehicle-sharing program and driven by anyone other than the insured or eligible family members
- Punitive damage awards
- Injuries that should be covered by workers' compensation or disability benefits laws

Part D excludes the following losses from coverage:

- Damage incurred while the vehicle is being used as a public conveyance, including use on a transportation network or ride-sharing platform
- Damage related to normal wear and tear, freezing, electrical issues, mechanical failure, or road damage to tires
- Damage caused by radioactive contamination or nuclear weapons
- Damage related to war or military action
- Loss or damage to equipment that is not permanently installed in a vehicle such as radios, stereos, tape and compact disc players, navigation systems, internet access systems, personal computers, video entertainment systems, telephones, TVs, two-way radios, scanners, or CB radios
- Total loss of an auto due to government action or intervention (this exclusion does not apply to a loss payee's interest in the covered auto)
- Damage to a non-owned auto that the insured or an insured family member was operating without reasonable belief he or she is entitled to use it
- Loss or damage to trailers, campers, or motor homes including any furnishings or related equipment
- Losses involving vehicles designed for or capable of flight
- Loss or damage to radar detection equipment
- Loss of damage to custom equipment or special decorations in excess of $1,500 (meaning there is a sublimit of $1,500 per loss for these items)
- Losses sustained while an insured is in the business of selling, repairing, servicing, or storing vehicles
- Damage to any auto while it is inside a facility designed for racing, driver skill training or events, or similar competitions
- Damage to vehicles rented by an insured unless the rental agreement precludes coverage by the rental company

OPTIONAL ENDORSEMENTS

Named non-owner coverage endorsement provides coverage for persons who rent or borrow their auto. This endorsement automatically covers private passengers, pickups, panel trucks, and vans for 14 days if they were acquired during the policy period.

Joint ownership coverage endorsement enables an auto policy to be issued to two or more people living in the same household, even if they are not married.

Extended non-owner coverage endorsement provides coverage for the insured and his or her family, even when they are operating vehicles not owned by the insured or excluded under the basic policy, such as work vehicles.

Towing and labor costs endorsement provides a minimum of $25 for the towing and labor costs that are incurred when a vehicle is disabled. Labor is only reimbursed if it is performed at the place where the vehicle was disabled.

Miscellaneous type vehicle endorsement covers vehicles that are not normally insured by the policy, such as motorcycles, mopeds, motor homes, and golf carts. Not all companies offer this endorsement. The insured may have to purchase a separate **specialized** policy to cover these vehicles.

Optional limits transportation expenses coverage endorsement reimburses the insured for transportation and/or loss of uses expenses incurred when a scheduled or non-owned auto is disabled due to a covered loss. The insured chooses the limits per day up to a 30-day maximum for this coverage. It is sometimes referred to as **rental reimbursement coverage**.

UNINSURED MOTORISTS' PROPERTY DAMAGE AND UNDERINSURED MOTORISTS' BODILY INJURY COVERAGE

Uninsured motorists' property damage coverage (UMPD) is usually an optional coverage on the PAP. It is added by endorsement and intended to provide coverage similar to that provided under Coverage D. This coverage part reimburses the insured for property damage caused by an uninsured driver. It can also pay for property damage sustained in a hit-and-run loss where the at-fault party cannot be identified. In most cases, the policyholder needs to select either collision coverage or UMPD coverage so as to avoid duplication of coverage under a single policy. UMPD is subject to a deductible just like collision coverage but can be a cheaper option since coverage only applies in limited circumstances.

Underinsured motorists' coverage (UIM or UMBI) is available as an endorsement on most personal auto policies. The endorsement form used is dictated by the state in which the policy is written. There is an important distinction between uninsured motorists' bodily injury coverage (UMBI) and UIM coverage; which coverage applies is based on whether the at-fault driver carried at least the state minimum liability coverage. If he or she carried no insurance, or insurance that was less than the state minimum, the claim falls under the UMBI. UIM applies when the insured is in an auto accident with a motorist whose coverage meets state requirements, meaning the motorist cannot be considered uninsured, but is insufficient to cover all the insured's losses. This coverage reimburses the difference between the actual loss amount and the amount paid out by the motorist's insurance. Depending on state law, it may be required or optional. In most states, the underinsured motorists' section of the policy will be similar to the uninsured motorists' policy language.

Commercial Auto Insurance

Commercial auto insurance, commonly called **business auto policy (BAP)**, provides liability and physical damage coverage for the insured business when it sustains a loss involving autos that it owns or uses. There are currently two revisions of the BAP in use, 2013 and 2020. Key differences between these policies will be noted. These policies may also provide medical payments, uninsured motorists', and underinsured motorists' coverage for bodily injuries. Commercial auto insurance policies include the following sections:

- Common policy declarations
- Common policy conditions
- Any number of four possible coverage forms: business auto, business auto physical damage, garage, or motor carriers'
- Corresponding declarations sections for the chosen coverage forms

COMMERCIAL AUTO COVERAGE SYMBOLS

Section I—covered autos provides information about how covered autos are designated by their numerical symbols. The symbol will be listed on the policy declarations for each coverage purchased to indicate which autos are covered for that specific coverage. The coverage symbols used are:

Symbol	Covered Autos
1	Any auto—This includes autos used, owned, leased, hired, rented, or borrowed by the insured.
2	Owned autos only—This includes autos owned by the insured.
3	Owned private passenger type autos only—This includes private passenger autos owned by the insured.
4	Owned autos other than private passenger autos only—This includes any trucks, buses, motorcycles, trailers, and similar vehicles owned by the insured.
5	Owned autos subject to no-fault law—This is used for autos that must have no-fault benefits under state law.
6	Owned autos subject to compulsory uninsured motorists' law—This is used for autos that must have uninsured motorist coverage under state law.
7	Specifically described autos—This is used for vehicles identified in the declarations section.
8	Hired autos only—This is reserved for autos that have been hired, borrowed, or rented by the insured.
9	Non-owned autos only—This is reserved for autos that are used in the insured's business, but not hired, borrowed, or rented by the insured, an employee, a partner, a member of the insured LLC, or any relatives of any of these parties.
19	Mobile equipment subject to compulsory or financial responsibility or other motor vehicle insurance law only—This is used when a land vehicle would meet the definition of "mobile equipment" under the policy if not for the statutory requirements in the location where the vehicle is registered or principally garaged.

This section also discusses newly acquired autos, trailers, mobile equipment, and non-owned autos. The provision regarding newly acquired autos is applicable to all symbols except for 8 and 9. For symbols 1 through 6 and symbol 19, any vehicle that is newly acquired during the current policy period is covered through the end of that policy period. If symbol 7 is indicated, newly acquired autos are only covered if the insurance company insures all of the insured business's other vehicles or it is a direct replacement for a vehicle described on the policy. The insurer must be notified of the newly acquired auto and ask for it to be insured within 30 days of taking ownership for coverage to continue. The 2020 version of the form makes some changes to the wording of this section. Rather than only addressing newly acquired owned autos, it is modified to be applicable to the insured's owned vehicles in general. It applies the same conditions as the previous version to newly acquired autos under symbols 1 through 7 and under symbol 19. The updated form provides additional clarification that autos the insured rents or leases without a driver for a period of at least six continuous months will be considered owned under the policy. These must be purchased using a written agreement requiring the insured to provide primary auto insurance.

With regard to trailers, liability coverage applies if the trailer has a load capacity of no more than 2,000 pounds and is meant to travel primarily on public roadways. The 2020 revision modifies the trailer liability coverage to apply to those with a gross vehicle weight rating of 3,000 pounds or less. This change was likely made as all commercially manufactured vehicles must include a gross vehicle weight rating in the specifications, so that number is more consistent than the load capacity.

One potential issue with this change is that some people build their own trailers. Homemade trailers are not required to provide specifications, so there is no gross vehicle weight rating for the policy to consider. The implication is that the automatic coverage for trailers will no longer extend to homemade trailers as a result of this change. Mobile equipment is covered while being hauled or towed by a covered auto. For a non-owned auto to be covered, it must be operated with the permission of the owner as a temporary substitute for a covered vehicle that is broken down, being serviced or repaired, is a total loss, or has been destroyed.

LIABILITY COVERAGE

Section II—covered autos liability coverage pays for property damage or bodily injury an insured is legally liable for as the result of an auto accident including losses related to the ownership and maintenance of an auto. BAP forms also reimburse any legal costs the insured may incur due to bodily injury or property damage resulting from owning, maintaining, or using a covered auto, as well as defense costs for the insured. The policy will also pay all the amounts legally owed by the insured as part of a **covered pollution cost or expense**. The insurance company only promises to pay for covered pollution costs or expenses when the same accident that incurred the expense caused property damage or bodily injury.

Section II of the BAP next explains "Who Is an Insured." This section includes a brief list of those parties who qualify as an **insured** for the policy. To begin with, the named insured is considered an **insured** for any covered automobile. Secondly, in most cases any person who is using a covered automobile with the permission of the insured is also covered. There are a few exceptions to this coverage. For instance, the owner or anyone else from whom the named insured party **hires or borrows** a covered auto is not covered by the insurance. There is an exception made for trailers connected to a covered auto. Autos owned by an employee, or a member of an employee's household, are not covered by the policy. Individuals using covered automobiles who are working in a **business** of selling, servicing, parking, repairing, or storing automobiles are not covered unless that business is the business of the insured party. Any person who is **moving** property to or from a covered automobile is not covered unless they are an employee, partner, lessee, or borrower of the employer. Any **partner** of the named insured is not covered if the vehicle is owned by the partner or by any member of his or her household. The final group to be covered by the standard business auto policy is any person liable for the conduct of the insured party. This coverage only applies to the extent of the insured's liability.

BAP forms also provide the following **supplementary payments**, which are paid in addition to the limits of insurance:

- $2,000 maximum for bail bond costs incurred due to a covered accident
- Bonds to release attachments not to exceed the limits of insurance
- Expenses incurred by the insured as a result of a lawsuit
- All reasonable expenses incurred by the insured party at the request of the insurance company, including reimbursement for loss of earnings up to $250 per day
- Post-judgment interest
- Other expenses the insured may incur due to a request from the insurance company

The **out-of-state coverage extension** applies when business autos are driven through more than one state. It alters the commercial auto insurance coverage to conform to a particular state's liability requirements.

LIABILITY EXCLUSIONS

BAP forms exclude the following liabilities from coverage:

- Injuries expected or intended by the insured
- Damages resulting from completed operations; work is defined as complete when all of the tasks indicated in the contract have been completed, when all the work at a particular job site has been completed, when the relevant part of the work at a job site has been put to its intended use by someone besides another contractor or subcontractor, or when the work has been abandoned
- Contractual obligations aside from those assumed in an "insured contract"
- Pollution damage that is not specifically stated as covered in the policy
- Bodily injury and property damage caused by self-propelled vehicles with cherry pickers, pumps, generators, air compressors, and similar permanently attached equipment
- Covered autos used in preparation for or participation in organized auto speed or driving skill competitions
- Losses stemming from war or any other military action
- Bodily injury to an **employee** of the insured that is related to the normal course of employment, including any liability the insured has as an employer; the policy also excludes coverage for injuries sustained by the spouse, parent, child, or sibling of an employee
- Bodily injury to a **fellow employee** of an insured that occurs in the course of the fellow employee's employment
- Injuries for which the insured is required to provide benefits under workers' compensation, disability benefits, or unemployment compensation law
- Property damage incurred when the property is being moved by a mechanical device
- Property damage when the insured owns, transports, or controls the property
- Damage or injury caused by the ownership, maintenance, or use of any unmanned aircraft *(new for 2020)*

LIMIT OF INSURANCE

The **limit of insurance** section states that the insurance company will not make payments in excess of the maximum amount of liability coverage indicated on the declarations page. This is true regardless of the number of insureds, covered autos, involved autos, premiums paid, or claims made. Any bodily injury, property damage, or covered pollution cost or expense that is caused by continuous or repeated exposure to the same conditions will be considered by the insurance company as resulting from a single accident. In other words, the policyholder may not receive duplicate payments for the same elements of loss that are covered in other portions of the auto policy.

PHYSICAL DAMAGE COVERAGE

Section III—physical damage coverage outlines the property damage coverage available for the vehicles the insured uses within his or her business. Typically, the insurance company will provide **comprehensive coverage** for losses to a covered auto, unless the loss is caused by the covered automobile's collision with another object, the covered automobile is overturned, or the cause of loss is excluded by the policy. If comprehensive coverage is purchased, it also covers broken glass, damage due to falling objects or missiles, and damage from hitting a bird or animal. Standard deductibles include $500 and $1,000. The insurance company will pay for losses under **specified causes** of loss coverage, specifically fire, lightning, or explosion; theft; windstorm, hail, or earthquake; flood; mischief or vandalism; or the sinking, burning, collision, or derailment of any conveyance during transport of the covered auto. Finally, the insurance company will assert that

88

losses will be paid under **collision coverage** when damage to a covered auto is the result of its collision with another object or due to it being overturned. The most common deductibles for collisions coverage are $500 and $1,000. In some instances, glass breakage is reimbursed as a collision loss rather than a comprehensive loss, thereby negating the possibility of paying two deductibles when a collision causes both glass breakage and another type of damage.

If indicated on the policy declarations, the policy will also reimburse the insured for **towing** costs related to the disablement of a covered vehicle. The policy will pay up to the limit indicated on the policy declarations. For the coverage to apply, the disabled vehicle must be a private passenger auto. The 2020 edition of the form renames this section to **towing and labor** and expands coverage to light- and medium-duty trucks. In both forms, any labor must be provided at the location the vehicle is disabled for the costs to be paid.

The BAP form offers the following extensions:

- **Transportation expenses**—This provides $20 per day up to a $600 maximum to cover the insured's transportation expenses after his or her auto is stolen. Reimbursement begins 48 hours after the auto is stolen and ends once the auto has been returned or the insurer repays the loss. The 2020 policy increases this coverage to $30 per day up to a $900 maximum.
- **Loss of use**—This provides $20 per day up to a $600 maximum to cover loss of use for rented autos for which the insured is legally liable. The 2020 policy increases this coverage to $30 per day up to a $900 maximum.

PHYSICAL DAMAGE EXCLUSIONS
The BAP form excludes the following from property damage coverage:

- War or military action
- Nuclear hazards
- Actual or perceived decrease in value of property due to its involvement in a direct physical loss, often referred to as diminution in value or diminished value
- Any electronic equipment that transmits sound, visual, or data signals; exception is made for equipment that is permanently installed in the auto and designed to only be powered by the auto's electrical system; such losses are limited to $1,000 per occurrence
- Tapes, records, and any other media designed for use with an audio, video, or data system
- Devices such as radar detectors, radar jammers, or laser detectors
- Natural wear and tear, mechanical or electrical breakdown, freezing, and tire damage from road use
- Damages incurred while participating in or practicing for any professional or organized racing, stunting, or demolition event

LIMITS OF INSURANCE AND DEDUCTIBLE
The **limits of insurance** section states that the maximum payment for any single accident is either the **ACV** of the damaged or stolen property at the time of the loss, or the cost of **repairing or replacing** the damaged or stolen property, whichever is less. This section also defines a special limit of $1,000 for any electronic equipment that meets the criteria for coverage discussed earlier in this section. For autos damaged to the extent of being a total loss, the insurer will make adjustments for depreciation and physical condition when establishing the ACV of the covered vehicle.

The **deductible** section states that any loss payment made will be reduced by the amount of the deductible. It also states that no deductible will be applied to fire or lightning losses when they are covered by Comprehensive coverage. The 2020 revision modifies the deductible section significantly. First, it reinstates the deductible for fire and lightning losses that had been waived in the prior edition. It also clarifies that any deductible is considered prior to applying the limits of insurance when the loss falls under Comprehensive or Specified Causes of Loss coverage. More simply put, for losses that exhaust the limits of insurance, the deductible is applied to the total amount of the loss rather than being subtracted from the limit of insurance. The newer version of the form explicitly states that the Specified Causes of Loss deductible will be applied only to losses caused by vandalism, mischief, or theft. For Comprehensive coverage, the deductible applies if the loss falls under the "all perils" coverage. When a loss occurs that is subject to the Comprehensive or Specified Causes of Loss deductible and multiple vehicles are damaged or stolen, the 2020 revision limits the deductible applied to five times the highest applicable deductible regardless of how many covered vehicles were affected. The amount of the highest deductible will be used even if the specific auto carrying that deductible was not involved in the covered loss.

CONDITIONS

In the BAP, the conditions section is applicable to all coverages unless specified otherwise within the section. They are split into **loss conditions** and **general conditions**.

There are three loss conditions specific to physical damage coverage. These are **appraisal for physical damage loss, loss payment—physical damage coverages**, and **no benefit to bailee—physical damage coverages**. The appraisal condition sets out the process for when the policyholder and the insurance company do not agree on the value of damaged property. The process is essentially the same as the appraisal process under the personal auto policy. The no benefit to bailee condition states that the policy will not make payment to the extent that it will benefit any party in possession of covered property in exchange for payment. The loss payment condition states that the insurance company has the option to handle losses in one of three ways:

- Pay the insured for the value of the property or pay for the repair or replacement of damaged property.
- If stolen property is recovered, the insurer may return the property, at their expense, to the insured; in this case, the insurer will also pay for any damage sustained in the course of the theft.
- Take possession of all or part of the property after payment to the insured of an appraised or agreed value.

The **duties in the event of accident, claim, suit, or loss** condition explains the steps the policyholder is obligated to take when a loss occurs. These duties are:

- **Alert** the insurance company as soon as possible to provide information about the loss, including the insured's **name and address**, the **location and time** of the incident, the **sequence of events** that led to it, and, if possible, the names and addresses of any **injured parties or witnesses.**
- **Assume no obligation** and **pay no expense** without the consent of the insurance company, unless this obligation or expense is intended to be borne by the policyholder.
- Promptly **send** the insurance company copies of any **request, demand, notice, order, legal paper, or summons** related to the claim or suit.
- **Cooperate** with investigation or defense of the claim or suit.

- **Authorize** the insurance company to obtain **medical records** or any other information that is relevant.
- If the loss involves **theft** of a covered auto or its equipment, the insured is required to **notify the police.**
- Take reasonable steps needed to avoid further damage to the covered property.
- Allow the insurer to inspect the covered auto and any documentation proving the loss prior to the repair or disposal of the damaged property.
- Submit to **medical examination** or **examination under oath** should the insurer request it.

The **transfer of rights of recovery against others** condition outlines the protocol for when the insured has a right of recovery against a third party. If the insured opts to take payment from the insurer transfers, his or her recovery rights transfer to the insurer to the extent of the payment made. The insured also has an obligation to protect the insurance company's right to recovery and assist in such recovery when requested. This is also known as a **subrogation clause**.

The **other insurance** condition explains how the policy will apply when multiple policies are covering the same loss. For owned covered autos, the BAP will be primary for the auto as well as for any trailers being towed by an owned covered auto. The BAP is also primary for Hired Auto Physical Damage coverage unless a driver was provided as part of the leasing, hiring, renting, or borrowing agreement. For non-owned autos and trailers towed by non-owned autos, the BAP will be excess over any other valid insurance. When a driver is provided via such an agreement, the vehicle involved is not considered a covered auto under the policy. If the insured assumes liability under an "insured contract," the BAP will be primary. When two or more forms cover a single loss on the same basis, the insurance company will only pay its proportional share of the loss based on the total coverage limits available. The insured cannot be reimbursed more than the highest single policy limit.

The **legal action against us** condition prevents the insured from suing the insurance company unless he or she has met all policy terms. For lawsuits stemming from liability, the insurer must agree in writing that the insured has an obligation to pay for a loss. The insurance company may not be named in a lawsuit intended to determine the liability of the insured.

The **bankruptcy** condition states that the bankruptcy or insolvency of the insured or the estate of the insured does not relieve the insurance company of any of the obligations indicated by the coverage form.

The **liberalization** condition states that, in the event that the insurance company revises the coverage form in such a way that more coverage is provided without raising the premium, the policy will be automatically adjusted on the same day that this revision goes into effect in the policyholder's state.

The **premium audit** condition describes the calculation of the **estimated premium**. Specifically, the insurance company typically states that the original estimated premium is based on the **reported exposures** at the time of the policy's initiation. Once the actual exposures are determined, the final premium can be calculated. The estimated total premium is credited against the final premium due, and either the insured or the insurance company will receive whatever difference exists. When the policy is issued for a period of more than one year, the premium for it is computed every year based on the rates or premiums that have been established at the beginning of that year.

The **policy period and coverage territory** condition states that the coverage form promises coverage for accidents and losses that occur within the dates specified on the declarations page and within the coverage territory. The covered territory consists of the United States, its territories and possessions, and Canada. **Worldwide liability coverage** applies when the insured hires, rents, borrows, or leases a private passenger auto. It provides worldwide liability coverage for such a vehicle when it is obtained **without** a driver. The auto cannot be hired, leased, borrowed, or rented for more than 30 days for this coverage to apply.

The **two or more coverage forms or policies issued by us** condition declares that the aggregate maximum limit of insurance under all the coverage forms or policies may not be higher than the highest applicable limit of insurance for any one coverage form or policy. The only exception to this rule is when one of the insurance policies has been issued specifically as excess insurance.

SELECTED DEFINITIONS

Accident—Any exposure to conditions, including repeated or continuous exposure to such conditions, that results in property damage or bodily injury.

Auto—A land motor vehicle, trailer, or semitrailer that was designed to travel on public roads, or any land vehicle that is required by law to carry liability insurance in its jurisdiction of licensing or primary garaging location. This definition does not include mobile equipment.

Bodily injury—Any injury, sickness, or disease sustained by a person. Death that results from any injury, sickness, or disease is also classified as bodily injury.

Covered pollution cost or expense—Any cost or expense that arises out of any request, demand, or order, or any claim or suit by a government authority, for the insured to clean up or dispose of pollutants. When the threatened, alleged, or actual release, migration, dispersal, discharge, seepage, or escape of pollutants results in expenses or costs, there are certain scenarios that do not fall within the definition of a "covered pollution cost of expense." This situation occurs when the pollutants or the containers in which they are stored are:

- Transported or towed by a covered auto
- Handled while being transferred onto or off of a covered auto
- In the course of transit by or for the insured
- Stored, treated, processed, or disposed of on or in a covered auto

If during any of the above, the escaped pollutants consist of substances used or expelled during the normal operation of a covered auto's electrical, hydraulic, or mechanical systems, and the pollutants escape from the areas of the auto intended to hold or dispose of them, the loss would be considered a "covered pollution cost or expense." This exception is not applicable to losses caused by the operation of certain mobile equipment, including cherry pickers, air compressors, pumps, generators, or equipment used in spraying, welding, building cleaning, geophysical exploration, lighting, or well-servicing.

The definition also excludes losses involving pollutants and, if applicable, their containers occurring:

- Prior to being moved to the location the insured intends to accept them for transfer into or onto a covered auto
- Subsequent to being unloaded from a covered auto at the location where they are to be delivered, abandoned, or disposed of by the insured

The two above exclusions are not applicable if, while the insured is away from any location they own or rent, the escape of pollutants is the result of damage, overturn, or upset of the pollutants and/or their containers caused by the maintenance or use of a covered auto. The escape of the pollutants must have been caused directly by such damage, overturn, or upset.

Employee—Any person performing tasks in the course of the insured's business, including leased workers but excluding temporary workers.

Insured—Any person or entity meeting the requirements outlined in the "Who Is an Insured?" portion of the applicable coverage. When coverage is afforded to multiple insureds, each insured is treated as a separate insured except for when applying the Limit of Insurance.

Insured contract—Includes all of the following:

- Leases for premises rented or temporarily occupied by the insured, exclusive of any portion of the lease mandating indemnification by the named insured for fire damage to such property
- Sidetrack agreements
- Licensing or easement agreements, excluding those taking place within 50 feet of railroad demolition or construction operations
- Any obligation imposed by ordinance in which the insured must indemnify a municipality, except when the contract relates to the insured performing work for the municipality
- Contracts with municipal entities, but only the portion applicable to assumption of tort liability for third parties
- The portion of any agreement or contract renting or leasing an auto for business use of any auto by the insured or any of the insured's employees, except for any obligation of the insured or the insured's employees to compensate for damage to the leased or rented auto

The following are not included in the definition of "insured contract":

- Any contract or agreement, or part of a contract or agreement, that obligates the insured to indemnify a railroad for losses occurring within 50 feet of railroad property and stemming from construction or demolition operations in that area relating to any railroad bridge, trestle, tracks, tunnels, roadbeds, crossings, or underpasses
- Any contract or agreement to rent or lease an auto when a driver is provided to the insured as a provision of the contract or agreement
- Any contract or agreement, or part of a contract or agreement, in which the insured agrees to hold harmless any party in the business of transporting property via auto for a fee

Leased worker—A worker provided to the insured under an agreement with a leasing firm to perform duties related to the furtherance of the insured's business, not including temporary workers

Loss—Damage or loss directly caused by an accident

Mobile equipment—Includes any of the following:

- Bulldozers, forklifts, farm machinery, or other vehicles designed to be used off public roads
- Vehicles that are propelled on crawler treads
- Vehicles that are maintained for use entirely on or adjacent to premises owned or rented by the insured

Moreover, mobile equipment includes:

- Any equipment that has the primary purpose of providing mobility to permanently mounted road construction equipment, resurfacing equipment, powertrains, shovels, diggers, or drills
- Any vehicles that are maintained primarily for purposes other than the transport of cargo or people

Mobile equipment does not include:

- Snow removal equipment
- Road maintenance equipment
- Street cleaning equipment
- Cherry pickers or other similar equipment designed to raise and lower people, when such equipment is mounted to an auto or truck chassis
- Air compressors
- Pumps and generators
- Equipment for spraying, welding, cleaning buildings, geophysical exploration, lighting, or well-servicing
- Any land vehicle subject to a financial responsibility or insurance law at the location where it is licensed or normally garaged

All of the items listed above are considered autos for the purposes of the business auto policy.

Pollutants—Any irritant or contaminant that is in solid, liquid, gas, or thermal form, including smoke, soot, fumes, chemicals, and waste. Waste includes materials being held for recycling, reconditioning, or reclaiming.

Property damage—Physical damage to tangible property or the inability to use it.

Temporary worker—A worker provided to the insured to handle seasonal or short-term increased workload or to act as a replacement for an insured employee on a leave of absence.

Unmanned aircraft *(new to 2020)*—Any aircraft that is not controlled by a person in or upon the aircraft.

Optional Endorsements

The **drive other car—broadened coverage for named individuals** endorsement provides coverage for autos that the named insured is using but does not own, hire, or borrow. This endorsement can be used to add liability, collision property damage, comprehensive property damage, medical payments, uninsured motorists', and underinsured motorists' coverage to the commercial auto policy. The specific type of coverage only applies when indicated on the policy declarations. Under all the coverages available in this endorsement, the named insured and his or her resident spouse are eligible for coverage. For liability, collision, and comprehensive, anyone other than the named insured or his or her spouse needs to be named in the endorsement to be covered. For medical payments, uninsured motorists', and underinsured motorists', coverage extends to resident relatives of the named insured. Individuals who are not resident relatives of the named insured may be scheduled on the form, but the coverage does not extend to any of their family members.

94

The **individual named insured** endorsement provides coverage for any auto that the named insured's resident family members personally use. Coverage under this endorsement is almost identical to a personal auto policy. This endorsement does not provide coverage for autos that are not listed on the policy when that auto is owned by the insured or any resident relative or when the auto has been provided to the insured's family member for business purposes.

The **employees as additional insureds** endorsement covers autos that an employee is using on behalf of the named insured or his or her business, but that are not owned, rented, or borrowed by the named insured.

The **additional insured—lessor** endorsement covers leased vehicles and grants insured status to the lessor.

The **specified hired autos** endorsement provides liability and property damage coverage for scheduled hired autos that is the same as that provided for autos owned by the named insured.

The **mobile equipment** endorsement covers scheduled mobile equipment for liability and property damage as if it were an auto.

The **primary and noncontributory—other insurance** endorsement states that the insured's BAP is primary when he or she has agreed in a contract to provide coverage for another party. When this endorsement is added to the BAP, the insurance company will not seek contribution or reimbursement from the party with whom the insured has the contract.

The **deductible liability coverage** endorsement allows the policyholder to have a deductible applied to liability losses in exchange for a lower premium. The insured can choose to have a deductible for only property damage liability losses or for all liability losses.

The **medical auto payments coverage** endorsement is used to add medical payments coverage to the BAP. The coverage is similar to that included in the personal auto policy.

In jurisdictions where **uninsured motorists' bodily injury** coverage is not compulsory, the policy holder may add it using an endorsement. **Underinsured motorists' bodily injury** coverage may also be purchased by endorsement.

Garage Coverage Forms

Garage coverage forms, also known as **auto dealer's coverage forms**, provide **liability coverage, garagekeepers' coverage**, and **physical damage coverage** for car dealerships, gas stations, parking garages, and other types of auto businesses. Covered autos are classified using the **following numerical symbols:**

Symbol	Covered Autos
21	**Any auto**—This includes autos used, owned, leased, hired, rented, or borrowed by the insured.
22	**Owned autos only**—This includes autos owned by the insured.
23	**Owned passenger autos only**—This includes private passenger autos owned by the insured.
24	**Owned autos other than private passenger autos only**—This includes any trucks, buses, motorcycles, trailers, and similar vehicles owned by the insured.

Symbol	Covered Autos
25	**Owned autos subject to no-fault law**—This is used for autos that must have no-fault benefits under state law.
26	**Owned autos subject to compulsory uninsured motorists' law**—This is used for autos that must have uninsured motorist coverage under state law.
27	**Specifically described autos**—This is used for vehicles identified in the declarations section.
28	**Hired autos only**—This is reserved for autos that have been hired, leased, borrowed, or rented by the insured.
29	**Non-owned autos only used in your auto dealership**—This is reserved for autos that are used in the insured's business, but not hired, borrowed, or rented by the insured. This includes autos hired, leased, borrowed, or rented by an employee, a partner, a member of the insured LLC, or any relatives of any of these parties. Coverage is only provided when the auto is being used in relation to the insured's business.
30	**Autos left with you for service, repair, storage, or safekeeping**—This is used for autos that are owned by customers, employees, or family members of employees when they are in the possession of the insured for the provision of auto services.
31	**Auto dealers' autos (physical damage coverages)**—This is used only for autos and the financial interest in these autos as described in Item 6 of the policy declarations.

Garage forms provide the following types of auto and business liability coverage:

- **Garage operation—covered autos**—This applies to owning, using, or maintaining covered autos. This coverage is identical to the business auto policy coverage, except that garage customers with their own liability insurance are not covered.
- **Garage operations—other than covered autos**—This applies to operating a garage, and includes the named insured as well as his or her employees, business directors, and shareholders as they are carrying out their duties in the business. This serves the same function as a commercial general liability policy.

Endorsements are available for uninsured motorists, underinsured motorists, and medical payments.

Garage physical damage coverage applies to either comprehensive or specific causes of loss and collision losses. It is normally purchased on a blanket basis so that it covers all vehicles the insured owns, regardless of whether each vehicle is specified. As a blanket coverage, garage physical damage excludes the following losses:

- Expected profits
- Collision damage for autos, if the collision occurs when the insured is transporting the auto from the purchase/distribution point to the destination point and the distance between the two points is 50 miles or more

Any type of garage physical damage coverage automatically excludes losses due to **false pretenses**, which occur when a dealer is tricked or deceived into giving away a covered auto.

The **garagekeepers' insurance section** provides liability coverage for damage to others' property, such as customer vehicles, when it is in the insured's control or custody for the purposes of service, parking, storage, or repair. This coverage is excluded under the form's regular liability section, and such vehicles are indicated by symbol 30. Garagekeepers' insurance can be on a **legal liability** basis or a **direct damage** basis. Legal liability garagekeepers' coverage only applies when the insured is legally liable for damage to other's property. If the insured does not carry legal liability for the damage, no payment will be made. Direct damage garagekeepers' coverage reimburses losses even when the insured is not legally liable for the damage. Direct damage garagekeepers' insurance can be purchased on either a primary basis or an excess basis, and it can cover losses under comprehensive, collision, or specified causes of loss coverage. Garagekeepers' coverage is not limited only to garage policies but may be added on to other commercial policies by endorsement, such as a business auto policy or a motor carrier policy.

The Motor Carrier Act of 1980 and Motor Carrier Coverage Forms

According to the **Motor Carrier Act of 1980**, trucking companies and motor carriers must be able to prove they can fulfill any financial liabilities resulting from injury or damage related to their business. As the act took significant steps to deregulate the motor carrier industry, minimum insurance requirements were put into place to promote safe operations within the less regulated environment the act created. The named insured must acquire the **MCS-90 endorsement** in situations where insurance is necessary to demonstrate financial responsibility. The limits of insurance are established by the weight of the vehicles and the property they are transporting.

Previously, motor carrier coverage forms were called truckers' coverage forms. The truckers' form was retired in 2010 and replaced by the motor carrier coverage form. The motor carrier form contains virtually the same coverages as the truckers' form but has a much broader application. It is available to any person who carries property in an auto as part of a business, even if he or she has not been hired expressly to transport goods. Motor carrier coverage can be obtained as a standalone policy or by adding the motor carrier endorsement to the BAP.

Like with the BAP and Garage policy, numerical symbols are used on the declarations page to designate what autos are covered by a policy. The coverage symbols for the motor carrier form are as follows:

Symbol	Covered Autos
61	**Any auto**—This includes autos used, owned, leased, hired, rented, or borrowed by the insured.
62	**Owned autos only**—This includes autos owned by the insured.
63	**Owned private passenger type autos only**—This includes private passenger autos owned by the insured.
64	**Owned commercial autos only**—This includes trucks, tractors, and trailers owned by the insured. When used for liability coverage, it also includes non-owned trailers attached to owned tractors.
65	**Owned autos subject to no-fault law**—This is used for autos that must have no-fault benefits under state law.
66	**Owned autos subject to compulsory uninsured motorists' law**—This is used for autos that must have uninsured motorist coverage under state law.
67	**Specifically described autos**—This is used for vehicles identified in the declarations section. When used for liability coverage, it also includes non-owned trailers attached to described autos.
68	**Hired autos only**—This is reserved for autos that have been hired, leased, borrowed, or rented by the insured or any employee, partner, or LLC member. Coverage also extends to members of such party's household.

Symbol	Covered Autos
69	**Trailers in your possession under a written trailer or equipment interchange agreement**—This is used for trailers the insured does not own but is legally responsible for pursuant to a written trailer interchange agreement.
70	**Trailers in the possession of anyone else under a written trailer or equipment interchange agreement**—This is used for trailers the insured owns but rents or loans to others under a written trailer interchange agreement.
71	**Non-owned autos only**—This is reserved for autos that are used in the insured's business, but not hired, borrowed, or rented by the insured, an employee, a partner, a member of the insured LLC, or any relatives of any of these parties. This includes private passenger autos.
79	**Mobile equipment subject to compulsory or financial responsibility or other motor vehicle insurance law only**—This is used when a land vehicle would meet the definition of "mobile equipment" under the policy if not for the statutory requirements in the location where the vehicle is registered or principally garaged.

Motor carrier coverage forms provide coverage for liability, physical damage, and trailer interchange. The liability and physical damage coverages are very similar to those provided in a business auto policy. Trailer interchange coverage applies when non-owned trailers are being transported by an insured under a written contract with the owner of the trailer. It is most often used when a trailer will be moved from one power unit to another during the course of transport. This coverage will pay for any physical damage to the non-owned trailer when it is in the insured's possession. Symbol 69 must be listed on the policy declarations for trailer interchange coverage to apply.

If the policyholder opts to purchase motor carrier coverage by endorsing a BAP, it is important that he or she also purchase the **truckers—insurance for non-trucking use** endorsement. This endorsement provides **bobtail liability** coverage, which is coverage for instances when the insured is using a tractor or other power unit without hauling a trailer or when not under the authority of a motor carrier. This insurance typically comes into play when the insured is traveling home or between pick-up points after delivering a trailer to its intended destination. The motor carrier policy can be endorsed with many of the same endorsements used with the BAP, including the deductible liability coverage endorsement, primary and non-contributory—other insurance endorsement, underinsured motorists' bodily injury endorsement, and the employees as additional insureds endorsement.

Commercial Insurance Policies

Commercial Package Policies

A **commercial package policy (CPP)** provides multi-line coverage for businesses. It consists of a common policy declarations section, a common policy conditions section, and two or more of the following coverages: commercial property, commercial general liability, commercial crime, commercial auto, commercial inland marine, farm, employment practices liability, professional liability, and boiler and machinery. While a wide array of coverages can be added to a CPP, certain coverages cannot be added. These are directors and officers liability insurance, workers' compensation insurance, life insurance, disability insurance, and health insurance.

In a CPP, the **common policy declarations** section provides the following information:

- Named insured's identity and mailing address
- Policy period
- Description of the business being covered
- List of coverages purchased, including their premium amounts
- Types of forms necessary for coverage

In most cases, a CPP also includes **interline endorsements**, which can be applied to multiple insurance lines. These endorsements can be optional or required under the policy.

COMMON POLICY CONDITIONS

The same **common policy conditions** form is used with nearly all standard commercial policies with the exception of the BOP and workers' compensation. This form lays out the responsibilities and obligations of the **first named insured** and is attached to all commercial package policies. The first named insured is the person who is listed first on the declarations page of the policy and who is responsible for payment of premiums, acts as the point of contact for the insurance company, is the payee on any premium refunds, and is the only party who can request changes to the policy.

- **Cancellation**—This condition explains the procedures for canceling policies. If the first named insured opts to cancel a policy, the insurance company must be notified in writing. The insurer may also cancel the policy. Written notice must be sent to the first named insured at least ten days prior to the cancellation effective date when the insured has not paid the policy premium. The notice must be sent 30 days in advance for all other cancellation reasons. The cancellation notice will be sent to the named insured's last known mailing address and will state the effective date of the cancellation. If any refund of premium is owed to the insured due to the insurer canceling the policy, it will be paid to the named insured on a pro rata basis determined by how much of the policy period has elapsed. Should the named insured initiate the cancellation, the refund may be less than the prorated amount. The insurer's proof of mailing is adequate to prove notice of cancellation was sent.
- **Policy changes**—Only the first named insured may request any policy changes, and such changes will only be executed with consent from the insurance company. The insurer reserves the right to amend or waive policy terms via endorsement.
- **Examination of your books and records**—This empowers the insurer to audit the insured's books and records upon request. An audit can be done at any time during the policy period or during the three years following the policy period's conclusion.

- **Inspections and surveys**—This clause entitles the insurance company to complete an inspection or survey at any time, report the findings to the insured, and recommend modifications based on the findings. The insurer has no obligation to perform these actions and will only do so for the purposes of calculating premiums and determining insurability. The insurance company's inspectors do not act as—nor are meant to take the place of—safety or regulatory inspectors. This condition does not apply to any actions taken to certify pressure vessels, boilers, or elevators subject to state or local laws, ordinances, or regulations.
- **Premiums**—The first named insured is obligated to pay all premiums and will be sent any premium refunds that may become due.
- **Transfer of your rights and duties under this policy**—Aside from death of an individual named insured, all transfers may only be done with the insurance company's written consent. In the event of a named insured's death, the rights will be assigned to the named insured's legal representative, but only for actions taken in the scope of being the legal representative. In the interim period between a named insured's death and the selection of a legal representative, parties with proper temporary custody of the named insured's property will possess the rights associated with the property being held.

COMMERCIAL PROPERTY INSURANCE

Commercial property insurance is part of the commercial package policy. It provides property insurance for businesses, and it covers both real property, such as buildings, factories, and garages, and business personal property, such as furniture, office equipment, and machinery. Commercial property policies consist of the following:

- Policy declarations
- Policy conditions
- Coverage form(s)
- Causes of loss forms
- Mandatory and optional endorsements

Coverage forms identify property that is covered and not covered, and they explain any limits, deductibles, and special conditions. Frequently used coverage forms include:

- Building and personal property (BPP)
- Builder's risk
- Extra expense
- Business income with extra expense
- Business income without extra expense
- Condominium association
- Condominium commercial unit-owners

COMMERCIAL PROPERTY CONDITIONS

All commercial property forms are subject to the **commercial property conditions** form. This form is attached to all commercial property policies alongside the common policy conditions form. The conditions described on this form are as follows:

- **Concealment, misrepresentation, or fraud**—States that if the insured commits fraud related to the policy at any time, the policy is void, including any misrepresentation or intentional concealment of material facts related to the policy, the covered property, or a claim made under the policy

- **Control of property**—States that coverage will not be impacted by any acts of neglect from a person who is acting beyond the scope of the insured's control; if this condition is violated at an insured location, the coverage for locations where the breach has not occurred will not be affected
- **Insurance under two or more coverages**—States that if a loss is covered by more than one coverage part within the policy, the insurance company will only pay the actual loss amount
- **Legal action against us**—States that any legal action against the insurance company must be brought within two years of the date of loss and that no such action may be brought unless the insured has fully complied with the terms described in the policy
- **Liberalization**—States that when the insurance company makes a change to the policy that broadens coverage without increasing the premium, the change applies to the existing policy automatically when the change goes into effect in the policy's jurisdiction, as long as the effective date is either within the policy period or within the 45 days immediately following the beginning of the policy period; this clause is not applicable to modifications to general program revisions that both expand and restrict coverage
- **Other insurance**—States that when a claim is covered by another policy of a similar type, the insurance company will only pay its fair share of the loss (usually determined by a pro rata share calculated as the percentage of coverage under this policy in relation to the sum of all coverage available); if the property is covered by any other sort of insurance, this policy will pay only on an excess basis
- **Coverage territory and policy period**—States that losses will only be covered if they occur during the active policy period and within the coverage territory; the coverage territory consists of the United States, its territories and possessions, and Canada
- **Transfer of rights of recovery against others to us (subrogation clause)**—States that when the insured has a right of recovery against a third party, that right gets transferred to the insurer when the claim is paid; the rights are only transferred to the extent that the loss was paid, and the insured also has an obligation to protect the insurance company's right to recovery and assist in such recovery when requested; any waiver of rights provided by the insured must be executed in writing and prior to the occurrence of a loss

CAUSES OF LOSS FORMS

The **causes of loss** forms list the perils that are covered by commercial property insurance, and are divided into three types: basic, broad, and special.

CAUSES OF LOSS—BASIC FORM

The **basic form** provides named peril coverage against the following perils:

- **Fire or lightning**
- **Windstorm or hail**
- **Explosion,** except for losses caused by the use or rupture of pressure-releasing devices, or the bursting of a building or structure due to water expansion
- **Riot and civil commotion**
- Collision with **aircraft** or objects falling from aircraft
- Collision with **motor vehicles,** including collision with items thrown by a motor vehicle; coverage is excluded for collisions with motor vehicles owned or operated by an insured
- **Smoke,** except from industrial operations or agricultural smudging
- **Vandalism,** including damage from burglary or attempted burglary
- **Sinkhole collapse**

- **Volcanic action**
- Damage caused by a leaking **fire sprinkler system**

The basic form outlines several **broad exclusions** that are not covered when a loss is caused directly or indirectly by the excluded peril. The exclusion also applies if any of these are within the chain of events that results in the loss. The broad exclusions are:

- Ordinance or law
- Earth movement, except that if any of these result in a fire or explosion, the policy will cover the damage caused by that fire or explosion; earth movement includes:
  o Earthquakes, landslides, and mine subsidence
  o Earth sinking, rising, or shifting, except for sinkhole collapse
  o Soil conditions or underground movement of water
- Volcanic eruption, unless it results in fire or broken glass
- Governmental action, except when performed to mitigate the spread of fire
- Nuclear hazards
- Failure of utility services off of the insured location
- War and military action
- Most types of water losses, including any waterborne substances or materials
- Fungus, bacteria, wet rot, and dry rot, except if they result from fire or lightning

The basic form also lists several **limited exclusions**. Coverage will not apply if the loss is caused by any of the following:

- Artificial electrical current or artificially generated energy
- Pipe rupture, except for automatic sprinklers
- Water or steam leakage caused by the breakage of water or steam systems
- Steam boiler, pipe, engine, or turbine explosion when the equipment is owned, leased, or operated by the insured
- Mechanical breakdown
- Neglect on the part of the insured, including failure to mitigate damage during and after a loss

The next part of the exclusions section explains the special exclusions that only apply to certain coverages. There are special exclusions for **business income, extra expense, leasehold interest, and legal liability**. These special exclusions are as follows.

Business income and extra expense, business income without extra expense, and extra expense coverages—no coverage applies to losses stemming from the following:

- Damage or destruction of finished stock or any time it takes to remake damaged stock
- Direct physical loss to radio and television antennas and any related equipment
- Delays in resuming operations when caused by interference of striking personnel or other people
- Losses from cancellation, suspension, or lapse of any lease, license, or contract
- Any other consequential damage or loss

Leasehold interest coverage—excludes losses caused by:

- The insured's cancellation of a lease agreement
- Any licensing cancellation, lapse, or suspension
- Any other consequential damage

Legal liability coverage—This optional coverage is not subject to the ordinance or law, governmental action, nuclear hazard, or war and military action exclusions listed in the special form. No coverage applies to:

- Any claim or action brought against the insured related to liability undertaken in a contract, except when there is liability assumed under a lease for physical damage stemming from an actual or attempted burglary or robbery
- Nuclear hazards

Limited coverage for "fungus," wet rot, dry rot, and bacteria is an additional coverage available on the basic form. The policy defines **"fungus"** as mold, mildew, spores, scents, mycotoxins, and fungal residue or by-products. It reimburses the following costs associated with removing mold: repairing direct physical property damage or loss caused by mold, removal and replacement of portions of the building to gain access to the mold, and testing to determine the presence of mold after property repairs or replacements have been completed. For this coverage to apply, the presence of fungus, mold, bacteria, or rot must have been the result of a covered cause of loss except for fire or lightning. The reimbursement amount cannot exceed $15,000 per year, no matter how many claims are filed. Coverage only applies if the damage occurs during the policy period and the mold is caused by a covered loss. Additionally, following the discovery of a mold occurrence, the insured must take reasonable steps to avoid further property damage.

CAUSES OF LOSS—BROAD FORM

The **broad form** insures against the following perils:

- All perils covered by the basic form
- Weight of ice, sleet, or snow
- Falling objects, except when damaged property was kept in the open; interior damage is only covered when there is a breach in the exterior of the building or structure
- Water damage due to release of water or steam from cracking or breaking plumbing, HVAC systems, other systems, or appliances

The broad form includes all the same broad exclusions listed in the basic form. The limited exclusions are slightly different. The limited exclusions under the broad form are:

- Artificial electrical current or artificially generated energy
- Explosion of steam boilers, pipes, engines, or turbines when the equipment is owned, leased, or operated by the insured
- Mechanical breakdown
- Neglect on the part of the insured, including failing to prevent further damage during and after a loss

In addition to the limited coverage for fungus, wet rot, dry rot, and bacteria, the broad form also provides **collapse additional coverage**. The section covers only abrupt collapse of a covered building when caused by:

- Any peril named in the broad form
- Glass breakage
- Weight of people and personal property
- Weight of rain on the roof
- Hidden decay, except when the insured is aware it exists before the collapse
- Hidden insect or vermin damage, except when the insured is aware it exists before the collapse
- Use of defective building materials or practices in construction, remodeling, or renovation
  - If the collapse occurs during the course of construction, it will be covered based on that alone.
  - If the collapse occurs after construction is complete, it is only covered if caused in part by one of the other covered perils.

The collapse additional coverage on the broad form covers the following outdoor properties when they sustain direct damage from a collapsed building:

- Radio or television antennas, satellite dishes, and their equipment
- Yard fixtures
- Awnings, gutters, and downspouts
- Piers, wharves, docks, and similar structures
- Fences
- Retaining walls
- Outdoor swimming pools
- Diving platforms
- Walks, roadways, and paved surfaces

Even in the absence of building collapse, personal property collapse is covered, provided the property is inside a building, the collapse was cause by a named cause of loss, and the property is not one of the outdoor items listed above. No coverage is provided for any building, structure, or personal property where a collapse is only threatened or likely. A collapse needs to actually occur for the loss to be covered.

CAUSES OF LOSS—SPECIAL FORM

The **special form** functions a bit differently from the other two forms, as it provides open peril protection against any direct physical loss not excluded under the policy. The special form excludes all the broad and special exclusions listed in the basic and broad forms. It also excludes the following additional perils:

- Artificial electrical current or artificially generated energy
- Pipe rupture, except for automatic sprinklers
- Delay, loss of market, or loss of use
- Industrial operations or agricultural smudging
- Normal wear and tear
- Corrosion, including rust
- Fungus

- Latent or hidden defects within the property, up to and including mechanical breakdown; exception is made for elevator collision
- Smog
- Insect, bird, or rodent damage
- Settling, shrinking, expanding, and cracking of buildings or personal property
- Steam explosion involving boilers, pipes, engines, or turbines when the equipment is owned, leased, or operated by the insured
- Water seepage occurring continuously for 14 days or more
- Criminal or dishonest activities carried out by the insured or his or her employees
- Leaking or discharge of water, liquids, powder, or molten material from plumbing, heating equipment, and other equipment due to freezing; exception is made for automatic fire sprinkler systems as long as the insured took reasonable steps to prevent freezing
- Property an insured voluntarily parts with as a result of a trick, scheme, or other deceitful act
- Snow, sleet, rain, or ice damage to personal property kept in the open
- Collapse that does not fall within the parameters of the collapse additional coverage
- Damage from release or discharge of pollutants; exception is made for losses resulting from a "specified cause of loss," when the pollution results in a "specified cause of loss," or losses related to the application of chemicals to glass
- The insured's failure to mitigate damage during and after a loss

The special form also outlines exclusions that apply to a loss even when caused in part by a covered cause of loss. These are sometimes called **anti-concurrent causation exclusions**. These exclusions are:

- Weather, but only when combined with a peril listed in the broad exclusions
- Acts or decisions of any person or organization, including the lack of action or decision
- Losses resulting from faulty, defective, or inadequate:
  o Planning, development, surveying, or zoning
  o Design, workmanship, repair, specifications, grading, remodeling, compaction, or construction
  o Materials used in repair, construction, remodeling, or renovation
  o Maintenance

There is an additional exclusion unique to the special form that applies to **loss or damage to products**. This exclusion states that the policy will not cover goods, merchandise, or products that are damaged due to errors or omissions that occur at any point in the development or manufacturing process. This extends to actions that occur outside of the insured's control, such as an offsite manufacturing facility.

Due to the nature of the open peril coverage, the special form also addresses some coverage limitations. These coverage limitations include:

- Losses caused by conditions internal to steam boilers, engines, pipes, or turbines; exception is made for damage caused by gases or fuels within such equipment
- Damage resulting from internal conditions of a water heating device or system; the exclusion does not apply if there is an explosion
- When property is inside of a structure or building, damage caused by snow, rain, sleet, ice, dust, or sand is only covered when there is damage to the exterior that exposes the interior; exception is made for damage caused by the thawing of sleet, snow, or ice

Mometrix

- Theft of uninstalled building materials except when being held for sale; this limitation does not apply to business income and extra expense claims
- Losses that are only supported by inventory shortage or other calculation; this is to prevent payment of losses for which there is no physical evidence of a covered loss occurring
- Property that is lost or stolen due to following unauthorized instructions
- Loss or damage of plant life that is part of a vegetated roof caused by atmospheric or soil dampness or dryness, frequent or extreme changes in temperature, diseases, or precipitation, including snow, rain, sleet, ice, or frost

Certain items are only covered when damaged by glass breakage or a **"specified cause of loss."** The policy states that "specified causes of loss" include:

- Lightning
- Fire
- Windstorm and hail
- Smoke
- Explosion
- Vandalism
- Riots and civil commotion
- Aircraft and other vehicles
- Volcanic eruption
- Leaks from fire extinguishing systems
- Sinkholes
- Water damage
- Weight of ice, sleet, and snow
- Falling objects

Property subject to this limitation is as follows:

- Statuary, marble, porcelain, chinaware, and other fragile items; exception is made for glass and containers holding property that is for sale
- Building machinery or equipment owned by the insured or in his or her care, as long as it is not covered by a Builder's Risk policy; this exclusion does not apply to business income and extra expense losses
- Animals that are killed by accident or destroyed out of necessity; this coverage does not extend to veterinary expenses

Some items are only covered for theft on a limited basis. Such property has the following coverage limitations:

- $2,500 limit for furs and garments lined with or made of fur
- $2,500 limit for dies, patterns, molds, and forms
- $2,500 limit for jewelry and watches worth more than $100, precious and semiprecious stones, jewels, gold, silver, and platinum
- $250 limit for stamps, credit letters, tickets, and lottery tickets for sale

The last limitation outlined in the special form relates to defective systems or appliances. When a defect leads to the release of water, liquids, powders, or molten materials, the insurance company will not pay to correct the defect. If the affected equipment is part of a fire extinguishing system, the damage will be covered when it is due to freezing or if there is any discharge from the fire

106

extinguishing system. Business income and extra expense coverages are not subject to this limitation.

The special form includes the limited fungus, wet rot, dry rot, and bacteria additional coverage and the collapse additional coverage. There are also a number of **coverage extensions** on the special form. These extensions are:

- **Property in transit**—This coverage only applies to personal property that is being moved by a vehicle the policyholder owns, rents, or leases, and loss must occur while the property is in or upon the vehicle. The perils covered by this section are fire, lightning, explosion, hail, windstorm, civil commotion, riot, and vandalism. Damage will also be covered when the loss results from the vehicle's collision with another vehicle or object or when it overturns. Theft losses are only covered when the personal property is stolen from a locked vehicle. Coverage is subject to a $5,000 per occurrence maximum that is paid in addition to the applicable limit of insurance.
- **Water, liquid, powder, or molten material**—When a covered loss is the result of released liquid, water, molten material, or powder, the insurer will pay any expenses related to tearing out and replacing parts of the building that prevent access to the appliance or system that caused the loss. These expenses are part of the policy limit of insurance.
- **Glass**—This covers costs associated with placing temporary glass or boarding up broken glass if there is a delay in the repair or replacement of the covered glass. The insurance company will also pay for removal of any obstructions blocking the path to the damaged glass.

BUILDING AND PERSONAL PROPERTY COVERAGE FORM
COVERAGES

The **building and personal property coverage form (BPP)** is the most common type of commercial property insurance form. It provides **building coverage** for the buildings, completed additions, outdoor furniture, floor coverings, select appliances, fixtures, personal property designed to maintain and protect the premises, materials and supplies used to construct the building, and additions, alterations, and repairs made during the construction process. This form also provides **business personal property coverage** for the following:

- Personal property used in the business
- Property within a covered building or structure
- Property outside of a covered building or structure that is either within 100 feet of a covered building or structure or within 100 feet of the insured premises, whichever is greater
- Labor, materials, or services to personal property of others
- Personal property of others for which the insured is contractually obligated to provide insurance
- Fixtures
- Machinery and equipment
- Furniture
- Personal property leased by the insured
- Stock including the insured's merchandise, raw materials, manufacturing materials, and packaging and shipping supplies
- Improvements and betterments made to a building that is occupied but not owned by the insured at the insured's expense; the insured must be unable to legally remove them

The building and personal property form excludes the following types of property from coverage:

- Accounts, money, securities, foods stamps, and similar monetary property
- Lottery tickets except when held for sale
- Contraband
- Paved surfaces such as roads, bridges, and walks
- Animals owned by the insured except when held as stock
- Non-owned animals unless the insured is boarding them
- Autos held for sale
- Expenses for excavating, grading, filling, or backfilling
- Airborne or waterborne personal property in transport
- Docks, piers, pilings, bulkheads, and wharves
- Property covered and explained more specifically under another policy
- Detached retaining walls
- Pipes, drains, and flues situated underground
- Electronic data, aside from that falling under additional coverages; exception is made for prepackaged software the insured is selling
- Repair or replacement cost of lost electronic or paper-based valuable records, unless included under additional coverages
- Vehicles, watercraft, and aircraft used primarily off the insured premises, subject to the following exceptions:
  - The insured is storing or manufacturing them
  - Non-auto vehicles, aircraft, and watercraft awaiting sale
  - Rowboats or canoes in storage
  - Trailers covered by the non-owned trailer coverage extension
- Grain, straw, hay, or crops
- Plant life unless part of a vegetated roof, except as covered by additional coverages
- Outdoor radio and television equipment not included in additional coverages
- Fences
- Ground-level or underground foundations of buildings, structures, or machinery

ADDITIONAL COVERAGES

Debris removal coverage reimburses the cost of removing debris from covered property, provided the debris was the result of a covered loss. Such expenses must be reported to the insurance company within 180 days of being incurred. The reimbursement amount is equal to 25% of the sum of the deductible and the amount paid to cover the direct loss to the property. The insurer will provide an additional $25,000 for debris removal under the following circumstances:

- The cost of debris removal is more than 25% of the sum of the deductible and the amount paid to cover the direct loss.
- The combined costs of debris removal and direct loss exceed the limit of insurance.

If debris removal is needed in the absence of direct property loss, the policy limits payment to $5,000 per location.

Preservation of property coverage insures property that has been removed from the insured location for the purposes of protecting it from a covered peril. This property is covered for a maximum of 30 days once it has been moved to the new location.

Pollutant cleanup and removal coverage reimburses the cost of extracting pollutants from the insured premises when their presence is the result of a covered loss. This additional coverage only applies if the insured submits an expense report within 180 days of the loss. The insurance company will not pay for monitoring, assessment, or testing for pollutants unless it is part of the extraction process. Reimbursement is limited to $10,000 per 12-month policy period regardless of the number of losses sustained or claims made.

Increased cost of construction coverage applies after a covered loss has damaged a building. It pays the additional construction costs necessary to bring the structure into compliance with new building codes. This additional coverage does not apply to additional construction costs when the building must be repaired, replaced, or rebuilt because of contamination by fungus, dry rot, wet rot, bacteria, or pollutants. The exclusion extends to expenses for evaluating the effects of any of these and any required testing, monitoring, treating, removing, or containing of them. Only buildings insured at replacement cost can receive this additional coverage, and the maximum reimbursement amount is 5% of the building insurance amount or $10,000, whichever is less. The limit is applied per building. Payment under the additional coverage is not subject to the policy limit and will be paid on top of it. If, prior to the covered loss, the insured was notified of required compliance measures, but failed to complete those measures, the insurer will not pay for the increased construction costs.

Fire department service charge coverage reimburses a maximum of $1,000 for payment of fire department services. This is in addition to the limits of insurance and is not subject to a deductible. This also covers the insured's liability for these expenses as required by law or when assumed in a contract that predates the loss.

Electronic data coverage reimburses the cost of replacing or restoring electronic data after it has been damaged or destroyed due to a covered cause of loss, including collapse and viruses. For insurance purposes, electronic data is defined as any information or computer program stored on computer software, disks, CD-ROMs, and similar kinds of electronic storage equipment. This definition does not include prepackaged software. If the lost data cannot be restored, losses are valued at the cost necessary to replace the damaged storage media with an identical blank storage medium. The maximum reimbursement amount cannot exceed $2,500 for all electronic data losses incurred during one policy year. If a single loss occurs over multiple years, it is covered as if the entire loss occurred during the year in which it started.

COVERAGE EXTENSIONS

This section outlines the **coverage extensions** afforded under the BPP. Unless specified otherwise, the extensions only apply to property located on the insured premises or within 100 feet of the premises when outdoors or in a vehicle. The coverage extensions are only valid on policies where there is a coinsurance of at least 80% or a value reporting period symbol on the policy declarations. The coverage extensions include:

- **Newly acquired or constructed property**—This extends $250,000 of coverage for each new building the insured constructs at the covered premises or acquires for uses outlined in the declarations section. This extension also provides $100,000 of coverage for business personal property, including newly acquired property stored at the new location. Coverage is limited to 30 days. For this coverage to be in effect, the policy must already cover property of the same type as that which is newly acquired. The coverage does not extend to property at exhibitions, fairs, or trade shows. If the insured is working on or installing the personal property of another or holding non-owned property temporarily during the course of wholesaling or manufacturing, the coverage extension does not apply.

109

- **Property off-premises**—This provides $10,000 for covered property that is temporarily stored at locations not owned or leased by the insured, space in a storage facility leased by the insured, and property taken to fairs, exhibitions, and trade shows. For items in leased storage, the lease must have started after the beginning of the applicable policy period. Coverage will not be granted for items within or upon a vehicle or in the possession of any salespeople when not at a trade show, fair, or exhibition.
- **Personal effects and property of others**—This extends $2,500 in coverage for the personal property of others and personal effects owned by the named insured, his or her partners, or his or her employees. This extension does not cover theft. The insured can receive this extension without purchasing personal property of others coverage. Any payment made under this extension will be issued to whoever owns the affected property.
- **Valuable papers and records—other than electronic data**—This insures papers and non-electronic records. It provides $2,500 when such documents are damaged, and the information contained in them must be repaired or replaced. The covered causes of loss under this extension are based on which causes of loss form is being used. Under the special form, only the specified causes of loss and collapse are covered perils. The broad form covers all named perils plus collapse. Coverage includes any expenses for blank media used in duplication of records, as well as any labor expenses for transcriptions or copies. Payments under this extension are made in addition to the policy limits of insurance.
- **Outdoor property**—This extension covers fences, antennas, signs, satellite dishes, trees, plants, and shrubs on a limited basis. Coverage only applies for losses due to fire, lightning, explosion, riot or civil commotion, and aircraft. Payment is limited to $1,000 per occurrence with a sublimit of $250 for any single tree, shrub, or plant.
- **Non-owned detached trailers**—Business personal property coverage will carry over to non-owned detached trailers so long as the trailer is used in the insured's business operations; it is in the insured's care, custody, and control at an insured location; and there is a written agreement that requires the insured to maintain insurance for the trailer. The coverage does not apply when the trailer is connected to another vehicle, or during the process of being connected to or disconnected from another vehicle. Coverage is normally limited to $5,000, but higher limits may be available. This coverage is excess over any other collectible policy.
- **Business personal property temporarily in portable storage units**—This extension requires the storage unit to be on the insured premises, within 100 feet of a covered building or structure, or within 100 feet of the insured location, whichever is the greatest distance. The extended coverage ends 90 days after the unit was brought to the insured location or 90 days after the property was first placed in the unit, whichever happens first. If the unit has been on the insured premises for more than 90 days before property is loaded into it, there is no coverage. This property is subject to a $10,000 limit that is included in the overall property policy limit and does not cover any personal property that is covered by any other part of the policy.

LIMITS OF INSURANCE AND DEDUCTIBLE

The BPP states that the maximum payment for loss or damage for a single occurrence is the amount listed on the declarations page. For outdoor signs that are attached to buildings, the limit is $2,500 for each sign per occurrence. Four of the additional coverages that are paid separately from the policy limit of insurance are: fire department service charges, pollutant cleanup and removal, increased cost of construction, and loss of electronic data. Only the increased cost of construction additional coverage does not increase the policy's limit of liability. If the amount of a loss is less than the applicable deductible, the insurer will not make any payment for that loss. If an occurrence involves loss to multiple pieces of covered property and multiple limits of insurance apply, these losses will not be grouped together for the purposes of the deductible. Instead, the deductible will be applied once for each occurrence.

<u>CONDITIONS</u>

In addition to the conditions listed in the common policy conditions and common property conditions forms, there are loss conditions included in the BPP form. These consist of:

- **Abandonment**—The insurance company is not required to take ownership of any property abandoned by the insured.
- **Appraisal**—States that when the insurance company and the insured party disagree about the amount of loss, either side may request an appraisal; the process is as follows:
  - Each side selects an impartial and qualified appraiser within 20 days; each side pays for their own appraiser.
  - The two chosen appraisers agree on an umpire to whom that matter will be presented should the appraisers be unable to agree on the loss amount; the sides split the cost of the umpire equally.
  - Each appraiser submits their assessment of the loss amount.
  - If they agree, that amount will be paid.
  - If they do not agree, the umpire will complete their assessment.
  - If the umpire agrees with either of the appraisers, this will be the amount paid.
- **Duties in the event of loss or damage**—The insured party has certain duties after a loss, including:
  - If a law has been broken or is suspected to have been broken, the insured must contact law enforcement.
  - Provide prompt notice to the insurance company, including advising what property is involved, how the loss occurred, where it occurred, and when it occurred.
  - Take reasonable action to avoid any additional damage to the covered property.
  - Furnish to the insurance company an inventory of all the property that has been damaged.
  - Allow the insurer to inspect all damaged property upon request.
  - Submit a signed and sworn proof of loss form to the insurance company within 60 days of request.
  - Provide requested records and documentation, and submit to an examination under oath as often as the insurance company reasonably requires.
  - Cooperate with any claims investigation undertaken by the insurer.
- **Loss payment**—States that the insurance company has four options to settle covered losses. These options are:
  - Reimburse the policyholder for the value of the property; valuation is dependent on the valuation condition of the applicable coverage form.
  - Pay to repair or replace the property.
  - Take possession of the property in exchange for an appraised or agreed value.
  - Pay to repair or replace the property with that of like kind and quality.

Once the insurer receives the proof of loss, the policyholder must be notified with 30 days of which option will be exercised. The insurance contract is intended for indemnification, and the insured may not intentionally or accidentally profit from a covered loss; thus, the insured will only be entitled to collect payment to the extent of his or her financial interest in the damaged or lost property.

The insurance company will handle all losses directly with the named insured unless the property is owned by someone else. Settlements are final and fulfill the insurance company's obligation under the policy. Payment must be tendered within 30 days of receiving the completed proof of loss and one of the following has occurred:

- An agreement is reached with the named insured.
- An appraisal award is made.

If a shared wall is damaged, payment will depend on how the insured and any co-owners of the wall decide to proceed. If all parties agree to repair or replace the wall, the insurer will make payment proportional to the insured's interest in the wall. If the co-owner(s) do not agree to repair or rebuild, the insurer will pay the full cost but retains the right to pursue the co-owner for their fair share of the cost.

- **Recovered property**—If property is recovered after payment is made under the policy, the recovering party must notify the other party. The policyholder has the option for the property to be returned to him or her, and the payment will be adjusted. If not, the insurer will take ownership.
- **Vacancy**—If an insured owns an entire building, it is considered vacant if less than 31% of the building's square footage is used for the insured's customary business. If the insured rents an owned building to others, it is considered vacant if there are not tenants in at least 31% of the total square footage. If a building is under construction or renovation, it may not be considered vacant. When a building has been vacant for more than 60 days immediately before the loss or damage, the insurance company will not pay for any expenses related to vandalism, sprinkler leakage, glass breakage, water damage, or theft. If the insured has taken the appropriate steps to protect the sprinkler system from freezing and the leaking is the result of freezing, the loss will be covered. Any loss or damage caused by any other covered cause of loss will be subject to a payment reduction of 15%.
- **Valuation**—This condition explains how lost or damaged property will be valued for payment. Valuation does not include any increased costs related to laws and ordinances. Most property will be valued at actual cash value (ACV), with the following exceptions:
  - When a loss to a building is less than $2,500, the insurer will reimburse the insured at replacement value as long as the property is sufficiently insured according to the Coinsurance additional condition.
  - Certain property is only paid at ACV whether it is attached to a building or not. This property consists of outdoor equipment and furniture, floor coverings, awnings, and appliances used for laundry, refrigeration, ventilation, cooking, or dishwashing.
  - Sold products pending delivery are valued at the net sale price minus expenses and discounts the policyholder would have incurred in the absence of the loss.
  - Glass will be replaced with safety glass only when required by law.
  - If a policyholder has performed or installed improvements to a property he or she rents from another, ACV is paid as long as the repairs are completed promptly. If this does not occur, the payment will be adjusted proportionally by calculating the cost of the loss per day based on the number of days between the occurrence date and the expiration of the lease. That amount is then divided by the number of days from the installation of the covered improvements to the end of the lease. If a party other than the insured ends up paying for the repairs or replacement of the installations, there will be no payment to the insured.

The BPP includes further conditions referred to as "additional conditions." These conditions are:

- **Coinsurance**—When there is a coinsurance percentage indicated on the declarations page, the policyholder is required to carry coverage that is at least equal to that percentage of the property's actual value to avoid a penalty for being underinsured. Common coinsurance amounts used are 80%, 90%, or 100%. A coinsurance is optional, but it does lower the premiums the insured is charged for coverage. When the coverage purchased does not meet the coinsurance requirement, loss payment will be calculated as follows:

Step 1:

Replacement Cost of Property × Coinsurance Chosen = Amount of Coverage Needed

Step 2:

$$\frac{\text{Amount of Coverage Carried}}{\text{Amount of Coverage Needed}} = \text{Coinsurance Percentage}$$

Step 3:

Loss Amount × Coinsurance Percentage = Proportional Loss Amount

Step 4:

Proportional Loss Amount − Applicable Deductible = Claim Payment

For example, a policyholder chooses a 90% coinsurance on his or her policy. The full value of the property is $600,000, meaning that the policy needs to have at least $540,000 in coverage to meet the coinsurance. The insured only purchases $405,000 in coverage and carries a $2,500 deductible. A loss occurs that causes $60,000 in damage. To calculate the penalty percentage that will be applied, divide $405,000 by $540,000. This calculation shows that the property was only insured for 75% of its full value. The next step is to calculate 75% of the total loss amount, which is $45,000. The last step is to apply the $2,500 deductible. Because the policyholder did not purchase insurance sufficient to meet the coinsurance selected, the loss payment will be $42,500. Had the property been adequately insured, the payment would have been $57,500.

- **Mortgageholders**—This condition is applicable to properties for which there is a mortgageholder. Trustees are considered to be mortgageholders by the BPP policy. The insurance company will compensate all mortgageholders listed on the declarations page in the order they are listed. The mortgageholder retains rights under the policy even if it has initiated foreclosure proceedings. The mortgageholder will still have the right to receive payment for losses even if the claim of the named insured is denied, so long as the mortgageholder pays any premium amounts that are due, submits a signed and sworn proof of loss within 60 days of receiving a request for such from the insurer, and notifies the insurance company of any relevant changes in ownership or occupancy. The insurance carrier will assume the mortgageholder's rights against the insured to the extent of the company's payment. The insurer also has the option to pay the entire balance of the mortgage, at which point the insurer becomes the mortgageholder and has the right to pursue the mortgage due from the insured. If the insurance company elects to cancel the policy, written notice of this decision must be provided to any mortgageholders at least 10 days in advance when cancellation is because of nonpayment of premium, or 30 days in advance for all other reasons.

OPTIONAL COVERAGES

Building and personal property forms offer a few optional coverages. To activate these coverages, the insured must pay an additional premium, and the coverages available are:

- **Agreed value**—Waives the coinsurance requirement and requires the insurer to reimburse the loss at the proportion which the limit of insurance holds to the stated value.
- **Inflation guard**—Increases the policy's limit of insurance on an annual basis. The yearly increase in coverage will be a percentage that both the insured and the insurer agree upon. This optional coverage only applies to the building policy limits.
- **Replacement cost**—Amends the policy to use replacement cost rather than ACV for most losses. Certain types of property listed under the declarations section are exempt from this coverage, including personal property of others, residential contents, works of art, antiques, rare articles, or property the insured is holding as stock. Replacement cost will not be paid until the repair or replacement of the property is completed. This must be done as soon as reasonably possible. Until the repair or replacement is completed, the policyholder will only be paid based on ACV. A claim for the additional payment may be made so long as the insurance company is notified within 180 days of the loss. The most the insurer will pay under this optional coverage is the lowest of the policy limit of liability, the cost to replace property with items of like kind and quality that are used for the same purpose as the damaged property, and the amount spent to complete repair or replacement of damaged property.
- **Extension of replacement cost to the personal property of others**—Removes the exclusion in the replacement cost optional coverage applicable to the personal property of non-insureds. The amount of liability assumed by the insured party determines the extent to which the owner of the property will be paid. If the policyholder's liability stems from an insured contract, the loss will be valued based on the terms of the contract, but the insurer will not pay more than the replacement cost of the damaged or destroyed property.

OPTIONAL ENDORSEMENTS

Earthquake and volcanic eruption endorsement—Amends the selected cause of loss form to include damage caused by volcanic eruption, explosion, or effusion, lava, ash, or airborne shock waves, and earth movement. For insurance purposes, a single instance of earthquake or volcanic eruption includes the initial shock or eruption and any proceeding shock or eruption over the next 168 hours. At the insured's request, coverage for this endorsement can be limited to sprinkler leakage. There are a few different endorsements available, which differ on how the deductible is determined. The deductible can be a flat amount or based on a percentage of the total loss amount. The deductible can be applied per occurrence, or the insured can opt to have each building scheduled separately, in which case there would be a deductible applied to each building damaged by an earthquake or volcanic eruption.

The **ordinance or law coverage endorsement** protects the insured when his or her loss amount is increased by ordinances and laws. This endorsement applies specifically to demolition costs, construction costs, and value loss to undamaged buildings. The insured may opt to add coverage for business income loss and extra expenses caused by enforcement of law or ordinance.

The **primary and noncontributory—other insurance** condition is used when the policyholder agrees to assume responsibility for the property of others under a contract. When attached to the BPP, the insurance company will not look for any contribution for loss payments from the other party or the other party's insurance company.

Spoilage endorsement is available on both the building and personal property coverage forms and the condominium commercial unit-owners coverage form, and covers the insured's perishable stock, which is defined as personal property that will spoil unless it is kept in a controlled environment. Covered items are listed on a schedule that is part of the endorsement form. The only causes of loss covered by this endorsement are contamination, breakdown, and power outage.

The **value reporting endorsement** is intended for property that is subject to regular changes in value, as well as property that is occasionally moved between locations, such as business personal property, others' personal property, and stock. This endorsement relies on a **value reporting form**, which the insured uses to report the actual value of his or her property at a specific time and location. These values are reported at regular intervals and are used to determine the premium payments and insurance amounts. Coverage will vary depending on risk at a specific location, and the insured normally carries more insurance than they need. The **peak season endorsement**, which is a type of value reporting form, allows the insured to have a higher amount of coverage at different times during the year.

DEFINITIONS

Fungus—Any fungus regardless of form, including mold, mildew, or any by-products released by a fungus such as spores, smells, or toxins.

Pollutants—Irritants or contaminants in any form, including soot, vapor, smoke, fumes, alkalis, acids, chemicals, and waste. Waste includes any items being held pending recycling, reconditioning, or reclamation.

Stock—Products or merchandise held for storage or sale, including unfinished goods, raw materials, finished products, and packaging supplies.

OTHER COMMERCIAL PROPERTY COVERAGE FORMS

Because of the customizable nature of commercial package policies, there are many coverage forms that can be combined to create a portfolio of insurance products that will meet the needs of each policyholder. Like the BPP form, each of these forms is subject to both the common policy conditions and commercial property conditions forms. This is not an exhaustive list due to the number of options available.

BUSINESS INCOME FORMS

Business income coverage forms reimburse any business income the insured may lose when he or she is forced to suspend business operations due to direct physical damage from a covered peril. This is sometimes referred to as **business interruption insurance**. Business income includes two components: net income the business would have earned if it had not been forced to shut down, and the cost of maintaining normal business operations, which could include completing tasks like payroll. Coverage begins on the date of the loss and lasts until the date business operations should be restored. Business income forms are divided into two types:

- **Business income with extra expense**—Reimburses the specific expenses the insured may incur to avoid suspending business operations.
- **Business income without extra expense**—Provides **expense to reduce loss** coverage rather than extra expense coverage. The insured is reimbursed the money he or she spends to reduce the overall loss.

Both forms offer business income coverage including rental value coverage, business income coverage other than rental value coverage, and rental value coverage only.

Extended business income additional coverage extends the reimbursement period for loss of business income to 30 days after business operations have resumed.

Order of civil authority additional coverage reimburses loss of business income and extra expenses. It applies when civil authorities prevent the insured from entering his or her property because damage to another property has rendered the insured property uninhabitable.

Alterations and new buildings additional coverage also reimburses loss of business income and extra expense. It insures new buildings and alterations against covered losses. Coverage includes building materials, machinery, equipment, and supplies that are used during construction, alteration, and occupancy of the building, and are located within 100 feet of the building. The coverage period begins on the date that business operations would have commenced if the damage had not occurred.

The **extended period of indemnity** optional coverage extends the reimbursement period for loss of business income to a certain number of days after business operations have resumed. This number of days, which can exceed the 30-day period under the extended business income additional coverage, is identified in the declarations section.

The **maximum period of indemnity** optional coverage states that reimbursement for extra expenses and loss of business income cannot exceed the total loss amount incurred during the first 120 days after the loss.

The **monthly limit of indemnity** optional coverage lets the insured select the amount he or she will be reimbursed for loss of business income for each 30-day period.

Agreed value optional coverage waives the coinsurance condition by requiring the insurer to carry an agreed value of insurance every 12 months. In order to establish the agreed value, the insured must submit a business income report or worksheet to the insurance company on an annual basis.

The **business income from dependent properties—broad form** covers direct physical loss to the following locations: **contributing locations, recipient locations, manufacturing locations**, and **leader locations**. This type of coverage may also be called contingent business income insurance. A contributing location is the insured's sole supplier of raw materials and merchandise. A recipient location is the only business that purchases the insured's products. A manufacturing location is contracted by the insured to deliver his or her products. A leader location is a business that brings in customers for the insured. Each of the above business locations is separate from the insured's business. However, because damage or loss to these locations may cause the insured to suffer a loss of business income or earnings, he or she can seek coverage under the business income broad form.

Extra expense coverage forms are intended for businesses that simply cannot afford to suspend operations, such as newspapers, utility companies, and other businesses whose services or products are very important. This form does not provide loss of business income coverage. Instead, it reimburses only those costs necessary for the business to continue operations. Insurance limits are expressed as percentages in the declarations section and assessed according to the period of restoration. Consider, for instance, a limit of 30%/70%/100%:

- For a restoration period of 30 days or less, the insurer pays 30% of the full insurance amount.
- For a restoration period of greater than 30 days, the insurer pays 70% of the full insurance amount.
- For a restoration period of greater than 60 days, the insurer pays 100% of the full insurance amount.

The following definitions are applicable to the business income coverage forms:

Finished stock—Products that the insured manufactures that are completed and pending sale or delivery. This does not include alcohol products or products that are away from the insured premises at a retail location.

Operations—Business functions of the named insured that take place at an insured location.

Period of restoration—The amount of time needed for covered property to be repaired, replaced, or rebuilt with reasonable speed and of quality equivalent to the property that was lost or damaged or the time it takes for the insured to restart business operations at new permanent premises. It begins immediately after a covered direct loss for the purposes of extra expense coverage. For business income coverage, it starts after 72 hours have passed. It terminates when there has been reasonable time to complete repairs or when the operations have commenced at a new location, whichever is earlier. It does not include any delays related to law, ordinance, or pollutants.

Rental value—Net business income, including profit or loss, that is obtained by renting the premises or part of the premises to tenants. It also includes any expenses that continue even when the rental premises are not habitable, such as payroll. Any legal obligation of the tenant that is assumed by the insured because of the inability to occupy the insured location is considered rental value.

Suspension—A slowdown or complete stoppage of business operations. If there is rental value coverage, this includes any time the insured's tenants are unable to use the premises because of a covered loss.

LEGAL LIABILITY COVERAGE FORM

Legal liability coverage covers the insured when he or she is found legally liable for damage to property that is in his or her care but owned by someone else. This coverage also reimburses for loss of use. Coverage does not apply to electronic data or records. What causes of loss are covered is dependent on the cause of loss form attached to the policy. The contract in which the insured assumes legal liability should list the causes of loss for which he or she is responsible so that the appropriate cause of loss form can be used. This coverage also makes use of a **schedule**. A schedule is a form that lists the property to which the insurance will apply. This is a requirement for the legal liability coverage because the coverage form does not provide a list of covered and not covered property.

The **supplementary payments** additional coverage states that certain expenses may be paid under the policy without affecting the available policy limits. These expenses include all claims and defense costs incurred by the insurance company, bond payments necessary to release attachments, court costs awarded against the insured, pre-judgment interest, and post-judgment

117

interest. If the insurance company requests the insured's presence at trials, hearings, or other events associated with handling the claim, the insured will be reimbursed up to $250 per day in lost wages as well as any other reasonable expenses incurred.

COMMERCIAL PROPERTY FLOATER

In some businesses, it is necessary for certain business personal property to be away from the insured premises on a regular basis. Some of this property can be extremely expensive to replace, such as specialized tools and laptop computers. Because the Building and Personal Property coverage form is primarily designed to cover property that is at the location listed on the policy, the coverage provided for off-premises property may be insufficient. To avoid this situation, the insured may add a **commercial property floater** endorsement to the policy. These floaters can be written for scheduled personal property or unscheduled personal property.

CONDOMINIUM COVERAGE FORMS

Condominiums have some unique coverage needs because of the ways a condo building can be used and the complexities surrounding ownership of a condo building. Like other commercial property coverage forms, these must be accompanied by a causes of loss form to determine which losses the policy will apply to. Condominium coverage forms are available in two types:

- **Condominium association coverage form**—This form can be used to cover both residential and commercial condominium associations. It insures the building against direct physical damage, including permanently attached indoor and outdoor fixtures and permanently installed equipment and machinery. Outdoor fixtures are items such as fences and light poles. Indoor fixtures are only covered when they are part of a common area, and they include property such as cabinetry and light fixtures. Business personal property is covered when in or on the condo building or other listed structure, or when it is within 100 feet of the building, structure, or premises. This form also extends personal property coverage to items the insured does not own but has in his or her care, custody, or control.
- **Condominium commercial unit-owners coverage form**—This is used only by commercial condominium unit-owners. It cannot not be used to insure entire buildings and is designed only to cover the unit or units the policyholder owns. Only the interior of the unit and the business personal property located inside the condo are covered. Covered personal property includes that owned by the unit-owner and others' personal property that is in the insured's care. When there is also a condominium association policy in effect for a loss, the unit-owners form is always excess coverage.

BUILDER'S RISK COVERAGE FORM

The **builder's risk coverage form** insures commercial, residential, and farm buildings as they are being constructed or renovated. It is also referred to as **course of construction insurance**. Builder's risk coverage is available under the commercial package policy or under commercial inland marine coverage. The forms are not identical, and this section will focus on the coverage form used with the commercial package policy. Coverage is typically written on a per-project basis and is subject to the cause of loss form attached to the policy. It covers the building and foundation, as well as any fixtures, machinery, or maintenance equipment, provided they are being permanently installed and are located within 100 feet of the structure. The policy also extends coverage to these items when they are inside a temporary storage unit. If not otherwise insured, temporary structures such as scaffolding are covered by the builder's risk form.

A builder's risk policy should be purchased prior to the beginning of the covered project. The effective date depends on the design of the building being constructed. If the building has no basement, the builder's risk form should go into effect no later than the first day of construction. However, if the building does include a basement, it should start no later than when construction on the floor immediately above the basement begins. Most insureds choose to have the coverage go into effect earlier than this so that materials that are delivered to the site in anticipation of the construction will be covered. Coverage ends immediately under the following circumstances:

- The policy period ends; a policy period is usually one year in duration.
- The coverage is canceled by the policyholder or the insurance company.
- The buyer of the building or structure accepts it.
- 60 days have passed after the building is put to its intended use.
- 90 days have passed from the date construction ceases.
- The insured no longer possesses a financial interest in the project.
- The project is abandoned, or construction ends without intention to resume.

Builder's risk insurance excludes coverage for land and water. There is no coverage for outdoor trees, plants, shrubs, radio and television antennas, satellite dishes, and signs. There is limited coverage for trees, sod, shrubs, and plants kept outside under the coverage extensions section. This coverage is limited to $1,000 per occurrence with a maximum of $250 paid for any single tree, shrub, or plant. These items are only covered when the loss results from fire, explosion, lightning, riot, civil commotion, or aircraft. A coverage extension of $5,000 is available for building materials and supplies that are not owned by the insured but are in his or her care. The builder's risk coverage form includes some of the additional coverages found in other commercial property forms, such as debris removal, preservation of property, fire department service charge, and pollutant cleanup and removal.

According to the **valuation condition**, builder's risk coverage reimburses losses at ACV. The **need for adequate insurance condition** states that the insurer will not reimburse an amount that is higher than the proportion of the limit of insurance to the completed building's estimated value. For instance, assume a building is worth $2 million. The insured purchases an insurance policy worth $1 million with a $10,000 deductible. Since the building is only insured for 50% of its value, losses will only be paid at 50%. This amount will then be reduced by the deductible. Consequently, if a covered loss is valued at $500,000, the policy will reimburse $240,000.

$$\$500,000 \times 0.50 = \$250,000$$

$$\$250,000 - \$10,000 = \$240,000$$

The **builder's risk reporting form** gradually raises the insurance amount on a building under construction based on reports from the policyholder, which are due every 30 days. As the building increases in value, the coverage amount also increases. If the insured misses a report and a loss occurs, the indemnity will be based upon the last reported value.

Equipment Breakdown Coverage

Equipment breakdown coverage, also called **boiler and machinery coverage**, insures losses caused by failure of covered equipment. Equipment breakdown coverage reimburses direct loss to business equipment, and some indirect losses, such as costs that are incurred due to business interruption. This coverage can be acquired as a monoline policy or as part of a commercial package policy with the following sections: commercial package policy declarations, commercial package policy common conditions, equipment breakdown protection coverage form, equipment breakdown protection coverage declarations, and endorsements.

COVERAGES

It should be noted that each category of coverage must be indicated on the policy declarations to be available under that policy. If the insured does not own the covered equipment, he or she must have a contractual liability for it in order for coverage to be afforded. The coverage parts of the equipment breakdown policy are:

- **Property damage**—Covers direct physical damage to covered equipment located at the insured premises
- **Expediting expenses**—Covers costs the insured incurs to continue operations or resume operations faster, such as express shipping charges, emergency service fees, and surcharges
- **Business income and extra expense**—Covers loss of income during the time that covered equipment is out of use, as well as any extra costs incurred by the insured related to the interrupted operations; extra expense coverage is also available alone
- **Spoilage**—Covers property that is spoiled or damaged due to an equipment breakdown that causes covered property to be exposed to an excess or lack of light, heat, power, steam, or refrigeration; coverage is limited to raw materials, finished products, and property still in processing
- **Utility interruption**—Extends coverage for spoilage, extra expenses, and business income to losses caused by utility failure
- **Newly acquired premises**—Covers property the policyholder obtains during the policy period; coverage is limited to the number of days shown on the policy declarations page, and it starts on the date the premises are acquired
- **Ordinance or law**—Covers costs associated with bringing property into compliance with an ordinance or law, including increased construction costs
- **Errors and omissions**—Provides coverage when certain information was omitted in error, such as not listing the description or location of a property, failing to disclose a location that was owned or occupied by the insured when the policy began, or coverage cancellation due to an error or omission of the named insured; these errors must have been made unintentionally, and the insured must report them to the insurance company as soon as he or she is aware of the error or omission
- **Brands and labels**—Obligates the insurance company to reduce the salvage value of branded or labeled items damaged by a covered breakdown; the insurance company will pay the full value of the branded products as long as the insured removes any labels and stamps the word "salvage" on the property
- **Contingent business income and extra expense**—Provides coverage similar to that under the standard business income and extra expense insuring agreement, but applies to equipment breakdown at a location the insured does not operate or own; such a breakdown must affect the insured business's ability to conduct business, such as slowing down manufacturing or causing a decrease in sales; extra expense coverage is also available alone

PROPERTY COVERED

With the exception of contingent business income and extra expense losses and utility service losses, insured equipment must be located at a location the insured leases, owns, or operates for coverage to apply. The following equipment is considered "covered equipment" under the policy:

- Equipment designed to work under internal pressure or in a vacuum
- Electrical or mechanical equipment that generates or transmits energy or is designed to use energy
- Equipment designed to provide a utility service exclusively to the insured, provided the equipment is owned by the utility company

- Computers
- Communication equipment

The policy lists several types of property that are not covered by the equipment breakdown coverage. These items are:

- Equipment or parts manufactured by the policyholder to be sold
- Excavation to inspect, remove, repair, or replace underground piping, vessels, or equipment
- Insulation or refractory material, unless it is glass that lines the inside of covered equipment
- Pressure or vacuum devices not made of metal
- Chemical catalysts
- Media
- Areas of vacuum or pressure equipment that are not under internal vacuum or pressure
- Cabinets, compartments, foundations, or other structures that provide support or contain parts of covered equipment
- Aircraft, vehicles, floating vessels, or other self-propelled equipment, including any that are mounted to or used exclusively on any of these
- Construction, dragline, and excavation equipment, including any that is mounted to or used exclusively on any of these
- Property used in the maintenance of covered equipment; this exclusion applies primarily to consumable or regularly replaced parts
- Any equipment used for medical, research, diagnostic, or dental purposes; coverage for this property may be added to the policy as diagnostic equipment if needed by the insured

EXCLUSIONS

Equipment breakdown protection coverage forms generally exclude losses that are both accidental and indirect in nature, as well as some losses for which risk is difficult to quantify. Excluded losses consist of those resulting from the following:

- Ordinance or law, except for that provided elsewhere in the policy
- War or military acts
- Nuclear hazards
- Earthquake or earth movement
- Natural wear and tear, deterioration, corrosion, erosion, or depletion in absence of a covered breakdown
- Aircraft, vehicles, lightning, sinkhole collapse, riot, civil commotion, freezing, smoke, vandalism, or weight of ice, sleet, or snow when the policyholder carries other coverage for such losses regardless of collectability
- Windstorm or hail
- Business activity interruption or delay, except for the coverage provided under business income, extra expense, and utility service coverages
- Fire or combustion explosion, even if it causes a breakdown
- Business operations stoppage that would have occurred without the occurrence of a breakdown (applies to business income, extra expense, and utility service coverages only)
- Delay in resuming operations caused by the insured's lack of action and urgency to resume operations (applies to business income, extra expense, and utility service coverages only)
- Restoration delays caused by the cancellation, suspension, or lapse of a contract following a breakdown loss (applies to business income, extra expense, and utility service coverages only)

121

- Damage caused by an explosion, except when the explosion results from covered equipment such as steam equipment, electric steam generators, gas turbines, and moving or rotary equipment that uses centrifugal force
- Spoilage caused by insufficient power, light, steam, heating, or cooling, except for coverage provided under the business income, extra expense, and utility service coverages
- Water damage caused by:
  - Flood, tidal waves, surface water, waves, or overflow of any natural body of water, including wind-driven spray and storm surges
  - Mudslide or mudflow
  - Discharge of water from drains, sumps, sump pumps, and sewers
  - Leakage from domestic water pipes or sprinkler systems
  - Seepage of or pressure from underground water into windows, doors, floors, surfaces, basements, and foundations
  - Waterborne materials
- Damage related to pressure or electrical testing
- Fungus, wet rot, or dry rot, except when it causes a covered breakdown
- Microorganisms such as viruses and bacteria
- Explosion within the furnace or pipes of a chemical recovery boiler
- Fire extinguishing substances, including water
- Utility service interruptions caused by:
  - Any act of sabotage
  - Deliberate load-shedding; this is intentionally reducing or stopping service to conserve power
  - Freezing from cold weather
  - Direct collision with aircraft, vehicles, or falling objects
  - Vandalism, lightning, riot or civil commotion, collapse including sinkhole collapse, smoke, or the weight of sleet, snow, or ice
- The insured's failure to preserve covered property
- Other indirect loss resulting from a breakdown, except for that provided under the business income, extra expense, and utility service coverages

CONDITIONS

The equipment breakdown policy contains many of the same loss conditions found in other commercial property policies, including:

- Abandonment
- Appraisal
- Duties in the event of loss or damage
- Insurance under two or more coverages
- Legal action against us
- Loss payable
- Other insurance
- Transfer of your rights of recovery against others to us

There are a few loss conditions that are not found in most other commercial property coverage forms. These include:

- **Defense**—Obligates the insurer to either settle or defend a lawsuit in which the insured may be liable for damage to others' property in his or her care.
- **Valuation**—Outlines numerous valuation methods that depend on the property damaged or some specific circumstance related to the property:
    - Most property will be valued based on the cost to repair, replace, or rebuild it. The insurance company is allowed to repair or replace the lost property with property that is of a kind and quality similar to the damaged property.
    - The insured may be reimbursed for up to an additional 25% of the loss value to purchase replacement equipment with enhanced safety features.
    - If covered equipment carried a warranty or service contract and it was damaged in a way that rendered the agreement void, the insurance company will only reimburse the amount that the insured would have been paid under the warranty or service contract.
    - The insurance company will only pay for replacement equipment at the price it was available for within the 24 months following the loss.
    - Media and data losses involving mass-produced, commercially available products will be paid at replacement costs. All other losses will be paid based on costs the policyholder sustains to reproduce the lost information on blank replacement media. No payment will be made on data or media that cannot be functionally replaced.
    - For spoiled property, raw materials will be paid at replacement cost, and finished items will be paid at sale price less any discounts or expenses. If property was spoiled during production, the loss will be paid at raw material replacement cost plus overhead and labor costs.
    - The value of any property the insured purchases to use temporarily after a loss will be deducted from the final settlement payment using its salvage value.
- **Reducing your loss**—The insured must minimize his or her loss following a breakdown and restore business operations as soon as possible. The insured is also obligated to take reasonable steps to make up for lost business once operations have resumed.
- **Privilege to adjust with owner**—This empowers the insurer to settle claims with the owner of property that is damaged while in the care, custody, or control of the policyholder.
- **Business income and extra expense coverage**—This lists conditions that only apply to losses under the business income and extra expense coverage. The policyholder may choose between coverage subject to a coinsurance or coverage subject to annual reporting requirements. These additional conditions state:
    - If coverage is on an annual reporting basis, the insured is mandated to provide a completed annual report of values form every year. This must be submitted within three months of the designated reporting date.
    - Once it is received, the insurance company uses the completed annual report of values form to calculate the earned premium for the applicable policy period. If the earned premium is more than the deposit premium, the insured will be billed for the difference. If it is less, the insurance company refunds the first named insured, but the refund cannot exceed 75% of the deposit premium amount.
    - If the insured fails to report annual values on time and a covered loss occurs, the insurer will apply a coinsurance penalty to any payment for that loss based on the proportion of the annual income to the estimated income for the time period for which the insured did not submit the appropriate report.

Like other commercial property policies, the equipment breakdown policy contains common policy conditions that apply to the policy in its entirety. Some of these conditions are similar to those found in other policies, including:

- Bankruptcy
- Concealment, misrepresentation, or fraud
- Liberalization
- Mortgageholder
- No benefit to bailee
- Policy period and coverage territory

General conditions specific to the equipment breakdown policy include:

- **Premium and adjustments**—The insured is required to report the full insurable value of each covered location on an annual basis. This report must be broken down by coverage. This information will be used to compute the renewal premium for the next policy period. Records that the insured uses to fill out the reporting forms must be retained and made available to the insurance company for examination during normal business hours within the applicable policy year and for up to one year after the policy terminates.
- **Suspension**—This empowers the insurer to suspend coverage when equipment has been placed in or presents an inherently dangerous situation. The suspension of coverage only applies to the specific equipment in question; coverage will continue for all other covered equipment. Although the insurer is not obligated to provide advance warning, it must send notification of the suspension to the address of the named insured or to the location of the equipment.
- **Joint or disputed loss agreement**—This condition applies when the same loss is covered by two different insurers, and they cannot agree on their respective reimbursement obligations. In most cases, both insurers will reimburse the insured the full amount of any loss that is indisputably covered under their own policies and half the amount of any disputed loss.

SPECIAL LIMITS

The equipment breakdown coverage forms contain a special limit of $25,000 per occurrence for each of the following types of losses:

- Spoilage or property exposed to ammonia due to a covered breakdown, inclusive of any salvage costs
- Consequential losses when undamaged parts are no longer sellable due to damage to covered parts or equipment
- Expenses related to the replacement, research, or restoration of lost or damaged media or data
- Water damage, except for that falling within the limited coverage for fungus, wet rot, and dry rot
- Expenses incurred for the repair, replacement, cleanup, or disposal of hazardous substance pollution

DEDUCTIBLES

There are numerous methods that may be used to determine the deductible under an equipment breakdown policy. The deductible may be a combined deductible, meaning that losses falling under different coverage parts will share a single deductible that is paid per occurrence. The deductible may also vary based on the type of equipment involved. When multiple types are damaged due to the same loss, only the highest deductible applies to that loss. The deductible options available are:

- Dollar deductible—The deductible is a flat dollar amount that is listed on the declarations page.
- Time deductible—There is a designated amount of time that must pass before the policy coverages will go into effect; any loss incurred during the time between the loss and the end of the time period is the responsibility of the insured.
- Multiple of daily value deductible—The amount is determined by calculating the daily amount of income the premises would have earned in absence of the covered breakdown, then multiplying this amount by the number of days shown on the policy declarations page; this is used to mitigate the significant losses and expenses that can take place immediately following the covered breakdown.
- Percentage of loss deductible—A set percentage is listed on the policy declarations; when a loss occurs, this percentage is applied to the total amount of the loss, and the resulting amount is the deductible.
- Minimum or maximum deductibles—Used in conjunction with the multiple daily value deductible and the percentage of loss deductible options, this sets a minimum deductible and a maximum deductible so that the policyholder has a range within which the deductible will fall; it applies as follows:
  - If the calculated deductible is less than the minimum deductible, the minimum deductible will be used.
  - If the calculated deductible is between the minimum and maximum deductible, the calculated deductible will be used.
  - If the calculated deductible is more than the maximum deductible, the maximum deductible will be used.

COMMERCIAL GENERAL LIABILITY INSURANCE

Commercial general liability insurance (CGL) protects businesses against claims made by others for which the policyholder has or may have liability. This coverage is extremely important for businesses because of the increased opportunity for liability due to business operations. Settlements and defense expenses can quickly deplete the resources of a company. The CGL allows the insured to transfer some or all of that risk to the insurance company. The CGL covers the following types of liability exposures:

- **Premises and operations liability**—This includes bodily injury, property damage, and other types of liability inherent to conducting business in a certain location or to carrying out certain business activities.
- **Products-completed operations liability**—This is the liability a business incurs through defective products, work, or operations.
- **Indirect or contingent liability**—This is the liability a business incurs through the actions of others, such as agents, employees, and contractors.
- **Personal and advertising injury**—This is injury caused by any of the following, including resulting bodily injury:
  - False arrest, detention, or imprisonment
  - Malicious prosecution
  - Wrongful eviction or entry by a landlord or on behalf of a landlord
  - Slander or libel, regardless of how such information is published

- Any form of oral or written publication of information that violates anyone's right to privacy
- Use of another's idea in the insured's advertisement
- Infringing on the intellectual property rights of others in the insured's advertising

Commercial general liability insurance policies consist of the following parts: common policy declarations, common policy conditions, CGL declarations, CGL coverage forms, and mandatory endorsements.

OCCURRENCE FORMS AND CLAIMS-MADE FORMS

CGL policies are written using either the **occurrence form** or the **claims-made form**. Both of these forms require the loss to occur within the coverage territory and not be excluded by the policy for coverage to apply, but they differ in how the policy determines whether a loss falls within the active policy period. Under occurrence forms, the date of loss is determined by the date the loss actually occurred. Even if a claim is not filed until after the policy has expired, the loss is still covered, as long as it occurred during the policy period. For example, if a policy is active from January 1 of a given year until January 1 of the next year, an accident or occurrence that happens between these dates would be eligible for coverage.

Under claims-made forms, coverage applies to any claim that is made and reported during the policy period. Most claims-made CGL policies include a **retroactive date**, which is the earliest date prior to the beginning of the policy period for which the insurer will provide coverage if it is notified during the policy period. Even a covered loss that occurs before the start of the policy period can receive coverage, as long as the claim was made during the policy period, notice is made in accordance with the provisions of the policy, and the loss occurred after the retroactive date. Using a retroactive date protects the insurance company from taking on excessive risk because it places a limit on how far into the past a loss can occur and still be eligible for coverage. In some cases, the retroactive date is the same as the policy effective date, in which case no losses occurring prior to the policy period will be covered. There is a subtype of claims-made policies that require not only that the claim be made to the insured during the policy period, but also that the insured must report the claim during the policy period in which the claim was made. These are called **claims-made and reported policies**.

Because claims-made forms do not rely on the occurrence date to determine coverage, the parameters for reporting a claim are more stringent. The policy does not consider a claim to be made solely based on when it was reported to the insurer. A claim is considered to have been made at the earliest of when the insured is notified of injury or property damage, when the insured receives a written or verbal demand for payment, or when the insured becomes aware of injury or property damage by any other means. This is key to determining the coverage period in which the claim falls, and to preventing an insured from being put on notice of a claim and then buying a claims-made policy after the fact.

It is important to note that coverage under a claims-made policy is not the same as coverage for **prior acts**, sometimes referred to as **nose coverage**. Prior acts are actions or conditions that existed before any injury or damage occurred. Prior acts coverage is based on when the loss occurred rather than when the claim was reported to the insured. It differs from an occurrence CGL in that it will still cover losses with an occurrence date before the policy inception, so long as it is after the chosen retroactive date. If there is no retroactive date for the prior acts policy, any claim occurring before the start of the policy period may qualify for coverage. Prior acts coverage is usually used for professional liability rather than for general liability.

RETROACTIVE DATE CHANGES ON CLAIMS-MADE FORMS

Changing or advancing retroactive dates on claims-made forms can create coverage gaps, which leave the insured without coverage for a period of time. These should be avoided whenever possible. When acquiring a new claims-made policy, the insured should make certain that the retroactive date on the new policy is identical to the old policy. Furthermore, retroactive dates cannot be advanced unless the insured provides written consent and one of the following criteria is present:

- A new policy is written by a different insurance company.
- The insured failed to provide the necessary material information, or omitted material information that would have affected the insurance company's decision to provide insurance.
- The insured's business has undergone a change that increases the insurer's risk exposure.

EXTENDED REPORTING PERIOD

Extended reporting periods are available for claims-made forms and are also referred to as **tail coverage**. They help eliminate coverage gaps by covering claims submitted after the policy has expired. Extended reporting periods are available only under the following conditions:

- The insured cancels or does not renew his or her claims-made form.
- The insured replaces the claims-made form with an occurrence form.
- The insurance company renews or replaces the current form with a form that lists an earlier retroactive date.

CGL policies may have a **basic extended reporting period (BERP)** or a **supplemental extended reporting period (SERP)**. The basic extended period is typically that which is already included in a claims-made policy. It gives the insured limited additional time after a policy expires to report a claim that was made between the policy's retroactive date and the expiration date. Depending on the insurer, BERP coverage provides extended reporting periods of 30 or 60 days at no extra charge or additional premiums to the insured. Under some policies, if the insured knows of a situation that may cause him or her to receive claims after the BERP has elapsed and reports it to the insurance company while the BERP is active, coverage will be extended to allow additional time for reporting of potential claims. In this case, the policyholder may be eligible for coverage for up to five years after the policy expires, when the claim made results from the conditions the insured reported to the insurer.

SERP coverage is optional and requires the policyholder to pay an additional premium. This option lengthens the extended reporting period beyond that provided under the basic coverage. SERP can be purchased in a variety of durations, up to and including an unlimited extended reporting period. This coverage can be very beneficial to businesses that are ceasing operations and thus have no need to continuing carrying CGL coverage, or for occupations in which it can take many years for claims to be made, such as medical malpractice and professional liability policies.

DEDUCTIBLE AND SELF-INSURED RETENTION

CGL policies may be endorsed to have a **deductible** or a **self-insured retention (SIR)**. Both of these set an amount that the policyholder is responsible to pay on a liability claim. An insured may choose to include these provisions on the CGL to reduce policy premiums. On a policy with a deductible, the insurance company will assume the expenses related to settling and defending a covered claim from the time it is reported. The deductible does not come into play until the claim is settled, it is denied, or a judgment is paid. Once the claim is resolved in one of these ways, the insurance company will seek reimbursement from the insured for an amount up to the deductible that is chosen. If the settlement or claims expenses do not exceed the deductible, the insured will be responsible for paying the insurer back for all payments made. If these costs exceed the deductible, the insured is obligated to compensate the insurer for the entire amount of the deductible, and any amount above the deductible will be assumed by the insurance company.

On policies with a SIR, the timing works differently than it does for a policy with a deductible. The insured must pay for claims, including defense costs, up to the amount indicated in the policy before the insurance company will start to pay any expenses associated with a covered loss. For example, if a policy carries a $25,000 SIR, the insurance company does not become involved in the settlement or defense of the claim until the insured has paid $25,000 for these expenses. Rather than reimbursing the insurance company on the back end, the insured will pay for the claim from the onset until the SIR amount has been paid.

SECTION I—COVERAGES
COVERAGE A—BODILY INJURY AND PROPERTY DAMAGE LIABILITY

This section states that the insurance company promises to pay any sums for which the insured becomes legally obligated to pay because of covered bodily injury or property damage caused by an **occurrence**. Also known as an **accident,** an occurrence includes injury that results from repeated or continuous contact with the same source of harm. The insurance company reserves the right to defend any suit seeking these damages, as well as to investigate precipitating events and settle any resulting claims or suits. The amount paid by the insurance company only extends up to the limits of insurance described in the third section of the policy. The insurance company's responsibility and duty to defend expire when the insurance company has paid the applicable limit of insurance.

Liability coverage for damage to the personal property of others is distinct from the coverage provided in the building and business personal property coverage form. Under the BPP, personal property that does not belong to the insured is covered regardless of any negligence on the part of the insured, so long as the loss meets the requirements outlined in the policy. Coverage is usually available by virtue of it being in the insured's possession or being located on the covered premises. The amount payable is usually subject to a sublimit within the policy. Under the CGL, the insured must have acted negligently in a way that resulted in property damage. The property does not need to be on the premises or in the insured's possession to be covered for liability. No sublimit applies for property damage claimed under the CGL, and these losses would fall within the occurrence limit on the policy.

Coverage A excludes liabilities that result from the following:

- Injury or damage intentionally caused by an insured
- Liability taken on by the insured in a contract or agreement that is not an "insured contract"
- Maintaining, owning, or using autos or aircraft
- Maintaining, owning, or using watercraft unless the watercraft meets the limited exceptions outlined in the policy
- Losses related to the consumption of alcohol if the insured is in a business involving the sale, furnishing, or distribution of alcoholic beverages
- Work-related injuries already covered under workers' compensation or similar laws
- Bodily injury to an employee of the insured that arises out of employment, regardless of whether the insured may be liable as an employer or in any other capacity
- Pollution that causes bodily injury or property damage, or results in cleanup costs
- Damage sustained by the insured's products due to some innate defect

- Damage sustained by the insured's work
- Personal and advertising injury
- Bodily injury or property damage that results from the transportation of mobile equipment
- Using an auto or mobile equipment to prepare for or participate in any race or contest
- Product recalls due to some known or suspected defect within the product
- Defects and dangers inherent in the insured's products or work
- Breach of contract
- Damage sustained by property that the insured owns, rents, occupies, or otherwise cares for, unless the property is being rented for less than seven consecutive days
- Losses occurring on a worksite where work is being performed by an insured or the subcontractor of an insured if the damages are the result of these operations
- Damage to property that has been given away or abandoned by the insured
- Bodily injury sustained by an insured
- War or similar activities
- Disclosure or breach of private data or information in violation of the law
- Recording or distributing material in violation of the Telephone Consumer Protection Act, the CAN-SPAM Act of 2003, the Fair Credit Reporting Act, or any similar law or regulation
- Property damage that falls within the "products-completed operations hazard" as defined by the policy

COVERAGE B—PERSONAL AND ADVERTISING INJURY LIABILITY

This coverage will pay the insured's liability expenses when he or she is found legally responsible for specific non-bodily injuries outlined in the policy. The policy defines personal and advertising injury as any injury including bodily injury that results from:

- False arrest or detention
- Malicious prosecution
- Wrongful eviction from or entry into a private occupancy
- Slander or libel
- Right-to-privacy violations
- Using another's advertising idea
- Copyright or trade dress infringement
- Advertising injury arising from the improper advertisement of the policyholder's goods, products, or services

Coverage B excludes liabilities that result from the following:

- Willfully and illegally violating the rights of another party
- Publication of knowingly false information
- Contractual liability, unless part of an "insured contract"
- Breach of contract
- Any publishing done prior to the policy's effective date
- War
- Criminal activities committed or ordered by the insured
- Listing incorrect prices for products and services
- Products and services failing to meet advertised quality standards
- Insured's business activities as a provider of internet service, search, or access
- Insured's business activities as an advertiser, broadcaster, publisher, or designer of web content for others

129

- Insured's unauthorized use of another's name in email addresses, meta tags, or domain names
- Insured's hosting, ownership, use, or control of an electronic chatroom or bulletin board
- Infringing upon the copyright, patent, intellectual properties, trademark, or trade secrets of others
- Any type of loss related to pollution
- Disclosure or breach of private data or information in violation of the law
- Recording or distributing material in violation of the Telephone Consumer Protection Act, the CAN-SPAM Act of 2003, the Fair Credit Reporting Act, or any similar law or regulation

COVERAGE C—MEDICAL PAYMENTS

This coverage reimburses medical costs resulting from bodily injury, regardless of who was at fault. This includes expenses related to reasonable medical treatment, hospital services, creation and fitting of prosthetics, ambulance services, first aid, and funeral services. The injury must have occurred on or adjacent to the insured's premises or in conjunction with the insured's business activities. Additionally, the insured must report the injury to the insurance company within one year of the accident date, otherwise, coverage does not apply.

Coverage C excludes injuries from coverage if they are:

- Excluded by Coverage A
- Sustained by the insured, his or her employees, his or her tenants, or anyone who else who is occupying an area of the premises he or she usually occupies; exception is made for volunteer workers
- Sustained by persons hired to complete work for the insured or for any tenant of the insured
- Sustained while performing athletic activities

SUPPLEMENTARY PAYMENTS FOR COVERAGES A AND B

The **supplementary payments** portion of the commercial general liability policy outlines the costs the insurance company will pay in addition to the payment of a settlement or judgment. They are paid on top of the regular liability limit of the policy, and normally include the following:

- Legal defense costs for the insured and, if applicable, any indemnitees
- First aid rendered to people during and immediately after the accident
- Costs resulting from claim investigation
- Bond premium payments, including appeal bonds, attachment bonds, and bail bonds; the maximum payment for bail bonds is $250
- Any reasonable costs incurred by an insured due to a request by the insurance company
- Loss of earnings incurred by an insured because he or she must miss work to appear in court, up to a maximum of $250 per day
- Pre-judgment interest if it is not listed as a damage under the insuring agreements section
- Post-judgment interest

Defense costs include the expenses of defending the insured against liability lawsuits, including lawsuits that are completely baseless. Liability insurance pays for defense costs in addition to the regular liability limit of the policy. However, the policy will cease to pay defense costs once it has reimbursed damages up to its limits.

Indemnitee defense costs are only paid when the insured has assumed liability and agreed to provide a defense for another party in a contract or agreement. This other party is called an **indemnitee.** The insured's obligation to defend an indemnitee may arise from a hold-harmless agreement or indemnification clause included in the contract. For the insurer to defend an indemnitee, the loss must be covered by the insurance policy, the contract must state that the insured must defend the indemnitee, no conflict exists in defending both the insured and the indemnitee, and both the insured and the indemnitee request that the insurance company provide a defense with permission to use the same counsel for both parties. The indemnitee must agree in writing to cooperate with the insurer in the defense of the suit, provide copies of all summonses and legal notices to the insurance company, put any other insurer that may cover the suit on notice, aid in resolving coverage disputes between the insurers who may afford coverage, and furnish written permission for the insurer to secure any documentation related to the suit. The insurer has the right to conduct and control the defense of the suit on the behalf of the indemnitee. If any of these conditions are not met, expenses paid to defend an indemnitee will reduce the applicable policy limit available for the loss. In some cases, this issue can be avoided by amending the CGL with an **additional insured** endorsement. This endorsement affords insured status to either a specifically named entity or to any party for which the conditions outlined in the endorsement are met. When a party is an additional insured, defense costs will be paid on top of the policy limits.

Pre-judgment interest is the amount in damages the injured party would have earned if he or she had started receiving payments immediately after the injury. In many cases, courts award pre-judgment interest to the injured. Policies generally cover pre-judgment interest either by including it as part of the insuring agreement or by making additional payments.

Post-judgment interest is the amount that accrues between the time the damage settlement is awarded and the time the company begins issuing payments. The insurance will not pay any amounts accrued following payment, offer of payment, or deposit of funds with the court.

SECTION II—WHO IS AN INSURED

This section defines the **people and companies** who are covered by the CGL insurance policy. The declarations section of the policy includes the following designations for named insureds:

- **Individual or sole proprietorship**—Includes the named insured and his or her spouse
- **Partnership or joint venture**—Includes the named insured, the company members and their spouses when they are performing business-related duties, and the company partners and their spouses when they are performing business-related duties
- **Limited liability company**—Includes the named insured, members when they are performing business-related duties, and managers when they are performing management-related duties
- **Organization other than partnership, joint venture, or limited liability company**—Includes the named insured, stockholders only for their liability as stockholders, and executive officers and directors when they are performing business-related duties
- **Trust**—Includes the named insured and any trustees when they are performing their duties as a trustee

In addition to those who qualify as named insureds, CGL policies also cover the following persons while they are performing duties for the named insured related to their jobs:

- Employees of the named insured, except for those included under named insured designations
- Volunteer workers

- Non-employees and organizations serving as real estate managers
- Persons or organizations with temporary custody of the named insured's property following the named insured's death; coverage only applies to the liability associated with using the property and only lasts until the estate appoints a legal representative
- The legal representative of the named insured after his or her death

CGL policies also provide automatic coverage for new organizations acquired or created by the insured if the new organization is not a partnership, joint venture, or LLC. For coverage to apply, it must not be covered by any other insurance and must be owned or under majority control by the insured. Coverage lasts for 90 days or until the end of the policy period, whichever is earlier. The insured can extend coverage by reporting the new organization to the insurer. Coverage only applies to losses sustained after the organization was obtained. No coverage applies to any current or prior joint venture, partnership, or LLC that is not listed on the declarations.

SECTION III—LIMITS OF INSURANCE

The **per occurrence limit** is the maximum amount Coverages A and C combined will pay out for bodily injury, property damage, and medical payments in a single occurrence. This limit is part of either the general aggregate limit or the product-completed operations aggregate limit.

The **general aggregate limit** is the maximum total amount available for payment under Coverages A, B, and C combined during any single policy period. This applies regardless of the number of insureds, or the number of claims made. Through endorsement, a separate general aggregate limit can be applied to each insured location or project. This limit does not include damages related to the products-completed operations hazard.

The **products-completed operations aggregate limit** is the maximum amount Coverage A will pay out for damages under the "products-completed operations hazard" during any single policy period. This is not included in the general aggregate limit.

The **personal and advertising injury limit** is the maximum amount Coverage B will pay out for personal or advertising injury to one person or organization for a single occurrence. This limit is included under the general aggregate limit.

The **damage to premises rented to the insured limit** is the maximum amount Coverage A will pay out for liability related to fire damage sustained by premises that the insured rents or occupies with permission from the owner. This limit applies on a per occurrence basis and is part of the general aggregate limit and per occurrence limit.

The **medical expense limit** is the maximum amount Coverage C will pay out for medical expenses related to bodily injury to a single person. Each person injured in a single occurrence is eligible to receive up to the limit for medical payments. This limit is part of the general aggregate limit and per occurrence limit.

SECTION IV—CONDITIONS

The CGL policy carries many conditions that are similar to those found in other types of liability policies. The conditions found in the standard CGL policy are as follows:

- **Bankruptcy**—States that bankruptcy or insolvency of the insured or the estate of the insured will not relieve the insurance company of its obligations for a covered claim
- **Duties in the event of occurrence, offense, claim, or suit**—This condition describes the actions the insured is obligated to take when a loss occurs. These actions include:

132

- o Notify the insurance company as soon as is practicable of any occurrence or offense that could possibly result in a claim; such notice should include the time, location, and circumstances of the occurrence, names and addresses of any injured persons or witnesses, and the nature of any injury or damage caused by the occurrence.
- o If an insured party receives a notice of a claim or lawsuit, he or she should immediately record the date and the specifics, and notify the insurance company as soon as practicable.
- o If an insured receives notice of a lawsuit or other legal action, he or she should immediately send copies of any papers, demands, summonses, or notices to the insurance company.
- o Authorize the insurance company to obtain records and other information pertinent to the investigation, defense, or settlement of a claim.
- o Cooperate with the insurance company in the investigation, settlement, or defense of all claims and suits.
- o Assist the insurer in the enforcement of their subrogation rights should the insurance company request such assistance.
- o Do not make any voluntary payment, assume any obligation, or incur any expenses without the consent of the insurance company; exception is made for first aid.
- **Legal action against us**—States that no person or organization may name the insurer in any suit requesting damages from an insured party nor may any party sue the insurer unless there has been full compliance with all the terms of the policy; the insurance company may be named in a suit to recover on an agreed settlement or final judgment, but the insurance company refuses to be held liable for payments that are not described in the policy or that are in excess of the limit of insurance
- **Other insurance**—States that when there is other insurance applicable to the loss that is valid and collectible, the insurer's obligation to pay a claim is limited as follows:
- o When the CGL is primary, coverage is only limited when another similar policy is also primary for the same loss; in such a case, loss payment will be shared per provisions of the **method of sharing** condition.
- o The CGL is always excess coverage when a loss is also covered by:
  - ❖ Fire insurance, extended coverage insurance, builder's risk, installation risk, or similar coverage related to the insured's products or work
  - ❖ Fire insurance that covers a location rented or temporarily occupied by an insured with the owner's permission
  - ❖ Insurance that covers the insured's liability as a tenant at a location that the insured rents or temporarily occupies with the consent of the owner
  - ❖ Insurance that covers autos, aircraft, or watercraft losses that are not excluded by the CGL policy
  - ❖ Any other liability policy on which the policyholder is an additional insured for damages resulting from the insured's premises or operations or the insured's completed products or operations
- o When the CGL is excess, the insurer has no duty to defend the insured for losses under Coverages A and B unless no other policy is providing a defense; if a defense is provided by this policy, the insurance company assumes the rights of recovery against the other insurer(s).
- o When the CGL coverage is provided on an excess basis, the insurance company will only pay the amount of the loss that exceeds the sum of all the other insurance applicable to the loss and any deductible or self-insured retention under those policies; any remaining loss payment will be shared with any other excess policies.

133

- o **Applicable only to the claims-made policy**: If there is another policy applicable to a loss and it is not a claims-made policy, this policy will be excess coverage, but only if the other policy does not have a retroactive date or the policy period on that policy is after the retroactive date for this policy.
- **Method of sharing**—Outlines how payments will be divided when multiple insurance policies apply to the same loss:
  - o **Contribution by equal shares**—When all involved policies allow the loss payments to be shared equally among the policies, each insurer will contribute equal amounts until each has paid either its applicable limit of insurance or the full amount of loss, whichever comes first.
  - o **Contribution by limits**—Also called **pro rata sharing**, this will be the sharing method used when any of the involved policies does not allow equal contribution; under this method, each insurer will pay a percentage of the loss based on the proportion of their policy limits to the sum of all applicable policy limits.
- **Premium audit**—Explains the protocol for handling premiums as follows:
  - o All premium calculations are based upon the insurance company's rules and rates for the applicable coverage part.
  - o Any premium paid in advance is considered a deposit toward the final premium.
  - o When requested by the insurer, the policyholder must provide documentation that the insurance company will use to determine the final premium.
  - o After the audit period expires, the insurer will send notice to the named insured advising of any additional premium owed and the date on which the additional payment is due.
  - o If the deposit premium is greater than the final premium, the difference will be refunded to the insured.
- **Representations**—When the named insured accepts the policy offered by the insurance company, he or she affirms that the statements made in the policy declarations are complete and accurate, that the information in those statements relies on representations made by the insured, and that the policy was issued under the assumption that those representations are truthful.
- **Separation of insureds**—States that each insured party will be treated as if he or she is the sole named insured under the policy and that the policy will apply separately to each insured party against whom a suit or claim is made; this condition does not apply to the provisions regarding the limit of liability or to any rights or duties specific to the first named insured
- **Your right to claim and occurrence information condition (applicable only to the claims-made policy form)**—States that the insurance company must provide the named insured with the following information related to the existing claims-made forms and any other claims-made forms the company has given the insured over the previous three years:
  - o A listing or record of occurrences that the insured has not reported to any other insurance company, but only if there is notification of an accident or occurrence in accordance with the policy conditions
  - o A yearly summary of amounts paid and reserved under the general aggregate limit and the products-completed operations aggregate limit
  - o This information must be provided under the following circumstances:
    - ❖ The first named insured sends a written request to the insurance company no more than 60 days after the expiration of the policy period; the insurance company must respond within 45 days.

134

❖ The insurance company cancels or opts not to renew the policy; the first named insured must be notified at least 30 days before the policy's expiration date.

- **When we do not renew**—States that if the insurer decides to not renew the policy, written notice must be sent to the first named insured at least 30 days before the policy ends

SECTION V—DEFINITIONS

Under the claims-made coverage form, Section V is dedicated to the extended reporting period provisions. This topic was discussed earlier in this chapter. In the occurrence coverage form, Section V lists definitions important to the policy.

Advertisement—Any publicly shared notice regarding the insured's products intended to attract business, including notices posted via the internet, including portions of the insured's website meant to gain customers or supporters.

Autos—Vehicles designed solely for use on public roads or required to carry insurance by law in the location of principal garaging. This includes motor vehicles, trailers, and semitrailers, as well as their attached machinery and equipment. It does not include "mobile equipment."

Bodily injury—Any sickness, injury, or disease suffered by a person, up to and including death.

Coverage territory—The area in which the commercial general liability insurance applies. This normally encompasses the United States, its territories and possessions, and Canada. International waters and airspace are also included if the injured party was traveling between the described territories when the damage or injury occurred. The rest of the world is included in the coverage territory when the loss results from:

- Goods or products created or sold within the described territory
- The actions of a person who lives in the described territory and was performing work on the insured's behalf outside of the described territory
- Publishing of information on the internet or similar means of communication that causes "personal and advertising injury"

Employees—People employed by the insured, including leased workers, but excluding temporary workers.

Hostile fire—Any fire that extends outside its intended boundaries or burns uncontrollably.

Impaired property—Includes two types of tangible property: products or works of the insured believed to be defective, dangerous, or flawed, and products that do not conform to contractual requirements. Impaired property cannot be classified as the insured's products or work, but it must be repairable by an adjustment or repair of the insured's products or work.

Insured contract—Includes all of the following:

- Leases for premises rented or temporarily occupied by the insured, exclusive of any portion of the lease mandating indemnification by the named insured for fire damage to such property
- Sidetrack agreements
- Licensing or easement agreements, excluding those taking place within 50 feet of railroad demolition or construction operations

135

- Contracts with municipal entities, but only the portion applicable to assumption of tort liability for third parties
- Elevator maintenance agreements

Leased workers—Workers who are acquired through an agreement with a labor leasing firm and perform work related to the insured's business.

Loading or unloading—Handling of property that is performed in the following situations:

- Moved or loaded onto an aircraft, watercraft, or auto after it has been approved for such loading
- Moved around, on, or in the aircraft, watercraft, or auto
- Unloaded off the aircraft, watercraft, or auto, and moved to its delivery location

It does not include property that is being moved with the assistance of a mechanical device, except for a portable hand truck.

Mobile equipment—Includes any of the following:

- Bulldozers, forklifts, farm machinery, or other vehicles designed to be used off public roads
- Vehicles that are propelled on crawler treads
- Vehicles that are maintained for use entirely on or adjacent to premises owned or rented by the insured
- Any equipment that has the primary purpose of providing mobility to permanently mounted road construction equipment, resurfacing equipment, powertrains, shovels, diggers, or drills
- Any vehicles that are maintained primarily for purposes other than the transport of cargo or people

Mobile equipment does not include the following; these are considered "autos" under the policy:

- Snow removal equipment
- Road maintenance equipment
- Street cleaning equipment
- Cherry pickers or other similar equipment designed to raise and lower people when such equipment is mounted to an auto or truck chassis
- Air compressors
- Pumps and generators
- Equipment for spraying, welding, cleaning buildings, geophysical exploration, lighting, or well-servicing
- Any land vehicle subject to a financial responsibility or insurance law at the location where it is licensed or normally garaged

Occurrence—Any accident resulting in injury or property damage, including ongoing or repeated exposure to a generally harmful condition.

Personal and advertising injury—Any harm or injury caused by the following, including resultant bodily injury:

- False arrest, detention, or imprisonment
- Malicious prosecution

- Wrongful eviction or entry by a landlord
- Slander or libel
- Violation of another's right to privacy via oral or written means
- Use of another party's advertising idea in an insured's advertisement
- Use of another party's intellectual property in an insured's advertisement

Pollutants—Any irritant or contaminant that is in solid, liquid, gas, or thermal form, including smoke, soot, fumes, chemicals, and waste. Waste includes materials being held for recycling, reconditioning, or reclaiming.

Products-completed operations hazard—Any loss or damage caused by the insured's work or products occurring away from locations the insured owns or rents. This excludes products still in the insured's physical possession and incomplete or abandoned work. It only extends to losses on the insured location when the insured's product is to be consumed on the insured's premises. The completion date for work is considered the earliest of the following: the date on which all work outlined in a contract has been performed, when the all work at a single jobsite has been completed (when the contract applies to multiple locations), or when the work performed at a job site is put to its intended use by any party other than contractors or subcontractors who are also working on that site. Work that is otherwise complete aside from maintenance, service, replacement, or repair is treated as complete by the policy. This definition does not include losses stemming from transporting any property unless loss results from a condition in or on a vehicle. The vehicle cannot be owned or operated by an insured, and the harmful condition must not have arisen from any insured loading or unloading such a vehicle. The definition also excludes damages due to the presence of tools, uninstalled equipment, or abandoned or unused materials. It does not include operations or products that are included in the general aggregate limit per the policy declarations.

Property damage—Damage to or loss of use of tangible property. Electronic data is not considered tangible property for the purposes of the CGL policy.

Temporary worker—A worker provided to the insured to handle seasonal or short-term increased workload or to act as a replacement for an insured employee on temporary leave.

Volunteer workers—Workers who do not receive payment from the insured or his or her associates. They do not charge a fee for their work, and they carry out job duties at the insured's discretion and direction.

Your products—Any goods or services that the insured, those operating under the insured's name, or any business owned by the insured sells, handles, distributes, manufactures, or disposes of. This definition excludes real property, but includes the following:

- Equipment included with the product, such as parts and containers
- Any product warranties and representations
- Any warnings or instructions provided with or omitted from the product

Your work—Any work that the insured or someone working under the insured's name performs, including the following:

- Any equipment, parts, or materials used in conjunction with the work
- Any warranties or representation regarding work quality or performance
- Any warnings or instructions the insured provided or omitted regarding the work

LIABILITY ENDORSEMENTS

CGL policies are used by many types of commercial entities, so they need to be customizable to a certain extent. This is accomplished by adding or eliminating coverage using endorsements and optional coverage forms. When an endorsement or optional coverage form is attached to the policy, the coverage and provisions in it supersede the sections within the policy that the endorsement is intended to alter.

Additional insured endorsements—There are many situations in which the policyholder needs to ensure that another party is covered by the CGL. This typically occurs pursuant to a contract. There are multiple additional insured endorsements that can meet this need. Endorsements vary based on the type of entity that needs to be covered and the reason why the coverage is needed. Some examples of these parties include:

- Grantors of franchises
- Lessors of equipment the insured rents
- General contractors when the insured is a subcontractor
- Vendors
- Governmental agencies or subdivisions
- Architects, engineers, and surveyors hired by the insured
- Property managers of rented premises owned by the insured

Deductible liability insurance endorsement—Adds a deductible to the CGL policy that the insured will need to reimburse the insurance company for at the conclusion of a covered claim. The insured may choose to have a separate deductible for each bodily injury or property damage claim presented, or a single deductible per occurrence.

Exclusionary endorsements—Used when the insured does not need insurance for a risk that is covered in the basic CGL and wants it excluded, or when the insured business presents a risk that the insurance company does not want to insure. Examples of such exclusions include:

- Acts of terrorism
- Communicable diseases
- Certain professional services, products, or work—the excluded items will be listed on the declarations page
- Personal and advertising injury
- Hazards associated with underground property or equipment
- Abuse, molestation, and corporal punishment
- Financial services
- Funeral services
- Amusement providers, such as theme parks, carnivals, circuses, and fairs
- Law enforcement activities
- Healthcare providers

Electronic data liability coverage endorsement—Amends the electronic data exclusion in the CGL so that it will cover data loss that is caused by physical damage to related equipment. It modifies the policy definition of property damage so that such losses can be covered.

Employee benefits liability coverage endorsement—Adds coverage for errors, omissions, and acts in connection with administration of a business's employee benefits. This coverage is only written on a claims-made basis.

138

Liquor liability endorsement—Used to provide liquor liability coverage to any insured by removing the liquor liability exclusion in the CGL policy form. It covers any damages that an insured may be legally responsible for related to the business of selling, serving, or furnishing alcoholic drinks to patrons. It is only appropriate when the policyholder's liquor liability exposure comprises limited losses that present minimal exposure.

Pollution liability coverage extension endorsement—Provides coverage for bodily injury and property damage caused by pollution. It negates Coverage A's exclusion on those types of damages. Pollution cleanup costs are not covered. This endorsement limits coverage only to areas of the insured location where there is no storage, handling, disposal, treatment, or processing of waste.

Primary and noncontributory—other insurance endorsement—Used when the policyholder agrees to assume liability of another in a contract. This endorsement states that the insurer will not pursue contribution or recovery from that other party or their insurer.

OTHER LIABILITY COVERAGE FORMS

Liquor liability coverage form—Used by those in the liquor business and covers the liabilities associated with selling liquor, including injuries that result from a customer consuming alcohol provided by the insured. This provides more robust coverage than the liquor liability endorsement. It also prevents liquor liability exposures from being included in the insured's general liability loss experience, allowing the policyholder to obtain coverage more easily for non-liquor exposures. Coverage is available on both an occurrence basis and a claims-made basis.

Owner's and contractor's protective liability coverage form—coverage for operations of designated contractor—Covers any liability that the insured may incur vicariously from the activities of independent contractors. In most cases, someone other than the named insured purchases this form to cover the insured.

Pollution liability-limited designated sites coverage form—Pays for bodily injury and property damage losses resulting from pollution emissions at a location specified by the insured. Coverage is only provided on a claims-made basis.

Pollution liability designated sites coverage form—Provides the same coverage as the limited pollution coverage form but extends coverage to include cleanup costs. Coverage is available on a claims-made basis only.

Products/completed operations liability coverage form—Used to cover losses that result from the insured's completed products or operations. It focuses on claims that result from alleged defects or deficiencies of the insured's work. Coverage is available on both an occurrence basis and a claims-made basis. For this coverage to apply, the loss must have occurred away from the insured premises.

Commercial Crime Insurance

Commercial crime insurance insures businesses and government entities against theft, robbery, employee dishonesty, and similar crimes. It can be acquired as either a standalone policy under a policy form, or as part of a commercial package policy.

Standard monoline policy forms for commercial crime insurance include the following:

- Commercial crime policy (discovery form)
- Commercial crime policy (loss sustained form)

- Government crime policy (discovery form)
- Government crime policy (loss sustained form)

Standard package coverage forms for commercial crime insurance include the following:

- Commercial crime coverage form (discovery form)
- Commercial crime coverage form (loss sustained form)
- Government crime coverage form (discovery form)
- Government crime coverage form (loss sustained form)

For the purposes of this guide, the discussion will focus on commercial crime forms. Each type of commercial crime insurance form can be divided into two versions: **discovery** and **loss sustained**. Under a loss sustained form, losses are covered if they are sustained or discovered during the policy period, or if they are discovered within a year of the policy's expiration date. Once the insured obtains a new commercial crime insurance policy, the yearlong discovery period ends. According to the **loss sustained during prior insurance condition**, these forms will pay losses that were discovered during the current policy period, even if they were sustained during the previous policy period. This condition does not apply unless three criteria are present:

- The previous policy's discovery period has ended.
- The current policy's effective date was the same day as the previous policy's expiration date.
- Both the current and the previous policy cover the loss.

Discovery forms cover any losses, no matter when they occurred, as long as they are discovered during the policy period or within 60 days of the policy's expiration date. This 60-day period is extended to one year for losses resulting from employee benefit plans. When a replacement policy is purchased, the discovery period ends as soon as a new commercial crime policy goes into effect. A named insured is considered to have discovered a loss when there is notice of an actual or potential claim, or when the named insured is aware of information sufficient to believe that a loss has occurred or that it will occur in the near future. The named insured does not have to know specific information about the loss for the insurance company to consider it discovered.

COVERAGES

The standard commercial crime insurance includes insuring agreements for seven different categories of coverage. It should be noted that these coverages do not apply automatically. The policyholder must select which coverages are needed, and those selected will be indicated on the policy declarations page. Theft coverages will typically cover property that disappears mysteriously as long as there is a likelihood it was stolen. Some insurance companies will decline to cover such losses. There are also many endorsements available for commercial crime coverage and policy forms that allow the insured to tailor coverage to his or her specific needs.

Employee theft coverage applies whenever an employee or employees steal company property, even if the employee is never identified. It reimburses loss of money, securities, and other types of property. For this coverage, theft includes forgery. Coverage does not apply in the following situations:

- Warehouse receipts are used in a fraudulent and dishonest manner.
- Someone trades in the insured's name or with a fictitious account.
- The only evidence of loss is inventory shortage or profit and loss calculations.

Losses can be reimbursed on a **per loss basis**, which pays out the maximum insurance limit without regard to the number of employees involved, or a **per employee basis**, which pays all losses for a single employee.

Forgery or alteration coverage reimburses losses that result when checks, drafts, promissory notes, and similar documents are forged or altered in the name of the named insured or his or her agent. Coverage applies worldwide and in situations in which fake signatures have been mechanically created. Additionally, the insurance company may pay the insured's court costs if he or she is sued for not paying for forged or altered documents.

Inside the premises—theft of money and securities coverage provides theft, disappearance, and destruction coverage for money and securities stored within the insured's premises. It also covers the interior or exterior of the premises, locked safes, vaults, cash registers, cash drawers, and cash boxes if they are damaged during theft, attempted theft, or forced entry.

Inside the premises—robbery or safe burglary of other property covers **other property** as defined by the policy when it is lost in either of the following situations:

- Robbery or attempted robbery of a custodian inside the premises
- Safe burglary or attempted safe burglary of a safe or vault inside the premises

Robberies that occur during normal business hours are also covered. This coverage also reimburses the damage to the premises' exterior or interior if the insured is legally obligated to insure it, and damage to locked safes and vaults contained within the premises when the damage results from actual or attempted robbery/safe burglary.

Outside the premises coverage reimburses the following losses:

- Money and securities that are stolen, lost, or destroyed while they are in the possession of a messenger or armored car company
- Loss of other property while in the possession of a messenger or armored car company that is lost during an actual or attempted robbery

Both types of inside the premises coverage and outside the premises coverage exclude losses if they result from the following:

- Errors or omissions in accounting or arithmetic
- Losses involving the exchange or purchase of any property
- Damage to motor vehicles, trailers, or related equipment
- Vandalism to any of the insured's property, including safes, vaults, or cash registers
- When the named insured or any representatives of the named insured voluntarily part with property due to a trick or deception
- Fire damage, unless it involves safes, vaults, money, or securities
- Malfunctions in money-operated devices, except for instances in which the device continuously counts money and records transactions
- Damage or loss that occurs after property is transferred or surrendered away from the insured premises or away from financial institution premises when such action is performed due to unauthorized instructions or because of a threat; exception is made for property in the possession of a messenger outside of the premises who had no knowledge of the threat

Computer and funds transfer fraud coverage applies when a computer is used to illegally transfer, deliver, or pay money, securities, or other property. The computer equipment used must be owned, operated, or leased by the named insured. It provides worldwide coverage against loss or damage. It will also reimburse the insured for money debited from a transfer account by a financial institution acting on fraudulent instruction in good faith. Transfer accounts allow the insured to electronically transfer funds via phone or written request. If the named insured engages a computer software contractor who makes changes or enters electronic data fraudulently, the policy will pay for such losses if these were executed in good faith by any employee. For this type of loss to be covered, there must be a written agreement between the named insured and the computer software contractor. Any losses of this type perpetuated by someone who is not a computer software contractor are not eligible for coverage. The following types of losses are excluded under this insuring agreement:

- Following fraudulent instructions, except in a situation as described above
- Transactions performed by anyone with authorized access to the system in question, unless it is an employee acting in good faith on information provided by specific types of contractors
- Losses resulting from the use of debit, credit, or other similar cards
- Property given up as part of a purchase or exchange
- Losses only identified via inventory shortage or profit/loss calculations

Money orders and counterfeit money coverage reimburses the insured when he or she takes counterfeit currency or invalid money orders in good faith as payment. Coverage only applies to money orders or counterfeit money accepted during the regular course of the insured's business.

EXCLUSIONS

Commercial crime insurance excludes losses from coverage under any insuring agreement if they result from the following:

- Nuclear hazards
- War or war-like actions
- Pollution
- Incurred legal costs, fees, or expenses outside of those specifically covered by the policy
- Indirect and consequential losses
- Disclosure of any personal or confidential information, including that of the named insured, or any dishonest acts that occur as a consequence of the information being disclosed
- Fines, fees, or penalties levied against the insured because of a data security breach
- Government authority seizing or destroying property
- Theft or dishonest acts committed by the named insured, or the named insured's partners, members, employees, directors, trustees, or authorized representatives, unless they are covered under employee theft coverage; this exclusion applies regardless of whether these people are acting alone or in collusion with others
- Acts committed by any employee whom the insured knows committed dishonest acts prior to the policy period
- Any loss of virtual currency, including but not limited to cryptocurrency

CONDITIONS

The following policy conditions apply to all coverages contained within the commercial crime policy or coverage form:

Consolidation—merger or acquisition—There is automatic coverage for employees and premises acquired due to a merger or consolidation. Coverage only lasts 90 days and is not available for government entities.

Additional premises or employees—Coverage is automatically afforded for employees and premises added to the insured's business during the policy period. This coverage is afforded without paying an additional premium. The insured is only required to report these additions to the insurance company when they are the result of a consolidation, merger, or acquisition.

Concealment, misrepresentation, or fraud—Any misrepresentation or concealment of material information committed by any insured is grounds for voiding the policy. Fraud committed by the named insured voids coverage provided by the policy.

Cooperation—The named insured is obligated to cooperate with the insurance company per the terms and conditions of the policy.

Duties in the event of a loss—The named insured has the following responsibilities when a loss occurs:

- Alert the insurance company of the loss.
- Alert the proper authorities if a crime has been committed.
- Provide sworn testimony or submit to examination under oath if the insurer requests it.
- Submit a sworn proof of loss within 120 days of discovering the loss.
- Cooperate with the insurer to investigate and settle the claim.
- Furnish the insurance company with any records requested for examination.

Employee benefit plans—Employee theft coverage extends to cover losses involving employee benefit plans. This condition modifies the definition of theft for this coverage to include fraudulent or dishonest acts.

Extended period to discover loss (loss sustained form)—Losses occurring during the policy period but not discovered until after cancellation may be covered if reported within one year of the cancellation. The extended discovery period terminates immediately if another crime policy goes into effect. Employee benefit plan losses have the full one-year discovery period regardless of any subsequent policy.

Extended period to discover loss (discovery form)—This is essentially the same as the condition in the loss sustained form except that the discovery period is 60 days from cancellation rather than one year.

Joint insured—When there is more than one named insured listed on the policy, the first named insured acts for himself or herself and all other named insureds. Any information pertaining to coverage that is known by one of the named insureds is deemed to be known by all named insureds. Payment to the first named insured satisfies any obligation the insurance company has to all named insureds. Employees of any insured are considered employees of all insureds. Each named insured is subject to the extended discovery period condition independently of all other insureds. The limit of insurance listed on the declarations applies regardless of the number of insureds.

Copyright © Mometrix Media. You have been licensed one copy of this document for personal use only. Any other reproduction or redistribution is strictly prohibited. All rights reserved. This content is provided for test preparation purposes only and does not imply an endorsement by Mometrix of any particular political, scientific, or religious point of view.

Legal action against us—No lawsuit can be filed against the insurer unless the insured has complied completely with the conditions of the policy. Actions must be filed no later than two years from the date of discovery.

Liberalization—If the insurer changes the policy in a way that broadens coverage without increasing the premium, the change applies to the existing policy automatically when the change goes into effect in the policy's jurisdiction, as long as the effective date is either within the policy period or within the 45 days immediately following the beginning of the policy period.

Loss sustained during prior insurance issued by us or any affiliate (loss sustained form only)—If a loss is sustained during a prior policy period but not discovered until after that policy period ends, the insurance company will provide coverage under the current policy period so long as there was continuous coverage with the same insurer or an affiliate of the current insurer. Coverage will be dated back to the initial policy inception, but each loss is subject to the per occurrence limit of the policy under which the claim is paid. If the occurrence spans two or more policy periods, the claim under the most recent policy will be settled first. Any remaining payment will be made under the previous policies. Only the current deductible will be applied to the entire loss settlement regardless of the number of previous policy periods involved. There will be no payment until that deductible is satisfied. When the occurrence is partly or entirely within a previous policy period, the limit will be the highest available from all periods in which the loss occurred.

Loss sustained during prior insurance not issued by us or any affiliate (loss sustained form only)—If a loss is sustained during a policy not issued by the current insurer or an affiliate, but not discovered until the discovery period for the applicable policy period has ended, the current insurer will cover the loss only when there has been no break in coverage. Any policy lapse between the policy period in which the loss was sustained and the current policy will void coverage under this provision. When a loss occurs across multiple policy periods and coverage was not continuously with the same insurance company, the lowest applicable limit of insurance will be used.

Other insurance—When a claim is covered by another policy with the same terms and conditions as this policy and both policies provide coverage on a primary basis, the insurer will only pay its pro rata share of the loss. If the property is covered by a policy with different terms and conditions, this policy will pay only on an excess basis.

Ownership of property and interests covered—Only specific property is covered under the policy: property the named insured leases or owns, property in the named insured's possession regardless of the reason for holding it, and property for which the named insured assumed legal liability in a contract predating the loss occurrence. Any claim, including that for property owned by others, may only be presented by the named insured.

Records—The policyholder is required to maintain and furnish records the insurance company needs to investigate and establish the value of a claim.

Recoveries—When there is recovery from another party, the insurer will recoup recovery expenses first. After this, any remaining payment will be distributed as follows:

- First, the insured will be compensated for any loss in excess of what the insurance company paid.
- Second, the insurer will be reimbursed for loss payments made.

- Third, the insured will be paid for the deductible applied to the loss.
- Fourth, if there is any payment remaining, it will be issued to the insured.

Territory—Except where specified otherwise, coverage is only available for claims that take place in the coverage territory: the United States, its territories and possessions, and Canada.

- Under the **employee theft coverage**, there is coverage for employees who are outside the coverage area, provided they have not been out of the coverage area for longer than 90 days.
- Under the **forgery or alteration coverage** and the **computer and funds transfer fraud coverage**, there is no specific coverage territory, and losses are covered worldwide.

Transfer of your rights of recovery against others—When the insured takes payment from the insurer, his or her recovery rights transfer to the insurer. The insured also has an ongoing duty to secure those recovery rights and take no action that would impair them.

Valuation—settlement—This outlines the method the insurance company will use to value different types of property. The methods are as follows:

- Money—Reimbursed at face value
- Securities—Reimbursed at face value as of the close of business on the day the loss was discovered
- Other property, including premises—Reimbursed at replacement value; payment will be the lowest of the policy limit, the cost to replace the property with functionally similar property, and the amount the insured pays to repair or replace the property

Replacement value is only paid after the completion of the repair or replacement in a reasonable amount of time. If the repair or replacement is not completed in a timely manner or the insured decides to not repair or replace the property, the payment will be made based on the actual cash value (ACV) of the property.

Termination as to any employee (employee theft only)—Coverage for any employee is terminated immediately when the insured or partners, directors, officers, members, or managers discover the employee has committed theft or another dishonest act, regardless of whether the act occurred before or after the employee was hired. The insurance company can also cancel employee coverage, provided it gives written notification to the insured at least 30 days before the effective cancellation date.

Deductible amount (forgery or alteration only)—Covered legal expenses are not subject to a deductible.

Electronic and mechanical signatures (forgery or alteration only)—Signatures that are produced or reproduced electronically or mechanically are considered as valid as handwritten signatures.

Proof of loss (forgery or alteration only)—When a claim is made under this coverage, the insured is obligated to provide the forged or altered instrument with the proof of loss.

Armored motor vehicle companies—This policy is excess over any recovery allowed under a contract with an armored motor vehicle company, whether that recovery is directly from the company or from the company's insurer.

Special limit of insurance for specified property (inside the premises—robbery or safe burglary of other property coverage and outside the premises coverage only)—Certain property is subject to a $5,000 per occurrence special limit when covered under these insuring agreements. These types of property are:

- Precious stones, pearls, precious metals, or any articles that incorporate them
- Semiprecious stones
- Furs and fur garments
- Manuscripts, drawings, or records

Special limit of insurance for specified property (computer and funds transfer fraud coverage only)—There is a $5,000 limit on each occurrence in which manuscripts, drawings, or records are damaged, inclusive of any costs to reproduce or reconstruct the information contained in them.

Policy bridge; Discovery replacing loss sustained (discovery form only)—Used for when an insured replaces a loss sustained form with a discovery form. It provides coverage for losses that were discovered during the loss sustained policy period but may not have been sustained until the discovery policy period. Coverage under the current policy will only pay when there is excess exposure over the sum of the limit of insurance and deductible.

COMMERCIAL CRIME POLICY FORM CONDITIONS

Because the commercial crime policy forms are designed to be standalone policies, they contain conditions that are not listed in the commercial crime coverage forms. These policies incorporate conditions that are also found in the commercial package policy common policy conditions. These conditions are:

- Cancellation
- Changes
- Examination of your books and records
- Premiums
- Transfer of your rights and duties under this policy

SELECTED DEFINITIONS

Counterfeit money—Coins or bills produced to imitate money with the intention to present it as real currency.

Employee benefit plan—A plan provided in whole or in part to employees by an employer that is subject to the Employee Retirement Income Security Act (ERISA) and listed in the declarations. Such plans include pensions, 401(k)s, unemployment benefits, and group health, life, or disability insurance.

Forgery—Unlawfully signing the name of another person or organization with the intent to deceive.

Premises—Includes only the interior area of a building that is used to conduct the insured's business.

Other property—Any tangible property that is valuable but is not money, securities, computer programs, or electronic data. If a type of property is excluded within the policy, it does not meet the definition of other property.

146

Robbery—Unlawfully taking property that is in another's possession. The act must involve causing harm to the person in possession of the property, a threat to cause harm to the person in possession of the property, or commission of an illegal act witnessed by the person in possession of the property.

Safe burglary—Burglary occurs when a person unlawfully enters or leaves the premises and removes property that was inside the premises and can only be proven by finding evidence of forced entry or exit. Safe burglary is a form of burglary in which someone unlawfully enters a locked safe or vault and removes property or removes the entire safe or vault from the premises. There must be evidence of forced entry into the premises or marks on the safe or vault. When property is stolen from a safe or vault that has been left unlocked or open, it is not considered safe burglary.

Theft—Unlawfully removing money, securities, or property including burglary, safe burglary, and robbery. Loss of the property must deprive the insured in some way to be considered theft. If the property taken does not have value, the act is not considered to be theft.

Federal Crime Insurance

The federal government offers insurance against crimes like burglary and robbery for geographic areas in which private insurance companies refuse to offer coverage. This policy is administered by the **Federal Insurance and Mitigation Administration** and the **Department of Housing and Urban Development**. In approved states, both businesses and homes may receive federal crime insurance. It is typical for buildings to require protective devices or security guards in order to be eligible for federal crime insurance. Like commercial and government crime policies, the federal crime policy has coverage forms for **discovery** and for **loss sustained** policies. It is also possible to obtain federal crime insurance for employee theft, both on a per loss and a per employee basis.

Cyber Insurance

With the evolution of the technology available to individuals and businesses, new opportunities for loss have emerged. Even those not directly involved in the technology industry still adopt products and technologies that can expose them to cyber risks. Commercial cyber insurance has been developed as a means of addressing these risks. Cyber insurance policies may provide coverage for first-party losses, liability losses, or both. The type of policy used depends on the size of the organization being insured, as the risks for a smaller business can be very different than those of a large corporation.

The **commercial cyber insurance** policy is intended for smaller organizations, and eligibility is limited to companies having less than $250 million in annual revenue, nonprofits with an annual budget under $125 million, insureds looking for no more than $5 million in aggregate coverage, or companies wanting a deductible more than $10,000. Entities not meeting these requirements will usually be covered under an **information security protection cyber** policy. Because of the variety of cyber risks that exist, specialized information security cyber insurance policies are available for media companies and financial institutions. Unlike with most other commercial policies, payment of defense costs erodes the aggregate policy limit, given the significantly higher likelihood of these types of losses leading to litigation or other legal proceedings.

SELECTED DEFINITIONS

Cyber extortion event—A demand for ransom payment directed at the "organization" related to the commission of or threat of:

- A "cyber incident" or "information security breach"
- Theft, publication, disclosure, use, or destruction of the confidential or proprietary information of the organization that is kept on the "organization's computer system" or a "third-party computer system"

Cyber extortion expenses—Costs related to actual or attempted extortion of the insured by another party. This covers expenses for:

- Costs of hiring a vendor agreed upon by the named insured and the insurance company who is tasked with determining whether the extortion risk exists
- Interest costs on loans obtained by the insured to pay a demand for ransom
- Payments for rewards to informants when that information causes the perpetrator to be convicted
- Any other costs the insurance company agrees, in writing, to cover

Cyber incident—A blanket term used to refer to any one of the following:

- Access or use of the insured organization's computer system, including use of "electronic data," that is unauthorized
- Introduction of a virus or any other harmful or malicious code to the insured organization's computer system or "electronic data" intended to destroy, use, corrupt, or otherwise disrupt the normal functioning of that system
- Denial-of-service attacks that prevent access to or otherwise disrupt the normal functions of the insured organization's computer system

Cyber incident or information security breach expenses—Costs incurred by the insured as the result of a covered cyber loss, including:

- Costs of services needed to determine whether a breach has occurred
- If a breach has taken place, the expense associated with investigating how it occurred, who was impacted by the breach, and how to resolve it
- Fees for any legal or other professional consultation needed to determine how to remediate the breach and how to respond to the breach
- Costs of public relations services needed to protect or remediate the insured company's reputation after suffering negative publicity
- Costs of sending notifications via approved channels to the parties who may have been affected by the breach
- Increased labor costs incurred due to employees working overtime to address the breach and coordinate with impacted parties
- Costs of hiring a call center that will handle incoming calls from affected parties
- Costs of credit and identity theft monitoring for the victims of the breach for the amount of time required by regulations
- Any other expenses that the insurance company has agreed in writing are reasonable and necessary

Data restoration expenses—Payment for services needed to restore or replace the company's electronic data or computer programs, including reprogramming, data entry, and computer consultation. For any data that cannot be repaired or restored, the insurance company will pay expenses to replace the media upon which the data was stored with substantially similar blank media.

Discover or discovered—The earliest time at which the insured becomes aware of an actual or potential cyber incident, information security breach, interruption, or cyber extortion event. Exact details on the loss do not need to be known for the loss to be considered discovered.

Electronic data—Data stored on, created on, used on, or transmitted by computer software to storage devices or media. This is not tangible property.

Extra expenses—Costs incurred by an insured to minimize the impact of an "interruption" which are not part of normal operations.

Information security breach—This occurs when there is unauthorized access, retention, use, or acquisition of "personal information" or the publication of any proprietary or confidential information of a third party that the general public does not have access to, that the insured had a duty to maintain under a written agreement. The breach must have occurred while in the insured's care, custody, or control.

Insured—The "organization" (as defined in the policy) and its employees.

Interruption—An unexpected slowing or stopping of business activities.

Liability loss—Events resulting in the insured being subject to:

- Compensatory judgments or awards, including interest
- Claim settlements
- Where allowed by law, exemplary or punitive damages

Named insured—Any individual or party listed on the policy declarations page.

Organization—The "named insured" and any "subsidiary."

Period of restoration—The period of time starting at the end of the policy waiting period and ending when the insured company's computer system should have been reasonably restored to normal operations; the maximum period allowed is 180 days.

Wrongful act—Any actual or claimed breach of duty, error, omission, or neglect committed by an insured that leads to a "cyber incident," a privacy regulation violation, transmission of a virus or other malicious code, or "information security breach."

COMMERCIAL CYBER INSURANCE POLICY

In most cases, commercial cyber insurance policies provide coverage on a discovery basis and do not include a retroactive date automatically. The policy can be endorsed to add a retroactive date for all coverages except for the public relations expense coverage. The insuring agreements are divided into two categories and provide coverage as follows:

Part A—first-party insuring agreements

- **Cyber incident or information security breach expense**—This provides reimbursement for expenses normally resulting from an "information security breach" or a "cyber incident."
- **Cyber extortion events**—This provides coverage for the "cyber extortion expenses" that result from a "cyber extortion event."
- **Replacement or restoration of electronic data**—This covers "data restoration expenses" related to data damaged, destroyed, or lost in a covered "cyber incident."
- **Business income and extra expense**—This compensates the insured for "business income loss" because of a covered "cyber incident" and for any "extra expense" costs incurred during the "period of restoration" after an "interruption" occurs.

Part B—liability insuring agreements

- **Cyber incident or information security breach liability**—This provides coverage for liability claims and expenses related to defending the insured against the claims. Coverage is provided on a claims-made basis. Under this coverage, the insurer has a right to defend and settle covered losses as it sees fit.
- **Regulatory proceeding liability**—"Regulatory loss" arising from regulatory proceedings initiated by any government agency with the authority to bring such action, including defense costs; the proceeding must have been initiated in response to a claim for a "wrongful act" or a series of interrelated wrongful acts.

INFORMATION SECURITY PROTECTION CYBER POLICY

The Information security protection cyber policy provides coverage that is more expansive than that provided by the commercial cyber insurance policy. This policy automatically includes a retroactive date for the liability coverages and can be endorsed to add retroactive dates to the other coverages on the policy. For all liability coverages, the insurance company has a right and duty to defend the insured for covered losses. The coverages included in the information security protection cyber policy are:

- All the coverages provided by the commercial cyber insurance policy.
- **Payment card industry liability**—This pays for amounts the insured is legally obligated to pay due to losses involving payment cards, including legal defense costs.
- **Media liability**—This covers liability arising from content published by the insured that results in a "liability loss."

EXCLUSIONS

Cyber insurance policies specifically exclude coverage for **property damage** and **bodily injury** losses. Both types of cyber insurance policies exclude certain types of loss, such as those resulting from:

- War
- Employment-related practices
- Acts of nature, including hail, lightning, earthquake, volcanic action, and similar uncontrolled events
- Liability taken on by the insured in a contract unless that liability would have existed without the contract

- Antitrust activities committed by the insured that are in violation of laws intended to prevent monopolization, unfair trade, and price fixing, such as the Federal Trade Commission Act, the Clayton Act, or the Sherman Antitrust Act
- Chemical, biological, and nuclear hazards
- Losses the policyholder was aware of before the policy inception
- Illegally recording or distributing material in violation of the CAN-SPAM Act of 2003, the Fair Debt Collection Practices Act, the Telephone Consumer Protection Act, the Fair Credit Reporting Act, the Fair and Accurate Credit Transactions Act, or any similar regulation
- Pollution
- Losses in which there was notice given under any prior policy
- Actions in violation of the Racketeer Influenced and Corrupt Organizations (RICO) Act or comparable laws
- Claims or losses related to transactions involving securities
- Infringement of any trade secret or patent
- Publishing material known by the insured to be false
- Actions brought by one insured against another insured
- Actions brought by government or regulatory agencies outside of those expressly covered by the policy
- Losses resulting from the insured performing or directing another to perform acts that are intentional, criminal, malicious, fraudulent, or dishonest
- Surges, reductions, or failures of power sources not controlled by the insured
- Contract breaches involving liability assumed by the insured
- Losses stemming from wrongful acts that took place before the retroactive date indicated on the policy
- Legal action initiated before the prior or pending litigation date listed in the policy declarations
- Any claim or action brought by a financial institution or credit card processor or company alleging violation of Payment Card Industry Security Standards

There are some exclusions in the information security protection cyber policy that are not found in the commercial cyber insurance policy that are applicable only to media liability. These are:

- Losses arising from promotional activities and contests such as sweepstakes, lotteries, coupons, discounts, or prizes
- Alleged or actual violation of another's music licensing and royalty rights, including actions initiated by the RIAA, BMI, ASCAP, or similar music licensing entity
- Claims made by independent contractors related to ownership of media content or services

CONDITIONS

Many of the standard policy conditions are contained in the cyber insurance policies. Such conditions are:

- Bankruptcy
- Changes
- Cancellation and nonrenewal
- Changes
- Examination of books and records
- Inspections and surveys
- Premiums

- Subrogation
- Legal action against us
- Separation of insureds
- Other insurance
- Valuation

Because of the nature of the exposures covered by cyber insurance, several of the conditions bear similarity to ones that are in the commercial crime policy. These include:

- Policy bridge—Discovery replacing loss sustained.
- Extended period to discover loss—Cyber insurance policies allow 60 days after the policy terminates for new losses to be discovered.
- Extended reporting periods—This only applies to the information security cyber insurance policy. The basic extended reporting period is 30 days from the end of the policy. An endorsement providing a specified supplemental reporting period can be purchased as late as 30 days after the policy expires. The length of the supplemental reporting period is indicated on the policy declaration page.

There are also conditions that are different from similarly named conditions in other policies, as well as some that are specific to cyber insurance policies. These conditions are as follows:

- **Representations and severability of the application**—This condition states that the insured acknowledges that the policy was issued based on representations made by the insured, that the information on the declarations and policy application is complete and accurate, and that such information was based upon the representations the insured made. Any material misrepresentation is sufficient for the insurer to void the policy with respect to the insured party that was aware of the misrepresentation being made.
- **Changes in exposures**—This condition addresses how the insurance company will handle changes that occur in the insured's business. It addresses three situations:
  - **Acquisition or creation of another entity**—When the insured obtains voting rights in another organization, creates a subsidiary, merges with another entity, or consolidates with an existing subsidiary, the insurance company must be notified within 60 days and pay any additional premium needed due to these actions; losses arising out of the newly acquired or created organizations will be covered under the policy, but only for wrongful acts happening after the creation or acquisition became effective.
  - **Merger or acquisition of named insured**—This condition applies when the company named on the policy merges with another company and ceases to exist as its own company, or when another entity gains majority control over the named insured; the insurer needs to be advised of the change within 60 days. Under both insuring agreements, coverage will only apply to wrongful acts that occurred prior to the date the merger occurred. Coverage ends as follows:
    - ❖ **Under first-party insuring agreements**—The insurance company will only provide coverage until the policy period ends.
    - ❖ **Under liability insuring agreements**—The policy remains active either until the end of the policy period or until the end of the run-off coverage period.
  - **Cessation of subsidiaries**—If any subsidiary owned by the named company stops being a subsidiary, coverage only persists as follows. Under both types of insuring agreements, coverage will only be provided for wrongful acts that took place before the change occurred. The policy termination will be as follows:

- ❖ **Under first-party insuring agreements**—The policy will only provide coverage until the policy period ends.
- ❖ **Under liability insuring agreements**—The policy will expire either at the end of the policy period or at the end of the run-off coverage period.
- **Confidentiality**—If a covered cyber extortion loss occurs, the named insured must make reasonable efforts to avoid disclosing that an insurance policy exists for the loss.
- **Territory**—Wrongful acts are covered worldwide, but litigation will only be covered when action is filed in the United States, its territories and possessions, and Canada.
- **Reporting, notice, and duties in the event of a cyber incident, cyber extortion event, information security breach, or interruption**—This applies to the first-party insuring agreements. Any actual or potential loss discovered by the insured must be reported to the insurance company as soon as practicable but no later than 60 days after the end of the policy period. If there is an extended discovery period, it must be reported within 60 days of the extended recovery period's end. Notice must be in writing, and the insured is obliged to cooperate with the insurance company in handling the claim.
  - o Under the "cyber extortion events" and "replacement or restoration of electronic data" insuring agreements, the insured must:
    - ❖ Alert local law enforcement.
    - ❖ Submit to examination under oath if requested.
    - ❖ Provide a sworn proof of loss within 120 days.
  - o Under the cyber extortion event insuring agreement, the insured has additional duties, which include:
    - ❖ Confirm that the covered event actually occurred.
    - ❖ Make all reasonable attempts to obtain data from any backup that exists, and perform ransomware remediation.
    - ❖ Make all reasonable efforts to put the insurance company on notice before making any ransom payments.
    - ❖ Give approval of any ransom payment to be made.
- **Reporting, notice, and duties in the event of a claim or a wrongful act that may result in a claim**—This condition applies to the liability insuring agreements. The reporting requirement is the same as under the previous condition. Additionally, the insured is required to:
  - o Cooperate with the insurer's investigation and settlement.
  - o Document the claim details, including when the claim was made.
  - o Provide the insurance company with copies of any demands, summonses, notices, or legal papers immediately.
  - o Provide authorization for the insurer to obtain needed documentation and records.
  - o Assist the insurance company with any efforts to enforce a right of recovery against a third party.
  - o If the policyholder discovers a wrongful act that could potentially lead to a claim, he or she is required to notify the insurer, including a description of the event, all relevant dates, names of all involved parties, the reasons for believing there could be a claim made, the nature of the damages, and how he or she first became aware of the wrongful act.
  - o Refrain from making any payments or assuming any obligations without the consent of the insurer.

Businessowners Policies

The **businessowners policy (BOP)** is typically a package insurance policy meant to provide the basic coverages needed for the owners of small to medium-sized businesses. The coverages provided are commercial general liability, commercial property, and business interruption. Commercial property coverage indemnifies the insured for damage to the business's real and personal property. This indemnification can be in the form of repair or replacement of the damaged property. Commercial general liability coverage is intended to protect the insured from claims being pursued by third parties on the basis of property damage, bodily injury, and personal injury. Medical payments coverage is usually available under the liability section of the policy. Business interruption coverage reimburses the insured for income lost as the result of a covered occurrence. This coverage is usually triggered when the insured business needs to be closed in order for repairs to be completed. There are many endorsements that may be used with the BOP to tailor it to an insured's unique coverage needs. A BOP is a single form containing property coverage, liability coverage, policy conditions, policy declarations, and optional endorsements.

ELIGIBILITY

A business is not eligible for BOP coverage unless its type is specifically identified by the **Insurance Services Office (ISO)** and it conforms to certain occupancy and size restrictions. Businesses that are eligible for BOP coverage can have no more than $6 million in gross sales annually, and no single location can exceed 35,000 square feet.

The following are businesses and/or properties that a BOP would be well-suited to cover:

- **Apartments** and **residential condominium associations**—Property coverage is available regardless of the building's size. The building must be used primarily for residential purposes. Some incidental business occupancies are allowed, such as mercantile, service, wholesale, and processing, so long as the total space devoted to these is less than 35,000 square feet. Offices are not subject to this limitation. Contractors may not occupy more than 7,500 square feet or 15% of the total square footage. Personal property owned by the building owner is covered while located in eligible apartments or condos.
- **Restaurants**—Eligibility for coverage depends on the category a restaurant falls into. All restaurants are limited to a floor area of 7,500 square feet to be eligible for a BOP. Seasonal restaurants, which are restaurants that are closed more than 30 consecutive days at a time, are also not eligible. Restaurants are categorized as limited cooking, fast food, casual dining, and fine dining. For example, limited cooking establishments may have a capacity of no more than 75 customers, while all other types are limited to 150 customers. There are many other factors used to determine restaurant eligibility.
- **Motels**—Property coverage is available regardless of the square footage; however, the building cannot be more than three stories tall. Annual sales may not exceed $6 million. Restaurants inside the building are also eligible for coverage and are subject to the same eligibility criteria as standalone restaurants. Motels that are open seasonally cannot be covered under a BOP. A business is considered seasonal if it is closed more than 30 consecutive days at a time.

- **Offices**, including **office and commercial condominium associations**—Coverage is available for buildings less than 6 stories high and less than 100,000 square feet in size. Business personal property contained in offices covering 35,000 square feet or less is also eligible for coverage. Eligible business occupancies, such as mercantile, processing, wholesaling, and service, are allowed as long as the total floor space devoted to these occupancies does not exceed 35,000 square feet. Contractors are also allowed but can only take up 7,500 square feet, or 15% of the total square footage. Apartments are allowed as incidental occupancies without limitation.
- **Contractors**—Contractors are subject to several limitations under BOP eligibility requirements. To be eligible, payroll cannot be more than $300,000, workers work at heights no more than three stories, and the contractor cannot lease or rent equipment to others. In addition, subcontracting cannot account for more than 10% of annual gross sales, and no more than 25% can be from activities that are not installation, service, or repair.
- **Convenience stores, grocery stores, and supermarkets**—All of these are eligible, except when filling of propane or kerosene tanks takes place on the premises. Any of these are also eligible if there is an accompanying gas station, as long as the floor area of the store is at least 3,000 square feet. The gas station cannot offer car washing services or automobile repair or servicing.
- **Wholesale risks**—These businesses are eligible as long as no more than 25% of the annual gross sales are from retail sales and no more than 25% of the total square footage is open to the public. Operations involving manufacturer's representatives or contractors are not eligible for the BOP.
- **Condominium commercial unit-owners**—The BOP may be used to cover personal property belonging to unit-owners when located in units used for eligible mercantile, service, wholesale, contracting, processing, service, or office operations.
- **Mercantile risks**—Coverage is available for eligible buildings and personal property.
- **Processing and service risks**—Coverage is available for select processing risks, select service risks, and those risks with a maximum of 25% of the gross annual sales generated off-premises.
- **Self-storage facilities**—There is no square footage limitation for these facilities, but the covered building cannot be more than two stories high. Locations that store industrial materials, waste, chemicals, pollutants, or refrigerated items are not eligible for a BOP.

The following types of businesses are completely excluded from coverage:

- Most types of auto repair and service stations
- Amusement facilities and parks
- Garages and parking lots
- Auto, motorcycle, motorhome, and mobile home dealerships
- Bars and pubs
- Banks and other financial institutions
- Manufacturing businesses and the buildings in which manufacturing occurs
- Self-storage facilities that are used to store motorized vehicles

CATEGORIES OF INSUREDS ON BUSINESSOWNERS POLICIES

BOP coverage applies to the following types of insureds:

- **Individual or sole proprietorship**—Includes named insured and his or her spouse
- **Partnership or joint venture**—Includes named insured, his or her partners and members, and their spouses

- **Limited liability company**—Includes named insured, his or her members, and his or her managers
- **Organizations other than those listed above**—Includes named insured, executive officer and directors, and stockholders
- **Trusts**—Includes those acting as trustees, but only with respect to their duties as trustees

Secondary insureds only receive coverage when they are performing their respective job functions in the insured business. BOP coverage extends to the following secondary insureds: the insured's employees or volunteer workers when performing their job functions, the insured's real estate manager when acting in such a role, legal representatives who are given temporary custody of the insured's property following the insured's death, anyone with temporary control of a deceased insured's property pending the appointment of a legal representative, and anyone operating the insured's mobile equipment with his or her permission. Secondary insureds are not afforded as many rights under the policy as a named insured because their status as an insured is based only on their activities that relate to the insured's business.

SECTION I—PROPERTY
POLICY DECLARATIONS
Like all other policies that have been discussed, the BOP begins with a policy declarations page. This page provides information about who the policy insures, the named insured, the named insured's address, and the dates the policy is effective. It also specifies which locations are insured, along with the information of any mortgageholders.

CAUSES OF LOSS
The BOP acts as a special form when it comes to covered causes of loss, meaning that any cause of loss not explicitly excluded or limited under the property section will be covered. BOP policies may be endorsed to reduce coverage to named perils only in exchange for a lower premium. Some types of property are only covered for "specified causes of loss." This means that such property is only covered for damage resulting from the following:

- Lightning
- Fire
- Windstorm and hail
- Smoke
- Explosion
- Vandalism
- Riots and civil commotion
- Aircraft and other vehicles
- Volcanic eruption
- Leaks from fire extinguishing systems
- Sinkholes
- Water damage
- Weight of ice, sleet, and snow
- Falling objects

PROPERTY COVERAGES

Coverage A—buildings covers the following types of property:

- Buildings and structures located on the insured premises
- Machinery and equipment that is permanently installed
- Completed additions
- Indoor and outdoor fixtures
- Personal property that the insured provides in rooms and common areas
- Personal property necessary to service and maintain buildings and structures on the premises
- Incomplete additions if they are not already covered by other insurance
- Repairs and alterations if they are not already covered by other insurance
- Equipment, temporary structures, and materials that are used for repairs, alterations, or maintenance that are located within 100 feet of the premises if they are not already covered by other insurance

Coverage B—business personal property covers the following classes of personal property:

- Business personal property used and owned by the insured
- Business personal property located in or on buildings or structures at the insured premises
- Others' personal property being held or controlled by the insured
- Tenant improvements and betterments, including additions, installations, alterations, and fixtures that are acquired and installed at the insured's expense; it must be unlawful to remove them
- Exterior building glass when the insured is a tenant who rents the insured premises and, as a result, does not carry building coverage
- Leased personal property that the insured is contractually obligated to insure, such as rented photocopiers and rented computer equipment
- Another's property in the insured's possession under the terms of a written agreement; loss will be paid to the extent of the liability the insured assumed, but payment will not exceed replacement cost or the policy limit for the applicable coverage

Coverage B protects personal property located within the building or on the premises. It also covers property kept outside in the open or in a vehicle within 100 feet of the premises or within 100 feet of an insured building or structure, whichever distance is greater.

PROPERTY NOT COVERED

BOPs do not cover the following property:

- Aircraft
- Watercraft and their equipment when they are on the water
- Vehicles requiring motor vehicle registration
- Computers that are permanently installed or are designed to be permanently installed in motor vehicles, except for items held as stock
- Electronic data, except for packaged software held as stock or any electronic data necessary to operate a building's essential systems, such as lighting, elevators, HVAC, or security systems, or that covered by the additional coverages
- Bills, accounts, food stamps, evidences of debt, and other monetary papers and records for which coverage is not provided elsewhere in the policy
- Money and securities

- Outdoor fences, shrubs, plants, and trees, unless they are part of additional coverages
- Illegally transported property and other contraband
- Land, water, lawns, and crops, except for lawns on vegetated roofs
- Outdoor signs detached from structures, unless they are part of additional coverages
- Outdoor fences, outdoor radio and television antennas, satellite dishes, and related equipment, unless they are part of additional coverages
- Animals owned by an insured, unless held as stock or being boarded at the insured location

ADDITIONAL COVERAGES

Debris removal reimburses the cost of removing debris, provided its presence was caused by a covered loss. To receive this coverage, the insured must submit an accident report within 180 days of the loss or the conclusion of the policy period. In most cases, debris removal has a maximum payout of 25% of the amount reimbursed for the direct physical loss plus the deductible. The insurer's total payout for the direct physical loss and debris removal cannot exceed the applicable insurance limit. However, the insurer may provide an extra $25,000 over the policy limit per occurrence if the following conditions are present:

- The insurance limit is insufficient to cover the combined cost of direct physical loss and debris removal.
- The maximum limit on debris removal is insufficient to reimburse the cost of debris removal.

If there is debris that needs to be removed without any accompanying direct physical damage, the policy will pay a maximum of $5,000 per loss event.

A **collapse** occurs when a building is rendered uninhabitable because all or a portion of it has fallen. This coverage insures against collapses that result from the following: building glass breakage, weight of people/personal property, weight of rain, and insect/vermin damage if the insured was unaware of the damage before the collapse occurred. A collapse is also covered when it occurs **during** construction or renovation due to poor-quality building materials. Certain outdoor properties (such as gutters, awnings, yard fixtures, swimming pools and related equipment, piers, docks, retaining walls, and various paved surfaces) are also covered if they are directly damaged by a building collapse. This coverage applies to collapsed personal property if the following criteria are present:

- The personal property is within the insured building.
- One of the causes listed above leads to the collapse.
- The personal property is not one of the outdoor items listed above.

The policy will not cover damage to personal property if it is only cosmetic or superficial.

Business income coverage reimburses the insured for income he or she loses when his or her business is forced to cease operations. This coverage only applies if the cessation was caused by direct physical damage to business property located on or within 100 feet of the insured premises. Additionally, the damage must have resulted from a covered peril. While the property is being repaired, the policy covers any income losses incurred within the 12 months directly following the day the damage occurred. Ongoing payroll costs for most employees will be covered for up to 60 days following the loss, including FICA payments, union dues, workers' compensation insurance premiums, and employee benefit costs. Depending on the circumstances of the loss, this coverage may offer **extended business income coverage**, which continues to issue payments even after business operations have resumed. For this coverage to be triggered, there must first have been a covered business income loss. The insured will receive payments until his or her previous earning level is restored, or until a condition outlined in the declarations section is met. The policy specifies that the time frame for restoring business operations must be reasonable for there to be continued payments under this coverage. Business income coverage is paid out independently of the limits of insurance.

Extra expense coverage applies when business operations are threatened by a covered loss. For a 12-month period immediately following the loss, this coverage reimburses money that the insured must spend to avoid or reduce suspension of business operations. Reimbursements are made in addition to the limits of insurance.

Increased cost of construction coverage covers additional costs the insured may incur when a damaged building must be repaired in accordance with some ordinance or law. This coverage has a $10,000 per building limit, and only provides coverage for buildings insured at replacement cost. If the insured chooses to rebuild the damaged building at a new location rather than the old location, the reimbursement amount is limited to what the increased cost of construction would have been at the old location. However, if the ordinance or law mandates moving to a new location, the reimbursement amount will cover the increased cost of construction at the new location.

Civil authority coverage applies when civil authorities are preventing the insured from accessing his or her property because a covered loss has damaged property at a location adjacent to the insured premises. This coverage reimburses any **business income** or **extra expense** losses incurred during the insured's absence from the covered property. For instance, assume that a fire is damaging a building adjacent to the insured's business. If the insured is denied access to his or her business because civil authorities fear the fire may spread, he or she is protected by civil authority coverage. Business income coverage begins 72 hours after civil authorities initially deny access to the property, and it continues for a maximum of three consecutive weeks. Extra expenses are covered immediately following the denial of access. Coverage for extra expenses continues for three consecutive weeks or for the duration of the business income coverage, whichever is longer.

Forgery and alteration coverage applies when someone forges or alters the insured's checks or similar documents. It covers any reasonable legal expenses incurred by the insured as a result of his or her refusal to pay for forged purchases or drafts. Coverage is limited to $2,500 or the limit shown in the declarations section.

Business income from dependent properties coverage applies when damage to a dependent property results in income loss. A **dependent property** is defined as a business that assists the insured in the following ways: delivering materials, accepting the insured's goods, manufacturing goods that will be delivered to the insured's customers, or expanding the insured's customer base. The insurance limit cannot exceed $5,000 or the amount listed in the declaration section. Income loss coverage starts 72 hours after the loss event occurs and lasts for the full period of restoration as defined in the policy forms.

Money orders and counterfeit paper currency coverage covers the insured when he or she accepts counterfeit currency and/or money orders in exchange for goods and services. Coverage is limited to $1,000.

Water or other liquid, powder, or molten materials coverage covers building damage when it is caused by indirect escape of these substances. It also covers the cost of removing and replacing the system from which the escape occurred if building damage is already covered by some other insurance; however, it will not pay to correct the actual defect that caused the substance(s) to escape unless that defect was created by a covered cause of loss. If the damage is caused by freezing or discharge from the automatic fire protection system, this coverage reimburses the cost of repairing or replacing damaged fire extinguisher equipment.

Pollutant cleanup and removal coverage covers the expense of removing or extracting pollutants from the insured's premises when they are placed there by a covered loss. Coverage is limited to $10,000 per 12-month policy period, and the loss must be reported within 180 days following the loss or 180 days before the end of the policy period, whichever represents the earlier date. Expenses related to government-ordered testing or monitoring are not covered.

Fire extinguisher systems recharge expense coverage covers the following costs:

- Recharging or replacing the insured's fire extinguishers and extinguisher systems
- Covered property damage resulting from accidental discharge of extinguisher systems

The coverage is limited to $5,000 per occurrence and only applies if the system discharge occurred within 100 feet of the insured's premises.

Preservation of property coverage applies when the insured moves property to a different location as a means of protecting it from a covered peril. This coverage lasts 30 days from the first date of removal and insures the property against direct physical damage by any cause of loss as it is being moved or stored.

Fire department service charge covers the charges and fees that may be incurred when the fire department is called upon to save or protect covered property. Coverage is limited to $2,500, and only applies when the insured is contractually or legally obligated to pay such a fee.

Glass expense applies when damaged glass cannot be repaired or replaced immediately. It reimburses the cost of boarding up and/or temporarily covering openings, as well as the cost of removing obstructions to the repair process.

Electronic data coverage is available in specific circumstances. The data must have been corrupted or destroyed by a covered cause of loss. The value of data that is unable to be repaired or restored will be based on the cost of replacing the media with blank media of the same or similar type. The covered causes of loss for electronic data are viruses or other detrimental code intended to damage or destroy a computer network or system. There is no coverage when such code was introduced to the insured's system by any insured employee or by a person or company hired by the insured to work on the system. Payment is limited to $10,000 per policy year unless the policyholder purchases a higher limit. This coverage does not extend to any stock of prepackaged software held by the insured or to electronic data integral to operating heating, lighting, air conditioning, elevator, security, or ventilation systems.

Interruption of computer operations coverage is triggered when an interruption causes the insured's normal business operations to stop. This additional coverage applies only when the loss is caused by collapse or a specified cause of loss. Any additional causes of loss added to the BOP by endorsement do not apply to computer operations interruption. The covered losses under this coverage are the same as those under the electronic data additional coverage, and losses are subject to a $10,000 per policy year maximum. Coverage is only available for the period of restoration even if the $10,000 maximum has not been reached. No coverage applies to electronic data required to operate heating, lighting, air conditioning, elevator, security, or ventilation systems.

Fungi, wet rot, or dry rot coverage applies to losses that were caused by a specified cause of loss, except for fire or lightning, that led to the presence or proliferation of fungi, wet rot, or dry rot. The insured must have made all reasonable attempts to preserve the affected property following a covered loss. Damage is only covered when directly caused by fungi, wet rot, or dry rot. The coverage includes expenses to remove affected property as well as any removal needed to gain access to the affected property. Testing performed subsequent to the removal of fungi or rot is only covered if there is a reasonable belief it may still be present. Payment is limited to $15,000 per 12-month policy period. The policy will only pay $15,000 total per loss even if issues persist beyond the end of the policy year. Any payment made under this coverage reduces the available property limit of insurance. If damage from fungi, wet rot, or dry rot increases the cost of a loss from another covered cause of loss, the amount of the increase will fall under this additional coverage. Payment for these loss types has no impact on the additional coverage provided for collapse or water damage, molten material, powder, or other liquids elsewhere in the BOP. This section also provides some limited coverage for business income loss and extra expenses when the presence of fungi or rot requires operations to be suspended. Coverage for income loss and extra expenses is limited to 30 days total. The 30 days do not need to be consecutive.

COVERAGE EXTENSIONS

Newly acquired or constructed property coverage extends coverage to new buildings ($250,000 per location) and new business personal property ($100,000 per location). This coverage applies to new construction on the insured location or buildings acquired by the insured away from the insured location. The duration of coverage is whichever of the following represents the shortest time period: 30 days from the date the property is acquired or construction begins, the remainder of the policy period, or the length of time before the insured reports new property values to the insurer.

Valuable papers and records coverage is an extension of business personal property coverage. It applies when the only existing copies of valuable papers and/or records are damaged, and it covers the expenses of researching and restoring the lost data. The limit for damages occurring at the insured premises is $10,000 (or the amount listed in the declarations section) and the limit for damages occurring outside the insured premises is $5,000.

Personal effects coverage is an extension of business personal property coverage. It provides $2,500 per location for the personal effects of the insured and his or her employees.

Accounts receivable coverage is another extension of business personal property coverage. It reimburses the following losses when they result from a covered loss:

- Customer payments the insured is unable to collect
- Interest fees on loans intended to compensate for loss of customer payments
- Excess collection expenses
- Reasonable expenses needed to restore accounts receivable documents

There is a $10,000 limit for losses at the insured premises and a $5,000 limit for losses to accounts receivable outside the insured premises.

Outdoor property extension provides coverage for debris removal, as well as outdoor items such as fences, trees, plants, shrubs, freestanding signs, and radio, television, and satellite antennas/dishes. This coverage only protects against fire, explosion, riot/civil commotion, aircraft, and lightning, and has a maximum limit of $2,500 and $1,000 per shrub, tree, and plant.

Business property temporarily off the premises is covered if property is being moved to or stored at a location that is not owned or controlled by the insured. Coverage cannot exceed $10,000.

Business personal property temporarily in portable storage units coverage is provided for items stored in this way, as long as the unit is within 100 feet of a covered building or within 100 feet of the insured premises, whichever is further. Damage to stored property from rain, sleet, sand, dust, ice, or snow is only covered when the exterior is damaged by a covered loss such that the interior is exposed. Property is covered up to either 90 days after the portable storage unit is placed on the property, or 90 days after the property was put into the storage unit, whichever comes first. There is no coverage to damage directly to the storage unit, nor is there coverage for occurrences covered elsewhere in the policy. The most the insurance company will pay for covered property under this extension is $10,000 unless a higher limit is shown on the declarations page. The amount paid for property covered by this extension applies to the property limit of insurance.

Additional coverages are part of existing coverages and do not require additional premium payments. Optional coverages are separate from existing coverages and do require additional premium payments.

EXCLUSIONS

The BOP acts as a special form when it comes to covered causes of loss. Businessowners policies divide the property exclusions into different categories based on how the exclusion applies to a loss.

The primary exclusions exclude losses from coverage if they result directly or indirectly from the following types of perils:

- Ordinance or law
- Earth movement, including earthquakes, landslides, and movement due to mine subsidence
- Earth sinking, rising, or shifting, aside from that meeting the definition of sinkhole collapse
- Settling, cracking, or derangement of foundations or other parts of real property
- Soil conditions such as contraction, expansion, freezing, thawing, erosion, deficient soil compacting, or underground action of water
- Volcanic eruption, explosion, or effusion that does not fall within the policy description of volcanic action
- Government action, except for that undertaken to prevent the spread of fire
- Failure of utility services, including but not limited to power, communication, or water utilities
- War or military action
- Water losses, including surface water, waves, tidal waves, tsunami, mudslides, tides, tidal water, and overflow of or spray from any body of water
- Water backup or spillover from a sewer, drain, sump, sump pump, or comparable equipment
- Damage to foundations, walls, floors, paved surfaces, paved or unpaved basements, and doors, windows, or similar openings when the damage resulted from subsurface water that has flowed into, pressed on, or seeped into those areas
- Waterborne material carried or moved by water

- Certain computer-related losses involving computer hardware, software, operating systems, networks, chips, or other components that fail or malfunction because of an inability to interpret or accept a date or time; there is also no coverage for expenses related to any attempts to correct or repair such a malfunction
- Fungi, dry rot, or wet rot that are not covered by the additional coverage for fungi, dry rot, or wet rot
- Viruses or bacteria

Businessowners policies exclude losses from coverage if they result from any of the following:

- Electrical equipment or apparatuses
- Steam boiler, engine, pipe, or turbine explosion
- Smoke, vapor, or gas
- Consequential losses including delay, loss of use, or loss of market
- Artificial electric current, unless it is generated within 100 feet of the insured premises
- Freezing that causes leakage of water, powder, liquids, or molten material from fire protective systems, unless the insured took appropriate measures to protect the system
- Any losses stemming from any insured engaging in criminal or dishonest behavior, including employees
- Being tricked or swindled into giving up property
- Rain, snow, ice, or sleet damage to personal property left exposed to the elements
- Pollution
- The insured's neglect or failure to protect covered property during and after a loss
- Normal wear and tear
- Rust, corrosion, or decay
- Hidden or latent defect that causes property to damage itself
- Damage resulting from nesting or infestation of birds, vermin, insects, or other animals
- Mechanical breakdown
- Poor planning, design, workmanship, or materials
- Decisions or failure to make a decision by any person, group, organization, or government body
- Weather conditions if combined with another excluded cause of loss
- Erasure of electronic media by electrical or magnetic sources
- Poor design, installation, maintenance, repair, or modification of computer and other systems
- Mistakes in programming, storing, processing, or copying of paper records or electronic records
- Damage caused by continuous seepage or leakage of water when the condition has persisted for 14 or more days
- Errors or omissions related to handling electronic data or valuable papers and records
- Personal property damaged or destroyed by atmospheric dampness or dryness, scratching or marring, or extreme changes in temperature
- Loss or damage to products when caused by any error or omission in development, production, use, planning, testing, processing, packaging, installation, repair, or maintenance of such products

163

PROPERTY COVERAGE LIMITATIONS

Steam equipment and **water heating equipment** are not covered when they are damaged by internal problems inherent in the equipment. However, they are covered if the damage is caused by gas or fuel explosions within the furnace or ducts that convey gas.

Missing property is not covered if there is no physical evidence showing why the loss occurred. The only exceptions are money and securities, for which optional coverage is available.

Property transferred beyond the covered premises without permission is not covered.

The **building interior** is covered when it is damaged by rain, sleet, ice, sand, or dust only if they entered through a hole in an exterior wall or roof that was created by a covered peril or if the damage was due to thawing of sleet, snow, or ice located on the building.

The policy does not provide coverage for **plant life** growing as part of a **vegetated roof** when the loss or damage is the result of dryness or dampness of soil or air, temperature changes, disease, hail, frost, rain, snow, or sleet.

Fragile articles, such as marble, glassware, porcelain, and chinaware, are only covered when damaged by "specified causes of loss." The limitations on these items are not applicable to glass that is part of a building or structure, fragile items when properly stored and awaiting sale, or lenses for scientific equipment or photography equipment.

Death or destruction of animals is only covered when due to a "specified cause of loss" or from breakage of building glass.

There is a **special limit** of $2,500 per occurrence when the following types of property are **stolen**: garments made of or lined with fur; dies, patterns, molds, and forms; jewelry worth $100 or more per item; watches worth $100 or more per item; or precious/semiprecious stones, precious metals, and bullion.

PROPERTY CONDITIONS

The property conditions section of the BOP outlines the conditions that only apply to the property coverage provided by the policy. They are separated into loss conditions and general conditions. Like in the previous section, many of the conditions are similar to those found in CPP forms. These include:

- Loss conditions:
  - Abandonment
  - Appraisal
  - Recovered property
  - Vacancy
- General conditions:
  - Control of property
  - Mortgageholders
  - No benefit to bailee
  - Policy period and coverage territory

164

Some of the BOP conditions, while similar to those in other commercial policies, do have distinct differences. There are also some that are unique to the BOP. Such conditions are:

- Loss conditions
  - **Duties in the event of an occurrence, offense, claim, or suit**—The policyholder is required to perform the following duties after a loss has occurred:
    - ❖ Notify police or law enforcement of any occurrence in which the law may have been violated.
    - ❖ Promptly notify the insurance company of any event that may result in a claim. This notification must include the location, time, and circumstances of the event, as well as a description of the damaged property.
    - ❖ Take all reasonable steps to protect or preserve the covered property.
    - ❖ If requested, provide the insurance company with a complete inventory of both damaged and undamaged property.
    - ❖ Allow the insurer to inspect and examine any damaged property, in addition to examining any pertinent books or records.
    - ❖ When the insurance company requests a sworn proof of loss document, the policyholder is mandated to supply it within 60 days.
    - ❖ Cooperate with any of the insurance company's attempts to investigate or settle a claim.
    - ❖ Resume business operations as quickly as possible.
    - ❖ If requested by the insurer, submit one or more examinations under oath as needed in relation to the claim or the insurance provided by the company.
  - **Legal action against us**—States that no legal action can be initiated against the insurer until the insured has met all the conditions of the policy. Such action must begin no later than two years following the loss in question.
  - **Loss payment**—Specifies how the insurer will value and pay for covered losses:
    - ❖ The insurance company has the discretion to indemnify for losses based upon the cost to repair or replace the damaged property, the value of the damaged property, the cost to replace damaged property with that of like kind and quality, or any agreed or appraised value. Payments are limited to the insured's actual financial interest in the covered property.
    - ❖ No payment may exceed the stated limit of insurance.
    - ❖ The valuation of the property will be at replacement cost so long as the policyholder carries insurance equal to at least 80% of the pre-loss replacement value.
    - ❖ Replacement is cost based upon the lowest amount of the cost to repair or replace damaged property with that of like kind and quality intended for the same purpose as the property being replaced, or the amount actually incurred to repair or replace the property.
    - ❖ If the insured fails to purchase sufficient insurance, the underinsured property will be paid at actual cash value (ACV) or at the percentage of coverage carried compared to the actual value of the property. If the second method is used, the portion for which the insured is responsible is the coinsurance. When a coinsurance penalty is applied, it is calculated the same way it is under the commercial property policy form.
    - ❖ Replacement cost payments are only made after replacement has been completed, and this must be done as soon as reasonably possible.

- An insured may choose to accept payment at ACV if he or she does not intend to rebuild or replace covered property. If the insured decides to proceed with replacement after taking payment at ACV, the insurance company must be notified of this intention within 180 days of the loss occurrence date.
- Replacement cost applies to losses of less than $2,500 regardless of insufficient coverage.
- Some items are only paid at **ACV** when replacement is necessary. Such items are secondhand and used products being stored or held for sale, property owned by non-insureds, household contents, works of art, rare articles, antiques, or manuscripts. For non-owned property, there is an exception made for any contractual obligation the insured may have related to the value of the property.
- For losses to property owned by persons other than the insured, the loss will be handled with the owner and the payment will be issued directly to the owner. The insurer may also opt to defend any claim or suit brought by the owner of such property.
- Glass will be paid at replacement cost, and safety glazing is covered only when law mandates it.
- Tenant's improvements and betterments will be reimbursed at replacement cost if the repairs are finished promptly. If not, the payment will be reduced in proportion to the number of days taken for completion of repairs in relation to the number of days remaining on the lease at the time of loss. If someone other than an insured pays for repairs, there will be no reimbursement by the insurance company.
- Accounts receivable claims are valued at the average monthly balance for the 12 months immediately before the loss if the policyholder is unable to provide an accurate value of the accounts as of the date of loss. The insurer will also account for any normal fluctuations that may have occurred for the month in which the loss occurred. A reduction will be applied to accounts receivable total for any portion not subject to damage or loss. The insurance company will also deduct the value of any accounts the insured is able to reestablish or collect from. The amount collected need only be for an amount that would be customarily collected under bad debt, and the insurer will not compensate the insured for any unearned service charges or interest.
- Payment will be made on any covered claims within 30 days of receipt of the sworn proof of loss so long as the insured has agreed to a settlement, or an appraisal award has been determined.
- If a covered loss involves damage to a shared wall, also called a **party wall**, the insurance will only pay damages in proportion to the policyholder's financial interest.

OPTIONAL PROPERTY COVERAGES

There are some coverages that are noted in the base BOP that are only applicable if the policyholder purchases the optional coverage. These optional coverages are subject to all the conditions outlined in the common policy conditions and the property conditions. Some have special conditions only applicable to the optional coverage. The optional coverages available under the BOP include:

- **Employee dishonesty**—Covers personal property, money, and securities that are lost due to dishonest acts of an employee or employees working in collusion. The employee must have intended for the policyholder to sustain damage or loss or must have sought financial benefit beyond that provided in the normal course of employment. Acts committed by the insured's members, managers, directors, or partners are excluded from coverage. Loss resulting from the dishonesty of any of these parties will not be covered if any insured was aware of any similar actions by that person prior to the inception of the policy. The insurance company will not pay for losses where there is no evidence of loss other than inventory shortage or profit loss. Coverage related to any specific employee will be deemed canceled as of the date the policyholder or any partners, manager, members, directors, or officers of the policyholder discovers that the employee has engaged in dishonest acts before or after being hired by the insured. The maximum limit for employee dishonesty coverage is listed in the declarations section. Losses involving a series of dishonest acts are treated as a single occurrence. Amounts paid under this coverage are included in the property limit of insurance. Some policies include a discovery period, which is a period of time after the policy expires during which a discovered loss will be covered. These can vary by insurer but are usually somewhere between 60 days and one year long.
- **Equipment breakdown**—Insures against direct damage from the sudden and accidental breakdown or electrical failure of any electrical, mechanical, or pressure equipment owned by the insured or in his or her care or custody at the insured premises. Purchasing this coverage essentially eliminates the BOP exclusions for electrical apparatuses, steam apparatuses, and mechanical breakdown. Coverage only applies if the equipment must be repaired or replaced. Additionally, mechanical breakdown only covers losses as outlined in the policy and excludes any damage that results from adjustment, alignment, calibration, cleaning, or modification. It also excludes damage due to leakage, glass or vacuum tube damage, or any malfunctioning safety device. If the insurance company finds the equipment is in an inherently unsafe or dangerous position, it may suspend coverage by notifying the insured in writing and sending a pro rata premium refund.
- **Outdoor signs**—This provides coverage for outdoor signs against direct physical damage or loss. These signs must be on the premises and must be either owned by the insured or in his or her care or custody. This coverage supersedes and replaces any other sign protection included in the policy. There is a maximum limit stated in the declarations section. The exclusions for governmental action, war and military action, and nuclear hazard still apply under this optional coverage. The policy excludes losses that result from mechanical breakdown, latent defect, wear and tear, rust, or corrosion.
- **Money and securities**—This covers money and securities against theft, destruction, or disappearance if they are used in the insured's business and stored within one of the following locations:
  - Banks and savings institutions
  - Insured premises
  - Residence quarters of the insured, his or her partner, or his or her employees
  - Any other location while they are being moved between these locations

There is no coverage for losses where the only indication of loss is an accounting discrepancy. There is also no coverage when money and/or securities were voluntarily paid during a purchase or exchange. The loss payment condition for this coverage states that for money and securities, money will be paid at face value, while securities will be paid based on the value at close of business on the day the loss was discovered.

Automatic Coverage Increases

The BOP provides an automatic increase in the building coverage limit. The increase will be in an amount equal to 8% of the existing coverage limit unless a different amount is specified on the declarations page. The policy also automatically increases coverage for business personal property when the insured's business is seasonal in nature. The increase will be for the amount listed in the policy declarations, or 25% if there is no percentage listed. This increase will only occur if the business personal property limit of insurance is at least 100% of the policyholder's average monthly values in the 12 months immediately before the date of loss or for the time period between the insured going into business and the date of loss, whichever period is shorter.

Selected Property Definitions

Computer—Programmable electronic equipment utilized for the storage, processing, or retrieval of electronic data, as well as any peripheral equipment that allows for input and output of data, but it does not include any computers used to operate production equipment or machinery.

Electronic data—Information used by or stored on a computer, including data, media, software, and programs, regardless of where these items are stored.

Fungi—Any fungus regardless of form, including mold, mildew, or any by-products released by a fungus, such as spores, smells, or toxins.

Manager—Anyone working in a managerial capacity in a limited liability company.

Member—Any owner of a limited liability company.

Operations—Business functions of the named insured that take place at an insured location.

Period of restoration—The amount of time needed for covered property to be repaired, replaced, or rebuilt with reasonable speed and of quality equivalent to the property that was lost or damaged, or the time it takes for the insured to restart business operations at new permanent premises. It begins immediately after a covered direct loss for the purposes of extra expense coverage. For business income coverage, it starts after 72 hours have passed. It terminates when there has been reasonable time to complete repairs or when the operations have commenced at a new location, whichever is earlier. It does not include any delays related to law, ordinance, or pollutants.

Pollutants—Irritants or contaminants in any form, including soot, vapor, smoke, fumes, alkalis, acids, chemicals, and waste. Waste includes any items being held pending recycling, reconditioning, or reclamation.

Specified causes of loss—Fire, lightning, explosion, windstorm, hail, smoke, aircraft, vehicles, riot, civil commotion, vandalism, sinkhole collapse, volcanic action, falling objects, leakage from fire extinguishing systems, and the weight of snow, ice, or sleet. This definition does not include:

- For sinkholes—collapse or sinkage into human-made underground spaces, sinkhole filling costs
- For falling objects—damage to items held in the open, damage to the interior of the building when there is no breach of the exterior that would allow the falling object to reach the interior

Water damage (included in the specified causes of loss definition)—Accidental leakage or discharge of steam or water directly caused by the breakage of any portion of a system or appliance. It also includes discharge or leakage of waterborne matter directly caused by the breakage of pipes located off the insured location that are components of a municipal sewer system or water supply system when the breakage is caused by wear and tear. The definition does not include any losses that fall under the water exclusion.

Valuable papers and records—Written or printed manuscripts, documents, or records, inclusive of maps, films, drawings, books, abstracts, deeds, or mortgages. Money and securities are not considered valuable papers.

SECTION II—LIABILITY
BUSINESS LIABILITY

Under BOP liability coverage, the insurance company agrees to pay the insured's court costs when he or she is legally liable for property damage, bodily injury, and personal and advertising injury. The insurer also agrees to pay for damages the insured is found to be legally liable for, up to the liability policy limit. The insurance company also has the right to investigate and settle claims. **Personal and advertising injury liability** may apply when the insured commits any of these offenses:

- Malicious prosecution
- False arrest or imprisonment
- Using the advertising ideas of another person
- Copyright/trade dress/slogan infringement
- Slandering or libeling a person or organization through oral and written publications
- Violating the right to privacy of another person
- Disparaging the goods and services of another person or organization
- Wrongfully evicting a person from his or her occupancy
- Wrongfully entering a person's occupancy
- Violating a person's right of private occupancy
- Consequential bodily injury

Under the **supplementary payments** clause, the insurance company will pay for certain expenses related to the handling and defense of liability claims brought against the policyholder or other insured. Supplementary payments include the following:

- Cost to release bond attachments
- Pre-judgment interest
- Judgment interest that is assessed after the ruling has been made, but before it is paid in court

---

- $250 maximum for bail bonds arising from bodily injury liability coverage on vehicles
- Reasonable expenses paid by the insured as he or she assists the insurance company in investigating or defending liability suits (the insured pays these expenses at the insurance company's request)
- Court costs paid by the insured during liability suits
- Expenses normally paid by the insurer
- Defense costs of an indemnitee, which is a party that provides goods and services for the insured but is not insured under the policy (this payment is only available under certain conditions)
- Up to $250 per day for wage loss incurred due to the insurance company requesting the insured's presence for or participation in the defense or investigation of a claim

With the exception of costs to release bond attachments, all supplementary coverages are offered in addition to the limits of the policy.

The insurer will also defend any **indemnitee** of the insured party so long as specific conditions are met. To be an indemnitee, the insured must have agreed in writing to defend or indemnify the party in an insured contract. The damages sought under the suit must be those the insured has assumed liability for in the contract, and the occurrence must be covered under the insurance policy. The insured and the indemnitee must request a defense and consent to being represented by the same counsel, and there must be no conflict of interest defending both the insured and the indemnitee. The indemnitee must submit written agreement to the insurance company to cooperate in the defense of the suit, provide forward copies of summonses and legal notices to the insurer, notify any other company that may have coverage for the loss, and assist in resolving any coverage disputes that may arise between insurers. Further, written authorization must be provided by the indemnitee allowing the insurance company to obtain any documents pertinent to the suit and for the insurer to conduct and control the defense of the suit for the indemnitee. Any obligation to the indemnitee ends when these conditions are no longer being met or when the applicable limit of insurance is exhausted.

MEDICAL EXPENSES COVERAGE

Businessowners policies cover the following **medical expenses**, no matter who is at fault:

- Surgical costs
- Ambulance costs
- Hospital costs
- First aid rendered at the time of the accident
- X-ray costs
- Nursing costs
- Dental costs
- Funeral costs

To receive coverage, these expenses must be necessitated due to a bodily injury sustained on or adjacent to the insured premises, or due to the insured's business operations. Additionally, the injured party must have been injured within the coverage territory during the policy period, and he or she must have reported the injury within a year of its occurrence. Because medical expenses coverage is intended for the general public, it usually excludes the following individuals from coverage: insured individuals, the insured's employees, people who normally reside on or occupy any part of the insured's premises, people injured during athletic activities, and people already covered by workers' compensation and/or comparable policies and laws.

170

EXCLUSIONS

BOP liability excludes bodily injury and property damages from coverage when they result from the following:

- Expected or intentional injury, unless the insured is protecting himself or herself using reasonable force
- Liquor-related activities, if the insured's business is involved in the sale, serving, or manufacturing of alcoholic beverages
- Injuries already covered by other contracts, workers' compensation, or other disability or benefit programs
- Bodily injury to the insured's employees during the regular course of their work, including any consequential injury to the employee's parents, siblings, spouse, or children
- Pollution
- Acts of war
- Aircraft, watercraft, or automobile ownership or maintenance
- Nuclear materials
- Damage to property that is owned, rented, or occupied by the insured; that the insured has abandoned or given away; that is loaned to the insured; or that is otherwise under the insured's care, custody, or control
- Loss of use, recall, repair, removal, disposal, or replacement of the insured's work, goods, or property
- Damages caused by the insured not performing work properly
- Property that is impaired, but not physically damaged, due to the insured's faulty work or products
- Rendering or failing to render professional services
- Damage to the insured's work or products
- Deficiency in or delay of the insured's products or work related to contract agreements
- Liability assumed under an agreement that is not an "insured contract"
- Losses resulting from mobile equipment being transported by any auto owned, leased, or operated by an insured, or from use during or in preparation for any planned racing, demolition, speed, or stunting activities
- Criminal actions committed by the insured or by those working under the direction of the insured
- Harm caused directly or indirectly by violation of the Telephone Consumer Protection Act, the CAN-SPAM Act of 2003, the Fair Credit Reporting Act, the Fair and Accurate Credit Transactions Act, or any other statute that governs the use of information
- Losses involving electronic data, such as those stemming from any inability to access, use, or manipulate electronic data or due to lost or corrupted data

In addition to the above exclusions, BOP liability excludes personal and advertising injury from coverage when they result from the following:

- Actions performed intentionally by the insured when he or she knows such actions will cause personal and advertising injury
- Oral and written statements made by the insured when he or she knows such statements are false
- Oral and written statements made before the policy period
- Actions for which the insured has contractually assumed liability, unless that liability would have existed without entering into the contract

- Breach of contract
- Unauthorized inclusion of someone else's name or product in the insured's email, meta tags, or domain
- Products and services of the insured that do not comply with quality standards
- Activities in electronic chat rooms or bulletin boards controlled by the insured
- False advertising of the insured's products and services
- Pollutant distribution or cleanup
- Activities of the insured's business related to advertising, broadcasting, and internet search, content, or service
- The insured's infringing upon the intellectual property rights of others, such as patents, copyrights, trade secrets, or trademarks, except when such use is in the insured's advertising

LIABILITY AND MEDICAL PAYMENTS CONDITIONS

As the liability and medical payments section of the BOP provides coverage similar to that provided by the CGL, the conditions are also similar. These include:

- Bankruptcy
- Duties in the event of occurrence, offense, claim, or suit
- Legal action against us

SELECTED LIABILITY DEFINITIONS

Advertisement—Any communication to the general public or specific markets that shares information about the insured's products or services to attract consumers or supporters. This is inclusive of online postings and the part of the insured's website dedicated to drawing in business.

Auto—Motor vehicles, trailers, and semitrailers designed to travel over land on public roadways or any other vehicle that is required to comply with registration, insurance, or financial responsibility laws. This includes any attached machinery or equipment but does not include "mobile equipment" as described in the policy.

Bodily injury—Physical injury, sickness, or disease to an individual, including death that results.

Coverage territory—The United States and its territories and Canada. It also includes international water and airspace when the loss occurs during travel between the covered territories. The definition extends to losses resulting from products that the insured manufactures within the coverage territory that are shipped to other areas, activities of an insured or employee traveling outside the coverage territory on business as long as that person lives in the coverage territory, and personal and advertising injury claims arising from internet communications.

Employee—Excludes temporary workers but includes leased workers.

Hostile fire—Any fire that extends outside its intended boundaries or burns uncontrollably.

Impaired property—Tangible property that cannot be partly or fully used for its intended purpose because of defects, inadequacies, deficiencies, or dangerous conditions in the insured's products or work. It also includes losses stemming from an insured's failure to meet the terms of an agreement or contract. To qualify as impaired property, there must be the possibility to restore the property by either repair, replacement, adjustment, or removal; or by complying with the terms of the pertinent contract or agreement.

Insured contract—Includes all of the following:

- Leases for rented premises
- Leases for premises temporarily occupied by the insured, except for of any part of the lease that requires the insured to indemnify the owner of the premises for fire losses
- Sidetrack agreements
- Licensing or easement agreements, except for those located within 50 feet of railroad demolition or construction operations
- Any legal requirement that the insured indemnify a municipality, except when it is related to the insured's work directly for the municipality
- Elevator maintenance contracts
- Contracts with municipal entities, but only the portion applicable to assumption of tort liability for third parties
- Any other contract or agreement related to the insured's business where the insured agrees to assume liability for bodily injury or property damage to others on behalf of another party; this does not apply to losses occurring within 50 feet of railroad demolition or construction operations

Leased worker—A worker provided to the insured under an agreement with a leasing firm to perform duties related to the furtherance of the insured's business, not including temporary workers.

Mobile equipment—Includes any of the following:

- Bulldozers, forklifts, farm machinery, or other vehicles designed to be used off public roads
- Vehicles that are maintained for use entirely on or adjacent to premises owned or rented by the insured
- Vehicles that are maintained for use entirely on or adjacent to premises owned or rented by the insured
- Vehicles that are propelled on crawler treads
- Any of the following when permanently mounted to a vehicle: road construction or resurfacing equipment, power diggers, loaders, cranes, shovels, or drills
- Any vehicles that are maintained primarily for purposes other than the transport of cargo or people
- Vehicles that are not self-propelled and are used to move the following permanently mounted equipment: air compressors, pumps, and generators used for spraying, welding, cleaning buildings, geophysical exploration, lighting, or well-servicing and cherry pickers or comparable equipment
- Any vehicles not described above used for primary purposes that does not include transporting property or people

When permanently mounted to a self-propelled vehicle, the following are considered autos:

- Snow removal equipment
- Road maintenance equipment
- Street cleaning equipment
- Cherry pickers or other similar equipment when mounted to an auto or truck chassis
- Air compressors, pumps, or generators, including equipment for spraying, welding, cleaning buildings, geophysical exploration, lighting, or well-servicing

Any land vehicle subject to a financial responsibility or insurance law at the location where it is licensed or normally garaged does not meet the definition of mobile equipment.

Occurrence—Any accident resulting in injury or property damage, including ongoing or repeated exposure to a generally harmful condition.

Personal and advertising injury—Injury caused by any of the following, including resulting bodily injury:

- False arrest, detention, or imprisonment
- Malicious prosecution
- Wrongful eviction or entry by a landlord or on behalf of a landlord
- Slander or libel regardless of how such information is published
- Any form of oral or written publication of information that violates anyone's right to privacy
- Use of another's idea in the insured's advertisement
- Infringing on the intellectual property rights of others in the insured's advertising

Pollutants—Contaminants and irritants in any physical state, including waste and materials meant to be recycled, reclaimed, or reconditioned.

Products-completed operations hazard—Any loss or damage caused by the insured's work or products occurring away from locations that the insured owns or rents. This excludes products still in the insured's physical possession and incomplete or abandoned work. It only extends to losses on the insured location when the insured's product is to be consumed on the insured's premises. The completion date for work is considered the earliest of the following: the date on which all work outlined in a contract has been performed; when all the work at a single jobsite has been completed (when the contract applies to multiple locations); or when the work performed at a job site is put to its intended use by any party other than contractors or subcontractors who are also working on that site. Work that is otherwise complete aside from maintenance, service, replacement, or repair is treated as complete by the policy. This definition does not include losses stemming from transporting any property unless loss results from the condition of a vehicle. The vehicle cannot be owned or operated by an insured, and the harmful condition must not have arisen from any insured loading or unloading such a vehicle. The definition also excludes damages due to the presence of tools, uninstalled equipment, or abandoned or unused materials.

Property damage—Physical damage to tangible property or the loss of use of damaged or undamaged property. Electronic data is not considered tangible property under this definition.

Temporary worker—A worker provided to the insured to handle seasonal or short-term increased workload, or to act as a replacement for an insured employee on temporary leave.

Your product—Items that the named insured sells, manufactures, or distributes, including those items sold, manufactured, or distributed by others using the insured's name. Also includes any party from whom the insured has acquired a business operation or assets, as well as the containers, materials, equipment, parts, warranties, and instructions furnished with sold goods. It excludes vending machines or any other property rented to others or intended for use off the insured's premises.

Your work—The operations or services provided by the named insured or an insured employee, inclusive of all materials and equipment used. It also extends to any warranties made by the insured, as well as the providing of or failure to provide warnings and instructions.

SECTION III—COMMON POLICY CONDITIONS

BOPs include **common policy conditions** that are applicable to all sections of the policy, as well as other conditions specific to the property and liability coverage parts. Most of the common policy conditions are similar to those included in the common policy conditions for a commercial package policy. The conditions that are largely the same include:

- Changes
- Premiums
- Transfer of your rights and duties under this policy

There are some other common policy conditions under the BOP that are comparable to property or liability conditions within the CPP. These are:

- Liberalization
- Concealment, misrepresentation, and fraud
- Insurance under two or more coverages
- Premium audit

Because the BOP provides both property and liability coverages, some of the common policy conditions are modified compared to those found in the CPP forms. These include:

- **Cancellation**—This condition explains the procedures for canceling policies. If the first named insured opts to cancel a policy, the insurance company must be notified in writing. The insurer may also cancel the policy. The policy may only be canceled at the request of the first named insured listed in the policy declarations. This can be done by sending advance written notice to the insurance company. The insurance company is also able to terminate the policy. In certain situations, the insurer is only obligated to provide notice of cancellation five days in advance:
  - When buildings have been vacant for at least 60 sequential days, except when under construction. There is an exception for vacancy on a seasonal basis. To be considered vacant, 65% or more of the floor area or rental units must be unoccupied.
  - When buildings have sustained a covered loss for which no permanent repairs have been initiated within 30 days of the first insurance payment.
  - When buildings have been deemed unsafe by a government authority or are subject to an active vacancy or demolition order.
  - When repaired or salvageable property is removed from the covered building with no intention of replacing such property, except when removal is necessary because of renovations or remodeling.
  - When the insured has failed to maintain utility service at a covered building for 30 or more consecutive days, or when there are delinquent property tax payments that have been due for more than one year. The former includes an exception for seasonal utility termination, and the latter does not apply when the insured is actively disputing the owed property taxes.

The first named insured must be notified at least ten days prior to the cancellation date when there is non-payment of premiums. For all other reasons not addressed previously, the cancellation notice must be sent no less than 30 days in advance. The cancellation notice will be sent to the last known mailing address of the first named insured and is required to list the cancellation effective date. If the cancellation results in overpayment by the insured, any premium refund will be sent to the first named insured. If the insurer cancels the policy, the refund amount will be prorated based on how much time was left in the policy period. If the insured cancels, the refund may be less than the pro rata amount. The insurance company's proof of mailing or delivery is sufficient to show that the notice was sent.

- **Transfer of rights of recovery against others to us (subrogation clause)**:
  - For property losses: When the insured has a right to pursue recovery against a third party, that right gets transferred to the insurer when the claim is paid. The rights are only transferred to the extent of the insurance company's payment for the loss. The insured also has an obligation to protect the insurance company's right to recovery and assist in such recovery when requested. Any waiver of rights provided by the insured must be executed in writing and prior to the occurrence of a loss. The insured only has the right to waive subrogation after a loss if the insured owns or otherwise controls the other business, if the other business owns or otherwise controls the named insured, or if the other party is a tenant of the named insured.
  - For liability losses (not applicable to medical payments coverage): The insured must ensure that any right of recovery held by the insurance company is protected. The insured must also do nothing to impair those rights and must assist the insurance company with enforcing those rights when needed. The named insured may waive recovery rights subject to a contract prior to a loss, in which case there are no rights that can be transferred to the insurer. Any agreement to waive recovery rights after a loss constitutes a breach of the insurance contract by the policyholder.
- **Examination of your books and records**—States that the insurer is entitled to examine the insured's books and records pertinent to the policy and retains this right for up to three years after the end of the policy period.
- **Inspections and surveys**—States that the insurance company is permitted to complete an inspection or survey at any time. The company may share the findings with the insured and suggest alterations. The insurer is not obliged to perform inspections or surveys, but when they do occur, the insurance company only seeks to get information needed to assess insurability or calculate accurate premiums. The insurance company does not intend nor has a duty to act as any entity that provides for the health and safety of workers or the general public. The insurer makes no assurance that the observed conditions are safe, healthy, or in compliance with the law. These conditions also apply to any party that performs insurance inspections, surveys, reports, or recommendations. Pressure vessels, boilers, or elevators subject to state or local laws, ordinances, or regulations are exempt from this condition.
- **Other insurance**—States that the insurance company is only obligated to pay any amount above that which is payable by the other insurance company. This condition applies regardless of whether the policyholder is able to collect those amounts from the other insurer. The business liability coverage is excess over any policy on which the insured is listed as an additional insured when a claim arises from the insured's premises or operations. It will also act as excess over any other coverage for direct physical loss or damage. In cases where the insurance company is providing coverage on an excess basis, it has no obligation to defend or handle any claim or suit that any other insurer has a duty to defend. If no other insurer provides a defense for the insured, the insurance company will provide a defense, but reserves the right to recover costs from any other insurer.

ENDORSEMENTS

Certain types of businesses require special endorsements to meet their coverage needs. Some operations have risk exposures that are not covered by the standard BOP, so the insured relies on the endorsements to bridge the gap. Such businesses include:

- Businesses involving selling, furnishing, and distribution of liquor or alcohol
- Pharmacists
- Businesses that sell optical products or hearing aids
- Funeral homes
- Veterinarians
- Hair salons and barber shops
- Beauty salons
- Snowplow operators
- Operations that require the insured to engage the services of an engineer, surveyor, or architect
- Restaurants
- Motels and hotels
- Self-storage facilities

Other endorsements can be used to enhance or limit coverage at the insured's option. Any endorsement that broadens or adds coverage will be subject to an additional premium. Some common endorsements are:

- **Protective safeguards endorsement**—This is used as a means to lower premium costs. The insurance company will only cover fire damage and other types of losses if the insured maintains the following protective safeguards:
  - **P-1: automatic sprinkler system**—Includes all automatic fire protection systems, such as sprinklers, pipes, and supervisory services
  - **P-2: automatic fire alarm system**—Any system that monitors the whole building and alerts a central, public, or private alarm station
  - **P-3: security service**—Requires that a guard make hourly rounds while the business is closed
  - **P-4: service contract**—Requires that a private fire department is contracted to protect the premises
  - **P-9: scheduled protective system**—Includes all other protective systems scheduled on the policy
- **Utility services—direct damage endorsement**—Insures against property damage or loss when it results from an interruption in utilities, such as water, communication, or power supply. This coverage only applies when the damaged property is covered by the policy and the utility service is interrupted by a covered loss. This form includes a schedule to list the insured locations for which the coverage will be active.
- **Utility services—time element endorsement**—Applies to lost business income and extra expenses incurred when utility services from a property outside the insured building are interrupted by a covered loss. The schedule included with this endorsement lists the specific utilities for which the insured is seeking coverage.

- **Hired auto and non-owned auto liability endorsement**—Provides liability coverage for bodily injury and property damage when they result from the insured or his or her employees using or maintaining a hired auto or any person using a non-owned auto. For coverage to apply, the driver must be performing work functions for the insured's business. When an auto is being used for the insured's business, but is not owned or rented by the insured, it is considered a non-owned auto. When an auto is leased, hired, or borrowed by the insured from someone other than his or her family or workers, it is a hired auto. This endorsement does not provide coverage for autos that are borrowed from employees or members of an employee's household, nor does it cover autos that are borrowed from partners or executive officers of the insured's business.

COMMERCIAL EXCESS LIABILITY AND UMBRELLA LIABILITY INSURANCE

Commercial excess liability insurance is purchased to cover any liability losses that exceed the limits on an underlying policy such as a CGL policy, business auto policy, or BOP. The intention of excess liability coverage is to only pay for losses where an underlying policy exists. The excess coverage does not go into effect until the underlying policy limits have been exhausted. All excess liability policies require the insured to carry a minimum amount of primary coverage for all perils covered. If this condition is not met, the insured will have to pay out of pocket for what the underlying policy would have paid. Excess policies do not generally carry a deductible due to the strict underlying policy requirements.

Commercial umbrella liability insurance provides excess liability coverage similar to that provided by an excess liability policy, but it can also cover perils outside of those the insured has an underlying policy for. Umbrella policies go into effect once the underlying limit is exhausted or the insured has liability for a loss not covered by an underlying policy, including those the underlying policy has an exclusion for or has denied coverage. Because umbrella policies cover many types of liability losses, they are not considered indemnity contracts. The insured is not required to pay a deductible, but if a required underlying policy lapses or is not purchased, the insured will have to pay what the underlying policy would have before the umbrella policy will go into effect. If the claim or loss is of a type that does not require an underlying policy, the umbrella policy may include a **retention limit**. The retention limit functions somewhat like a self-insured retention. It is an amount that the insured chooses when the policy is purchased, which he or she agrees to pay before the umbrella coverage will apply to a loss. A retention limit can range from $250 to $10,000 depending on the insured's coverage needs.

EMPLOYMENT PRACTICES LIABILITY INSURANCE

Employment practices liability insurance (EPLI) is a risk management tool used to share financial risk associated with employee lawsuits. EPLI is insurance purchased to protect against some of the legal costs faced if an employee brings a civil suit against the organization. There are many situations in which an employee may bring a lawsuit because of perceived rights violations such as allegations of discriminatory employment practices. If they do occur, the organization will pay huge costs in legal fees, even if it wins the suit. EPLI can be extremely useful in covering these unexpected costs. Unlike many other liability policies, defense costs and legal expenses are included in the limit of liability for the policy. This means that payments made for these items reduce the limits available for that exposure.

PROFESSIONAL LIABILITY COVERAGE

Professional liability policies are specialty liability insurance policies that are popular in certain occupations. Professional liability policies cover loss due to negligence, error, or omission during the **performance of professional services**. Professional services are generally defined as any services that require specialized education or knowledge to properly provide. There is no standardized form for the professional liability policy. Some of the most common professional liability policies are for accountants, insurance agents, dentists, doctors, lawyers, pharmacists, and real estate agents. There are also some occupations that one might not expect to fall under a professional liability policy, such as law enforcement, morticians, funeral directors, beauticians, and barbers. The standard exclusions to a professional liability policy are for **fraudulent, intentional, dishonest, or criminal acts**. There are some specialized versions of the professional liability policy for directors and officers. There is also a policy for the **fiduciary liabilities** that may be incurred during compliance with the Employment Retirement Income Security Act.

Professional liability policies are available for:

- **Directors and officers liability (D&O)**—This provides coverage for an organization's directors or officers when they are alleged to have not executed their duties properly. Claims of this nature are usually brought by a company's stockholders. Directors and officers are obligated to act in the best interests of the stakeholders, so allegations of wrongful or negligent actions are not unusual. Most corporations will include an indemnification clause in their charters or by-laws that promises to repay directors and officers for any expenses they incur while defending or otherwise handling a matter involving such allegations. This coverage is split into two sections. The first section will pay claimants on behalf of covered directors and officers when it is found that a wrongful or negligent act has been committed. The second section reimburses the insured company for expenses they have paid to or for covered directors and officers while handling a wrongful act allegation.
- **Errors and omissions liability (E&O)**—This coverage is used to insure an entity against allegations of negligence or error by its clients. For a loss to be covered, the client must have incurred damages, usually some sort of financial loss. It is most appropriate for occupations that require the insured to provide expert advice or services to his or her customers, such as lawyers, insurance agents, and financial planners. Covered losses may include breach of contract, failure to meet a deadline, or professional negligence. This policy will also pay defense costs for the insured.
- **Medical malpractice liability**—This provides coverage for medical professionals against claims of bodily injury or property damage resulting from the insured's work in the medical field. Claims of personal injury may also be covered by medical malpractice insurance. Examples of claims that may be covered include treatment errors, prescribing errors, misdiagnosis, and performing unnecessary procedures. This coverage is available in both claims-made and occurrence variations. It covers defense and claim costs in addition to providing indemnity payments. These policies typically exclude coverage for intentional acts, sexual misconduct, criminal acts, and punitive damages.

LIQUOR LIABILITY COVERAGE

Another specialized form of liability insurance is for **liquor liability**. CGL excludes coverage for liquor liability when the insured is in a business involving liquor. This coverage is intended for businesses that sell, manufacture, serve, furnish, or distribute beverages that contain alcohol. There are policies that provide this coverage on either a claims-made basis or an occurrence basis. The liquor liability coverage applies to losses where the insured is alleged to have done any of the following:

- Caused or contributed to the intoxication of another person
- Provided alcohol to anyone under the legal drinking age

- Provided alcohol to anyone who was already intoxicated
- Violated any law relating to distributing, selling, or providing alcoholic beverages

In addition to covering claims for bodily injury or property damage, liquor liability coverage will also pay the insured's defense costs when a lawsuit or other legal action is filed against him or her. For a loss to be eligible for coverage, the insured must have had a valid liquor license when the accident or loss occurred. Losses that do not involve alcohol in some way are not covered by this policy.

Farm Insurance

Farm insurance, sometimes called **farm owners' insurance**, provides personal and business coverage for farm businesses and homes. It is designed to provide coverage similar to a homeowners policy for the residential areas of the farm while also addressing the unique coverage needs of a farmer. It can be acquired as a monoline policy or as an inclusion in a commercial package policy. Farm insurance package policies are designed to cover smaller farms and ranches where the owner of the farm also has a dwelling on the farm property. Owners or operators of large commercial farms would need to purchase a **farm combination policy**, in which farm-specific forms can be combined with commercial insurance forms to create a portfolio of insurance coverage that is tailored to the special coverage needs of a large commercial farming operation.

COVERAGE FORMS

There are several **farm property coverage forms**, which offer the following:

- **Coverage A**—dwellings
- **Coverage B**—other private structures appurtenant to dwellings
- **Coverage C**—household personal property
- **Coverage D**—loss of use
- **Coverage E**—scheduled farm personal property
- **Coverage F**—unscheduled farm personal property
- **Coverage G**—farm property—barns, outbuildings, and other farm structures

Crops, trees, plants, shrubs, and lawns are excluded from coverage unless the insured acquires extensions under Coverages A, B, and C.

Farm liability coverage forms provide the following:

- **Coverage H**—bodily injury and property damage liability
- **Coverage I**—personal and advertising injury liability
- **Coverage J**—medical payments

These coverages exclude losses resulting from pollutants, injuries to farm employees, vehicles that are not identified by the policy, aircraft spraying, products of the insured, and action or failure to take action by the insured.

CAUSES OF LOSS FORMS

The **farm property—causes of loss** form identifies the perils against which farm property is insured, and provides three types of coverage: basic, broad, and special. The insured selects the type of coverage he or she needs.

The **basic form** covers losses from the following perils:

- **Fire or lightning**
- **Windstorm or hail**
- **Explosion,** except for steam boilers, steam pipes, steam engines, steam turbines, and alcohol stills owned, leased, or operated by the insured
- **Riot and civil commotion**
- Collision with **aircraft** or objects falling from aircraft

181

- Collision with **motor vehicles,** including collision with items thrown by a motor vehicle; this is only applicable under Coverages E and F, and the vehicle must not be owned or operated by an insured
- **Smoke,** except from industrial operations or agricultural smudging
- **Vandalism,** except when the building has been vacant for 60 or more consecutive days immediately preceding a loss
- **Theft,** subject to many exclusions and limitations
- **Sinkhole collapse**
- **Volcanic action**
- Livestock loss from **earthquake** or **flooding**

Some losses due to theft are covered; however, there are several scenarios where theft would not be covered. The policy considers attempted theft to be theft for the purposes of property damage. The exclusions are broken down by coverage part as follows:

Excluded Items	Applicable Coverage Part
Building materials at a dwelling being constructed	A, B, G[1]
Property in a part of the dwelling being rented to a non-insured	A
Household personal property away from the insured location and at another residence used by the insured (exceptions are made for temporary residences and students away at college)	A, B, C
Watercraft and related equipment away from the insured location	A, B, C
Trailers, campers, and semitrailers away from the insured location (semitrailers were added in the 2016 revision)	A, B, C
Electronic equipment within a vehicle or mobile equipment that is not permanently installed, including media for such equipment	All coverage parts[1]
Property transferred to a person or other property without authorized instruction	All coverage parts
Property owned by an insured that is voluntarily surrendered by the insured or any other party under fraudulent pretenses *(new in 2016 revision)*	All coverage parts
Dishonesty or criminal acts of any insured, officers, managers, trustees, or authorized representatives, including those performed by employees of any type *(new in 2016 revision)*	All coverage parts[1]
Acceptance of counterfeit money or money orders issued by a post office or similar entity	E, F, G[2]
Acceptance of checks or promissory notes that are not paid upon presentation	E, F, G[2]
Property only discovered missing via inventory without any evidence of theft	E, F

182

Excluded Items	Applicable Coverage Part
Disappearance of a portable building or structure without evidence of where or by whom it was taken	G

- [1] Under Coverage G, these exclusions *do not apply* to livestock, poultry, or other animals covered by Coverage E or F.
- [2] Under Coverage G, these exclusions *only* apply to livestock, poultry, or other animals covered by Coverage E or F.

The **broad form** includes the standard perils in the basic form plus the following risks:

- **Dog or wild animal attacks** on covered livestock
- Covered livestock **electrocution**
- Covered livestock **drowning**
- **Accidental shooting** of covered livestock
- **Loading/unloading accidents** that result in the death of covered livestock
- **Falling objects**
- **Weight of snow, sleet, or ice**
- **Accidental and sudden tearing** apart of HVAC, steam, water heating, or sprinkler systems
- **Accidental discharge of steam or water** from HVAC, plumbing, or water heating systems
- **Freezing,** so long as the insured has taken appropriate measures to prevent freezing
- **Artificially generated electrical current**

The **special form** covers property on an open peril basis subject to the exclusions outlined in the form. Such exclusions include:

- Tobacco barn fires
- Collapse, outside of the limited coverage described within the policy
- Windstorm or hail damage to property kept out in the open
- Damage to property left out in the open caused by rain, snow, ice, or sleet
- Interior personal property damaged by rain, snow, sleet, sand, or dust, unless the exterior of the building has been breached
- Supports of covered structures due to freezing, thawing, pressure, or weight of water; this exclusion applies only to Coverages A, B, and G
- Accidental discharge or overflow of water or steam from plumbing, heating, air conditioning, or automatic fire protective systems or within a household appliance if caused by freezing (unless the insured took reasonable steps to prevent freezing) or if the source of the water or steam is off the insured premises
- Explosion of alcohol stills, steam boilers, steam pipes, or steam engines owned, leased, or operated by the insured
- Rupturing, bursting, or operating of pressure relief devices
- Rupturing or bursting of any building or structure where expansion was caused by water
- Theft from any portion of the insured location that is rented to and occupied by a non-insured; this exclusion only applies to Coverages A, B, and C
- Personal property theft occurring at any unlisted residence owned, rented, or occupied by an insured, except when the insured's residence is temporary; this exclusion only applies to Coverage C
- Losses incurred as the result of following unauthorized instructions to transfer property to another entity

183

- Property of the insured that is voluntarily given away due to any trick or scheme
- Vandalism or theft of electronic equipment within any vehicle or piece of farming equipment unless it is permanently installed
- Losses arising from dishonest or criminal acts perpetrated by the named insured, any other insured, temporary and permanent employees of the insured, leased employees, trustees, officers, managers, or authorized representatives
- Losses from wear and tear, marring or scratching, rust, or corrosion
- Losses due to fungus, decay, deterioration, or hidden or latent defect
- Damage from the nesting, infestation, discharge, waste, or secretions of birds, vermin, rodents, insects, or domestic animals
- Rupturing or bursting caused by centrifugal force
- Any type of mechanical breakdown
- Losses arising from smog, settling, crackling, shrinkage, or expansion
- Damages sustained due to the intake of foreign objects by machinery
- Agricultural smudging or industrial vapor, gas, or smoke
- Inadequate, faulty, or defective:
  - Planning
  - Zoning
  - Development
  - Surveying
  - Siting
  - Design
  - Specifications
  - Workmanship
  - Repair
  - Construction, renovation, or remodeling
  - Supplies and materials used in repairing, constructing, renovating, or remodeling
  - Maintenance
- Pollution losses not covered elsewhere in the policy
- Damage to farm personal property that occurs while transporting the property, except when the damage resulted from the collision or overturn of a motor vehicle that the farm personal property was in or upon
- Damage to electrical devices, wires, or appliances from artificially generated electrical current
- Losses caused by any quality in the property that causes it to damage or destroy itself

EXCLUSIONS COMMON TO ALL CAUSES OF LOSS FORMS

Some exclusions are applicable to all causes of loss forms. Many of these are similar to exclusions on other property coverage forms. These exclusions are:

- Ordinance or law
- Earth movement, including earthquakes, landslides, and movement caused by human-made mines
- Earth sinking, rising, or shifting, except for sinkhole collapse
- Soil conditions or underground movement of water
- Volcanic eruption, effusion, or explosion that does not fall under the volcanic action coverage
- Governmental action

- Intentional loss
- Failure of utility services
- Neglect on the part of the insured, especially failure to mitigate damage after a loss
- War and military action
- Most types of water losses, including any waterborne substances or materials

Farm Property Coverages

COVERAGES A, B, C, AND D

Under farm insurance policies, these coverages function very similarly to a personal homeowners policy. These coverages combine to provide coverage for the residential dwelling, any detached appurtenant structures, household personal property, and costs associated with a dwelling being uninhabitable after a covered loss. A key difference between the farm policy and the homeowners policy is that the farm policy only covers household personal property while it is on the insured premises. Some types of property are excluded from coverage entirely.

Coverage A excludes coverage for land, water, and plants that do not fall within the limited coverage for trees, shrubs, and plants. Coverage B also excludes coverage for water and land, as well as any structures rented to someone who is not a resident of the covered dwelling. An exception is made for renting out a private garage. Coverage C contains more exclusions than Coverages A and B. Property excluded under Coverage C consists of:

- Aircraft and related equipment
- Animals, birds, and fish
- Plants, including lawns
- Business property
- Farm personal property, except for office equipment, furniture, and fixtures
- Electronic data processing media in excess of the cost to replace it with prepackaged software or blank media
- Portable electronic equipment in or on a motor vehicle, or motorized equipment that is not powered by the electrical system of that vehicle or equipment
- Motor vehicles or their parts
- Cards and devices used to electronically transfer funds
- Contraband
- Property used for agritainment purposes

Coverage D does not have any explicit exclusions, but it will only cover additional living expenses and, if applicable, fair rental value. In the case of government intervention preventing the insured from accessing the residential portion of the farm, these expenses will only be covered for up to two weeks.

Farm policies contain coverage extensions similar to those found in a homeowners policy, including:

- Trees, shrubs, plants, and lawns, excluding those used in farming operations (Coverages A and C only)
- Household personal property away from the insured location; this is subject to a limit of $1,000 or 10% of the Coverage C limit, whichever is larger

- Refrigerated products that are not farm personal property when spoilage is caused by power failure or mechanical breakdown; this is subject to a $1,000 limit (Coverage C only)
- Improvements, additions, and alterations that the insured makes to a property that he or she is renting; this is subject to a limit of 10% of the Coverage C limit (Coverage C only)

Farm policies also provide additional coverages as follows:

- Removal of fallen trees; this is subject to a limit of $1,000 per occurrence, with a maximum of $500 for any single tree
- Theft or unauthorized use of credit cards or electronic funds transfer cards and losses related to forgery, check alteration, or counterfeit US or Canadian currency that was accepted in good faith by the insured; this is subject to a limit of $500 per occurrence
- Water or steam damage related to plumbing, heating, air conditioning, or fire sprinklers
- Damage to grave markers or mausoleums; subject to a $5,000 limit
- Up to $2,000 without a deductible for the cost of researching, replacing, or restoring important records (Coverages E and F only)
- Rented or borrowed farming equipment for up to 30 days after taking possession; this is subject to a $10,000 limit and only applicable under the special causes of loss form (Coverages E and F only)

COVERAGES E, F, AND G

Coverage E only provides coverage for personal property that is specified on the Coverage E schedule. To be covered, a limit must be indicated on the policy declarations for the type of property covered. The list of property that can be scheduled under Coverage E is extensive. Some property that may be covered in this way includes grains, beans, seeds, hay, straw, products and materials related to farm operations, poultry, wood crates, computers, software, farm vehicles and equipment, and permanent fixtures attached to a covered structure.

Coverage F covers all farm personal property except for that explicitly excluded and requires that damage must have been the result of a covered cause of loss. Most property is only covered while at an insured location, but there are some exceptions made for livestock, livestock feed, threshed beans and seeds, hay, straw, herbicides, pesticides, and grain. Farming equipment, machinery, tools, implements, and supplies are covered unless they fall under the property not covered clause or are being transported by a common or contract carrier. Dealer-owned equipment or machinery loaned to the insured for demonstration purposes is not covered, nor is any equipment while it is located at the owner's premises.

Coverage G covers farm structures and barns located on the insured premises. Examples of other farm structures include fences, pens, radio and television equipment, portable structures and buildings, uninstalled building materials, and improvements and betterments that the insured makes to the insured location as a tenant. Silos are only covered when scheduled on the policy. There are some specific items that Coverage G does not cover: land, water, field and pasture fencing, light and electrical poles, foundations below ground level, piers, wharves, pilings, and docks. It also excludes any expenses related to grading, excavating, filling, or backfilling. Under the loss conditions for Coverage G, some items are paid based on the ACV of all property within a category in proportion to the coverage carried. This is applied to property that is insured by category instead of by individual items. There is one category for fences, corrals, pens, feed racks, and chutes. The other category handled this way is portable buildings and structures. For instance, if the insured has a coverage limit of $50,000 for portable buildings and structures but the sum of the ACV for all covered items is $80,000, the insured only carries 62.5% of the coverage he or she actually needs.

Any losses to portable buildings and structures in this scenario would only be paid at 62.5% of the loss amount.

For valuing other property, except for betterments and improvements, the protocol depends on what the insured chooses. There are options for ACV valuation and replacement cost valuation. Like in other forms, the property must be adequately insured for replacement cost to be paid without penalty. Property is adequately insured if the coverage limit is at least 80% of the covered property's actual value. Improvements and betterments to premises that the insured rents are covered at replacement cost as long as repairs are completed within 12 months. Otherwise, the payment will be reduced in proportion to how much time remains on the insured's lease. For broken glass, the insurance company will only pay for safety glazing material if mandated by law.

There are some coverage extensions and additional coverages afforded under Coverages E, F, and G. These are as follows:

- Coverage extensions for Coverage E only:
  - For miscellaneous equipment related to or used in the farm operation, when it is away from the insured location, coverage is limited to 25% of the Coverage E limit of insurance.
  - Coverage for other farm personal property away from the insured location is limited to 10% of the Coverage E limit of liability.
  - When equipment is acquired during the policy period, there is limited coverage available. For equipment intended to replace already-scheduled equipment, the policy will provide up to an additional $75,000 in coverage. Payment is limited to the ACV as of the time of loss. The coverage extension for added equipment provides coverage based upon what equipment is already scheduled on the property. Coverage will apply based on the equipment that the newly acquired equipment is most comparable to. The limit for additional equipment is $100,000; however, the form indicates that this is included in the Coverage E limit of insurance rather than in addition to it. This coverage will end at the end of the policy period or 30 days following the acquisition of the property, whichever comes first.
  - When additional livestock is acquired by the insured, there must already be coverage for livestock on the policy for the coverage extension to apply. It may be listed via specific description or by class on the declarations. Coverage is only afforded for 30 days following the insured's procurement of the additional livestock. The coverage under this extension is limited to the ACV of the livestock or to 25% of the listed coverage limits, whichever is smaller.
  - For farm products kept in the open, only losses caused by fire, lightning, windstorm, hail, vehicles, or theft are subject to coverage. Payment is limited to 10% of the farm personal property limit. This extension covers grain kept in piles, shocks, stacks, or swaths. When hay, straw, or fodder is stored in stacks, windrows, or bales, there is coverage; however, no more than $10,000 will be paid for a single stack. There is coverage for unharvested grains, soybeans, and sunflowers, but only for losses resulting from fire or lightning. There is no coverage for seed or foraged crops. This coverage extension does not increase the limits of insurance.
- Coverage extension for Coverages E and F only:
  - Farm personal property that is in the custody of a contract or common carrier is covered up to a maximum of $1,000 per loss.
- Coverage extensions for Coverage G only:

- o Losses involving private light and power poles are subject to a $1,000 limit per occurrence. This is in addition to the limit of insurance, and a deductible does apply.
- o When the insured has new permanent structures built on the insured premises for the purposes of farming, there is up to $100,000 in coverage available for it as long as it is not covered by other insurance. There is only coverage for losses due to aircraft, riot or civil commotion, smoke, fire, lightning, explosion, windstorm, hail, vehicles, or vandalism. This coverage terminates the earliest of the following: 60 days after construction begins, the end of the policy period, or when the new property is reported to the insurer.

- Additional coverages:
  - o Up to $2,000 is available for costs associated with researching, replacing, or repairing farm operations records. (Coverages E and F only.)
  - o If the insured rents or borrows any farm machinery, equipment, or vehicles, the policy will provide an additional $10,000 per occurrence for damage to such property, but only for the first 30 days after the insured takes possession of it. This coverage does not extend to private passenger vehicles, motorcycles, motorized bicycles or tricycles, dirt bikes, snowmobiles, or mopeds. After that point, the insured must request coverage for it to continue. (Coverages E and F only.)
  - o Extra expenses incurred by the insured to continue or resume farming operations are covered when they are needed as the result of a covered loss. The coverage must be shown on the declarations page for it to apply. There is no deductible, but coverage is limited to the time it would reasonably take the insured to replace, repair, or rebuild the covered property. This does not apply to expenses related to pollutants or compliance with ordinance or law.
  - o If a covered water or steam damage loss occurs, the insurance company will also pay any costs to remove and replace areas of the building that are blocking access to the area where the loss occurred.

Farm Property—Other Provisions Form

Farm property insurance is subject to the provisions listed in the individual coverage, which specify that for the policy to be valid, it must include a competed covered causes of loss form. These forms also state that all coverages are subject to the limits of insurance and deductible clauses listed in the "farm property—other provisions" form. This form is used with all farm property coverages and outlines some further additional coverages as well as the conditions applicable to all farm property coverage forms.

ADDITIONAL COVERAGES

The additional coverages provided in the other provisions form include:

- **Debris removal**—Coverage applies if debris results from a covered loss. These expenses must be reported to the insurer within 180 days of the covered loss. Payment is limited to 25% of the sum of the limit of liability and deductible. There is no coverage for any costs related to pollutants cleanup. Payments are included in the limit of insurance for the loss in question. If the expenses for debris removal exceed the 25% or direct loss payments have exhausted the limits, an amount equal to 5% of the policy limit will be made available for further debris removal expenses.

- **Reasonable repairs**—This covers repairs that the insured must take on following a loss that are reasonable and necessary to mitigate further damage following a covered event. This is included in the policy limits.
- **Removal of property**—This covers costs associated with damage to property that has been moved away from the loss location to protect it from an actual or expected covered loss. Coverage is limited to 30 days following the removal of the property. This is included in the policy limits.
- **Fire department service charges**—This provides coverage for the costs of calls made to the fire department to protect covered property from a covered cause of loss. For these expenses to be paid, the services must not be available from public fire protection. Payments for such services are in addition to the policy limits, and no deductible will be applied.
- **Limited collapse coverage**—For a loss to be considered a collapse under this coverage, there must have been an abrupt or sudden falling or caving in of all or part of a building. Predicted or expected collapse is not eligible for this coverage, nor are any parts of the building that remain standing. For there to be coverage for a collapse loss, it must be caused by a covered cause of loss specified in the policy, glass breakage, hidden damage inflicted by animals, hidden decay, weight of rain on the roof, weight of people or property within or upon the structure, or defective materials used during construction. If the insured was aware of any decay or insect damage before the loss, there is no coverage.
- **Pollutant cleanup**—Under this coverage, losses are only reimbursable when triggered by a covered cause of loss. There is an aggregate policy limit is $10,000 per 12-month policy period. No payment will be made for testing unless it is necessitated by the extraction procedure. The insured must report these costs within 180 days of the occurrence for them to be covered.
- **Glass or safety glazing material**—To be covered, the glass must be part of another covered building, structure, storm door, or storm window, or there must be damage to covered property caused by pieces, fragments, splinters of broken glass, or safety glazing material that are part of any of these. The cause of loss must be one covered by the policy or caused by earth movement. If glass is broken due to a combination of a covered loss type and earth movement, the damage will be covered. There is no coverage if the building sustaining the damage is on the insured location and has been vacant for more than 60 days. Payments under this coverage reduce the limit of liability on the policy.

CONDITIONS

The farm property policy shares many of the same conditions as personal residential insurance policies. These include:

- Liberalization
- Concealment, misrepresentation, or fraud
- Deductible
- Limits of insurance
- Duties after loss
- Loss to a pair or set
- Appraisal
- Other insurance and service agreement
- Suit against us
- Loss payment
- Abandonment of property

- Mortgage clause
- No benefit to bailee
- Recovered property
- Policy period
- Transfer of your interest in this policy (subrogation clause)
- Control of property
- Insurance under two or more coverages

The farm property policy also contains an **unoccupancy and vacancy** condition, which states that if a building or structure is vacant or unoccupied for 120 consecutive days, there will be a 15% reduction for loss payments associated with an unoccupied or vacant location, including its contents. The form defines these terms in the Definitions section.

Farm Liability Coverage

COVERAGE H

Coverage H of the farm insurance policy insures the policyholder against liability for property damage or bodily injury to others. It is very similar to the liability coverages provided under the personal and commercial liability policies and contains many of the same exclusions, such as:

- Expected or intended injury or loss, except for using reasonable force to protect property or people
- Liability assumed in a contract or agreement, except for an "insured contract"
- Pollution
- Losses involving motor vehicles that are subject to legal registration and insurance requirements
- Watercraft liability, aside from the exceptions outlined in the policy; these are the same as the exceptions listed for the 2013 revision of the homeowners liability coverage
- Communicable diseases
- Losses subject to workers' compensation or similar laws
- Employer's liability
- Damage to property owned or controlled by an insured
- Controlled substances
- Physical, mental, or sexual abuse, including corporal punishment
- Personal injury
- Losses caused by defects in the insured's work or products
- Costs of recalling, withdrawing, or repairing of impaired work or products
- Business pursuits (outside of those that are part of the farming operations)
- Rental of the insured premises, outside of that covered in the policy
- War
- Occurrences involving mobile equipment used during or in preparation for any planned racing, demolition, speed, or stunting event, or any mobile equipment transported by a motor vehicle that is owned, operated, rented, or leased by an insured

Some exclusions unique to the farm liability form are:

- **Release or discharge from aircraft**—There is no coverage for losses resulting from the release or dispersion of any substance from an aircraft. This exclusion does not apply to model or hobby aircraft.

- **Aircraft, motor vehicle, motorized bicycle, or tricycle**—There is no coverage for any loss stemming from the ownership, maintenance, use, or entrustment to others of any of these items. The exclusion extends to loading and unloading activities, as well as any vicarious liability an insured may have as the parent or guardian of a minor.
- **Use of livestock or other animals**—The policy excludes damages arising from the use of animals in any racing or strength contests. It also excludes any use of animals in which rides are provided in exchange for compensation.
- **Custom farming**—No coverage will apply for losses related to the insured's performance of or failure to perform custom farming operations. This exclusion applies if the insured has income from custom farming that exceeds $5,000 in a 12-month period.
- **Bodily injury to an insured**—There is no coverage for injury to any person who meets the policy definition of an insured.
- **Professional services**—The policy does not apply to any bodily injury or property damage related to the performance or nonperformance of professional services. This extends to any allegation of an insured being negligent in supervising, hiring, employing, training, or monitoring others.
- **Rental of premises and ownership or control of premises**—An exclusion also applies to losses occurring at locations owned, rented, or controlled by the insured party, but which are not listed as insured locations. This exclusion does not apply to bodily injury or property damage sustained by a residence employee during the course of employment by the insured.
- **Building or structure under construction**—Coverage does not apply to any bodily injury sustained on the premises where a building or structure is being constructed. This exclusion does not apply to bodily injuries sustained by people who do not meet the definition of an insured or residence employees during the course of their employment. For this exception to apply, the building being constructed must be a dwelling or related to farm operations of the insured, and the construction must be occurring on an insured location.
- **Agritainment**—No coverage exists for bodily injury or property damage that occurs while the insured is engaging in agritainment activities as defined in the policy.

COVERAGE I

Coverage I of the farm liability policy pertains to losses resulting from personal injury or advertising injury. It provides coverage very similar to that provided under Coverage B of the commercial general liability policy. It contains many exclusions comparable to the ones found in the CGL, including the following.

Applicable to both personal and advertising injury losses:

- Knowingly violating another person's rights
- Publishing information an insured knows is false
- Contractual liability, except when part of an "insured contract"
- Statements made before the policy was in effect
- War
- Criminal activities of an insured or anyone taking direction from an insured
- Pollution losses
- Infringement of the copyright, patent, intellectual property, trademark, or trade secret of another
- Activities related to the insured hosting, using, owning, or controlling electronic chatrooms or bulletin boards

- An insured's use of another entity's name in email addresses, meta tags, or domain names with the intention of misleading customers
- Recording or publishing information that violates of the Telephone Consumer Protection Act, the CAN-SPAM Act of 2003, the Fair Credit Reporting Act, or any similar law or regulation

Applicable only to advertising injury losses:

- Breach of contract
- Losses stemming from products whose quality is not consistent with statements made in advertisements
- Advertising products and services using inaccurate prices
- For insureds working in media and internet businesses, the policy also excludes:
  o The insured's actions when conducting business as an internet service, search, or access provider
  o The insured's business activities as an advertiser, broadcaster, publisher, or designer of web content for others

The exclusions for personal injury under the farm liability policy are a bit different than those in the CGL. There is an exclusion for **agritainment** that is similar to the one under Coverage H. Additional exclusions consist of:

- **Business pursuits**—There is no coverage for the insured's business activities that are unrelated to the needs of the farming operations.
- **Civil or public activities for pay**—There is no coverage for personal injury losses occurring in connection with any insured's duties related to public or civic activities undertaken as part of a government or civic organization. Examples of such activities are serving on a city council, being a member of a local school board, or working for a fire department.
- **Personal injury to an insured**—Losses involving personal injury to anyone who meets the policy definition of an insured are not covered.

COVERAGE J

Coverage J of the farm liability policy provides coverage for **medical expenses** regardless of the insured's liability or negligence. The insurance company will pay for reasonable medical expenses, which are those incurred within three years of the date of loss and deemed necessary. Covered medical expenses include first aid at the scene of the accident, as well as medical, surgical, x-ray, ambulance, hospital, nursing, and funeral services. Medical payment coverage only applies to individuals who are on the insured premises with permission, people who are injured because of a condition on the insured location, due to the actions of an insured or an insured's farm employee in the course of his or her employment, or a residence employee in the course of his or her employment. This coverage also applies to injuries caused by animals owned or being cared for by an insured.

There are a number of exclusions pertaining to medical payments coverage. These exclusions include:

- All losses excluded under Coverage H
- **Farm employees or others who maintain the farm**—There is no coverage for injuries sustained by employees of the farm or any other person working to maintain the farm.
- **Injury to resident**—The policy does not cover injury to anyone who lives on the insured premises or within the insured's household, with the exception of residence employees.

ADDITIONAL COVERAGES AND COVERAGE EXTENSION

The farm liability policy offers some additional coverages for Coverages H and I. As in other types of liability policies, there is coverage for **supplementary payments**. The insurer agrees to reimburse these items on top of the applicable limit of liability. Covered items include:

- Expenses related to the investigation or settlement of claims made against an insured
- Costs that are taxed against the insured as part of a suit, except the portion of court costs that is for attorney's fees or expenses
- Pre-judgment interest that is charged to the insured in relation to a judgment paid by the insurance company
- Up to $250 toward the cost of bail bonds that are required because of the use of a vehicle covered under Coverage H
- Costs of any bonds necessary to release attachments, so long as these bond amounts are less than the limit of insurance
- Interest that accrues after the judgment has been rendered but before the insurance company has made the required payment

In the event that the insured has entered into a contract that requires them to indemnify a party that is also named in a lawsuit, the insurer agrees to provide such a defense so long as all of the following are true:

- The suit against the indemnitee seeks damages for which the insured has assumed liability in a contract or agreement.
- The insurance is applicable to the liability the insured assumed.
- The contract requires the insured to defend the indemnitee.
- There is no conflict in defending both the insured and the indemnitee.
- Both the insured and the indemnitee ask the insurer to defend against the suit and allow the insurer to use the same counsel to provide defense for both parties.

The indemnitee must also provide written agreement to cooperate with the insurer in the defense of the suit, send copies of all summonses and notices to the insurer, report the suit to any other insurance that is available to the indemnitee, assist in coordinating coverage with any other insurance that may apply, and provide written permission to obtain documentation related to the suit as well as conduct and control the defense of the suit. If any of these conditions are not met, the insurance company may still provide a defense to an indemnitee, but the costs may be treated as damages instead of supplemental payments. When this happens, the indemnitee's defense costs will reduce the amount of coverage available for the loss.

The second additional coverage under Coverage H and I of the farm liability policy relates to **damage to the property of others**. The insurance company will pay a maximum of $1,000 for each instance of property damage caused by an insured to the property of others, regardless of liability.

The insurer will pay the ACV of the property or the cost to replace or repair the property. The policy will not pay for damage to the property of others when it is caused intentionally by an insured who is at least 13 years old. This coverage does not extend to property owned by or rented to an insured or a member of his or her household, nor to property damage related to agritainment or to the ownership, operation, or use of motor vehicles, motorized bicycles, farm machinery, watercraft, or aircraft.

The only coverage extension in the farm liability policy applies to Coverages H, I, and J. It amends the definition of "you" under the policy to include the named insured's cohabiting spouse as a named insured under the main coverage, as well as for any endorsement that is attached to the liability policy.

CONDITIONS

The farm liability policy contains conditions very similar to those found in commercial general liability policies and the liability section of the BOP. These include:

- Bankruptcy
- Duties in the event of occurrence, offense, claim, or suit
- Legal action against us
- Insurance under two or more coverages
- Transfer of rights of recovery against others to us
- Liberalization
- Representations
- Separation of insureds

The **other insurance** condition states that losses covered by more than one policy will be shared proportionally between the insurers based on the sum of all coverage available. If the loss involves mobile equipment used at an insured-owned premises, watercraft, or motor vehicle, the farm policy will only provide coverage when there is no other coverage available, and coverage will only apply to such property when it is eligible for coverage under the farm liability policy. The **no admission of liability with medical payments** condition asserts that payment of medical expenses under Coverage J does not constitute an admission of guilt or liability by the insurance company or the insured.

Farm Policy Selected Definitions

Advertisement—Any publicly shared notice regarding the insured's farm products intended to attract business, including notices posted via the internet, including portions of the insured's website meant to gain customers or supporters.

Advertising injury—Any injury caused by slander or libel, violation of privacy rights, use of another's idea in the insured's advertisement, or infringing on the intellectual property of others in the insured's advertising, without regard to how the message or information is communicated.

Agritainment—Any activity that is agricultural or aquacultural in nature that is operated primarily at the insured location for tourism or entertainment purposes for which the insured receives compensation.

Agritainment property—Property owned by the insured used primarily for agritainment, except for buildings, structures, land, water, and growing crops, aside from those available for purchase as nursery stock.

Bodily injury—Any sickness, injury, or disease suffered by a person up to and including death.

Business—Activities performed by the insured for money or other compensation that are not related to farming or custom farming; agritainment is not included in the definition of "business."

Business property—Property used for any business that is not farming operations, excluding agritainment property.

Custom farming—Any services the insured provides to other farmers, including but not limited to planting, cultivating, and harvesting on a non-owned location and which is directed by the farmer who owns that location.

Dwelling—Any building used as a family residence, excluding those that serve as storage for products, livestock, or poultry.

Farm employee—A person employed by the insured and whose principal duties are to maintain or use the insured location as a farm; employees engaged in non-farming business or agritainment are not considered farm employees.

Farm personal property—Equipment, supplies, and products used in farming or ranching operations.

Hostile fire—Any fire that extends outside its intended boundaries or burns uncontrollably.

Insured (property policy forms)—When the named insured is an individual person, the following parties qualify as insureds:

- The named insured and his or her resident spouse
- Any relative residing within the named insured's household
- Any non-relative under the age of 21 and in the care of the policyholder or a resident relative
- Students living away from home to attend school full-time if under age 24 and a relative of the policyholder OR under 24 and in the care of the named insured or a resident relative

Insured (liability policy form)—Includes all of the above, as well as:

- For a **partnership or joint venture**—All partners, members, and their spouses, but only to the extent of their activities in the farming operations
- For a **limited liability company (LLC)**—All members when conducting the operations of the farm, and managers when executing managerial duties
- **Any other organization**—Executives and directors in the course of their duties in the farming operations, and stockholders but only related to their interest as stockholders
- **Employees** are considered insureds when in the course of their employment by the insured, so long as the injury caused by the employee is not suffered by the named insured, partners, members, or other employees; executive officers and LLC managers are not included in the definition of "employee"
- **Real estate managers** or anyone acting as such, so long as he or she is not an employee
- **Anyone responsible for animals or watercraft owned by an insured,** so long as the animal or watercraft is eligible for coverage and is used with the insured's permission, and is not used for business purposes or for agritainment activities
- Any person using a vehicle on the listed location with the insured's permission, but only if the vehicle in question is covered under the policy

Insured contract—Includes all of the following:

- **Leases for premises rented or temporarily occupied** by the insured, exclusive of any portion of the lease mandating indemnification by the named insured for fire damage to such property
- **Sidetrack agreements**
- **Licensing or easement agreements,** excluding those taking place within 50 feet of railroad demolition or construction operations
- **Contracts with municipal entities,** but only the portion applicable to assumption of tort liability for third parties
- **Any other contract or agreement related to the insured's farming operations** in which the insured agrees to assume liability for bodily injury or property damage to others on behalf of another party, excluding occurrences within 50 feet of railroad demolition or construction operations

Insured location (property policy forms)—Any location specified in the declarations as an insured location, inclusive of private ways into the property.

Insured location (liability policy form)—Includes the above, as well as:

- Portions of other locations used as a residence or newly acquired during the policy period
- Premises used in the maintenance of any of the above locations
- Locations not owned by the insured being used as the insured's temporary residence
- Vacant land rented or owned by the insured
- Land where a dwelling is being constructed for the insured, farm employees, or residence employees to occupy
- Buildings intended for use in the farm operations that are under construction
- Insured-owned cemetery or burial plots
- Locations rented by the insured on occasion, except if rented for business purposes or for agritainment purposes
- Farming premises newly acquired by the named insured or his or her spouse within the policy period

Livestock—Cattle, sheep, swine, goats, horses, mules, and donkeys.

Occurrence—Any accident resulting in injury or property damage, including ongoing or repeated exposure to a generally harmful condition.

Personal injury—Harm or injury caused by the following, including resultant bodily injury:

- False arrest, detention, or imprisonment
- Malicious prosecution
- Wrongful eviction or entry by a landlord
- Slander or libel, regardless of how such information is published
- Violation of another's right to privacy via oral or written means, regardless of how or where the information was made public

Pollutants—Contaminants and irritants, regardless of physical state, including waste and materials meant to be recycled, reclaimed, or reconditioned.

Poultry—Birds kept by the named insured intended for sale or use, not including fowl kept as pets only.

Property damage—Damage to or loss of use of tangible property; electronic data is not considered tangible property.

Residence premises—The primary residence of the named insured, including the surrounding grounds and structures on such grounds, that are not used for business purposes or agritainment.

Specified causes of loss—Defined as the following:

- Under the **basic** or **broad** causes of loss form:
    o Fire
    o Lightning
    o Explosion
    o Windstorm or hail
    o Smoke
    o Impact from aircraft or vehicles
    o Riot or civil commotion
    o Vandalism
    o Leakage of fire-extinguishing equipment
    o Weight of ice, snow, or sleet
    o Falling objects, excluding loss or damage to:
        ❖ Personal or agritainment property in the open
        ❖ Building or structure interiors or personal property contained within a building or structure, unless the damage was caused by a breach of the exterior by a covered cause of loss
        ❖ The object that fell
    o Sinkhole collapse—The abrupt sinking or collapsing of land into hollow underground spaces caused by erosion of limestone or dolomite by water; this definition does not include:
        ❖ Sinkhole filling expenses
        ❖ Sinkhole collapse of land into man-made underground cavities
    o Water damage—Accidental discharge or escape of water or steam caused directly by the cracking or breaking apart of heating, air conditioning, plumbing, or other appliances or systems at the insured location and holding water or steam. Sump systems and their associated parts and equipment are excluded from this definition.
- Under the **special** causes of loss form:
    o All the loss types covered under the basic and broad forms.
    o Water damage—Definition is broadened to include accidental discharge or leakage of water or waterborne material directly caused by the cracking or breakage of pipes not on the insured location that are components of a municipal water or sewer system, if the failure of such pipes was caused by wear and tear. Causes of loss and damages subject to the water exclusion are not considered water damage by this definition. If the discharge or leakage meets the criteria previously described in the definition, the resulting water is not excluded by the water exclusion provision pertaining to surface water or water beneath the surface of the ground.

197

Unoccupancy or unoccupied—Any dwelling not being lived in, or any building or structure not being used for its intended purpose, except when such locations are under construction, regardless of whether there are furnishings or personal property at the location customary to its use.

Vacancy or vacant—The condition created when any building or structure does not contain sufficient property or furnishings for the building or structure to be used for its intended purpose.

Your product—Items that the named insured sells, manufactures, or distributes, including those items sold, manufactured, or distributed by others using the insured's name. Does not include any unsold product, but does include the containers, warranties, and instructions furnished with sold goods.

Your work—The operations or services provided by the named insured or an insured employee, inclusive of all used materials and equipment as well as provided warranties and instructions.

Inland Marine Insurance

INTRODUCTION

Inland marine insurance is designed to cover property as it is being transported over land. It can be added to an existing policy, such as a commercial package policy, or be issued as a standalone policy. Inland marine coverage is available in both personal lines and commercial lines options. Personal lines coverage is typically used for items of value that may be frequently moved between locations or stored off the insured location, or that accompanies an insured who is traveling. Commercial inland marine insurance is usually purchased to cover property that is transported during business operations, property kept at offsite storage, or business property that is highly susceptible to damage or theft. Coverage is typically purchased based on the type of property that needs to be insured, so there are many different coverage forms available. In order to standardize the definition of **marine**, the NAIC created a definition of this term that is used throughout the United States. It breaks down the term into six different elements:

- Imports—Property that originates outside of the US for which there is coverage until one of the following occurs: it is delivered by the importer, it is combined with the purchaser's existing stock, or it is delivered to the importer's location
- Exports—Property designated for export or prepared for export outside of the US; it ceases to meet this definition once it is integrated into the domestic trade market in the destination country
- Domestic shipments—Property being transported between points within the US or its territories; coverage only applies while it is in transit to its final location
- Bridges, tunnels, and other property needed for transportation and communication—This includes property vital to transport property or facilitate communication; it excludes any buildings, building betterments and improvements, furniture and furnishings, supplies in storage, and permanently installed contents
- Personal property floater risks—Items of non-business personal property, regardless of location
- Commercial property floater risks—Items of business personal property, regardless of location

Personal Inland Marine Insurance

Personal inland marine insurance (PIM) is often used to supplement the coverage for personal property that is provided under a homeowners, renters', or dwelling policy. These forms contain many limitations on covered property, so they may not be sufficient to meet a policyholder's coverage needs. They also limit how much can be paid when property is damaged or lost away from the covered premises. Personal inland marine insurance can be used to provide broader coverage for property that is subject to the limitations of residential coverage or losses that are excluded entirely. PIM coverage and policy forms, commonly known as **floaters**, consist of a declarations page, a common policy provisions form, and one or more personal inland marine coverage forms.

The coverage forms available for PIM policies include:

- Personal articles
- Personal effects
- Jewelry and furs

- Cameras
- Musical instruments
- Silverware
- Stamp and coin collections
- Fine art
- Bicycles
- Golfer's equipment
- Personal property
- Outboard motor and boat
- Motorized vehicles for handicapped person
- Motorized ground maintenance vehicles
- Motorized golf carts
- Motorized snowmobiles

COMMON POLICY PROVISIONS

All personal inland marine policies must be accompanied by the **common policy provisions** form. This form contains the insuring agreement, definitions, exclusions, and conditions pertaining to all PIM coverage forms. Many of the provisions outlined are similar to those found in other personal lines policies. The following causes of loss are excluded by the common policy provisions:

- War
- Nuclear hazard
- Governmental action
- Intentional loss
- Neglect

Loss conditions included in the PIM provisions that are similar to those found in other policies are:

- Loss settlement
- Loss payment
- Duties after loss
- Loss payable clause

There are three different loss settlement conditions listed in the common policy provisions:

- **Standard loss settlement**—This applies to property for which the policyholder has chosen for losses to be settled under the standard method. For scheduled property and newly acquired property, the insurer will pay the lowest of the ACV, the cost of reasonable restoration or repairs, the cost of a replacement item that is identical or substantially identical to the loss property, or the limit of insurance applicable to the loss property. When covered property is part of a pair or set and only a portion of the pair or set is damaged, the insurance company may replace or repair the damaged portion, the pre-loss ACV, or an amount representative of the value of the lost or damaged item. If any portion of the property is recovered following payment, whoever recovers the property must notify the other party. The insured then decides if he or she wants to take possession of the recovered property or allow the insurance company to keep it. If the insured chooses to keep the recovered property, he or she will need to return some or all of the loss payment to the insurer.

- **Agreed value loss settlement—scheduled property only**—This condition states that when property is scheduled with value agreed upon by the insured and the insurance company, this will be the amount paid to this insured in the event of loss involving that property. The insured is obligated to relinquish any remaining property to the insurer if requested. When the damaged property is a part of a pair or set, the insurance company pays the agreed value for the entire set and takes possession of any remaining portion of the pair or set. If the property is recovered subsequent to payment, it must be surrendered to the insurance company. If the insured wishes to retain the recovered property, he or she must negotiate a price with the insurance company, which he or she will then pay.
- **Unscheduled property—blanket insurance**—This condition contains two separate clauses, one for collections of stamps or rare coins and one for fine art, cameras, golfer's equipment, musical instruments, and silverware. Both clauses state that when there is loss to unscheduled property, payment will be determined by the proportion of the ACV of the property to the entire blanket limit for that category of property. For an unscheduled coin collection, the policy will pay a maximum of $1,000. For any single piece of a stamp or coin collection, the policy will pay no more than $250. For fine art, cameras, golfer's equipment, musical instruments, and silverware, the proportional payment is subject to a $500 per item limit.

Other conditions included in the PIM provisions that are similar to general conditions found in other policies are:

- Policy period
- Insurable interest and limit of liability
- Appraisal
- Other insurance and service agreement
- Suit against us
- Changes in policy
- Liberalization
- Concealment or fraud
- No benefit to bailee—called "insurance not to benefit others" under the PIM form

The **cancellation** provision is essentially the same as those found in other policies, except that the insurance company only needs to give the policyholder 10 days advance notice, no matter the reason for canceling. The **nonrenewal** condition states that the insurance company must provide the insured with 30 days advance written notice if declining to renew the policy. The **death** condition states that the named insured's interest in the insurance policy is transferred to an appointed legal representative of the insured's estate when the insured dies. While appointment of a legal representative is pending, anyone with legal temporary possession of the covered property is treated as an insured. Members of the insured's household will also be considered insureds after the death of the insured, but only while a resident of the insured's premises.

PERSONAL ARTICLES FORM

The **personal articles form**, also called a **personal articles floater**, is available in either the standard loss settlement form or the agreed value loss settlement form. It covers property that has a higher value because of its rarity or desirability. Personal articles present more risk than other types of property because they are frequently carried, worn, or transported by the insured. This form also includes a schedule of the categories of property the policy will cover, and the limit of insurance purchased for each category. The categories listed are:

- Jewelry, excluding unmounted stones and precious metals not part of a piece of jewelry
- Furs, including garments lined or trimmed in fur
- Musical instruments, including accessories, sheet music, and other equipment
- Silverware, including silver-plated ware, gold-plated ware, pewterware, platinumware, and any dinnerware plated or embellished with any of these materials
- Golfer's equipment, including clubs, clothing, and accessories
- Fine art
- Stamp and rare coin collections, including any property used to display or mount these items
- Cameras, including both still and video cameras, as well as any accessories and related equipment

When newly acquired property falls under the jewelry, furs, cameras, musical instruments, or fine art categories, it is automatically covered under the policy with the following stipulations: All newly acquired property other than fine art is covered for 30 days at either 25% of the insurance limit or $10,000, whichever is less. Newly acquired fine art is covered for 90 days at 25% of the insurance limit. After the applicable coverage period elapses, the insured must notify the company of the new property for coverage to continue. Although personal articles forms require an appraisal immediately after the policy is issued, they are not agreed value policies. Only fine art property is covered on an agreed value basis. All other property is subject to the standard loss settlement valuation condition in the common policy provisions.

Most coverage under the personal articles floater is provided on an open perils basis. Excluded causes of loss are:

- Any defect inherent to the property that causes it to damage or destroy itself, referred to in the form as **inherent vice**
- Natural deterioration and expected wear and tear
- Insects or vermin
- Nuclear hazards
- War
- Governmental actions
- Losses intentionally caused by an insured
- Neglecting to preserve property during and after a loss

There are some special exclusions that only apply to specific categories of property. These include:

- Musical instruments—There is no coverage for breakdown or failure of a permanently installed organ or for damage caused by service, maintenance, repairs, or adjustments.
- Fine art—Breakage of especially fragile pieces such as art glass, marble, and statues is only covered when caused by vehicle overturn or derailment, fire, lightning, collision or explosion of aircraft, earthquake, flood, windstorm, malicious mischief, or theft.
- Stamp and rare coin collections—No coverage applies to losses resulting from handling or working on the property. Marring, fading, creasing, tearing, or thinning losses are also excluded. There will be no payment for losses involving color transfer, depreciation, extreme temperatures, or inherent defects. Coverage is excluded for disappearance of individual items unless the mounting also disappears.

PERSONAL PROPERTY FORM AND PERSONAL EFFECTS FORM

The **personal property form** can be used to provide open perils coverage for personal property by adding it as an endorsement or purchasing a standalone policy. Only the comprehensive homeowners forms, the HO-5 and HO-14, provide open perils coverage for personal property, so an insured with a policy other than these may not have coverage broad enough for his or her needs. The personal property form can also be used for property that would not fall within the scope of the personal articles form. In addition, certain items are covered on a limited basis under the homeowners or dwelling policies, and that amount may not be sufficient to cover the insured's actual risk. This form allows insureds to increase coverage only for the types of property they need it for. Another benefit to using the personal inland marine personal property form is that it covers personal property while it is away from the insured residence without the limitations in the homeowners or dwelling policies. This coverage is subject to the common policy provisions form.

The **personal effects form** is another option for personal inland marine coverage. It is primarily used to protect personal property that is frequently carried by an insured. The items insured under this form typically do not carry as much value as items that would be covered under the personal articles form. This form is a good option for insureds who travel frequently or for extended periods of time, live in an RV on a regular basis, or temporarily live outside the coverage territory specified in other types of policies. For coverage to apply, the property must be owned and used by the insured. It provides open peril protection for cameras, clothing, souvenirs, and other types of property that tourists often carry. It can also be used to cover costume jewelry, frequently worn jewelry such as wedding rings, sports equipment, and medical items that are not excluded by the policy. This coverage excludes certain types of property that are either better insured by a different policy or carry exceptional risk of loss. These types include:

- Aircraft and watercraft
- Vehicles and trailers
- Animals
- Valuable documents such as tickets, passports, deeds, letters of credit, accounts, and securities
- Bicycles
- Currency, bank notes, and other financial instruments
- Household furniture
- Prosthetic limbs, dentures, hearing aids, and contact lenses
- Property while at the policyholder's residence or in storage
- Property of students living away from the insured's residence
- Contraband
- Sales samples and merchandise
- Theatrical property
- Physician's or surgeon's equipment

Like the other forms, this one must be accompanied by the common policy provisions form.

Commercial Inland Marine Insurance

Commercial inland marine insurance (CIM) is used to cover specific property while it is being transported or when it is away from the insured's primary location. Commercial inland marine policy forms are classified as either **filed** or **non-filed**. Filed classes encompass property that more frequently needs to be insured while being transported, whereas non-filed classes can provide more niche coverage. Only filed classes can be used with a commercial package policy. When used in this way, the intention is typically to supplement or increase coverage provided by another part of the commercial package policy. When commercial inland marine coverage is purchased on its own, the policy includes the common policy declarations, the common policy conditions form (the same form used with the commercial package policy), the CIM declarations form, the CIM conditions form, and any applicable coverage forms with their respective declarations. All coverage forms provide open perils protection subject to the exclusions and limitations described in each individual form. The filed commercial inland marine coverage forms are as follows:

- Commercial articles
- Mail
- Theatrical property
- Film
- Physicians and surgeons equipment
- Camera and musical instrument dealers
- Equipment dealers
- Accounts receivable
- Valuable papers and records
- Jewelers block
- Signs
- Floor plan

COMMERCIAL INLAND MARINE CONDITIONS

The CIM conditions include many conditions identical or functionally similar to conditions found in the CPP common policy conditions or the commercial property conditions. These conditions consist of:

- Loss conditions:
  - Abandonment
  - Appraisal
  - Duties in the event of loss
  - Insurance under two or more coverages
  - Other insurance
  - Pairs, sets, or parts
  - Recovered property
  - Transfer of rights of recovery
- General conditions:
  - Concealment, misrepresentation, or fraud
  - Control of property
  - Legal action against us
  - No benefit to bailee
  - Policy period and coverage territory—The standard coverage territory consists of the United States, its territories and possessions, and Canada. Any deviations from the standard territory will be noted.

There is an additional loss condition that relates to **reinstatement of limits after a loss.** This states that after payment of a claim, the applicable limit is restored to its full amount. The only exception is for property that is completely lost or destroyed. In this case, the limit is decreased to account for the item being deleted from the policy. The insured is refunded any unearned premiums for the deleted property.

STANDARD EXCLUSIONS TO FILED INLAND MARINE COVERAGE FORMS

Because there are multiple options available for CIM coverage, the exclusions can vary from form to form. The following primary exclusions are found in all filed forms:

- Government action
- War or military action
- Nuclear hazard (*except* the mail coverage form)

The following secondary exclusions are listed in all filed forms *except* the mail coverage form:

- Delay, loss of use, and loss of market
- Voluntary parting
- Unauthorized instruction
- Neglect

The following other (anti-concurrent causation) exclusions are listed in all filed forms *except* the mail coverage form:

- Weather conditions
- Acts or decisions
- Faulty, inadequate, or defective planning
- Collapse, aside from that covered by limited collapse coverage, if applicable

An exclusion for **wear and tear** is included in all coverage forms except mail, film, and accounts receivable. This exclusion also eliminates coverage for damage caused by inherent vice, latent defect, depreciation, deterioration, insects, vermin, rodents, rust, corrosion, dampness, and hot or cold temperatures. There is also an exclusion for **theft** that is committed by anyone entrusted with covered property that applies to all forms except mail and jewelers block. This exclusion makes an exception when the property is in the possession of a hired carrier. Except for the mail and accounts receivable forms, any **criminal or dishonest acts** committed by the insured or anyone working on the insured's behalf are not covered.

ADDITIONAL COVERAGE—COLLAPSE

Several of the filed CIM forms provide additional, but limited, coverage for collapse losses. Payment under this coverage does not increase the applicable limit of insurance. This will only pay for losses resulting from a sudden or abrupt collapse of all or part of a building. There are only specific causes of loss that the insurance will cover for a collapse. These causes are:

- Hidden decay, insect, or vermin damage that the insured was not previously aware of
- Defective construction methods or materials after construction is completed, but only when in conjunction with one or more of the following:
  - Hidden decay, insect, or vermin damage
  - Certain named perils if also covered by the CIM form:
    - Fire or lightning
    - Windstorm or hail
    - Collision with aircraft, vehicles, or falling objects
    - Explosion
    - Smoke
    - Riot or civil commotion
    - Vandalism

* ❖ Fire extinguisher or device leaks
* ❖ Sinkhole collapse
* ❖ Water damage
* ❖ Earthquake
* ❖ Weight of sleet, ice, or snow
  * ○ Weight of persons or personal property
  * ○ Weight of rain on the roof of the building

FILED COMMERCIAL INLAND MARINE COVERAGE FORMS

COMMERCIAL ARTICLES COVERAGE FORM

The **commercial articles coverage form** is part of the commercial property floater risk category. While similar in name, the types of property covered under the commercial articles form are much more limited than those under the personal articles form. The commercial articles form provides worldwide open peril protection for covered property. This form only applies to commercial cameras, musical instruments, and similar commercial property that is owned by the insured or in his or her care or custody. When the insured acquires new property that is included under the policy form, it receives limited coverage for 30 days. Afterward, the insured must report it to the insurer or lose coverage. In addition to the typical exclusions, this form also includes primary exclusions for earthquake and water damage losses. It is also subject to the collapse additional coverage.

MAIL COVERAGE FORM

The **mail coverage form** is part of the domestic shipment category of commercial inland marine insurance. It covers property loss on an open peril basis if the property is in the care or custody of a government postal service or a common carrier during transport from one location to another. A **common carrier** is a company that offers a service to the general public in exchange for compensation. The property may be conveyed via registered mail, first class mail, express mail, or certified mail via the US Postal Service (USPS). This coverage is not intended for singular or special shipments. It is meant for entities that frequently use the post office or common carrier services to transport items of value. Eligible businesses include financial institutions, insurance companies, security brokers, investment companies working primarily in fiduciary capacities, and companies that maintain their own transfer agents or registrars.

Coverage lasts until the property reaches its final location and applies to stamps, money orders, checks, stock certificates, bonds, deposit certificates, and various other security certificates. Money, food stamps, and unsold traveler's checks are not covered. Bullion, platinum, precious metals, watches, jewelry, and precious and semiprecious stones are covered when transported by registered mail. Transportation of contraband or other illegal items is not covered. The only exclusions under this form are for losses caused by government action, war, military action, or use of weapons. For first class, certified, and USPS express mail, the coverage territory is limited to the United States, its territories and possessions, and Canada. Registered mail is covered while en route to destinations worldwide.

Property loss is valued on an actual value basis, but the value reported on the policy cannot be less than the property's market value. The policyholder is required to report items mailed at an interval specified in the policy declarations. The report must be submitted within 30 days of the end of that period and must include a listing of the types of items that were sent. This is necessary in determining how the claims related to those items will be covered. There are separate limits depending on which method of mailing was used. They are split into the categories of first class and certified mail, USPS express mail, and registered mail. If the property loss exceeds the limit of insurance, the reimbursement amount will equal the proportion of the limit of insurance to the actual value. The loss recovery formula is as follows:

$$\left(\frac{\text{Limit of Insurance Carried}}{\text{Limit of Insurance Required}}\right) \times \text{Amount of Loss} - \text{Deductible} = \text{Loss Recovery}$$

Loss payment for most items also includes reimbursement for postage cost and loss of interest earnings. Recovery for bonds, certificates, and securities is limited to 125% of the recorded value. If the policy is canceled, any items shipped before the cancellation date will be covered until they reach their destination.

THEATRICAL PROPERTY COVERAGE FORM

The **theatrical property coverage form** provides open peril protection for scenery, props, and costumes that a theater group is using in a production specified under the policy's declarations section. The property can be owned by the insured or be in his or her care or custody. This form includes the collapse additional coverage. In addition to the standard exclusions already discussed, the following perils are excluded from coverage:

- Theft from an unattended vehicle, unless there are signs the vehicle was locked, such as forced entry marks; exception is made for property in the possession of a hired carrier
- Damage from light exposure, marring, or scratching
- Damage occurring while the property is being worked on or otherwise processed
- Inventory shortages
- Unexplained disappearances
- Artificially generated energy or current

Additionally, these forms do not cover certain property, such as buildings including improvements and betterments, vehicles, animals, contraband, jewelry, currency, money, deeds, accounts, bills, admission tickets, and securities. This form is subject to the standard coverage territory, and there is the option to add a coinsurance to this form.

FILM COVERAGE FORM

The **film coverage form** insures exposed motion picture film, soundtracks, videotapes, and magnetic tapes on an open peril basis. The property must be part of a production identified in the declarations section and must be owned by the insured or under his or her care. Film coverage forms also provide additional collapse coverage, but do not cover positive prints or films, library stock, cutouts, or unused footage. A positive print is essentially the opposite of a negative print. Positive prints show the image as it would appear on a developed print with accurate coloration. This form is subject to all the standard exclusions, but the following perils are also excluded from coverage:

- Light exposure to negative film
- Temperature changes, atmospherically induced wetness, or deterioration
- Erasure or damage to electronic records and videotapes caused by electric or magnetic sources other than lightning
- Damage caused by developing chemicals
- Film cutting, developing, printing, or other lab processing
- Damage due to electricity or magnets

The reimbursement amount is determined by adding the cost of reproducing the damaged property to any value the undamaged portions of the production may have lost. The coverage area is limited to the United States, its territories and possessions, and Canada, and any area within 50 miles of these locations.

PHYSICIANS AND SURGEONS EQUIPMENT COVERAGE FORM

The **physicians and surgeons equipment coverage form** provides coverage for items that are commonly used by medical and dental professionals. These parties are eligible for this coverage, but dealers, hospitals, medical schools, and clinics are not. Eligible items may be covered under the policy even if the insured does not own them, and he or she is only required to use them to purchase the coverage. Coverage for such equipment is not limited to losses occurring on the insured premises, and coverage is applicable anywhere within the standard coverage territory. This form includes the collapse additional coverage and covers the following items on an open perils basis:

- Medical and dental equipment used by the insured
- Medical and dental supplies, materials, or books
- Office fixtures and furniture owned by the insured and located at the insured location
- Improvements and betterments to a rented insured location paid for by the insured

Most covered losses are paid at the lowest of the ACV, restoration cost, or cost to replace with functionally similar property. Building property damage due to attempted theft is covered when the insured rents the premises and is required by the lease to cover such damage. This kind of damage is reimbursed at ACV, unless the insured pays for the replacement or repair and it is completed within a reasonable time period. This coverage extension does not apply to fire losses or damage to glass. If any protective safeguards, such as security and sprinkler systems, were in place at the beginning of the coverage period, they must be maintained by the insured. Otherwise, the insurer may suspend coverage until they are in working condition. If desired, the policyholder may add the coinsurance condition to the policy.

All the standard exclusions apply, but there are additional exclusions as follows:

- Contraband
- Losses involving radium in any form
- Electrical damage caused by artificial currents
- Damage to property while it is being worked on or processed

CAMERA AND MUSICAL INSTRUMENT DEALERS COVERAGE FORM

The **camera and musical instrument dealers coverage form** provides open peril coverage for the insured's stock-in-trade when the insured sells cameras and musical instruments. It also provides coverage for cameras and musical instruments that are owned by others but are in the insured's possession or care. The standard coverage territory applies, but there are separate limits of insurance depending on where the property is located at the time of loss. A separate limit applies to each of the following:

- Property at the insured's business premises
- Property away from the insured's location but in the care of the insured or an employee
- Property being transported
- Property off the insured premises, other than that listed above
- Property at all locations—Usually only applicable to catastrophe losses

Certain property is entirely excluded from coverage on an unendorsed policy:

- Sold property that has been delivered to customers such that the insured no longer holds any financial interest
- Fixtures, office supplies, and furniture (optional coverage is available)
- Improvements and betterments (optional coverage is available)
- Machinery (optional coverage is available)
- Money, accounts, and other types of securities
- Property sent via mail, unless it is sent via registered mail or is covered by government mail insurance
- Tools, patterns, dies, molds, fittings, and models (optional coverage is available)
- Contraband

This form contains all the typical exclusions, but does contain additional exclusions as follows:

- Losses resulting from earthquakes or water damage
- Theft from an unattended vehicle, unless there is evidence of forced entry; an exception is made for property in the custody of a hired carrier
- Marring, scratching, and light exposure
- Damage caused by processing or work performed on the property
- Losses involving artificially generated electrical power
- Breakage of glass items except for lenses

This form provides additional collapse coverage and also requires the insured to maintain protective safeguards and inventory lists. Losses are reimbursed differently depending on the property's status at the time of loss:

- **Unsold property**—The lowest of ACV, replacement cost, and restoration value
- **Property of others**—The lower of ACV and the insured's liability amount
- **Sold property not yet delivered**—Net selling price, which is gross selling price minus discounts and allowances

Negatives and prints are valued at the cost of unexposed film plus labor and materials.

EQUIPMENT DEALERS COVERAGE FORM

The **equipment dealers coverage form** provides open peril coverage for mobile agricultural equipment and construction equipment that is part of the insured's stock-in-trade, or equipment owned by someone else but in the insured's care. It protects property both inside and outside the insured location, during transit, and while at other locations.

Certain property is specifically excluded from coverage:

- Autos, motorcycles, and trucks
- Currency, securities, deeds, accounts, bills, and evidences of debt
- Property that the insured manufactures
- Property not in the custody of the insured or a hired carrier after it has been leased, sold, or rented
- Contraband

The following items are excluded, but coverage may be added as an additional coverage if the policyholder chooses:

- Fixtures, office supplies, and furniture
- Improvements and betterments
- Machinery
- Tools, patterns, dies, molds, fittings, and models

This form includes the additional coverage for collapse but contains all the standard CIM exclusions. It describes additional exclusions for:

- Water damage
- Property damaged during processing or work on the insured premises
- Loss caused by artificially generated electrical current

The equipment dealers form has some additional coverages to supplement the protection provided by the CIM coverage:

- **Theft damage to buildings**—Covers damages caused by actual or attempted theft when the insured is a rental tenant and is required by the lease to cover such damage; coverage does not apply to damaged glass or damage caused by fire.
- **Pollutant cleanup and removal**—Applies when a covered peril has caused pollutants to discharge onto the insured's property. It provides $10,000 per 12-month policy period to cover the cost of extracting and removing pollutants. Only testing related to extraction and removal is covered. Testing for any other reason will not be paid for by the insurer.
- **Debris removal**—Covers the cost of removing debris from the insured's property when the debris is caused by a covered loss. The reimbursement limit equals 25% of the amount of the sum of direct physical loss and the deductible. This limit can be increased by $10,000 in the following situations: the total cost of debris removal and direct loss is greater than the limit of insurance, or the cost of debris removal is greater than the 25% limit. The limits are applicable to each location. Debris removal coverage excludes costs related to pollutant cleanup.

For both debris removal and pollutant cleanup to apply, the insured must submit an expense report within 180 days of the loss or the end of the policy period, whichever is earlier.

Valuation for losses under the equipment dealers form is essentially the same as for the camera and musical instrument dealers form. Losses are reimbursed as follows:

- **Unsold property**—The lowest of ACV, replacement cost, and restoration value
- **Property of others**—The lower of ACV and the insured's liability amount
- **Sold property not yet delivered**—Gross selling price minus allowances and discounts, also referred to as **net selling price**

ACCOUNTS RECEIVABLE COVERAGE FORM

The **accounts receivable coverage form** provides coverage when a company's accounts receivable records are damaged and the insured is unable to collect payments from customers. This form reimburses lost customer payments, as well as any extra collection expenses the insured incurs beyond those that would be customary for the business. It will also cover any reasonable expenses the insured pays to try to restore or reconstruct the lost records. If the insured needs to acquire a loan to maintain business operations during the restoration period, the policy will cover the associated interest. Only account records stored at premises specified on the declarations are covered. Some policies require that accounts receivable records must be stored in containers identified in the declarations section when they are not being used or the business is closed. Accounts receivable coverage excludes records stored at locations not listed on the policy, as well as any illegal items or contraband.

The accounts receivable CIM coverage form contains all of the standard exclusions, except for the exclusion related to unexplained disappearances. In addition, the policy excludes the following:

- Changing, falsifying, destroying, or concealing documents or records as a means of covering up illegal or wrongful behavior
- Errors in bookkeeping, accounting, or billing
- Erasure of electronic data or recordings due to:
  o Electrical or magnetic interference
  o Errors in programming
  o Power surge or failure occurring more than 100 feet from the insured premises
  o Any other problem occurring more than 100 feet from the insured premises
  o Defective installation or repair of data processing equipment
  o Incorrect or flawed machine instructions
- Losses without physical evidence and only supported by inventory or audit findings

This form also includes the additional coverage for collapse and is subject to the standard coverage territory. There is a coverage extension for **removal** of covered records to an alternate location to protect them from a covered peril. Coverage also applies while the records are being transported. The insured must provide written notification to the insurance company within 10 days of the removal.

There are a few conditions within the accounts receivable form that are not part of the typical CIM conditions. These conditions are as follows:

- **Determination of receivables**—This takes the place of the valuation condition found in the commercial inland conditions form. This condition explains a special reimbursement method used when an accurate accounts receivable amount cannot be determined following a loss. The insurer calculates an average monthly amount for accounts receivable from the previous 12 months, then adjusts this average for any applicable variances and fluctuations. For all covered losses, the insurance company will subtract the following amounts from the loss payable:
  o Accounts that have sustained no loss
  o Unearned interest and service charges
  o Accounts the insured is able to recover or re-establish
  o Estimated bad debts the insured usually cannot collect
- **Recoveries**—If the named insured recovers any account funds after the claim has been paid, he or she is required to repay the insurer for the amount issued. Any remaining recovery is kept by the insured.

The policy may be amended to add the **coinsurance** condition if the policyholder chooses to add it.

VALUABLE PAPERS AND RECORDS COVERAGE FORM

The **valuable papers and records coverage form** covers the costs of replacing lost deeds, books, manuscripts, films, maps, and drawings that are owned by the insured or in his or her care. The floater provides open perils coverage and will pay up to $5,000 for such records when they are away from the insured premises. Coverage also extends to documents that have been relocated from the insured location as a means to preserve them from a covered peril, if the policyholder informs the insurer of the relocation within 10 days. The valuable papers and records form is subject to the standard coverage territory. This form provides the collapse additional coverage. Property that the policy does not cover includes:

- Property not declared on the policy declarations page, except when the property cannot be replaced with substantially similar property
- Property used as samples
- Property that is sold but pending delivery
- Property located at a location not listed on the policy

These forms include all the CIM exclusions, as well as some additional exclusions. These additional exclusions are:

- Loss of electronic data due to erasure
- Electrical interference or disturbance
- Copying and processing errors or omissions

Coverage only applies if the papers and records are stored in accordance with the requirements listed in the declarations section. Each covered item has an insurance limit that coincides with its value listed in the declarations. After the loss is settled, the insured may be required to pay back the reimbursement amount to the insurance company if he or she recovers the property and wants to retain ownership.

JEWELERS BLOCK COVERAGE FORM

The **jewelers block coverage form** is a dealers policy, though it does not say it in the name. This coverage is intended for smaller jewelry retailers and applies on an open perils basis. Any commercial jeweler with an average inventory valued at more than $250,000 is not eligible for this coverage. There are several other businesses that are ineligible to use this form, including:

- Auction houses
- Businesses that primarily work with raw materials such as bullion and loose diamonds
- Industrial diamond operations
- Watch repairers
- Fine art or antique sellers
- Jewelry exhibitioners

Unlike most types of inland marine insurance, this form covers property that is on the business premises as well as property off-premises and in transit; however, there are separate limits that apply based on the location of the property when the loss occurs. The standard coverage territory applies. The location options are:

- Property at the insured's listed premises
- Property within a safe deposit vault at a trust, bank, or safe deposit company location
- Property away from the insured's location that is in the care of a processor, dealer, or similar bailee
- Property during transport—The limit for this scenario is further broken down by how the property is being transported:

- o Armored vehicles
- o Merchants parcel delivery services
- o Registered mail
- o Waterborne carriers, air carriers, railroads, and passenger bus lines, but only to the extent allowed by the coverage form
- Property at any other premises not listed above

The following types of property are covered:

- Stock used in the insured's business, such as precious and semiprecious stones, precious metals and alloys, jewelry, watches, and watch movement mechanisms
- Any of the above that has been sold that is awaiting shipment or delivery to the buyer and is on the insured premises
- Similar property of others in the insured's care when the owners are not in the jewelry business
- Similar property of others in the insured's care when the owners are in the jewelry trade, but only to the extent of the insured's legal liability for such property

There is no coverage for any of the following property:

- Property that is sold under a deferred payment arrangement and has been removed from the insured location
- Items on display in showcases or show windows at locations other than the insured's premises
- Property on display at exhibitions produced or funded by trade associations or public authorities
- Jewelry worn by the insured, the insured's family members, the insured's employees, or any other people involved in the jewelry business, including their family members; the only exception is when a watch is worn during a sizing adjustment
- Property shipped by express carrier or mail other than registered mail
- Property in transit by an air, water, or railroad carrier, except when under a passenger parcel service or baggage service
- Property while being transported by a motor carrier that is not a merchant parcel service, armored vehicle service, bus parcel transportation, or bus baggage service
- Contraband

The following items are excluded, but coverage may be added as an additional coverage if the policyholder chooses:

- Fixtures, office supplies, and furniture
- Improvements and betterments
- Machinery
- Tools, patterns, dies, molds, fittings, and models

This form contains the standard CIM exclusions, but its **theft** exclusion differs from the one found in other forms. While it still excludes theft committed by anyone entrusted with covered property, there are some additional exceptions. This exclusion does not apply to property that the named insured—or any of the insured's salespeople, officers, or members—deposits for safekeeping while traveling. There is also an exception for property that is in the possession of the USPS or other carrier. The last exception made is for property while it is held by a helper or porter who is not included in the insured's payroll. The form also includes several other coverage exclusions:

- Earthquake losses
- Water damage
- Property stolen from any vehicle, except when the insured or any other person tasked with attending to the vehicle is within or on the vehicle at the time of the theft; another exception is made for property in the possession of the USPS or any other carrier for which there is coverage
- Property shipped in a package to a consignee that arrives with the packaging intact but does not contain all the property that was claimed to be sent
- Attempted or actual theft of property displayed in a show window that has been broken or cut to allow access to the property (optional coverage is available)
- Damage occurring while property is being worked on or processed
- Defective or inadequate packaging
- Damage to highly breakable items

The jewelers block coverage form includes the additional collapse coverage as well as a coverage extension for damage to a building caused by a theft or attempted theft. The coverage extension only applies for insureds who rent the premises from a landlord, and only when the lease contractually obligates the insured to repair such damage. Payments under this coverage extension are included in the overall limit of insurance. Some coverages are optional and are only in effect if the insured chooses to purchase them. The jewelers block form can be enhanced with the following optional coverages:

- **Show window coverage**—Insures against theft of stock that is being displayed in a window that has been broken or cut; when purchased, this coverage overrides the exclusion in the base form
- **Money coverage**—Provides theft coverage for money stored in safes and vaults located at the insured location

The jewelers block coverage **valuation** condition states that losses will use whichever of the following options is the lowest amount:

- ACV
- Replacement cost
- Costs to restore the property to its pre-loss condition
- The lowest value of the property as in the insured's inventory report or other documents

Other special conditions in this form are:

- **Protective safeguards**—Coverage will be suspended if the insured fails to maintain the property's protective safeguards as reported to the insurer at the beginning of the policy. These systems are only required to be functioning during closing hours.

- **Records and inventory**—The insured is required to maintain accurate records throughout the policy period and for up to three years after the policy ends. Required records include itemized inventories, a report of others' property that is in the insured's possession, a list of property removed from the insured location for any reason, purchase and sale records, and itemized listings of travelers stock. The insured is obligated to perform a physical inventory on covered stock at least annually. If there is a change in the risk of an insured premises due to expansion or relocation, the insurance company must be notified in writing for coverage to apply.
- **Changes to premises**—If there is any substantial change in the risk related to covered property or the policyholder expands his or her premises, the insurance company must agree in writing to provide coverage.
- **Attachment of proposal**—This states that the policy must be accompanied by a completed "proposal for jewelers block coverage" form. This is the only filed CIM policy that has this requirement. The proposal form includes extensive and detailed questions regarding the insured premises, the property to be covered, security measures, and the insured's loss history, among many other items.

SIGNS COVERAGE FORM

The **signs coverage form** provides open peril coverage for neon, fluorescent, automatic, and mechanical electric signs or lights that are owned by or in the care of the insured business. The only property excluded is contraband, since the scope of coverage is so limited. Aside from the standard exclusions, the only other causes of loss exclusions are for damage resulting from artificially generated electrical current or breakage during transport or installation. The typical coverage territory applies, and the insured has the option to add a coinsurance provision. The deductible is usually $0 or 5% of the damaged sign's value.

FLOOR PLAN COVERAGE FORM

The **floor plan coverage form** is another dealers form used for CIM insurance. It covers the **encumbered property** described on the declarations page. This is merchandise or product the policyholder has purchased using funds borrowed from a bank or other type of lender. This is known as a floor plan arrangement. Floor plan coverage can apply to both the dealer's interests and the lender's interests. The policy will not cover the following property:

- Contraband
- Property for which the insured no longer carries a financial interest
- Property that has been sold, delivered, or disposed of

It also provides additional collapse coverage and contains the standard CIM exclusions. There are some additional causes of loss for which the policy will not provide coverage:

- Water damage occurring at the insured's premises
- Losses related to foreclosure, bankruptcy, or other similar legal proceedings
- Property damage resulting from open exposure to rain, sleet, snow, freezing, or hail
- Damage to breakable items, including glass; exceptions are made for direct damage due to fire, lightning, explosion, vandalism, windstorm, falling aircraft or objects, rioters and striking workers, building collapse, theft, or accident involving a transporting vehicle
- Electrical damage to covered property caused by artificial currents

Floor plan coverage carries the standard coverage territory condition, but is subject to a number of additional conditions, including:

- **Valuation**—This overrides the valuation condition in the commercial inland marine conditions form. It states that property will be assessed based on its value at the time of loss. Sold and unsold property are subject to different valuation protocols.
  - **Unsold property**—Value is based on the lowest of the cost to replace the property with substantially comparable items, reasonable restoration costs, and the price the dealer paid for the property plus any applicable transportation expenses.
  - **Sold property**—This provision applies to property that has not yet been delivered to the buyer. Such property will be valued at net selling price, which is the gross selling price less any discounts or allowances.
- **Loss limitation—single interest**—When the coverage is written only for the insured's interest in the property, reimbursement will be limited to the amount of the insured's interest.
- **Dual interest**—States that all parties must abide by policy provisions. It also protects the interests of the lender even when other insured parties fail to fulfill policy provisions, so long as the lender has tried to fulfill its obligations under the policy.
- **Transit coverage in the event of cancellation**—If property is in the process of being transported when the policy is canceled, the policy will cover the property until it reaches its destination.
- **Records and inventory**—States that the insured must maintain accurate records for the entire policy period and retain them for up to three years after the policy expires. Mandated records include itemized inventory reports, records showing property of others that is in the care of the insured, a list of property sent to others for any reason, all purchase records, and a ledger of payments, outstanding balances, or values at risk. The policyholder is required to perform a physical inventory at least once per year.
- **Reports and premium**—This condition outlines all the conditions relating to reporting requirements and calculation of premiums. It states:
  - Named insureds must submit required reports within 30 days of the end of the month.
  - Premium is calculated monthly, and any deposit premium is applied to the earned premium balance. Any additional premium owed will be billed to the insured monthly and must be paid by the due date on the statement.
  - If there is a minimum premium for the policy, this will be the amount owed, regardless of whether the calculated premium is a lower amount.
  - If the insured has not properly submitted the required reports at the time a loss occurs, there will be a penalty applied to the payable amount. If no reports were submitted, there will be a 10% penalty applied to the value of the loss. If reports were previously submitted but are currently overdue, valuation will be based upon the most recent records submitted.
  - When the reported amounts are more than the limit of insurance, the policy limit is still the most that will be paid for the loss. Premium calculations will be based on the reported value and not the limit of insurance.
  - If the amount reported ends up being less than the value of the covered property at the time of loss, loss payment will be subject to a penalty. This penalty is calculated by determining the percentage of the reported value in relation to the actual value of the property. That percentage will be applied to the loss payment. This is similar to the coinsurance condition present in other policies.

- Policies will be re-rated annually at the policy anniversary date. Reports needed to re-rate the policy must be provided to the insurance company within 30 days of the anniversary date.
- When the policy is canceled, the policyholder still must submit total value reports covering the period up to and including the cancellation date.

NON-FILED INLAND MARINE FORMS

Non-filed commercial inland marine forms are not subject to state filing rules because of the many variables that make the risks insured difficult to quantify. They are not standardized because of the vast array of risks they can be used to cover. There are no common policy provisions or conditions for this class of insurance. Only a few forms will be addressed here, but the available forms are as follows:

- Animal mortality
- Annual transit
- Bailees customers
- Boat dealers
- Builders risk
- Computer systems
- Contractors equipment
- Difference in conditions
- Drone coverage
- Exhibition
- Commercial fine art
- Fine art dealers and galleries
- Fine art museums
- Furriers block
- Furriers customers
- Installation
- Installment sales
- Jewelers block
- Machinery and equipment
- Marine supplies dealers
- Miscellaneous articles
- Motor truck cargo carriers
- Motor truck cargo owners
- Parcel post
- Patterns and dies
- Processors
- Radio and television towers and equipment
- Railroad rolling stock
- Riggers liability
- Salespersons samples
- Scientific and medical diagnostic equipment
- Signs
- Tank storage
- Trip transit

- Warehouse operators legal
- Wireless communications equipment

DOMESTIC TRANSIT FORMS

The **parcel post form** provides coverage similar to the filed mail coverage form but includes coverage for items sent via unregistered mail or parcel post. Coverage is on an open perils basis and requires the insured to keep records of the items shipped.

The **annual transit form** can be used to provide open peril coverage for goods as they are being transported. This coverage is available to both the shipper and receiver, and it applies to all shipments made over a one-year period. The limit of insurance is applied separately based on the method of transport used. These methods are contract carrier, non-owned vehicles, owned vehicles, messengers, railroad, and air carrier. There are also options to cover property at the named insured's premises, property located at a single unlisted location, or all property damaged in a single occurrence regardless of location. The last option is used to cover catastrophes and other wide-scale events that can result in extensive damage. There is an extensive list of non-covered items. Such items would typically be insured by another coverage form or under a specific transit policy. These exclusions include:

- Money, securities, and other financial instruments
- Jewelry
- Furs and fur garments
- Collectible coins and stamps
- Vehicles used to transport covered property
- Works of art
- Live animals
- Property the insured handles as a contract or common carrier
- Property sent through US Mail
- Jewelry, precious metals, watches, bullion, and precious and semiprecious gems
- Contraband
- Property transported by water, except when incidental to land transport

The **trip transit form** provides nearly the same coverage as the annual transit form, but only covers a single shipment. It is available for shipments through contract carriers and specified non-contract carriers, including air carriers, railroads, and messengers. Shipments in which a vehicle owned by an insured is used are also eligible for this coverage.

The **motor truck cargo carriers form** provides liability coverage for carriers who are in the business of transporting the property of others. This form protects the carrier against damage sustained by property it has been hired to transport. Services must be provided under a contract, tariff, bill of lading, or other shipping agreement for coverage to apply. Property must be in the insured's care, custody, or control at the time of loss. The policy will not provide coverage in certain situations, including damage caused by improper stowage or packing, rough handling, or refrigeration equipment failure.

The **motor truck cargo owners policy** provides coverage for direct damage to property owned by and transported by the insured. For property to be covered, it must be indicated on the policy declarations. Most of the property exclusions under this policy are for items that should be covered under another property floater form.

BAILEE'S CUSTOMER COVERAGE FORM

Bailee customer policies are a subcategory of the commercial property floater risk category and include only non-filed classes of inland marine insurance forms. The **bailee's customer policy** provides liability coverage for bailees. When a bailee is in possession of a customer's property, and that property is damaged or destroyed by a covered peril, the policy reimburses the bailee so he or she may repay his or her customer. Different versions of the bailee's customer policy are available for different types of businesses. One such type is the **cleaners, dyers, and laundries policy**, which provides **misidentification of property coverage,** also referred to as **confusion of goods coverage.** This coverage applies when the bailee (in this case, the owner of the laundry service) suffers damage from a loss and is subsequently unable to differentiate between the garments of individual customers that are under his or her care.

CONTRACTOR'S EQUIPMENT COVERAGE FORM

The **contractor's equipment floater** is a non-filed form under the equipment floater subcategory of inland marine insurance. It provides named or open peril coverage for any tools, machinery, and equipment that are owned by the insured or in his or her care. Coverage only applies when the property is being stored temporarily, being used on the job site, or being transited between locations. Coverage is provided on an open peril or a named peril basis and, depending on policy conditions, can apply to property that is on the premises, off the premises, or being transported. The **installation policy** covers property such as machinery, equipment, supplies, and building materials as they are in the process of being built, tested, installed, repaired, or renovated. Coverage only applies if the property is being used or transported in conjunction with the above tasks. Owners, sellers, and contractors can all obtain installation policies. The **electronic data processing equipment floater** covers computer hardware, software, servers, media, and data on an open peril basis. The property can be owned by the insured or in his or her care and can be in transit. Standard coverages include business interruption and extra expenses, while optional coverages include breakdown, which protects against mechanical breakdown, temperature fluctuations, and electrical damage.

JEWELERS BLOCK COVERAGE FORM

The filed version of the jewelers block coverage form is limited to smaller jewelers and many entities in the jewelry business do not meet the eligibility requirements for the filed form. For these businesses, the **non-filed jewelers block coverage form** is best suited to meet their coverage needs. Despite their different uses, the two jewelers block forms supply similar coverage and have similar conditions, provisions, and exclusions.

FURRIERS BLOCK COVERAGE FORM

The **furriers block coverage form** is used for businesses who deal in furs, fur garments, and clothing trimmed with fur. It is necessary for such businesses to carry this coverage because the protection offered under other commercial property policies is limited for these items. It functions similarly to jewelers block coverage in that it not only covers products while they are being moved from one location to another, but also while they are on the insured premises. It contains the option for show window coverages but does not cover items at public or government-sponsored trade shows or exhibitions.

DIFFERENCE IN CONDITIONS COVERAGE FORM

The **difference in conditions coverage form (DIC)** is a unique form that is used to provide supplemental coverage in relation to more traditional commercial property policies. The **conditions** referred to in the form name means coverages, so this form essentially provides coverage for losses to the extent that the coverage under the DIC and the coverage under the commercial property policy differ. For exposures that are covered by both the commercial property policy and the DIC, the DIC will cover any elements of the exposure that fall within the DIC coverage but are not covered by the commercial property policy. The coverage provided under the DIC form is not as restricted as in other policies. Some exposures that are usually excluded under commercial property policies, such as earthquakes, are covered by the DIC form. It can be used by insureds who want to increase coverage for losses that may not be covered sufficiently by other policies and fill gaps in coverage that may exist. It is used to cover buildings, structures, indoor and outdoor fixtures, completed additions, permanently installed equipment and machinery, and the personal property used to service and maintain the listed premises. It also covers business personal property both when it is being transported and when it is at the insured location. Personal property not owned by an insured is covered when it is in the insured's possession. It contains many of the special limits, exclusions, and coverage limitations seen in other commercial property coverage forms.

Ocean Marine Insurance

INTRODUCTION

Ocean marine insurance is the oldest type of insurance and was developed due to the risks inherent to transporting large amounts of cargo on a single ship. Ocean marine insurance is subject to the same NAIC nationwide definition of **marine** as inland marine insurance is. Ocean marine insurance is fairly similar to commercial inland marine insurance, but there are a few important differences. Inland marine insurance is primarily concerned with risks applicable to personal property while it is being transported over land. Ocean marine insurance offers protection for property, cargo, and ships while in transit over bodies of water, including seas, lakes, rivers, harbors, and oceans. Ocean marine insurance usually provides some level of liability coverage as well. While inland marine insurance typically offers open peril protection for personal property, ocean marine has both named and open peril options. In most cases, coverage for eligible property begins when the vessel departs the point of origination and ends once it has reached its intended destination.

TERMINOLOGY

Because there are many terms used in the maritime vernacular that are not used in other insurance areas, it is important to know some of the special language used.

All risks—Refers to policies in which any cause of direct loss is covered as long as it is not excluded by the policy; typical exclusions to all risks coverage are nuclear hazards, seizure and detention, strikes, riots, and war.

Assailing thieves—People other than a ship's crew or officers who commit theft by threat or physical force.

Barratry—Actions taken by the crew of a vessel, including the master, that are done to intentionally cause the owner financial loss; such acts must be perpetrated without the owner's knowledge.

Carrier—Any commercial entity that transports the property of others, usually in large quantity, in exchange for compensation.

Freight forwarder—A party who acts as a liaison between carriers and shippers; they organize the logistical details of moving cargo between its origin point and its destination. Freight forwarders work with all types of carriers, so their operations are not limited to ocean marine transport.

General average loss—Refers to when a loss is shared between involved parties, usually the shipper and the cargo owner(s), when action is taken to mitigate a loss and that mitigation is beneficial to all involved parties. This can apply to partial losses resulting from jettisoning or a similar act to preserve a vessel from catastrophic loss. It can also apply to situations in which an extremely high expense is incurred that benefits all parties, such as costs to free a stranded ship. These losses are usually split proportionally between the parties.

Implied warranties—Part of the ocean marine policy addressing conditions commonly accepted as necessary to ensure safety and compliance with public standards. Though not always written in

221

the policy, they are as valid as any other policy conditions. Failure to fulfill them can result in contract voidance. There are several implied warranties:

- **Seaworthiness**—This requires that the vessel be fit, properly loaded, and operated by a competent crew. Insurers will not cover losses if the ship is overloaded or stowing contraband.
- **Conditions of cargo**—This requires that cargo be sound, warranted, and packed correctly.
- **Legality**—This requires that the trip's enterprise be lawful.
- **No deviation in voyage**—This requires that the ship follow a predetermined route without destination changes or untoward delays.

Jettison—Refers to any situation in which cargo must be dropped from the vessel to prevent more extensive loss; for example, dropping heavy cargo into the sea to prevent a breached ship from sinking.

Particular average loss—Refers to situations in which one party assumes the responsibility of another party's property and must reimburse that other party if a loss occurs. This is usually used when there is a partial property loss in which the damage is not shared by every involved property owner. Most often, it is the shipper who takes on the liability for a particular average loss.

Perils of the sea—Any risks inherent to traveling by sea, sometimes referred to as **acts of God** because they involve circumstances that are largely outside the control of a ship's crew. What risks are included in this definition can vary depending on which policy form is used. These perils often include:

- Collision
- Capsizing and sinking
- Stranding
- Severe weather, including storms and tempests
- Fire and explosions
- Acts of piracy, including hijacking, attacks, and holding a ship or its crew for ransom
- Jettisoning
- Acts of assailing thieves

Pilferage—Ongoing theft of lower-value items from a shipment; these thefts are usually committed by employees or crew.

Inchmaree—Refers to a clause that expands ocean marine coverage to losses involving latent defects of equipment, boiler explosion, breakage of drive shafts, vessel management and navigation errors, and mechanical failures.

Shipper—The party that hires a carrier to transport cargo or property.

Shore perils—Causes of loss when vessels are ashore, or cargo is on land or being transported over land when it is incidental to the ocean marine travel plan. These perils include collapse or sinking of docks or wharves, fire, lightning, fire sprinkler leaks, hurricanes, tornadoes, floods, earthquakes, and accidents involving cars, trucks, or trains.

Stranding—When a ship or vessel runs aground accidentally and cannot be freed without assistance.

TYPES OF OCEAN MARINE INSURANCE

Ocean marine insurance includes three categories. Not all entities with ocean marine risks need all of these types of coverage. The coverages offered are:

- **Hull insurance**—An insurance policy that covers direct physical loss to a ship or vessel. It is most needed by entities who own and operate marine vessels, but it can also be appropriate for owners and operators of stationary floating property such as an oil rig or a docked riverboat casino. The **running down clause** provides limited liability insurance when the insured's vessel is legally liable for damaging another vessel.
- **Cargo insurance**—An insurance policy that covers losses to property that is being transported by ship or vessel. It may be purchased by the owner of the property being shipped or the carrier engaged to transport the property. Who is obligated to purchase cargo insurance depends on the terms of the shipping contract. When purchased by the carrier, it serves as **freight insurance** to cover the cargo in the carrier's care. This type of coverage is most applicable to importers, exporters, any owner of cargo that is shipped whether it be the shipper or receiver, and freight forwarders. It provides coverage on a trip or voyage basis for a specific shipment or an open cargo basis, which covers a specific period of time. The **warehouse to warehouse clause** extends coverage to protect the shipment as it stays at both its point of origin and its destination. It will also cover costs associated with storing and rerouting cargo when a covered loss results in the ship stopping at a place other than its intended destination.
- **Protection and indemnity (P&I) insurance**—Insurance that protects ship owners and operators from liability losses occurring in the course of maritime operations. Unlike most commercial liability coverage, this coverage may apply to employees and crew if they are not covered by any other type of occupational compensation act, such as the Merchant Marine Act of 1920 or the United States Longshore and Harbor Workers' Compensation Act.

COVERED PERILS

In most cases, ocean marine hull and cargo policies provide coverage on an all risks basis. Common exclusions include:

- For hull insurance:
  - Wear and tear
  - Damages caused by an insured's willful misconduct
  - Expected leaks
  - Loss of weight or volume
  - Losses caused by inherent vice of cargo
  - Losses due to insolvency or default of the carrier
  - Inadequate or defective packaging by the insured or at the insured's direction
  - Losses caused by the insured's lack of due diligence:
    - ❖ Bursting of boilers
    - ❖ Shaft breakage
    - ❖ Negligence of officers, pilots, or crew
    - ❖ Negligence of bailees, such as repairers and charterers
    - ❖ Barratry or mutiny
    - ❖ Latent defects in covered property
- For cargo insurance:
  - All perils excluded by hull insurance

223

- Breach of **free of capture and seizure warranty**—This includes any losses due to arrest, capture, requisition, detainment, confiscation, nationalization, or preemption, whether successful or attempted; damage from nuclear and non-nuclear weapons of war; encountering hostile operations or acts of war; and acts of rebellion, including civil war and revolution.
- Breach of **free of strikes, riots, and civil commotion warranty**—This applies to any damage or loss caused by terrorists, strikers in labor disputes, or rioters.
- Breach of **delay warranty**—This includes consequential losses resulting from delivery delays, regardless of whether they are caused by a covered peril.
- Breach of **nuclear/radioactive contamination exclusion warranty**—This applies to damage caused by any nuclear hazard or release of radioactive substances, even those caused by fire.

Ocean marine P&I coverage is usually on a named peril basis, given the extensive liability risks inherent to water transport operations. Covered losses include:

- Injury or illness, including those resulting in death, sustained by any person except employees subject to a workers' compensation law or other similar law; injuries to seamen are covered, and other employees can be covered by endorsement
- Collision damage to other vessels or property—This is excluded because these losses fall under the hull insurance coverage
- Non-collision damage to other vessels or property if the insured has a contractual obligation to cover it
- Damage to any fixed or movable property caused by the insured vessel
- Repatriation costs that are required by law
- Damage to cargo, unless it is of a type excluded by the policy
- Removal and disposal of debris resulting from an obstruction or wreck
- Fines and penalties related to immigration and customs
- Mutiny and other misconduct—This also covers expenses to defend the insured against meritless allegation made by officers and crew, as well as any expenses pursuing criminal prosecution of such parties
- Quarantine expenses, except when the insured had knowledge of disease at a location but directed the vessel to go there anyway
- Expenses incurred while diverging from the intended route to take an ill or injured seaman ashore
- The insured's portion of general average cargo losses
- Costs incurred by the insured with the insurance company's permission
- Defense and legal expenses related to a covered claim

Workers' Compensation and Employer's Liability Insurance

INTRODUCTION AND GENERAL CONCEPTS

Workers' compensation insurance is used by employers to protect themselves against losses involving workplace injuries. It is mandatory in most states for businesses that employ more than a certain number of workers. These states are called **compulsory states**. In **elective states**, compliance with workers' compensation laws is optional. Employers who decide not to abide by these laws sacrifice certain incentives, such as common law defense and caps on their liability exposures in the event of a worker injury. For certain types of employers, workers' compensation is federally mandated and thus applies regardless of the state in which the worker lives. Workers' compensation laws only cover **compensable injuries**, which are injuries that arise out of employment or in the course of employment. In some states, workers' compensation is the **exclusive remedy** for someone injured while working, meaning that the state law does not allow a worker to pursue a liability claim against his or her employer at all. Some states will only allow a worker to make a liability claim or a workers' compensation claim, but not both.

Employer's liability insurance protects a business against allegations of negligence or liability made by employees. The biggest advantage of having employer's liability coverage is that it will cover defense and legal costs related to any covered claims made. Litigation involving employees can be very expensive and time-consuming, and the employer's liability policy allows an employer to transfer most of that risk to the insurance company.

Workers' compensation and employer's liability coverages are typically purchased under one policy from a private insurance company. There are four states that handle workers' compensation under a **monopolistic system:** Ohio, Wyoming, North Dakota, and Washington. In a monopolistic state, workers' compensation policies may only be purchased through the state. The claims are handled by the applicable state agency. Workers' compensation policies in monopolistic jurisdictions do not include employer's liability coverage, so it must be obtained separately if an employer wants to carry that coverage. This section will focus on policies purchased from private insurance companies, since this is how the vast majority of employers obtain their coverage.

There are four levels of disability used for workers' compensation losses:

- **Permanent total disability**—These disabilities are those that make the injured party completely unable to work and persist for the remainder of the worker's lifetime.
- **Permanent partial disability**—These disabilities leave the injured party with a limited ability to work, and the limitations are expected to be permanent.
- **Temporary total disability**—These disabilities render the injured party entirely unable to work for a period of time but are not expected to persist for the remainder of the worker's life. The worker should recover completely over time.
- **Temporary partial disability**—These disabilities temporarily impair the injured party's ability to work at full capacity, but he or she is still able to perform some work activities. The worker is expected to resume full work duties once fully recovered.

These are generalized descriptions of these terms. The definitions of "total" and "partial" depend on whether the state abides by the industrial disability standard or the medical disability standard. Under the industrial disability standard, a total disability means the worker no longer has any

225

ability to work, while a partial disability means the worker can still do some sort of work. Under the medical disability standard, a total disability means the worker has lost all physical function, while a partial disability means the worker retains partial physical function. If an injury results in partial disability, a worker can no longer perform their current job, but may be able to perform another, lower-paying job. When this occurs, workers' compensation would reimburse the income difference between their old job and their new job. If the injury results in total disability, a worker can no longer perform any job, and workers' compensation would reimburse their entire income. The income reimbursement for permanent disability will last until the age at which the worker is expected to retire.

INFORMATION PAGE

The workers' compensation and employer's liability (WC & EL) policy consists of seven sections plus an **information page**. The information page is similar to the policy declarations on other types of insurance policies. The information page includes the following:

- **Item 1**—Name and address of the employer/insured and type of business, such as partnership, joint venture, corporation, LLC, or sole proprietorship.
- **Item 2**—The policy term, which starts at 12:01 a.m. standard time at the policy address.
- **Item 3**—This is broken down into four sections:
  - **Section A—workers' compensation insurance**—A list of states in which the WC coverage will apply; this list should include all of the states where the employer has a permanent location and where he or she regularly has employees working on his or her behalf.
  - **Section B—employer's liability insurance**—Indicates the EL coverage limits. These are usually shown as a split limit; for example, $100,000/$500,000/$100,000 means $100,000 per accident for bodily injuries, $100,000 per employee for occupational disease, and a $500,000 annual aggregate limit for occupational disease claims. These are the standard EL limit amounts, but higher limits may be purchased.
  - **Section C—other states insurance**—A list of any additional states in which the insured may have exposure as an employer.
  - **Section D—endorsements and schedules**
- **Item 4**—Contains the information needed for premium calculations, including classifications and codes, estimated payrolls, premium bases, estimated annual premium, and rates.

GENERAL SECTION

The **general section** of the WC & EL policy includes policy definitions and conditions. It begins with a preamble indicating that payment of the premium will guarantee the provision of insurance in accordance with all the terms of the policy. This section continues by stating that the policy provided is complete and includes any applicable endorsements or schedules indicated on the information page. The policy is effective as of the date listed on the information page. Finally, this portion of the policy asserts that no terms of the policy may be waived or changed unless an endorsement doing so is issued by the insurance company.

The next part of the general section describes who is considered an insured under the policy. It states that a person or entity is insured when named on the information page. If the employer is a partnership, the individual partners are only insured in their capacity as employers of the partnership's employees. The general section goes on to indicate that workers' compensation law as referenced in the policy pertains to the **workers' compensation law and occupational disease law** within each jurisdiction named on the information page. Any amendments to such legislation that are in effect during the policy period are applicable. The standard policy does not include any federal workers' compensation law, any federal occupational disease law, or any law that provides non-occupational disability benefits.

The last part of the general section states that coverage applies for the workplaces listed on the information page. For any additional states listed under "Part Three—other states insurance," the policy will cover all insured workplaces so long as there is no other applicable insurance available and the location is not self-insured.

PART ONE—WORKERS' COMPENSATION INSURANCE

Part one of the WC & EL policy is dedicated to the workers' compensation coverage provided by the policy. It begins by stating that workers' compensation insurance applies only to bodily injury, including death caused by accident or disease. Any accidental bodily injury must occur during the policy period to be eligible under the WC coverage. Bodily injury by disease is any disease caused or exacerbated by the conditions of employment. In order for the workers' compensation policy to apply, the last day of the last exposure to the conditions that caused or exacerbated the disease must be within the stated policy period. The insurance company promises to promptly pay the benefits required by the applicable workers' compensation law. WC insurance generally pays medical expenses, income benefits, death benefits, and rehabilitation expenses. There are no limits for workers' compensation losses stated in the policy. Any limitation is determined by the applicable state law.

Next, the policy states that the insurer will defend, at its own expense, any claim or proceeding related to a covered loss. When providing coverage or defense, the insurance company is entitled to investigate, defend, and settle any claim as it sees fit. There are additional costs the insurance company will pay, including:

- Reasonable expenses incurred by the policyholder at the request of the insurer related to a claim; this does not include loss of earnings incurred during an investigation
- Premiums for bonds that are within the limit of insurance; covered items are bonds to release attachments and appeal bonds
- Court costs levied against the insured related to a covered loss
- Interest accrued on judgments up to the date the insurance company offers to pay the judgment due
- All costs the insurance company sustains in relation to a covered suit, action, or claim

When there is more than one insurer that may provide coverage for a single loss, the insurance company will not pay more than its equal share of the benefits and costs covered by other insurance or under a self-insurance arrangement. Payments will be made by each involved carrier or insurer until the limits are exhausted.

The next section outlines damages and costs the insurance will not pay. The employer is typically responsible for making payments for these amounts. The insurance company will not pay for losses arising from serious and willful misconduct on the part of the employer, conscious employment of an individual in violation of law, the employer's failure to comply with a health or safety law or regulation, or discrimination against any employee in violation of workers' compensation law. If the insurance company makes any payments in excess of the regularly provided benefits, the employer must reimburse the insurance company promptly.

The policy next addresses the insured's rights to recover from others. This section serves as a **subrogation clause**. When benefits are paid under the policy, the insurance company assumes the named insured's rights to recover funds from any third party liable for the injury. The employer is responsible for assisting the insurance company in protecting those rights and enforcing them. This prevents the injured employee from collecting from both the insurance company and the negligent third party.

The final section outlines six important statutory provisions. These provisions only apply when required by the applicable state law. They are all included so the policy can account for most conditions without needing to write a separate policy for every state in which they write coverage and so that policies do not have to be revised every time a regulation or law changes. These provisions are as follows:

1. The insurance company is considered to have **notice of an injury** when the employer has notice. The notice of an injury given to the employer by the worker has the same legal effect as notice given to the insurer.
2. The insurance company will not be relieved of its duties under the policy even if the employer or the employer's estate **goes bankrupt** or **becomes insolvent**.
3. The insurance company agrees to be **directly and primarily liable** to anyone entitled to benefits payable by the insurance policy. This obligation may be enforced by the rightful recipient of benefits, as well as by any agency authorized by law. This enforcement may be leveled against the insurance company alone, or against both the insurance company and the employer.
4. Any workers' compensation law having **jurisdiction** over the employer also has jurisdiction over the insurance company. The insurance company agrees to be bound by any rulings made against the employer under workers' compensation law.
5. The insurance policy will abide by applicable **workers' compensation law** with respect to benefits payable by the insurance, special taxes, payments into security or other special funds, and assessments payable under workers' compensation law. The insurance company is obligated to pay amounts incurred for these items.
6. Any terms of the insurance policy that conflict with workers' compensation law will be changed automatically to conform to that law.

PART TWO—EMPLOYER'S LIABILITY

Part two of the WC & EL policy outlines the employer's liability coverage provided by the policy. Employers' liability insurance applies to any bodily injury, including death, caused by accident or disease. In order to be covered by the insurance, the bodily injury or disease must arise out of and in the course of the injured party's employment by the employer. If the injury or disease occurs in a state not listed under Item 3 on the information page, then the work the employee performs must be necessary or incidental to the employer's business in one of the states named on the information page. Any bodily injury by accident must occur during the policy period, and disease must be either caused or exacerbated by the conditions of employment. For disease losses to be covered, the employee's last day of exposure to the conditions causing or aggravating the disease must occur during the policy period. Because the effects of disease can be cumulative, only the EL policy effective on that date will cover the loss. Finally, the policy states that any suit or legal action against the employer must be brought in the United States, its possessions, or Canada.

This coverage applies when the insured is liable as an employer under tort or common law to pay damages that are covered under the policy. Not all states allow an employee to recover liability damages from an employer in relation to a loss that falls under workers' compensation, so the state must allow this type of action for coverage to apply under the EL coverage part. The only payable damages are those that are due to the following:

- **Third-party-over claims**—When an injured employee pursues a claim against a third party who, in turn, pursues payment from the insured.
- **Dual capacity claims**—When the injured employee makes a claim for damages against the insured for liability unrelated to the insured's capacity as an employer.
- If a claim is made under either of these two circumstances, certain close relatives of the injured employee may pursue consequential claims against the insured for loss of care and services or consequential bodily injury.

In addition to the above damages, the EL policy will pay the same supplemental expenses as Part 1 covers. It is also subject to the same other insurance and subrogation provisions as the workers' compensation coverage. There is an additional condition that addresses legal action taken against the insurance company. The insurer can only be directly named in a legal filing if the named insured has fully complied with all policy terms and conditions and there has been a final judgment or settlement that determines the amount the insured is liable for.

Employer's liability coverage is subject to the following exclusions:

- When the injured employee is hired in violation of the law; for this exclusion to apply, the injured employee and the named insured—including any executive officers—must have knowingly acted illegally
- Exemplary or punitive damages related to illegally hiring the injured worker

Fines or penalties imposed due to violation of state or federal law

- Liability assumed as part of a contract
- Injury to the master or crew of a seafaring vessel
- Claims falling within the scope of employment practices liability, including discrimination, coercion, defamation, harassment, wrongful termination, or other employment practices usually prohibited by law
- Injuries outside the coverage territory, unless the worker is a US or Canadian citizen who was only temporarily outside the area
- Injuries that the insured intentionally causes or exacerbates
- Injuries already subject to federal workers' compensation or similar laws, including:
  o The United States Longshore and Harbor Workers' Compensation Act
  o The Defense Base Act
  o The Outer Continental Shelf Lands Act
  o The Nonappropriated Fund Instrumentalities Act
  o The Federal Coal Mine Health and Safety Act
  o The Migrant and Seasonal Agricultural Worker Protection Act
  o The Federal Employers' Liability Act
- Obligations that the insured carries under workers' compensation laws, disability laws, and other applicable laws

PART THREE—OTHER STATES INSURANCE

Part three outlines the coverage for losses that occur in a state listed under Item 3, Section C on the information page. If there are no states listed under that section, there is no coverage under Part 3. This provision indicates that the workers' compensation insurance will apply to any work that begins in one of the named states after the effective date of the policy. Coverage will be afforded as if the state was listed under Item 1, Section A, as long as the employer is not self-insured or covered by another policy. If the law in that state does not allow the insurance company to compensate the injured worker directly for payable benefits, it will issue the payment to the employer instead. If the employer has active operations in any of the other states listed on the information page on the date the WC policy goes into effect, coverage will only be provided for the first 30 days of the policy period. The named insured must report such operations to the insurance company during that 30-day period. If this is not done, there is no coverage for losses that happen after the 30-day mark.

PART FOUR—YOUR DUTIES IF INJURY OCCURS

Part four of the workers' compensation and employers' liability insurance policy explains the duties of the insured employer when an employee is injured. First, the employer must provide immediate medical attention, or any other services that are mandated by the applicable WC law. The employer is then responsible for notifying the insurance company immediately when an injury that may be covered by the policy occurs. The notification should include names and addresses of any injured persons and any witnesses. The employer should also provide the insurer with any notices, demands, or documents received in relation to the injury, claim, suit, or proceeding. The employer should assist the insurance company in the investigation or defense of any claim or suit. The employer should refrain from any actions that may interfere with the insurance company's right to recover from others. Finally, the employer should not voluntarily make payments, incur expenses, or assume obligations with the expectation of reimbursement from the insurance company.

PART FIVE—PREMIUM

Part five of the WC & EL policy describes the procedures and methods used to calculate the premium amount for the policy. It states which manuals are used in rating and how business classifications are applied to rate computations. The named insured is required to pay the premium even if the applicable workers' compensation law is rendered partially or entirely invalid. If a policy is canceled, the final premium will be calculated on a pro rata basis, meaning that the insurance company will determine how much of the policy period remained at the time of cancellation and determine what percentage that is of the length of the policy period. That will then be applied to the final premium calculation for the entire policy period. If the cancellation is initiated by the insurer, the named insured will be refunded for the full amount of the deposit premium that was not applied to the final premium. If the named insured cancels the policy, the refund will be subject to a short-rate surcharge penalty because of the early cancellation. The insured is also responsible for keeping records that the insurance company needs to make premium calculations. Finally, the insurance company is entitled to audit any of the insured's records that relate to the policy when determining the premium.

PART SIX—CONDITIONS

Part six of the workers' compensation and employers' liability insurance policy outlines the conditions applicable to the policy as a whole. The conditions are as follows:

- **Inspection**—The insurance company has the right, but no obligation, to inspect the employer's place of business at any time. These are not safety inspections per se, but rather investigations into the insurability of the workplace and the appropriate premium to be charged. The insurance company may provide a report related to this inspection and may recommend alterations in the workplace. These inspections are not intended to replace the responsibility of the employer to create a safe and healthy work environment. Inspections do not indicate that the workplace is safe or healthy, or that it conforms to codes, laws, regulations, or standards. The entitlements granted under this condition also extend to inspectors from insurance rate service organizations.
- **Long-term policy**—This asserts that if the policy period is longer than 1 year and 16 days, the provisions of the policy will be applied as if a new policy were being issued on each yearly anniversary during which the policy is in effect.
- **Transfer of your rights and duties**—The employer's rights or duties under the policy may not be transferred to any other party without the written consent of the insurance company. If the named insured dies, the insurance company must be given notice within 30 days, or else the legal representative of the named insured will not be covered after the 30 days expire.
- **Cancellation**—If the insurance company elects to cancel the policy, it must give at least 10 days prior notice to the named insured. If the named insured cancels the policy, he or she must notify the insurer prior to the cancellation effective date, but there is not a specific time in which this must be done. Should any portion of the cancellation provision be in conflict with the laws of the jurisdiction, the law will take precedence over the policy.
- **Sole representative**—This states that the insured named first on the information page is treated as the representative for all other insureds with regard to policy changes, premium refunds, and cancellation notices.

EMPLOYMENT PRACTICES LIABILITY INSURANCE

Employment practices liability insurance (EPLI), sometimes called **employment-related practices liability**, provides liability insurance for employers but is quite different from the employer's liability coverage in terms of the risks it covers. The risks covered by EPLI are almost always excluded from employer's liability coverage. EPLI can be obtained as a standalone policy or as part of a commercial package policy, or it can be added to other commercial liability policies by endorsement. Standalone policies give the insured the choice between a **duty to defend** policy and a **no duty to defend** policy. "Duty to defend" policies entitle the insurance company to select defense counsel and control the handling of the claim or lawsuit. "No duty to defend" policies do not require the insurance company to provide a defense for the insured. These are mostly used by very large companies who have counsel on staff to handle legal matters. The exposures that fall under the EPLI are usually related to how the employer hires, dismisses, or behaves toward employees. Covered exposures may include discrimination, wrongful termination, retaliation, defamation, obstruction of career advancement, and sexual harassment. It may also cover circumstances in which one employee has behaved inappropriately toward a fellow employee. These policies usually exclude actions that are in direct violation of applicable laws. They also exclude liabilities that are best covered by a different type of policy.

EPLI is most frequently used to cover litigation and defense costs incurred when an employee sues an insured for infractions that are covered by the policy. Lawsuits can be brought by current and former employees, so the costs associated with employment practices liability claims can be extensive, regardless of whether the employer actually engaged in any wrongdoing. These policies can be written to include defense costs within the policy limit or to pay for such expenses on top of the policy limit. Policies that pay defense costs in addition to the limit carry higher premiums, so most insureds opt for the defense costs to be included in the liability limits. If a claim is found to have merit and qualify for coverage, the EPLI policy will also cover settlements and judgments. One benefit of standalone EPLI policies is that the policy limits are dedicated only to claims that fall within the coverage of the policy. When this coverage is added to another policy by endorsement, there is a risk of the limits being eroded by non-EPLI claims since there is no separate liability limit for EPLI claims when the coverage is added to another type of policy.

Surety and Fidelity Bonds

INTRODUCTION

Bonds are a risk management tool used to mitigate the risk of one party when there is a contract with another party. They are usually purchased from an insurance company to ensure the contractual obligations between two or more entities are met. Essentially, bonds serve to add the insurance company as a third party to the contract involved, especially when one party is at risk of financial loss when the other party does not execute on the terms of the contract. The parties to a bond are:

- **Principal or obligor**—This is the party who purchases the bond. The bond is purchased to ensure that a specific contractual obligation of the principal is fulfilled. Principals usually purchase bonds as a condition of the applicable contract.
- **Obligee**—This is the party who carries the risk of financial loss if the principal fails to execute the requirements of the contract.
- **Surety or guarantor**—The insurance company or other entity from whom the bond is purchased. Issuance of a bond by the surety indicates that they are vouching for the principal's willingness and ability to fulfill the terms of the contract. If the principal does not satisfy the contractual obligations, the surety promises to compensate the obligee for their loss.

SURETY BONDS

A surety bond states that unless a principal performs an action outlined in a contract, the surety will make payment to the obligee to indemnify them for the loss they incurred. Surety bonds are included as a standard part of many common business agreements. There are different types of surety bonds available, and which type is used depends on the needs of the parties involved.

The following bonds are most used when the contract involves a building project or other construction work. In these cases, the principal is the contractor, and the obligee is the client.

- **Performance bond**—This bond guarantees that the contractor will perform the work according to the specifications outlined in the contract or otherwise provided to him or her by the client.
- **Bid bond**—This bond provides assurance that the bidding contractor will obtain a performance bond and do the required work if he or she is awarded a contract.
- **Labor and material payment bond**—This bond guarantees that the contractor will pay for labor and material costs as they are incurred.
- **Maintenance bond**—Also called a **warranty bond**, this is used to guarantee the quality of the principal's work. This type of bond is in force for a specified time frame, and the cost of any workmanship issues or defects discovered during that time will be paid by the principal.
- **Supply bond**—This bond assures that the contractor will provide all of the required supplies, products, and equipment for the project. A supply bond may also require the contractor to install specific equipment.

There are also bonds used in other areas, such as government operations, financial services, and legal practice. These bonds include:

- **Judicial bond**—Otherwise known as a **court bond**, this bond is used to guarantee that the principal will comply with a court order or surrender a specified amount of money if he or she does not comply. Judicial bonds can be categorized into **fiduciary** and **litigation**.
- **Fiduciary bond**—These bonds are obtained by the guardians, administrators, or trustees appointed to act on the behalf of another party, usually due to either death or incapacity. They guarantee proper management of the property belonging to that other party. They are sometimes called **probate bonds**.
- **Litigation bond**—This is a general term used to describe bonds that are used when a principal is involved in litigation. Generally, litigation bonds are used to ensure that some type of obligation required of the principal is met. Examples of litigation bonds include:
  - ○ **Appeal bond**—This bond is used when a trial has been completed and a judgment is entered against the principal. To file an appeal of the judgment, the principal will need to deposit the amount of the judgment with the court to ensure that the judgment is paid if the appeal should fail.
  - ○ **Injunction bond**—This bond is used by a principal named as a defendant in a litigation action. An injunction is a judicial filing in which one party asks the judge to order another party to stop doing a particular action, or to order that an action be performed. The injunction bond is purchased to protect the principal from the financial loss incurred by complying with an injunction in the event the litigation is dismissed by the court.
- **License and permit bond**—These bonds involve licenses issued by government agencies. These are usually required to ensure compliance with laws, regulations, and the specifications of the license or permit being issued.

FIDELITY BONDS

Fidelity bonds are utilized by employers at risk for fraud, theft, or other dishonest acts committed by employees. They are important in some industries because the criminal or illegal acts of employees can result in significant fines and penalties. Fidelity bonds are divided into two types:

- **First-party**—Used when the employee is directly employed by a company and the company needs protection for any wrongful acts an employee may perform
- **Third-party**—Used when a business needs protection from wrongful acts committed by contract workers

Like surety bonds, there are several types of fidelity bonds that can be used:

- **Business services bond**—This bond protects the property of clients when an employee of the principal goes to the client's premises. It is often used when the business involves working at the site of a client, as with janitorial work and security personnel.
- **Employee dishonesty bond**—This bond is used to protect a business from employee misuse of sensitive information, such as committing identity theft or fraudulently using a customer's credit card. There are several different categories of employee dishonesty bonds that may be used:
  - ○ **Name schedule bond**—This outlines a certain amount of coverage for every employee scheduled on the policy. Each employee may have a different coverage amount.

- o **Position schedule bond**—This is similar to the name schedule bond, but rather than putting employees by name, it lists specific positions held within the company. A coverage amount is then assigned to each position listed. When a new employee is hired, he or she will immediately receive the coverage inherent to his or her position.
- o **Blanket position bond**—This bond provides protection against dishonest acts committed by employees. Coverage is provided by position rather than by employee. The same coverage limit applies to all positions regardless of how many employees hold that position.
- o **Commercial blanket bond**—This will reimburse losses the insured may incur when employees commit dishonest acts. The limit of liability applies on a per occurrence basis, regardless of the number of employees involved in that occurrence. No specific employees or positions are named in the policy.

Other Types of Insurance

The National Flood Insurance Program (NFIP)

Flood insurance covers virtually any walled or roofed building that is fixed to a permanent, above-ground location. The standards for the National Flood Insurance Program were established by the Federal Emergency Management Agency (FEMA); however, rate, eligibility, and coverage parameters are established by the Federal Insurance and Mitigation Administration. Under the NFIP, communities receive two types of flood insurance programs—emergency and regular. **Emergency coverage** applies as soon as the community submits the application and provides limited coverage for buildings and their contents on a subsidized basis. **Regular coverage** applies after the NFIP receives the application and determines rates for the community. The standard NFIP policy covers residential homes. There are also policies that provide coverage to commercial properties and condominium associations.

ELIGIBILITY, RATING, AND COVERAGE

In order to be **eligible** for flood insurance under the NFIP, the property must be located in a **participating community**. Any community that meets the requirements established by FEMA may be eligible. Qualifying communities will receive a **flood insurance rate map**. The zones outlined in the maps each fall into one of two categories: low- to moderate-risk areas and high-risk areas. For those located in a high-risk zone, flood insurance is required if the property carries a federally backed mortgage. Premiums are determined by the building's age, the risk of flooding, proximity to a flood source, frequency of past floods, elevation, and rebuilding costs.

The NFIP defines a **flood** as an excess of water on land that is normally dry. To be considered a **flood event**, there must be a significant accumulation of water over two or more properties or over at least two acres of normally dry land. Floods include those caused by overflow of inland or tidal waters, rapid accumulation or runoff of surface water, mudslides and mudflows, and the collapse of land along a shore. The standard flood insurance policy includes building and contents coverages for residential homes and commercial buildings. Coverage for condominium associations does not cover contents or personal property, even property that is in common spaces. Individual unit-owners may opt to purchase separate flood insurance to protect their personal property. The commercial NFIP policy does not provide coverage for business income loss or extra expenses. There is no coverage for property that extends over water. When personal property is moved to a different location to protect it from flood damage, it is covered for a maximum of 45 days at the new location. **Debris removal** is covered as long as the policy limit is large enough to cover both the expense amount and the direct loss amount.

Coverage for a building's basement and any personal property stored in a basement is limited to the types of property specified in the NFIP policy forms. A **basement** is defined as any area of a building with a floor that is beneath ground level on all sides, including sunken or partially sunken rooms. The NFIP will only cover the following property when it is installed in its functional location and connected to a power source, when needed for the property to operate.

- Under **Coverage A—building property**:
  - Central air conditioning units
  - Drywall that is nailed to the framing
  - Water tanks and cisterns, including the water contained within them
  - Electrical boxes

- ○ Electrical switches and outlets
- ○ Elevators, dumbwaiters, and related equipment, except for equipment installed below grade after September 30, 1987
- ○ Fuel tanks and fuel
- ○ Furnaces and heat pumps
- ○ Water heaters
- ○ Fireproof insulation
- ○ Solar energy system tanks or pumps
- ○ Attached stairways and staircases
- ○ Sump pumps
- ○ Parts integral to the plumbing system, including water filters, faucets, water softeners, and water softening chemicals
- ○ Well water pumps and tanks
- ○ Utility connections required for any covered item
- ○ Building support structures
- Under **Coverage B—personal property**:
  - ○ Portable or window air conditioners
  - ○ Clothes washers and dryers
  - ○ Freezers, except walk-in freezers, and food within them

EXCLUSIONS, LIMITS, AND DEDUCTIBLE

The NFIP does not cover the following types of property:

- Personal property not located within a building
- Any buildings constructed or substantially improved after September 30, 1987, that are over, in, or on water, including any personal property contained in such a building
- Open structures such as boathouses
- RVs, except for certain travel trailers
- Self-propelled vehicles or machines, except those not registered for use on public roads and used either to assist handicapped persons or service the location listed on the policy
- Land, including lawns, trees, plants, shrubs, and growing crops
- Animals
- Accounts, manuscripts, deeds, valuable papers, and most types of currency or financial instruments
- Underground equipment such as septic systems, septic tanks, and wells
- Decks, driveways, walkways, patios, and other similar surfaces outside the exterior walls of the insured building
- Fuel tanks, containers, and related equipment
- Hot tubs and spas, except for bathroom fixtures
- Swimming pools and any related equipment
- Aircraft, watercraft, and any related equipment or furnishings
- Fences, retaining walls, wharves, seawalls, bridges, docks, and piers

The NFIP offers different **limits** for various situations. The maximum limits for buildings under the emergency program are $35,000 for single-family homes and $100,000 for other residential and nonresidential buildings. With regard to the contents of a building, the maximum limits for the emergency program are $10,000 for residential buildings and $100,000 for nonresidential buildings. The standard deductible for emergency coverage is $1,000. For the regular program, the combined maximum limits for buildings are $250,000 for residential buildings and $500,000 for nonresidential buildings. As for contents, the maximum limits in the regular program are $100,000 for residential buildings and $500,000 for nonresidential buildings. The standard deductible for regular coverage is $500. The deductible applies to both the building and the contents. Most policies include **increased cost of compliance** coverage, which pays for expenses related to elevating, relocating, or demolishing buildings to ensure compliance with code or to make the new building less susceptible to flooding in the future. Coverage is provided for up to $30,000 in addition to the building policy limit.

CLAIMS

As with any other type of claim, a flood loss should be reported to the insurance company or agent as soon as reasonably possible. The insured may ask for an advance payment if up-front costs need to be paid. If the location has experienced a flood in the past, the insurance company will most likely request receipts showing that the prior damages were repaired. The insured should move undamaged property to a safe location, if possible, to avoid damage. If damaged property must be thrown away for safety reasons, the policyholder will need to take photographs of it prior to disposal. NFIP policies reimburse losses based on ACV.

Personal Watercraft Insurance

When an insured owns or frequently operates boats or other watercraft, it is important for them to have appropriate boat and watercraft insurance. There is only limited watercraft liability coverage available under personal liability coverage provided in dwelling and homeowners policies. There are numerous restrictions on what those policies will cover, so an insured should consider a separate watercraft policy to ensure that his or her coverage needs are met.

SELECTED DEFINITIONS

It is important to understand how the insurer defines certain items within a watercraft policy. Such items include:

- **Covered watercraft**—Watercraft that the insured owns and that is scheduled on the declarations of the policy; it also pertains to watercraft the insured obtains during the policy period, but the insurance company must be notified of new watercraft within 14 days; watercraft leased or rented under contract for six months or more are deemed owned by the insured for the purposes of the policy
- **Non-owned watercraft**—Boats, boat trailers, and boat motors possessed by an insured that he or she does not own nor has regular access to
- **Outboard motor**—A motor that is attached to the exterior of a craft that propels it across water
- **Personal watercraft**—A recreational water vehicle powered by an inboard motor, designed to accommodate at least one rider, and propelled by a jet of water generated by the motor; passengers may be in standing, kneeling, or sitting position during use
- **Yacht**—This is any vessel or boat including its integral machinery and equipment, maintenance equipment, masts, sails, rigging, spars, and tackle; related smaller boats such as dinghies are included under the definition so long as they are under 16 feet long and have horsepower of 35 or less

TYPES OF PERSONAL BOAT AND WATERCRAFT INSURANCE

There are a few different coverage options an insured can choose from when it comes to insuring watercraft. What the insured needs is determined by the type of watercraft being insured and the nature of the insured's use of it. Coverage can be added by endorsement to other personal lines policies or purchased as a monoline policy. Watercraft coverage typically offers liability coverage, medical payments coverage, and property damage coverage, sometimes called hull coverage. The coverage purchased will be indicated on the policy declarations page. For the property damage portion of a watercraft policy, there are collision and comprehensive coverage options, and the insured can choose to have losses reimbursed at ACV or at an agreed value.

Watercraft liability endorsement—This is available to add to personal residential policies so that liability resulting from the ownership or use of watercraft is covered. The endorsement is intended to replace the limitations in the base policy so that watercraft that was otherwise excluded can be covered. It extends coverage to watercraft with one or more motors that output more than 25 total horsepower and to sailing vessels longer than 26 feet.

Boat insurance—This insurance is used to insure boats for personal use that the insured owns or has leased long term. Depending on the policy or coverage form used, there may or may not be a limitation on the length of the covered boat. It also extends coverage to trailers used with the covered boat. An unendorsed boat policy does not cover losses involving personal watercraft. Boat policies can be endorsed with **uninsured boater coverage,** also called **uninsured watercraft coverage**, which provides protection to an insured when he or she is in an accident with another watercraft that does not have insurance. This coverage only applies to bodily injury suffered by an insured.

Personal watercraft insurance—This can be added to a boat or other watercraft policy to fill the coverage gap created by the exclusions those policies have for personal watercraft. In most cases, this insurance only covers watercraft used for personal enjoyment. Examples of personal watercraft include jet skis and water scooters. Coverage does not apply when the craft is being used for transportation in exchange for a fee, being chartered out, or being used for racing contests.

Personal yacht insurance—Personal yachts are usually covered by standalone policies. These policies are used for watercraft that do not fall within the eligibility requirements for boat insurance. To be eligible, the covered yacht must only be used for pleasure. Yacht policies provide open peril coverage for inboard boats, large pleasure boats including houseboats, self-powered sailboats, and high-value smaller boats in good condition. Yacht policies can also be endorsed with uninsured watercraft coverage.

Aircraft Insurance

Aircraft insurance, often called **aviation insurance**, is rather niche, and a limited number of insurers write this coverage. Aircraft insurance coverage is available for four different kinds of aircraft owners and operators. These parties are defined as follows:

- **Business and pleasure operators**—Individuals or businesses that own and operate aircraft for both business and pleasure purposes; aircraft are normally operated by one of the owners, as it is not common for these operators to employ full-time pilots
- **Fixed base operators (FBO)**—Businesses typically operating out of airports that lease, own, operate, sell, and rent aircraft, along with other services related to aircraft, such as flight instruction, repairs, and fueling
- **Flying clubs**—Groups of three or more people who jointly own and operate all aircraft that are part of the flying club; the aircraft are only used for pleasure, and these are mostly nonprofit organizations
- **Industrial aid operators**—Companies or corporations that own aircraft and that employ full-time professional pilots to operate them

Similar to watercraft insurance, aviation policies include hull coverage, liability coverage, and medical payments coverage. Hull coverage can be categorized based on where the covered aircraft is when a loss occurs. Personal aircraft policies may combine hull coverages under one section of the policy. The categories are:

- **In-flight insurance**—This covers property damage that occurs while the covered aircraft is in flight.
- **Ground risk hull insurance in motion**—This covers damage incurred by the covered aircraft while it is in motion on the ground, except for that occurring during taking off or landing.
- **Ground risk hull insurance not in motion**—This covers damage sustained when the aircraft is on the ground and stationary. It can cover losses caused by perils such as hail, fire, hangar collapse, and animals, but it will also provide coverage when the insured's aircraft is struck by an uninsured aircraft or vehicle.

Commercial and personal aircraft policies may handle liability coverages differently. A personal policy will typically cover all liability exposures under one blanket coverage. Commercial policies differentiate by who sustains the liability loss. The options for liability coverage are:

- **Passenger liability insurance**—This coverage is required by law for most large aircraft, and it covers medical costs and funeral expenses for passengers that are on the aircraft when a loss occurs. It also covers damage to the passengers' property. It is normally written on a per passenger basis with an aggregate limit per loss.
- **Public liability insurance**—This covers essentially any other type of property damage or bodily injury that an aircraft can cause a third party. This includes damage to hangars and airports. It does not cover losses sustained by passengers of the covered aircraft. This coverage is mandated in most jurisdictions.
- **Combined single limit liability insurance (CSL)**—This combines passenger liability and public liability into one coverage that is subject to a single limit of liability.

Because of the breadth of exposures related to aircraft, aviation policies can be amended by endorsement to cover many different losses that are not covered under the base policy. Examples of such optional coverages include non-owned aircraft liability, pollution liability, drone coverage, cargo legal liability, and renter's liability coverage.

Texas-Specific Content

Texas Department of Insurance

INTRODUCTION

Because insurance is mostly regulated at the state level, each state has its own set of rules, regulations, and practices. In Texas, this regulation generally falls to the **Texas Department of Insurance (TDI or "the department")**. To work in insurance in Texas, one must have a thorough understanding of how Texas regulates insurance and what the state expects from insurance personnel. Texas insurance regulation is primarily governed by the **Texas Insurance Code**, but other laws may also come into play, such as the **Texas Administrative Code (TAC)** and the **Texas Labor Code**.

With respect to state regulation, there are three basic types of insurers under Texas law. How a company is classified depends on the company's geographical location. **Domestic insurers** are those both licensed and incorporated within the state of Texas. **Foreign insurers** are those that are incorporated in another state but licensed to do business in Texas. **Alien insurers** are incorporated outside of the United States and licensed to conduct business in Texas.

Insurance companies are also categorized based on who owns the company. A **stock insurance company** is owned by stockholders or shareholders and has the ultimate goal of generating profits for these parties. A **mutual insurance company**, in contrast, is owned by the company's policyholders. Profits are used to directly benefit policyholders, usually by either reducing premiums or paying periodic dividends.

The Texas Department of Insurance performs its duties under the supervision of the **Commissioner of Insurance (the "commissioner")**. The TDI is made up of officers and employees tasked with implementing and enforcing laws applicable to the insurance business. The department has broad regulatory powers that apply to most insurance transactions taking place within the state. The department regulates:

- Property and casualty (P&C) insurance
- Title insurance
- Life insurance and annuities
- Accident and health insurance
- Workers' compensation insurance
- Credit insurance

The basic responsibilities of the TDI consist of:

- Regulating the insurance business conducted within the state of Texas
- Overseeing the workers' compensation system for the state of Texas in accordance with Texas Labor Code
- Assuring that insurance companies and any other entities working in the business of insurance operate in compliance with Texas laws and codes
- Safeguarding insurance consumers against unfair treatment by insurance providers and personnel
- Promoting fair competition between insurers to encourage a competitive insurance marketplace

The commissioner acts as both the chief executive officer and the administrative officer of the TDI. The obligations and duties of the commissioner are provided by the Texas Insurance Code, Title 5 of the Texas Labor Code, and any other insurance or workers' compensation law in force at the state level. These responsibilities include the oversight of all insurance companies operating in Texas. The commissioner serves a term of two years and is appointed by the governor with the approval of the Texas State Senate. The commissioner's term ends on February 1 of odd-numbered years.

The Texas Insurance Code defines in great detail what activities are considered to be conducting the business of insurance. Such activities include:

- Proposing or making insurance contracts as an insurer
- Proposing or making a guaranty or surety contract as a guarantor or surety professional
- Accepting applications for insurance coverage
- Collecting money or other consideration in exchange for providing insurance coverage
- Issuing insurance contracts to parties residing in Texas or authorized to conduct business in Texas
- Acting as an agent directly or indirectly on behalf of an insurance company or insurance consumer by engaging in:
  - Soliciting, negotiating, obtaining, or effectuating insurance coverage for both new and existing insurance customers
  - Providing information on insurance rates or coverage
  - Presenting insurance applications to insurers
  - Furnishing insurance policies to consumers
  - Risk inspections
  - Rate setting
  - Claim or loss investigations or adjustments
  - Handling matters arising from an insurance contract
  - Any other means of assisting or representing an insurer or consumer with an insurance transaction within the state
- Handling of contracts intended to reimburse the medical expenses for a resident of the state of Texas or for risks within the state
- Any activities substantially similar to those listed above when performed in a way meant to circumvent insurance laws
- Any of the aforementioned activities when performed by an unlicensed or unauthorized entity within the state of Texas that applies to residents of other states or jurisdictions

CERTIFICATES OF AUTHORITY

The primary means by which the department regulates insurance companies is through licensing. There is further regulation to monitor the financial health of the company as well as to guarantee that business is being conducted in a fair and ethical manner.

The TDI holds considerable power when it comes to determining which insurance companies operate within the state of Texas. This regulation is carried out using **certificates of authority**, sometimes called applications for registration. For the purposes of issuing certificates of authority, the Texas Insurance Code defines "insurer" as follows:

> "The issuer of an insurance policy that is issued to another in consideration of a premium and that insures against a loss that may be insured under the law."

The definition applies to all of the following types of companies engaged in the business of insurance:

- Fraternal benefit societies
- Mutual companies including statewide mutual assessment associations, county or farm mutual insurance companies, and local mutual aid associations or burial associations
- Reciprocal or interinsurance exchanges
- Health maintenance organizations (HMOs)
- Stock companies
- Group hospital service corporations
- Lloyd's plans
- Nonprofit legal services corporations

HANDLING OF FUNDS

Another function of the TDI is handling money that it collects in the form of taxes, fees, and other types of reimbursement. These funds are held in the TDI operating account, and the commissioner has the authority to manage the funds at his or her discretion so long as it is done in accordance with Texas law. The commissioner is allowed to add and remove monies from the account using **electronic funds transfers (EFTs)**. EFTs can be used to collect fees, deposit guarantee funds, and disburse any other money held by the department for the benefit of the state. An EFT is required for any debits or deposits in excess of $500,000. The accounting procedures related to the TDI's operating account, including recordkeeping, may be handled by either the commissioner or the **comptroller**, if necessary. The Texas state comptroller is an elected official who maintains the public financial accounts of the state.

When an insurer domiciled in Texas wishes to do business outside of Texas, including international business, it might have to make a monetary deposit, as some jurisdictions outside of the state require such a deposit as a condition of transacting insurance in that venue. The Texas commissioner has the authority to accept and hold these deposits for other jurisdictions. Insurers may do this voluntarily if they do not want to deposit funds outside of Texas. Deposits can be in cash or in securities. The insurance company may designate that the funds be held to safeguard only customers and creditors in a specific state or jurisdiction, or it may designate that the funds are held to protect customers and creditors regardless of location.

Once the funds are deposited, only authorized officers of the insurance company are allowed access to them. Such access only allows examination of the deposit and collection of interest payments. For tax purposes, the funds deposited are governed by the tax code of the location in which the insurer's charter places its main office. In some instances, the insurance company may want to withdraw some or all of a deposit after it is made. In most cases, the commissioner must approve withdrawals. Withdrawals can be done to substitute different securities than those that were originally deposited. Withdrawals without substitution of funds are only allowed if the insurance company ceases to do business in the location that required the deposit or if the insurer withdraws from the business of insurance entirely. In the former scenario, the insurance company must provide evidence that there are no outstanding obligations to policyholders or unsecured liabilities to any other party within the state or jurisdiction the insurer was operating. In the latter scenario, the evidence must show that the company does not have outstanding unsecured liabilities or policyholder obligations in any location.

When insurance companies merge or consolidate, the deposit requirements are also consolidated. If there are deposits made previously that become duplicative after a merger or consolidation, the

243

duplicative deposit may be withdrawn in full. If an insurer is being dissolved, it may cede all of its business to a **reinsurer** including assets and liabilities. A reinsurer is essentially an insurance company that protects the liabilities of another insurance company. When another insurer cedes business to a reinsurer, the reinsurer can request withdrawal of any deposits made by the defunct insurance company except for the largest deposit that was made. Deposits may also be returned to an insurance company if the jurisdiction outside of Texas changes its laws such that a deposit is no longer required. In all of these cases, there must be documentation proving that these changes have occurred before any of the funds can be withdrawn. Once the commissioner issues an order approving the return of the deposits, the comptroller is then responsible for releasing and delivering the funds to the appropriate party.

Regulation of Insurance Companies

INTRODUCTION

The state insurance commissioner and the department of insurance regulate insurance companies to protect insurance consumers throughout the state of Texas. Part of that duty is to ensure the financial solvency of insurance companies that operate within the state. Insurance companies must also operate in ways that are fair not only to the consumers but also to the fellow companies in the Texas insurance industry. Insurance companies are held to high ethical standards in their business practices, such as with the sale of insurance and the adjudication of claims.

LICENSING PROCEDURES

As mentioned in the previous chapter, most insurers must be granted a certificate of authority to transact insurance in the state of Texas. Texas is a participant in the Uniform Certificate of Authority Application (UCAA) program administered by the **National Association of Insurance Commissioners (NAIC)**. This means that Texas uses the uniform application process developed by the NAIC. The UCAA was established to streamline and promote consistency in the application process. Before a domestic company can submit an application, it must be incorporated in the state of Texas. The certificate of authority application must specify which line or lines of insurance the company plans to do business in.

The process for obtaining a certificate of authority begins with the company submitting an application along with the required filing fee, if applicable. Any fee collected is deposited into the operating account of the department. An application is required for all insurers regardless of if they are domestic, foreign, or alien. What information must accompany the application varies based on the type of company looking to be certified. This can include biographical affidavits and fingerprinting of key company officers. Such officers may include chief executive officers, presidents, chief financial officers, controllers, executive directors, medical directors, or board members.

Some lines of insurance are also required to submit proof that **capital stock** and **paid-in surplus** minimums are met. Capital stock is the face value of the stock, also called the **par value**, multiplied by the number of stocks sold. The paid-in surplus is the difference between the par value of the stock that is sold and the amount for which the stock sells. In Texas, the requirements are as follows:

- Property and casualty insurance: $2.5 million in capital stock and $2.5 million in paid-in surplus
- Life and health insurance: $700,000 in capital stock and $700,000 in paid-in surplus
- Title insurance: $1 million in capital stock and $1 million in paid-in surplus

Once the application is received by the TDI, a review will be completed. If all requirements have been met, the certificate will be issued. The state is authorized to give preference to domestic applicants to encourage growth of the insurance industry in Texas. Once a certificate is issued, it remains in force until it is revoked or suspended. If the application is denied, the applicant may submit a request to the commissioner for a hearing. The commissioner must then request a hearing date within 30 days. Once an application is approved, the applicant is classified as an **admitted insurer**, which is sometimes referred to as an **authorized insurer**. While most insurers must obtain a certificate of authority in Texas, some insurers are allowed to do business as **non-admitted insurers**. Entities allowed to operate as non-admitted insurers are usually surplus lines carriers or those insurers from which a Texas-based insured independently obtains coverage.

After an insurance company is admitted, the commissioner retains the right to modify or revoke the certificate of authority. This can occur if an insurance company ceases to satisfy any conditions or requirements related to the certificate that was granted. Modifying or revoking a certificate of authority can be necessitated by an insurance company having violated Texas insurance law, a company leaving the Texas insurance market, or the department needing to restrict a company's business within the state. In cases where the company is not withdrawing from the state, whether the action will be a modification or revocation depends upon the severity of the offense and the reasons for which the action is being taken. Once the commissioner determines that the certificate will need to be modified or revoked, a notice must be provided no less than 10 days before the change goes into effect. This notice must explain in specific detail the reason the action is being taken.

FINANCIAL REGULATION OF INSURERS

The commissioner's duty to monitor the financial health of insurance companies is carried out via financial report filings and periodic **examinations of records**. Financial statements must be filed with the department annually, while examinations are carried out at least once every five years. For annual financial filings, an insurer must retain an independent **certified public accountant (CPA)** to conduct an audit of financial records and generate reports that are to be submitted to the department for review. These reports are required to follow the statutory accounting practices of the location in which the company is domiciled and must provide a summary of the company's financial condition, including the overall financial results of the company, any changes in fiscal position, and any changes in capital or surplus held. As outlined in the insurance code, the CPA's reporting must include the following information:

- The CPA's audit report
- A comprehensive balance sheet listing admitted assets, liabilities, capital, and surplus
- A statement regarding any gains or losses sustained from operations
- A statement of cash flows
- A statement detailing any changes in capital and surplus
- Notes pertinent to any submitted financial statements such as:
  - Notes explaining any discrepancies between the audited statements and the annual statement filed with the department
  - Any notes required under the NAIC's annual statement instructions or by generally accepted accounting principles (GAAP)
  - A summary of the ownership of the insurance company and the company's relationship with any affiliates
- Any supplemental information or data as requested by the commissioner

An examination of a carrier's records is carried out by a member of the TDI or an examiner appointed by the department. The insurance code requires that the department conducts an examination of all domestic and foreign insurers, including physically visiting the primary office of each insurer. An examination covers the period between the last day covered by the prior examination and December 31 of the year prior to the year in which the examination is being executed. For example, if an examination is taking place in 2015 and the prior examination period ended on December 31, 2012, the examination period would be from December 31, 2012, through December 31, 2014. It is left to the department's discretion how frequently examinations occur, but once every five years is the minimum requirement.

During an examination, the examiner is entitled to freely access pertinent books and records for review. If needed, the examiner also has the authority to request examination under oath of any employee, officer, or agent of the company. If the company holds real estate assets, the TDI is authorized to obtain information to confirm the market value of such assets, including appraisals, tax records, income records, and data on sales of comparable properties. The information gathered and the reports generated from the examination are confidential except in cases where the examination is related to the liquidation or receivership of an insurance company. In the event that a company fails to comply with examination protocol or refuses to provide information requested during an examination, the company may be subject to disciplinary action. If there is a dispute between the insurer and the TDI regarding the findings of the examination, the carrier may file a request for judicial review of the examination.

Texas law allows the department to submit reasonable data and information inquiries to insurance companies at any time. Such requests may include information relating to the company's financial condition or any other issue the department deems necessary to appropriately perform its duties or for the good of the public. Upon receipt, an insurer has 15 days to respond. If more time is needed, the insurer must notify the TDI in writing of the need for an extension. An extension will allow an insurance company 10 additional days to respond to the inquiry. The information gleaned from an inquiry is treated as confidential and privileged unless it is introduced into a court or administrative action. The department is obligated to maintain records of all inquiries made and responses received.

HAZARDOUS FINANCIAL CONDITION

Once an audit has been completed, the department determines the financial health of the insurer being examined. A company whose financial health is in such a state that it poses risks to policyholders, creditors, or the general public can be declared in **hazardous financial condition** by the department. For the purposes of declaring a company in hazardous financial condition, the term "insurer" is explicitly defined. Insurers include:

- Capital stock insurance companies
- Reciprocal or interinsurance exchanges
- Farm or county mutual insurance companies
- Fraternal benefit societies
- HMOs
- Group hospital service corporations
- Lloyd's plans
- Mutual companies including mutual assessment companies
- Risk retention groups
- Title insurance companies
- Fidelity, surety, or guaranty companies
- Statewide mutual assessment associations
- Local mutual aid associations
- Stipulated premium companies
- Burial associations
- Any other person or organization engaging in the insurance business

The insurance code outlines the criteria that may be reviewed to establish an insurance company's financial state. The commissioner and department may use any of the following information to make a determination:

- The types and nature of the risks insured
- The insurer's ownership and loss experience

- The ratio of total annual premium and net investment income to commission costs, general insurance expenses, claims or benefits payments, and required reserve increases
- The insurance company's methods of operating, affiliating, and investing
- The insurer's agreement to any contracts that lead to or could lead to contingent liability
- Guaranty and surety agreements

Upon review of these criteria, the commissioner will issue a notice of hearing to the potentially compromised carrier. If after the hearing is completed, the commissioner maintains the position that the company is in a risky state, he or she may issue an order compelling the insurer to take certain reasonable actions to remediate the issues of concern. The measures that may be ordered include:

- Using reinsurance to reduce current and future liabilities
- Lowering the volume of new business written
- Temporarily restricting or suspending writing new business
- Cutting general expenses and commissions using methods specified by the department
- Raising the carrier's surplus and capital via contribution

If the commissioner believes the insurer is in such a dire position that reasonable remedies are unlikely to resolve the issues at hand, he or she may order the suspension or termination of the carrier's certificate of authority.

STOCK AND SURPLUS IMPAIRMENT

The department lays out requirements for stock and surplus holdings for insurers. Insurers are obligated to comply with such requirements continuously while conducting business within the state of Texas. For stock insurance companies, this means maintaining the amount of stock and surplus required by the department, For mutual companies, reciprocal or interinsurance exchanges, and for Lloyd's plans, this means ensuring that minimum aggregate surplus requirements are met. With the exception of life insurance companies, the commissioner will use reinsurance reserve requirements and the number of claims and debts the carrier has outstanding to decide if impairment exists.

The commissioner may order the insurer to increase the surplus to be in compliance with the requirements established by law. In some cases, the commissioner may order the insurance company to stop engaging in the insurance business entirely. For stock insurance companies, this can occur if the surplus is less than 50 percent of the required amount or fails to meet the minimum amount established by the commissioner's rules. For Lloyd's plans, the commissioner considers the aggregate amount of the carrier's guaranty fund and held surplus. For a mutual company's reciprocal or interinsurance exchange, again with the exception of life insurance, the commissioner uses the aggregate surplus amount. In either case, the insurer may have its ability to do business terminated if the surplus is impaired by more than 25 percent or falls below the minimum amount established by the rules the commissioner adopts.

RECEIVERSHIP AND LIQUIDATION

If an insurer is found to be in such poor financial condition that it is at risk of insolvency or poses a risk to policyholders, creditors, or the public, the TDI is allowed to take possession and control of the insurer's assets and take over the company's business activities. This can also happen when a carrier fails to appropriately remediate its impaired position. When this occurs, the insurer is placed into a **receivership**. During the receivership, the TDI and its appointed receivers may attempt rehabilitation of the company. In cases where rehabilitation is not possible, the company will be liquidated. **Liquidation** is a process in which the company's assets are sold to raise funds to pay outstanding liabilities.

SURPLUS LINES INSURERS

Surplus lines insurance, also referred to as **excess and surplus lines (E&S) insurance**, is a subcategory of P&C insurance designed to cover risks that traditional insurers do not have an appetite to assume. Surplus lines insurers can be influential in developing policies for emerging lines of business. Consumers look to surplus lines carriers when they are denied coverage in the mainstream insurance market, when there is limited data available about the risk presented, when the property to be insured is unique or of extreme value, or when there is an exceptionally high risk of loss. Typically, surplus lines coverage is treated as an insurer of last resort after an applicant has been rejected by one or more admitted insurers.

Although surplus lines insurers do not need to be admitted in Texas, it does not mean that there is no regulation of this line of business. Because surplus lines carriers do not participate in any Texas guaranty fund, they must adhere to stricter financial requirements than other insurers. These insurers are mandated to hold a minimum amount of capital to operate in Texas. These requirements are as follows:

- Non-admitted domestic insurers: $15 million in capital and surplus
- Non-admitted foreign insurers: $15 million in capital
- Non-admitted alien insurers: $45 million in capital

One benefit for a surplus lines carrier when it is admitted to the Texas insurance market is that these requirements are reduced substantially. When such an insurer is admitted in Texas, it only needs to maintain $5 million in net worth to operate.

Unlike other insurers, surplus lines companies are not regulated for financial health by the TDI but rather regulated by the **Surplus Lines Stamping Office of Texas (SLTX)**. The STLX is a nonprofit organization that subjects surplus lines insurers to financial examinations in addition to enforcing the minimum capital requirements. Surplus lines coverage is usually sold by a licensed general agent working in cooperation with a wholesale insurance broker. These wholesale brokers are responsible for filing policy information with the STLX. The STLX then requires the broker to pay a **stamping fee**, which is an amount paid per policy issued. It is through the stamping fees that the STLX is funded. Surplus lines agents are required to file documentation regarding active surplus lines policies no later than 60 days following the effective date of a new or renewed policy or the date that the policy is issued, whichever is later. If the information is filed after 60 days, but before 180 days, the agent is charged with a late filing fee. The amount charged depends on the agent's history of filing policies in a timely manner. If for the prior calendar year, the agent filed 95 percent or more of policies within the 60-day period, the fine is $50 per late-filed policy. If the agent's late filings for the prior calendar year exceeded 5 percent of the total filings, the fine is increased to $100 per late-filed policy. In cases where the information is filed after the 180-day mark, but before the 365-day mark, a fine of $200 per late-filed policy is assessed, but only if the agent filed at least 98 percent of policies in the prior calendar year on a timely basis.

TEXAS LLOYD'S PLANS

While treated very similarly to traditional insurance companies under Texas law, a **Lloyd's plan**, often called simply **Texas Lloyd's**, is structured in a unique manner. Lloyd's plans companies consist of an individual or a partnership or association of individuals that organize into a Lloyd's company with the intention of selling and writing various types of insurance. All lines of business that can be written under Texas law can also be written by a Lloyd's plan with the exception of life insurance. The parties who make up the membership of a Lloyd's plan are called **underwriters**. To qualify as a Lloyd's plan, the association must have at least 10 underwriters. The underwriters then select an **attorney-in-fact** to act on their behalf when conducting insurance business in Texas. An attorney-in-fact is appointed under a **power of attorney**. The parties involved must then draft **articles of agreement**. This document, which is used in place of an articles of incorporation document, outlines the structure of the association, the obligations of all parties involved, and the processes that will be used in the operation of the company.

Like most insurance providers, a Lloyd's plan must be issued a certificate of authority; however, that certificate is issued to the attorney-in-fact rather than the company as a whole. To qualify as an attorney-in-fact, the person selected must reside in Texas and operate an office within the state. The application for a certificate of authority must include:

- The attorney-in-fact's name
- The name under which the Lloyd's plan intends to operate
- Addresses and names of all underwriters
- The address of the principal office
- A listing of the types of insurance that will be written
- Copies of each policy form or insurance contract that will be used
- A copy of the executed power of attorney granting authorization for the attorney-in-fact to act on behalf of and bind insurance for the underwriters
- A copy of the articles of agreement signed by the attorney-in-fact and all underwriters
- A financial statement
- Documents signed by each underwriter allowing the attorney-in-fact to accept service of process for any litigation falling under an insurance contract or policy
- A $10 filing fee

Like other insurers, Lloyd's plans are subject to minimum capital requirements depending on the business in which the plan will engage. This amount can be increased at the discretion of the commissioner, and the failure to maintain capital and surplus requirements is subject to corrective action. The commissioner may order the company to be placed under the conservatorship or supervision of the state, declare the company to be in hazardous or impaired condition, or impose any other penalty as allowed under the insurance code. Lloyd's plans are also subject to many of the same financial reporting and examination requirements as other insurance companies. Lloyd's plans are exempt from insurance laws to a limited extent, but for the most part must follow the same regulations as other insurers.

INSURANCE FILINGS

Under the Texas Administrative Code (TAC), insurance companies are required to file rates, rating manuals, and policy forms with the insurance department. The TDI also requires insurers to file underwriting guidelines for certain lines of business. All filings must be submitted electronically using the **System for Electronic Rates and Forms Filing (SERFF)**. SERFF is owned and managed by the NAIC to provide a streamlined and consistent process for handling insurance filings across the country.

RATE AND RATING MANUAL FILING

A **rate** is defined as the cost of insurance per exposure unit adjusted to consider expenses, profits, and insurer loss experience. This is the base amount an insurer uses to determine insurance premiums, and then the premiums are adjusted based on each insured's individual risk level. For property and casualty insurance rates, Texas operates under a file-and-use system. This means that an insurance company can put the filed rates and/or rating manuals into use on the date the filing is submitted. A **rating manual** is the resource that contains the rules, classifications, territory codes and descriptions, rates, premiums, and other information an insurance company uses to calculate the premiums charged for each insured. The Texas Insurance Code mandates that rates and rating manuals be filed with the state for a number of reasons. These reasons include:

- Prohibiting inadequate, excessive, or unfairly discriminatory rates and rating procedures in order to promote the welfare of the public
- Supporting the availability of insurance within the state
- Encouraging competition among insurance companies to produce rates and premiums that are responsive to market conditions
- Prohibiting behavior that suppresses competition such as price-fixing agreements
- Creating guidelines for maintaining information reporting systems

Nearly all common P&C lines of business are required to file rates and rating manuals. There are some exceptions made for some commercial lines of business such as professional liability, product liability, errors and omissions liability, surety and fidelity bonds, and inland marine. In most cases, the rates and rating manuals can go into effect as soon as they are filed, but the commissioner has the authority to require preapproval in specific situations. Preapproval can be required if the commissioner determines the insurer's financial condition or rating practices need to be supervised or if there is a statewide insurance emergency.

When setting rates, an insurance carrier is only allowed to consider factors permitted under Texas law. Only some expense categories may be used in rate calculations. The insurance code specifically excludes the following expenses from being used in rate calculations:

- Administrative expenses in excess of 110 percent of the industry median for such expenses aside from the costs related to acquisition, loss control, and safety engineering
- Lobbying expenses
- Advertising expenses except for those related directly to the products the insurer sells or those designed to promote loss prevention
- Payments for claims of bad faith, fraud, or any other extracontractual issues including fines, penalties, or exemplary damages for violations of civil or criminal law
- Donations to social, religious, political, fraternal, or legislative advocacy organizations
- Fees and assessments paid to advisory organizations except for those exempted under commissioner rule
- Any premiums the commissioner finds to be excessive
- Any unreasonably high expenses as declared by the commissioner following a notice and hearing

Insurers may use the following information as a basis for rates:

- Past and potential future loss experience within Texas—information for outside of Texas is allowed if the data for losses in Texas is insufficient
- Unusual hazards or loss experience from individual risks
- Historical premium, exposure, loss, and expense experience
- Catastrophe risks within the state
- Operating expenses except for those explicitly disallowed
- Income from investments

- Reasonable profit margins
- Any other factors the commissioner deems relevant

After rates and the corresponding rating manual are filed through SERFF, the commissioner has until the earlier of the rate's effective date or 30 days after the rate was filed to reject the proposed rate and/or rating manual. If needed, the commissioner has the authority to extend this period by an additional 30 days. If a filing is denied, the commissioner will file an order to the insurer explaining the reasoning for the denial. The insurance carrier has the right to request a hearing within 30 days of the order. If the commissioner determines that additional information is needed to make a decision on the filing, the insurance company will be notified. Disapproval of a filing after it has gone into effect requires a hearing, and a notice will be sent to the insurer at least 20 days in advance of the hearing. If the commissioner determines the filing still cannot be approved after the hearing, an order must be issued within 15 days.

POLICY FORM FILING

As with rate and rating manual filing, policy form filing seeks to make insurance accessible to the residents of Texas. It is also done to ensure that the policies sold to consumers are fair and equitable and not unjust, misleading, or deceptive. The exceptions to policy form filing requirements for certain commercial lines of business are very similar to the exceptions for rate and rating manual filings.

Policy form filing requirements also apply to endorsement forms and standardized policy forms. For insurance policy and endorsement forms, the insurer must obtain approval from the commissioner before the form can be put into effect. Forms must be filed no later than 60 days before the carrier intends to use them. Forms are also filed through SERFF, and the commissioner has 60 days to approve or disapprove them. If the insurer has not received notice of disapproval from the commissioner after 60 days, the form may be used under the assumption that it was approved.

Filings are reviewed to ensure that none of the provisions are in violation of Texas insurance law or contain wording that is deceptive, misleading, or breaches public policy. If a form is found to be in violation of the TDI's requirements after it was approved, the commissioner may call a hearing and withdraw any prior approval. Forms for residential or commercial property insurance are permitted to outline a contractual statute of limitations for losses within the policy provisions. Insureds must have at least three years from the date of loss or two years from the date the insurance company accepted or rejected the claim to file legal action against the insurer. Insurers may also require that policyholders report claims within a certain period of time, but it cannot be less than one year from the date of loss.

UNDERWRITING GUIDELINES

Texas law requires insurers to file **underwriting guidelines** for certain lines of business including personal auto, residential property, and workers' compensation. Underwriting guidelines are the rules, standards, guidance, or practices an insurer uses when determining whether or not to accept or reject an application for insurance. The method or methods an insurance company uses to classify applicants or insureds for the purposes of rate calculation are also considered part of underwriting guidelines. Guidelines may be written, verbal, or electronic in form and must be filed with the state whenever any changes are made. The underwriting guidelines used by an insurance carrier must not be arbitrary and need to be actuarially supported and result in rates that are commensurate with the anticipated risk the insured presents. Underwriting guidelines are prohibited from being unfairly discriminatory.

Filing of underwriting guidelines is necessary to ensure that the methods being used align with the requirements imposed by the Texas Insurance Code and other laws. Filed guidelines are generally treated as confidential, but the TDI is permitted to publicly publish summaries of a carrier's underwriting guidelines so long as the identity of the insurer is not disclosed in the summary. Aside from the insurance department, the Office of Public Insurance Counsel is entitled to copies of filed underwriting guidelines as necessary.

Regulation of Insurance Professionals

INTRODUCTION

Insurance professionals and entities must be licensed in Texas to make certain that minimum educational and ethics requirements are met. Licensing is also an effective tool for ensuring that people who engage in criminal behavior, especially those involved in crimes of dishonesty, are not allowed to work in the business of insurance.

LICENSING REQUIREMENTS

Texas law imposes licensing requirements on many different types of insurance professionals so that all transactions involving insurance are completed in accordance with the standards set by the department. This includes **agents**, **claims adjusters**, and **risk managers**. Agents who are focused primarily on selling insurance are commonly called **producers**. Licenses may also be categorized by the line of business in which the professional works. The insurance code gives the commissioner the authority to adopt any rules needed to enforce licensing requirements and ensure compliance with federal law.

AGENTS

The insurance code describes the activities that, when performed, constitute acting as an insurance agent. Many of these overlap with the code's definition of transacting insurance addressed previously. A person engaging in any of the following activities is considered to be acting as an agent under Texas law:

- Soliciting insurance on behalf of an insurance company or HMO
- Handling insurance applications transmitted to or from an insurance company, including advertising the service of handling applications for insurance policies
- Receiving or transmitting policies for an insurance company
- Collecting insurance premiums from customers or delivering insurance premiums to an insurance company
- Creating or forwarding building diagrams for insurance purposes
- Inspecting or examining risks
- Adjusting claims on behalf of an insurance company
- Any other activity intended to result in the making of an insurance contract with or for an insurance company or HMO

While this definition is broad, there are explicit exceptions listed in the insurance code that narrow down the application of the term agent. Exceptions include:

- Regular employees of an insurer who devote their time fully to tasks other than the solicitation of insurance, annuities, or memberships, who do not earn a commission based on the sale of these items, and who do not solicit or accept applications for such items from the public
- Administrators who solely handle employee benefit plans for the company for which they work as long as there is no direct or indirect compensation from the insurer who issues the insurance contracts
- Financial institutions and their employees who handle premium funds for an insurer
- Contractors retained by HMOs to provide only management, administrative, or health care services

Pertaining to the licensing of agents, the Texas Insurance Code provides an extensive list of entities that meet the definition of "insurer" under the code. This definition includes all of the following:

- Fraternal benefit societies
- Mutual life, health, accident, fire, or casualty insurance companies
- Statewide mutual assessment companies
- County and farm mutual insurance companies
- Local mutual aid associations
- Local mutual burial associations
- Reciprocal or interinsurance exchanges
- HMOs
- Stock life, health, accident, fire, or casualty insurance companies
- Group hospital service corporations
- Lloyd's plans
- Nonprofit and for-profit legal services corporations
- Mexican casualty insurance companies
- Stipulated premium companies
- Nonprofit hospital, medical, or dental service corporations

When an individual solicits applications from the public for insurance coverage, he or she is deemed to be an agent of the insurance company to whom the application is being delivered. This is an important distinction because if a dispute arises between the company and the insured, the agent is treated as an extension of the insurance company. Generally, agents do not have the authority to waive or alter any of the policy conditions or terms contained in an insurance policy. Because of the strict rules and requirements for both agents and insurers in Texas, agents risk being held personally liable if policies are written with an insurance company prior to that company complying with insurance laws. This means that if an agent sells insurance from an unauthorized or otherwise noncompliant carrier, he or she could be held financially responsible for claims made that the company fails to properly pay.

To apply for an agent license in Texas, the applicant must intend to solicit and sell insurance to the general public. This is to prevent someone from obtaining a license solely to sell coverage to him- or herself, family members, or business partners. Selling insurance in this way is considered **controlled business**, and Texas law limits the amount of controlled business an agent may write. Generally, insurance agents are limited to 10 percent of their annual premium volume coming from controlled business. This limitation is in place to avoid conflicts of interest and encourage fair competition in the insurance market.

TYPES OF AGENTS

While the term "agent" is used broadly to refer to persons working in the insurance industry, especially those who sell insurance, there are a few different types of agents under Texas law pertaining to licensure. Some of these types of agents require special licenses to engage in insurance transactions.

GENERAL AGENTS

General agents are the most common type of insurance agent. General agents are allowed to transact insurance within the category of insurance for which they are licensed. An agent may be licensed for P&C insurance or for life, accident, and health (LAH) insurance. However, these categories may overlap if permitted by the insurance code. For example, a general P&C agent may also sell accident or health insurance if his or her appointing insurance company is authorized to write such business in the state of Texas. General agents are authorized to sell both commercial lines and personal lines insurance.

MANAGING GENERAL AGENTS

A **managing general agent (MGA)** is a special type of agent that has duties and authority beyond that of a general agent. The specifics of the MGA's responsibilities are outlined in the MGA agreement made with the insurance company. MGAs are most frequently used for niche lines of P&C business. Under life and health lines of business, such an agent may be referred to as a **managing general underwriter (MGU)**. Typically, MGAs are granted underwriting authority by the appointing insurer. They may also have the power to bind insurance coverage, enter into reinsurance agreements, issue insurance contracts, and make producer appointments for the insurer.

In Texas, an MGA is more narrowly defined, and permitted activities are outlined in the insurance code. It is defined as an individual, corporation, or firm that acts in a supervisory capacity for the local field and agency operations of an insurer that operates in Texas. The MGA is endowed with the authority to accept and process insurance applications from other agents on behalf of the insurance company. Other permissible activities include:

- Receiving and forwarding daily reports and monthly accounting
- Receiving and managing agency balances
- Adjusting losses and claims
- Appointing or directing other agents including local recording agents, state agents, and special agents

Insurance law also imposes requirements on MGAs relating to the contracts they make with insurance carriers. MGA agreement contracts must be in writing, and any alterations to the agreement must be written and include the effective date of the outlined changes. The specific function for each party to the agreement must be stated explicitly in the contract. The contract must also include a clause describing the process for terminating the agreement and a provision allowing the insurance company to suspend the authority of the MGA during disputes concerning defaults. The schedule for the MGA to deposit funds with the insurer must be stated in the contract language, with a deposit occurring no more than 90 days after the last day of the month in which a policy is issued. The law also mandates that the MGA submit monthly account statements to the insurer detailing all insurance transactions completed within a calendar month. Once a month has ended, the MGA has no more than 60 days to submit the reporting to the insurance company. Account documentation must be maintained by the agent for at least three years.

If the MGA has the authority to appoint agents for the insurers, this must be stated in the contract. Certain activities can only be undertaken with the prior written approval of the insurance company. Such activities include binding reinsurance, agreeing to participate in an insurance or reinsurance syndicate, collecting payments from a reinsurer, and settling claims with a reinsurer. The contract is also required to state that the MGA cannot directly or indirectly assign the duties under the contract to another party unless the insurance carrier consents to it in writing. If claims files are maintained electronically, then the protocol for transferring that data to the insurer must be outlined in the contract. For any authority that is granted to the MGA, the extent of that authority needs to be stated in the agreement. Types of authority that must be addressed include:

- Maximum premium volume allowed per year
- Lines of business that can be written
- Maximum limits of liability on policies sold

- Maximum policy period for policies sold
- The ability to alter policy exclusions, coverage territory limitations, and cancellation conditions

The MGA contract must state that reinsurance may only be ceded to companies that are not eligible for reinsurance credit under the Texas Insurance Code. The conditions under which the MGA can place reinsurance need to be outlined in the contract as well. For commissions, the agreement is required to state that the MGA is not obliged to refund any commissions to the insurance company that are more than the total commission that has been paid to the MGA.

If the agreement includes a provision under which profits will be shared between the MGA and the carrier prior to the closure of all reported claims, including loss payments and claims expenses, the profits can only be distributed after a specific amount of time has passed. The length of time depends on the line of business involved. Additionally, if the MGA has claims settlement authority or the authority to set loss reserves, the insurance company must audit and verify all pending claims and loss reserves before any profit sharing may be paid out. The carrier does have the option to not pay any profit sharing before all claims within the payment period have been closed or pay in installments based on when the reporting periods close. The method chosen by the insurer must be specified in the agreement.

The contract is also required to include a stipulation that the documentation for each insurer the MGA works with must be stored separately and held for a period of at least five years. In cases where the MGA has the authority to settle claims, the contract must state that the insurance company must be notified of claims in writing within 30 days when a claim involves any of the following:

- A demand in excess of the applicable policy limits
- Allegations of bad faith
- Alleged violations of the Deceptive Trade Practices Act or Article 21.21 of the Texas Insurance Code
- A coverage dispute

The MGA agreement requires a clause regarding examinations of the MGA by the carrier. If the MGA is not an affiliate of the insurance company, examinations must be completed semiannually. If the MGA is an affiliate of the insurer, the examinations can be conducted annually. In cases of atypical premium volume increases, the contract is required to state that an examination must be carried out within 90 days if the increase exceeds 30 percent for any 30-day period. Examinations that may be conducted pursuant to the MGA contract include:

- Policy inventory reconciliation
- Timely premium reporting and collection
- Compliance with underwriting guidelines
- Claims procedures
- Timely payment of claims

The contract must include a stipulation that the insurance company is notified of certain major changes with the MGA, including a change in ownership involving 10 percent or more of the MGA's outstanding stock or changes of any principal officers or directors. The agreement must prohibit offsetting balances under one contract with balances due under another contract. The MGA agreement must also establish the fiduciary duty of the MGA to the carrier. Finally, the contract must state that in claims matters including settlement and loss reserves, the insurer has the final authority to resolve disputes.

Because MGAs can handle significant amounts of money on behalf of the insurer, the insurance code also sets requirements for the handling of such funds. There must be a separate escrow account for each insurer the MGA works with, and the monies may only be held in a bank that is FDIC insured. Funds cannot be invested in common stock, preferred stock, or junk bonds with a security rating of category 3 or below from the NAIC's Securities Valuation Office. All money accepted by the MGA must be deposited in the appropriate escrow account, and all withdrawals must be documented in detail. While the escrow account is considered the property of the MGA, withdrawals may only be taken for approved purposes. Those purposes consist of:

- Payment of amounts due to the insurer(s)
- Agent commissions and expenses
- Premium refunds
- Loss settlements and adjustment expenses
- Recovering amounts deposited in error
- Reclaiming amounts belonging to the MGA
- Making legally permissible investments
- Payment of reinsurance premiums

SURPLUS LINES AGENTS

In Texas, a separate license is required for **surplus lines agents**. If an agent resides in Texas and wishes to obtain a surplus lines license, he or she must already have a valid general P&C license or a managing general agent license. If an agent does not reside in Texas, a standalone surplus lines license may be issued if the agent's home state does not require a general P&C license.

TYPES OF AGENT LICENSES

NONRESIDENT AGENT LICENSE

A **nonresident agent** is someone who works in the insurance business within the state of Texas but does not reside there. Such agents are usually licensed in the state where they reside. When there is a **reciprocity agreement** between Texas and the other state in which the applicant is licensed, the applicant must still meet any requirements in Texas that are not satisfied by his or her home state license; however, he or she does not need to duplicate efforts in areas where the licensing requirements overlap. A reciprocity agreement is an arrangement between states that the satisfaction of one state's licensing requirements constitutes meeting some or all of the licensing requirements of another state.

TEMPORARY AGENT LICENSE

Permanent agent licenses require the licensee to pass the state licensing exam before the license can be issued. In some limited circumstances, an individual can obtain a **temporary license** that allows him or her to transact insurance prior to sitting for the applicable licensing exam. An applicant may need a temporary license because his or her employer wants to evaluate his or her work before deciding to appoint the applicant as an agent for the company. That employer can be an insurance agency, another insurance agent, an insurance company, or an HMO. An application for a temporary license can only be approved if the candidate is sponsored by an employer.

Temporary agent licenses are only valid for 180 days from the date of issue and are not eligible for renewal. They are also not appropriate for individuals who do not have any intent to pursue a permanent license. When applying for the license, the sponsoring employer must submit a certificate stating that the applicant is being sponsored, that the company is requesting a temporary license be issued, and that it will provide the education required by Texas law. The state mandates that an applicant completes at least 40 hours of agent training within the 30 days after the license application is received by the TDI. At least 10 of those hours must be taught in a classroom setting such as at a college, business school, or a class sponsored by the insurer. The topics that must be covered include:

- General insurance principles
- Texas insurance regulations and licensing laws
- Broad principles of HMOs including laws, regulations, and membership requirements
- Agent ethical duties and obligations

To avoid abuse of the temporary licensing option, the TDI sets specific requirements for companies who sponsor applicants for temporary licenses. In any two consecutive calendar quarters, at least 70 percent of a company's applicants must sit for a licensing examination. Of those applicants, at least 50 percent must pass the test. Generally, one company may only appoint up to 500 temporary licensees in a calendar year. The commissioner may allow an exception to this limit if the employer is able to effectively monitor the appointed temporary agents. Once the 180-day period has expired, the applicant may not continue working as an insurance agent unless he or she has successfully completed the examination for a permanent license.

EMERGENCY AGENT LICENSE

An **emergency agent license** is a special license issued when a general P&C agent dies, is disabled, or becomes insolvent. An agent is deemed insolvent if he or she is unable to pay the premiums that have been collected to the insurance company when they are due. An emergency license grants agent status to an individual who takes over the business of a deceased, disabled, or insolvent agent. This is done in an attempt to preserve the impaired agent's business while protecting consumers who may be impacted by the inability of the original agent to conduct business as expected. An emergency license is valid for 90 days within any period of 12 consecutive months. It may be renewed for an additional 90 days within that time period, if necessary.

LIMITED LINES AGENT LICENSE

In contrast to a general lines insurance agent, a **limited lines insurance agent** is only permitted to write insurance business for the specific lines of business designated by the license. Limited lines licenses are available for both property and casualty lines of insurance and life, accident, and health lines of insurance. A limited lines license can be used for agents who deal exclusively in a particular type of insurance or for those who write only less common types of insurance.

For a P&C limited lines license, such a license may be used if the agent writes exclusively crop, auto, personal manufactured home, or industrial fire insurance. There are some constraints on the industrial fire insurance that may be written with a limited lines license. Firstly, the policies offered must cover dwellings, household items, and apparel. Secondly, the coverage may only be written on a weekly, monthly, or quarterly basis with the premiums being paid pursuant to a continuous payment plan. Finally, the insurer for whom the agent works must be a county mutual insurance company that was in operation as of May 22, 1953. Credit insurance, prepaid legal services contracts, and job protection insurance may also be written under a limited lines P&C license.

There are also limitations on what types of LAH business may be written under a limited lines license. Limited lines agents can write policies or provide policy riders that offer lump-sum cash payments for accidental death and dismemberment, payment for ambulance services due to accident or illness, prepaid legal service contracts, and credit insurance. For both P&C and LAH limited lines agent licenses, the insurance commissioner may permit additional lines of business to be written under such a license if it is needed to sufficiently protect insurance consumers.

FIDUCIARY CAPACITY AND DUTIES OF AGENTS

Generally, insurance personnel act in a **fiduciary capacity** when it comes to consumers. Acting in a fiduciary capacity entails always putting the interests of another party above one's own interests. Like in any other state, insurance agents in Texas are held to a standard of behavior to ensure that consumers are protected and insurance business is conducted in good faith. While the explicit duties of an agent are not outlined in the insurance code, case law has determined that insurance agents have a **general duty to act reasonably**. This means that agents are expected to treat clients in a way that any reasonable agent would. Agents owe a great duty to insureds because they provide information and advice that insureds rely upon to make important financial decisions. Agents are expected to make certain insureds receive the coverage they need from a company that is able to meet those needs. Agents are also expected to keep insureds updated on any material changes that could affect coverage. The carrier with whom the agent writes coverage should be solvent and readily able to pay claims promptly when they arise. While agents are not explicitly required to explain policy coverages and provisions to insureds, it is still prudent for agents to do so.

In contrast to other jurisdictions, the fiduciary duties most agents owe to clients are not formalized under law. This does not mean that agents are held to no fiduciary standards, rather there is an overall expectation that agents engage in reasonably prudent business practices when dealing with customers. If an agent fails to act in a way that a reasonable consumer could expect, the agent could be held liable for the loss associated with such a breach of duty; however, legal action against insurance agents for fiduciary failures or errors are generally unsuccessful.

Under Texas law, some contracts are seen to create a **special relationship** between the parties. Special relationships are those that require utmost good faith and fair dealing for the parties involved, especially if the power between the parties is unbalanced or unequal. In the context of insurance, the relationship between the insurer and the policyholder is often considered unbalanced in favor of the insurer. This is generally due to the insurer's position of dictating the terms of the insurance contract and the significantly higher amount of resources an insurance company has in comparison with a customer. This is something that an agent needs to keep in mind when dealing with clients.

When it comes to the relationship between an agent and the insurance company he or she represents, the existence of a special relationship is more well-defined. Agents have a fiduciary duty to the insurer, which could result in civil liability if not upheld. Agents are expected to avoid making mistakes, follow the direction of the insurer fully, provide information in a timely manner, disclose all material information pertaining to policies sold, and work within the underwriting authority the insurance company grants.

INSURANCE ADJUSTERS

The Texas Insurance Code also requires **insurance adjusters**, usually referred to as **claims adjusters**, to be licensed. The insurance code defines an adjuster as a person who is either an employee or independent contractor of an insurance company who investigates and settles losses on that insurer's behalf. The definition also includes those who supervise others who handle claims. In Texas, there are three types of claims adjuster licenses:

- Property, casualty, and surety adjuster
- Workers' compensation, employer's liability, and US longshore and harbor workers' compensation adjuster
- All-lines adjuster: an all-lines adjuster can handle any of the claim types listed above

To be considered an adjuster, the individual must be working for a general or personal lines P&C agent, an adjustment bureau, an association, a managing general agent, an insurance company, or an independent contractor. Persons who investigate, adjust, settle, or supervise the handling of workers' compensation claims are also considered adjusters under Texas law.

Licensing is also required for those working as **public insurance adjusters**. Public insurance adjusters are hired by insureds to negotiate and settle claims on their behalf. Public adjusters are also allowed to work on behalf of another public adjuster. A license is required even to advertise one's services as a public insurance adjuster. Public adjusters may only handle claims for real or personal property losses.

RISK MANAGERS

A **risk manager** is a trained professional who specializes in identifying and assessing risks, providing advice for risk reduction and/or remediation, creating and implementing a risk management program, and monitoring risk management programs that are already in place. Risk managers can evaluate organizations for event risks and operational risks. Event risks are those attributable to a loss event, such as an injury that results from a car accident or property damage caused by a natural disaster. Operational risks are those inherent to the operations of the organization being examined that can cause interruption of business. Examples of operational risk include fraudulent activities, technology or equipment failure, and defective processes.

In Texas, a risk manager is a person who publicly advertises risk management services and who provides those services to parties looking to acquire insurance coverage or renew an already existing insurance policy. Risk managers are limited to providing services related to P&C insurance under the insurance code. A risk manager is exempt from licensing requirements if he or she works for an authorized liability insurer, a single employer, or a public self-insurance pool.

PROPERTY AND CASUALTY LICENSING PROCEDURES

This section will detail the process that must be completed for an individual agent, claims adjuster, or agency to become licensed in the state of Texas. Features unique to specific types of licenses will be outlined where applicable. Any person wishing to apply for any type of Texas insurance license must be at least 18 years old and legally authorized to work in the United States. Other specific requirements will be set forth in their respective sections.

OBTAINING A LICENSE
INDIVIDUAL AGENTS

To qualify for any insurance agent license, an individual must not have a history of committing acts for which the license application can be denied. Such activities include:

- Intentionally violated Texas insurance laws
- Knowingly made untrue statements of material fact in a license application
- Acquired or attempted to acquire a license using fraud or misrepresentation

- Mishandled funds belonging to an insurance carrier, HMO, or customer by misappropriation, conversion, or illegal withholding; misappropriation is the act of illegally using another party's funds for unauthorized purposes, while conversion is unlawfully taking possession of another party's money or property
- Committed dishonest or fraudulent acts or practices
- Misrepresented material terms and provisions of an insurance contract, including contracts pertaining to HMO membership
- Made or issued a statement including falsified or incomplete comparisons of an annuity or insurance contract that was legally issued by an insurer or HMO to encourage a consumer to cancel or surrender the contract or allow it to lapse so that the consumer is persuaded to replace it with another policy or annuity
- Provided a rebate or offered a rebate of insurance commissions or premiums to an insured or enrollee
- Committed a crime that resulted in a felony conviction
- Failed to engage in actively selling or writing insurance for the general public as required by the terms of the license; agents are prohibited from securing a license for the sole purpose of obtaining insurance coverage or annuity contracts for themselves, members of their family, or their own business associates

All of these actions are also grounds for disciplinary proceedings when committed by an agent who is already licensed.

If all of the aforementioned criteria are met, the candidate can start the application process. For an insurance agent license, this begins with passing an examination. There are courses and study materials that may help an applicant in passing, but using them is not a prerequisite to sit for the exam. However, there is a nonrefundable fee for each testing attempt, so most candidates opt to complete some type of exam preparation. As of 2024, the general lines P&C agent exam has 150 questions consisting of 130 scorable questions and 20 pretest questions that are not considered in exam scoring. All questions are multiple choice. The scored questions are split into two sections. These sections consist of 100 questions about general P&C insurance concepts and 30 questions based on Texas-specific insurance concepts. To pass, a score of 70 percent or higher is needed on each section of the test. Candidates are allotted two and a half hours to complete the licensing examination.

Once the licensing exam is completed successfully, the license application must be submitted within one year. For most people, completing the application begins by submitting a complete set of fingerprints. The applicant's fingerprints will be used as part of the background check completed for all applications. First, the applicant must make an appointment with IdentoGO, a vendor used by the state for handling the capture and submission of fingerprints. This process consists of making an appointment at an IdentoGO location. Applicants are required to bring documentation showing proof of identity. During the appointment, the candidate is fingerprinted and receives a receipt confirming the fingerprints were sent to the Texas Department of Public Safety. During the application process, the applicant will submit this receipt to the department of insurance. Failure to complete this step in an expedient manner can result in denial of the license application. Finally, the candidate must submit a licensing application online via either the **National Insurance Producer Registry (NIPR)** or **Sircon**. The license application must be accompanied by the applicable fee. If everything is in order, the application will be approved, and the agent license will be issued. A license is good for two years before needing to be renewed.

REQUIREMENTS FOR CERTAIN LINES OF BUSINESS

Due to the unique nature of some types of insurance, the agent licensing requirements may be supplemented with additional education depending on the type of insurance or financial products an agent intends to sell. Most of the time, an agent will secure this necessary education through a one-time certification course. Like other prelicensing training programs, these certification courses must meet minimum curriculum requirements and be approved by the state. Once the course is completed, the state must be notified so that the appropriate certification can be added to the agent's license. Available certifications include:

- Medicare-related product certification
- Small employer benefit health plan certification
- Long-Term care partnership certification
- Annuity certification

In order for agents to sell annuity products, Texas law mandates that agents complete an approved course to ensure that they have sufficient knowledge of these products. This course provides the equivalent of four continuing education hours. Texas law outlines the information that must be included in the training:

- Types and classifications of annuity products
- Identifying the parties to an annuity
- The impact of product-specific features on consumers
- Taxation of qualified and nonqualified annuities as income
- The primary uses of annuity products
- Standards of conduct for sales practices, disclosure requirements, and replacement requirements

When an agent finishes the approved course, it must be reported to the state. Insurers who work with an agent to sell annuities are mandated to confirm the educational requirements are met before they can allow the agent to sell their products.

INSURANCE ADJUSTERS

Claims adjusters are required to complete 40 hours of education prior to sitting for the exam. The all-lines adjuster license exam consists of 150 multiple choice questions about both general and state-specific insurance concepts. On this exam, all 150 questions are considered in the score, and 70 percent of them must be answered correctly to pass. Like the P&C general lines agent exam, examinees are allotted two and a half hours to complete the test.

The process of submitting the application is essentially the same as for agents, including fingerprinting. For adjusters, the circumstances under which a license application is denied are not defined as clearly. An adjuster's license application can be denied under any rule ratified by the insurance department or under applicable state law.

Certain parties are exempt from claims adjuster licensing requirements while conducting work related to claims. Such parties include:

- Practicing attorneys who only adjust claims occasionally and incidentally at their law practices as long as they do not represent themselves as claims adjusters
- Salaried insurer employees who do not adjust, investigate, or supervise insurance claims on a regular basis

- Persons retained by a licensed adjuster for technical assistance only, such as private investigators, attorneys, photographers, engineers, estimators, and other experts
- Agents or general agents of a licensed insurance carrier who process claims for uncontested losses on behalf of the insurer under a policy issued by that agent
- Persons who only perform clerical tasks related to claims
- Adjusters who handle only life, accident, or health insurance claims; claims under workers' compensation policies are not considered life, accident, or health insurance claims
- Right-of-way agents, including right-of-way claims agents, who principally handle the acquisition of easements, leases, permits, or real property rights or claims associated with the operations under easements, leases, permits, or other contractual obligations
- Persons employed only to investigate potentially fraudulent insurance claims who do not adjust or pay claims
- Licensed public adjusters
- Persons who only enter data into an automated claims management system including collecting claims information from or providing claims information to claimants and insureds, including any licensed agents who supervise such employees
- Persons employed by a licensed independent adjuster to perform the above duties so long as no more than 25 people are working under that licensed independent adjuster's supervision
- Employees of an insurer or an affiliate of an insurer who handle first party P&C losses of no more than $500 or claims for which the coverage limit is no more than $500
- Nonresident adjusters who are acting as a temporary replacement for a licensed adjuster, who adjust claims related to a single catastrophic event, or who adjust Texas claims on a one-off basis
- Adjuster trainees registered with the department working under the supervision of a licensed claims adjuster but only for a period of 12 months or less

AGENCIES

For an agency license, the process is more focused on making sure that all of the pieces are in place for an agency to operate properly. The application is completed online via Sircon or the National Insurance Producer Registry and with the necessary application fee. To apply for an agency license, at least one of the agency officers or partners must be a **designated responsible licensed producer (DRLP)** who holds a Texas insurance agent license for the line of business in which the agency intends to work. Information must also be furnished about the executive officers, directors, and/or partners who administer the agency's operations in Texas and about any party or entities who manage those operations. Officers, directors, and partners who are not licensed as insurance agents are required to submit fingerprints the same way an individual applicant would. An agency must be registered as a business in the state of Texas prior to applying for a license, and proof of such registration must accompany the application. If the business is a limited partnership or limited liability partnership, a copy of the partnership agreement must also be provided. If the business uses a name other than its legal name, also known as a **doing business as name** or **DBA name**, the application must include a copy of the certified articles of incorporation or articles of organization as well as all amendments to these documents. An agency also must provide proof of financial responsibility such as a copy of an errors and omissions insurance policy or a bond.

AGENT APPOINTMENTS

For an individual licensed as an insurance agent to perform the business activities of an insurance agent, he or she must have an **appointment** from one or more insurance carriers. An appointment is when an insurer has formally designated an agent to handle insurance transactions on its behalf.

Insurers must file agent appointments using Sircon or the National Insurance Producer Registry. When an appointment from an additional insurer is made, the TDI must be notified within 30 days of the agent beginning to work for that insurer. Appointments continue until they are terminated or withdrawn by the insurance carrier. If an appointment is ended due to improper agent behavior, the insurance carrier or the agent must file a statement with the TDI immediately outlining the circumstances surrounding the termination. In all other cases, the termination notice is submitted using either of the online systems noted above.

RISK MANAGERS AND MANAGING GENERAL AGENTS

The process for becoming licensed as a risk manager is similar to that of an individual agent. The applicant must successfully complete a licensing examination. The application must be completed with information about the candidate's identity, experience, business history, and personal history. It is left to the discretion of the department if information beyond this is required. Applicants must also comply with fingerprinting requirements and maintain a place of business within the state of Texas to qualify for the license. Like agent and adjuster licensing, risk manager licenses expire after two years. When the applicant is a business entity, an application must be submitted that includes information about all executive officers, partners, or directors who administer the entity's business in Texas as well as information on all persons and entities who manage the entity's operations.

For the purposes of licensing, a managing general agent may be an individual person, a firm, or a corporation. Individuals must pass a licensing examination and go through the same application and background check process as the licenses addressed previously. A corporation is exempt from MGA licensing under specific circumstances including:

- The corporation is authorized to conduct business in the state.
- The entirety of the corporation's outstanding stock is owned only by an insurer authorized to conduct business in Texas, and the insurer exercises exclusive control over the corporation's business affairs.
- The corporation was formed with a principal purpose of handling collection and distribution of commissions between an agent and the insurer or any of the insurer's affiliates and does not engage in any other acts constituting the duties of an MGA.

MAINTAINING A LICENSE

Once an individual is granted a resident insurance agent or adjuster license, the license must be renewed every two years. These licenses expire on the licensee's birthday during the year in which the license expires. As part of the renewal process, an agent or adjuster must complete 24 hours of **continuing education (CE)**. No less than half of these hours must be completed in a classroom setting or using a classroom equivalent. Of the 24 hours, there must be three hours devoted to ethics. Courses must be approved by the state to fulfill continuing education requirements. If a license expires with CE hours still outstanding, the licensee will be fined $50 for each CE hour that has not been completed. All fines must be paid and the missing CE hours completed before the license can be renewed. If the agent decides to leave the insurance industry, they should file the voluntary surrender form to reduce fines and continuing education requirements. Continuing education hours may be completed at any time while a license is active, but the renewal payment cannot be submitted more than 90 days before the expiration date. For nonresident licenses, the agent or adjuster must follow the procedure of his or her domicile state. Licensees are mandated by law to maintain records relating to prelicensing or continuing education courses for at least four years after completion. Such information must be presented to the department upon request. In cases where a licensee's compliance with educational requirements is being audited or investigated, the records must be retained for the duration of the audit or investigation. The department reserves the right to investigate or audit a licensee at any time.

If there is a change in a licensee's legal name, address, or contact information, the TDI must be notified immediately. Failure to notify the department of these changes within 30 days may result in administrative actions or fines. If a nonresident licensee relocates to Texas, he or she must complete an application for residency change to convert the nonresident license to a resident license. This application may be submitted up to 30 days prior to the licensee relocating. Prior to applying, the nonresident licensee must terminate his or her status as a resident licensee of the state he or she is leaving. In addition to notifications about personal information, an agent or adjuster must alert the TDI if he or she has been convicted of a felony or has been the subject of administrative or disciplinary action by any financial or insurance regulating entity within the United States.

Corporations or partnerships licensed as agencies also have notification requirements. The department must be alerted within 30 days following any events that require reporting. One event that must be reported to the department is the addition or removal of any officer, director, partner, member, or manager. The TDI must also be notified if any of these parties is convicted of a felony. Felony convictions involving licensed insurance agents working for the agency need to be reported as well. If the agency does business in a different state, any disciplinary action arising out of activities in that other state must be reported to the department, including copies of any applicable orders or judgements.

Agents, including nonresident agents and managing general agents, have financial reporting requirements to maintain licensing as well. Because of the strict rules surrounding who agents can accept compensation from, they are mandated to report commissions and other compensation to the state. Generally, an agent is only permitted to accept direct compensation from an insured in the form of service, application, or inspections fees that are used to offset the costs associated with procuring insurance for that customer. If for some reason the agent is compensated directly by the insured, he or she is not entitled to additional payment from an insurance company or any other third party. An agent may only collect further payment from such parties if, prior to the insurance being purchased, the customer provides written acknowledgement that a specific amount will go directly to the agent and is provided a written explanation of the methods and factors used in determining the amount that will be paid to the agent. Exception is made for agents who act solely as a go-between for the insurance carrier and the customer's broker or agent. There is an additional exception for agents who are only compensated for insurance placements by commissions, salary, or other payments made by the insurer.

License Renewal and Expiration

As discussed previously, insurance licenses are valid for two years. If the licensee is not an individual, it expires two years from the date of issue. For individual licensees, the expiration dates are staggered. If the license was issued in an even-numbered year, it expires on the licensee's birthday in each even-numbered year. If it was issued in an odd-numbered year, then it expires on the licensee's birthday in each odd-numbered year. If multiple licenses are held by a single licensee, all licenses expire on the expiration date for the license that expires first.

When a license is due for renewal, an application must be submitted to the department. As long as the application is filed prior to the expiration date of the license, the license will remain in effect until the license renewal is issued, denied, or the commissioner orders the license to be revoked. If the application was submitted no more than 90 days after the expiration date, a penalty of 50 percent of the renewal fee must be paid in addition to the renewal fee. If the license has been expired for more than 90 days but less than one year, an application for a new license must be filed. The application must be accompanied by the license fee plus a penalty equal to 50 percent of the license fee. As long as the expiration date was less than one year ago, the applicant does not need to repeat the licensing examination. Once a license has been expired for one year, the applicant completes the entire process for obtaining a new license including retaking the exam.

LICENSE TERMINATION

Insurance agent and adjuster licenses can be terminated voluntarily or via disciplinary action. If a licensee opts to cancel his or her license voluntarily, such as when moving to another state or discontinuing employment in the insurance industry, he or she must simply complete the **Voluntary Surrender of Texas Insurance License** form and submit it to the department. Once this form is completed and submitted, the licensee is required to immediately stop engaging in any business activities for which the license was needed. It is also possible to let a license expire when it is due for renewal, but this course of action can result in the accumulation of fines related to not meeting CE requirements. If at any point, a former licensee wants to reinstate his or her license, any outstanding fines must be paid before the reinstatement will be granted.

A licensed agent may have his or her license terminated via disciplinary action. This occurs when the agent is found to have engaged in prohibited behavior as outlined earlier in this chapter. A license can be terminated via revocation or by the TDI refusing to renew it. A revocation occurs when the department rescinds a license that was previously granted. This can happen at any time if there is justifiable cause for such action. Revocation is usually reserved for serious violations of law when the TDI or commissioner determines that an agent's ability to transact insurance must be stopped as soon as possible. In other cases, the commissioner may decide to deny the agent's renewal application when the license is due to expire. Even when a license is surrendered voluntarily, the agent is still subject to disciplinary action for any violations that occurred while the license was active.

FELONY CONVICTIONS

Texas law does not entirely prohibit persons with criminal backgrounds from obtaining an insurance license, but it does dictate the offenses that render an applicant ineligible for a license. If a person is already licensed and is then convicted of an offense that would prevent a license from being granted, then his or her license may be revoked, suspended, or have its renewal refused. Unless a conviction relates to a crime that would specifically prohibit someone from being granted a license, the department has the authority to accept or deny an application at its discretion. To deny an application, the department must issue a notice of hearing, and the applicant must be given the opportunity to respond.

The crimes that would cause a license application to be denied include, but are not limited to:

- Crimes in which deceit or dishonesty are essential elements
- Financial crimes, including violations of the Texas Insurance Code
- Fraud, including insurance and health care fraud
- Money laundering
- Engaging in unauthorized insurance business
- Felonies related to breaches of fiduciary duties
- Criminal homicide or manslaughter
- Sexual offenses, including solicitation
- Arson or intentionally damaging property
- Perjury

- Robbery, burglary, or theft
- Domestic offenses
- Kidnapping or human trafficking
- Possessing, delivering, or manufacturing controlled substances
- Organized crime

Unfair Trade Practices and Insurance Fraud

Like all states, Texas closely regulates the activity of insurers to ensure that consumers are treated fairly. The insurance code addresses prohibited trade practices and claims settlement practices at length. While these regulations apply to the insurance industry broadly, including life and health lines of business, the discussion in this chapter will focus on property and casualty insurance. Texas also imposes statutory requirements for the handling and investigation of insurance fraud.

UNFAIR TRADE PRACTICES

Trade practices are concerned with the marketplace activities of an insurer and are intended to promote a fair and competitive insurance market in the state of Texas. Under Texas insurance law, unfair trade practices are referred to as **unfair methods of competition** and **unfair or deceptive acts or practices**. These restrictions apply to the insurance industry in general and focus largely on the sales and business practices of insurers.

The first prohibited practice is **misrepresentation** regarding an insurance policy or an insurer. The Texas Administrative Code (TAC) defines misrepresentation as any of the following:

- Any untrue statement of a material fact
- Any omission of information from a statement of material fact that would cause that statement to be misleading
- Any statement made in such a way that would mislead a reasonable person to a false conclusion about a material fact
- Any material misstatement of law
- Any failure to disclose material information when disclosure of such information is required by law

Insurers are forbidden to distribute information or documents that are knowingly untruthful about certain aspects of an insurance policy. Insurers are also not allowed to make misleading or untrue representations about the terms of a policy, the advantages or benefits of a policy, or how surplus funds are distributed. Regarding surplus sharing, the insurer is also prohibited from misrepresenting how dividends or surplus amounts have been paid on a comparable policy in the past. Insurance companies are also legally bound to represent their financial health in a truthful manner. Any misrepresentation of this is banned by Texas law. Insurers are not allowed to use the name or classification of an insurance policy to mislead consumers about the true characteristics of the policy. In addition, insurers are barred from making false representations to a policyholder to encourage the policyholder to allow an existing policy to lapse or to surrender or forfeit a policy.

Secondly, Texas insurers are not permitted to engage in the distribution of **false advertising or information** about an insurance company or a person who works in the business of insurance. This restriction applies to any advertisement, announcement, or statement presented to the public. False advertising is forbidden in essentially any format, including printed materials, television and radio advertisements, and the internet. The insurance code leaves room for covering other methods of information sharing regarding false advertising by making the law applicable to any other manner in which such information can be disseminated. Further, Texas law prohibits certain advertising tactics. Insurance advertisements may not present comparisons between insurers when those comparisons are unfair or incomplete with respect to the policies, benefits, dividends, or rates. Insurers also cannot compare policies that are not comparable in the coverage or benefits offered. P&C insurers are not allowed to use the word "dividends" in advertising at all if done in such a way that implies that payment of dividends is guaranteed.

Next, Texas law prohibits **defamation** of insurers or those working in the business of insurance. Defamation entails making direct or indirect statements about another party with the intention of harming that party's insurance business. This includes statements that are malicious, derogatory, or false. Such conduct is banned in both written and oral forms. Insurers are also not allowed to behave in ways that restrict competition or support the creation of a monopoly. Prohibited behaviors include **boycotting, intimidation,** and **coercion**. Boycotting occurs when there is intentional refusal to do business with a company or entity in order to remove a competitor from the market or cause a competitor to be prevented from doing business in a particular market. Intimidation takes place when a party is inclined to perform an action due to a perceived threat of harm. Coercion means to force a party into an agreement or action by using force or threats

Texas law continues by stating that use of **false financial statements** is an unfair or deceptive practice. Such statements must have been created to deceive the public or government officials about the insurer's financial standing. This includes omitting factual information from reports to conceal detrimental information from a public official to whom the insurer is obligated to report financial data or a lawfully appointed agent or examiner. Insurers are also prohibited from using **rebating** or **inducements** to encourage consumers to purchase coverage. While this is mostly applicable to life, health, and accident insurance, it is important to understand what these practices entail. Rebating is promising to return funds to a customer in exchange for entering into an insurance contract. This can be in the form of dividends or a premium rebate. Inducement is to offer something other than money to a customer to incentivize him or her to purchase insurance coverage. This can be offering stock, shares, benefit certificates, securities, or any contract that promises profits or returns.

Unfair discrimination is not allowed in relation to life insurance and annuity contracts. Unfair discrimination occurs when a consumer is denied coverage or offered coverage with higher premiums or less favorable terms compared to other consumers with comparable traits and risk levels. As a general example, if you have two women of roughly the same age, socioeconomic standing, and health condition, it would be unfairly discriminatory to charge one woman more for a life insurance policy based on her race or ethnicity.

Finally, insurers are not allowed to use **deceptive names, words, symbols, devices,** or **slogans**. This applies to both advertising practices and insurer communications. Use of these items is considered deceptive if it could lead a reasonable person to believe there is a connection or affiliation with another insurer when there is not one. Names, logos, and slogans must be distinctive enough that consumers cannot be easily misled as to what company he or she is dealing with. If there is a dispute over the use of one of these items, the insurer who can prove it continuously used the item first will be given the approval to continue using it. Consumers should be able to readily discern between companies when presented with names, logos, slogans, or other identifying material.

Texas Unfair Claims Settlement Practices

The TAC provides a lengthy list of behaviors that are considered unfair within the context of claims handling and settlement. Additionally, the Texas Insurance Code includes a section called the **Unfair Claim Settlement Practices Act (the Act)** that outlines the obligations of insurers when handling and settling claims. While there are many parallels between the NAIC's Unfair Claims Settlement Practices Act and the activities described under the TAC and the Act, they are not identical. The overarching goal of these statutes is to ensure that insurance claims are handled promptly, comply with state law, and consider the insured's best interests. A first-party claimant is a party making a claim on an insurance policy in which they are the policyholder or in which they meet the definition of "insured" under the policy. A third-party claimant is a party making a claim against an insurance policy that is held by another party. In this section, the term "claimant" will be used to describe both first-party and third-party claimants. There are a number of behaviors classified as unfair claims settlement practices in the TAC:

- Failure to promptly provide insureds with claim forms required by the policy as a precondition for settlement
- Failure to make good faith attempts to settle a claim under one coverage part of the policy where liability is reasonably clear as a means to influence settlement under a different coverage part of the policy
- Failure to confirm or deny insurance coverage for a claim to a policyholder within a reasonable amount of time
- Unless otherwise stated in the policy provisions, refusal or failure to provide a settlement offer to a first-party claimant, including unreasonably delaying making an offer under the assertion that a third party is legally liable or that there is other coverage available
- Settlement or attempted settlement of a claim for an amount less than what a reasonable person would believe a claimant or insured is entitled to recover based on advertising by the insurer or someone working on behalf of the insurer
- Requiring an insured to execute a full and final release when a claim has only been partially paid, except when the claim involves a compromised settlement
- Failure to establish and follow proper policy and controls guiding the calculation of premium refunds that are due following a cancellation
- Refusal to pay claims when there has not been a proper investigation and consideration of all available evidence or information
- For personal auto policies, refusal or delay of settlement solely due to the availability of coverage of another type that will pay the claim in full or in part; when a claimant is entitled to recover from more than one insurer, the claimant may recover from one or all insurers and choose the order in which the claim is paid
- Requiring a claimant to produce federal income tax returns as a condition of settlement except when ordered by the court, the claim concerns arson, or there is an alleged loss of profit or income
- Any action committed by an insurer that violates the Texas Unfair Claim Settlement Practices Act

The Act further restricts how insurers handle claims and bans them from doing the following:

- Intentional misrepresentation of facts or policy provisions in relation to a claim
- Failure to acknowledge a claim in a reasonably prompt manner
- Failure to adopt and employ reasonable guidelines for prompt claims investigations
- Not making good faith attempts to settle a claim in a prompt, fair, and equitable manner in cases where liability is reasonably clear
- Inducing an insured to file a lawsuit by making a settlement offer that is significantly less than the amount that is eventually recovered through such legal action
- Failure to maintain information and documentation as required by the Texas Insurance Code
- Any other act established to be unfair by rule of the commissioner

PROMPT CLAIMS PAYMENT GUIDELINES

Most insurance companies are subject to the prompt claims payment requirements of the Act with some notable exceptions. The Act contains exceptions for mortgage guaranty insurance, title insurance, guaranty associations, most marine insurance, HMOs that only offer a single health insurance plan, and fidelity, surety, and guaranty bonds. Some requirements are expressed in calendar days, while others are expressed in business days. Under the TAC, a business day is any day that is not a Saturday, Sunday, or a holiday observed by the state.

Once a claim has been reported, the insurer has up to 15 days (30 days for surplus lines policies) to acknowledge the claim's receipt. The acknowledgement does not have to be in writing, but the claim file should clearly reflect when and how it was acknowledged along with the information provided to the claimant in the acknowledgement. During this period, the insurer is also required to begin its investigation and request any forms, statements, or other items needed from the claimant. Texas law allows an insurer to make subsequent requests for information if the need arises.

The Act also dictates the guidelines for an insurer accepting or rejecting a claim. In most circumstances, the insurer has up to 15 days to advise the claimant of acceptance or rejection. If there is a reasonable belief that the claim involved arson, this period is extended to 30 days. If the claim is accepted in full or in part, the claimant must be notified of this. Payment for the full amount of the claim or, if the claim is accepted in part, the undisputed portion of the claim payment, must be issued no later than the five business days after the insured is alerted that the claim has been accepted. Surplus lines insurers have up to 20 business days to issue payment. If acceptance or rejection of the claim is contingent on an action required of the claimant, the payment must be issued within five business days of the claimant completing the necessary action.

If the claim is being rejected, a notice must be sent to the claimant that explains the basis for the rejection. If more time is needed, the insurer is required to advise the claimant that additional time is needed and provide an explanation as to why. Once this notice is made, the insurer has an additional 45 days in which it can accept or reject the claim. For most lines of insurance, if a claim payment is delayed more than 60 days after all pertinent information is received, the insurer is mandated to pay interest on the amount due. When a lawsuit is filed, the claimant may also be entitled to collect legal and attorney's fees. The insurance code allows prejudgment interest going back to when the claim should have been paid to be awarded as well. These penalties are not applicable when the claim is deemed invalid by a litigation or arbitration proceeding. When a claim is related to a natural disaster or catastrophic weather event, these deadlines are extended by 15 days.

When a settlement offer is made to a third-party claimant under a casualty insurance policy, the named insured on that policy must be notified of the offer that has been made. This notice must be sent within 10 days of the first settlement offer being made. When a settlement is completed, an additional notice must be sent to the insured within 30 days of the settlement date. This requirement does not apply in cases where the policy obliges the insurer to obtain the insured's consent to settle claims, nor does it apply for marine insurance policies or surety, fidelity, or guaranty bonds.

INSURANCE FRAUD

Because the TDI has a vested interest in maintaining a healthy insurance marketplace, the insurance code outlines expectations for handling actual or suspected fraudulent activity involving insurance. These expectations apply to any person or entity engaged in the insurance business within the state. In addition to regulating how fraud is handled, the commissioner is also empowered to develop and employ fraud prevention educational programs to inform the general public about fraud.

If an individual who works in insurance reasonably suspects or has confirmed fraudulent insurance activity, he or she must report it to the department within 30 days of discovery. If applicable, a report can be made to the insurance department of another state and this would meet the Texas reporting requirement. Persons who report fraudulent activity are granted protection from civil liability as long as the report was made to an authorized entity, including the state insurance department, law enforcement, the NAIC, or the special investigation unit of the insurance company in question.

Once a report has been made, the commissioner can investigate it at his or her discretion. If deemed necessary, the commissioner may launch an investigation to establish if fraud occurred or to assist in enforcing laws against insurance fraud. If the commissioner's investigation concludes that insurance fraud has occurred, the commissioner has a duty to report his or her findings to the government agency authorized to take action on it. The TDI employs its own investigators who are tasked with conducting fraud investigations. These investigators are required to be commissioned as **peace officers**. They are generally police officers or other members of law enforcement. In addition to using its own investigators, the department may leverage the assistance of local law enforcement agencies. The commissioner carries the power to subpoena involved parties for documents, depositions, or any other relevant evidence. When information is required from an insurance carrier, the carrier has 15 days to comply with the request.

Insurers are also permitted to request TDI assistance with their own fraud investigations. A request may be submitted once the insurer has compiled sufficient evidence that there may be fraudulent activity taking place. The request must be accompanied by a report outlining the evidence collected as of the date of the report. The insurance company's investigation does not need to be final or complete before reporting. Any information the TDI collects during the course of an investigation is confidential unless the department determines otherwise.

Violations and Disciplinary Action

INTRODUCTION

Aside from requiring the licensing of insurance companies and personnel, the Texas Department of Insurance also has mechanisms in place to identify, investigate, and remediate behavior that is in violation of the insurance code. The methods through which these actions are accomplished vary based on the entity in question. While the powers of the department to enforce the insurance code are broad, there are some limitations in place. Firstly, the insurance code imposes time limits on how long the department can take to initiate an action against an insurer, agent, or any other licensee.

For suspected violations of the insurance code or any other Texas insurance law, action must be commenced before the earliest of:

- Five years after the violating action occurred
- Two years after the department discovers conduct violations
- Two years after the department is notified of conduct violations

If the potential violation involves the suspected commission of fraud, the TDI has up to five years from the date the conduct is discovered by the department or the department is notified of possible fraud, whichever is earlier. These time limits are inapplicable in certain circumstances. If the conduct is continuous and ongoing when the action is initiated, there is no time limit imposed. The same is true in cases involving unfairly discriminatory conduct. Violations of the Texas Labor Code are also exempt from time limitations.

DETECTING PROHIBITED ACTIVITY

The TDI uses a few methods for identifying violations of the insurance code. Employees of insurers can file reports with the department if there is suspected or actual violation of Texas insurance laws or rules. This can be done anonymously if the employee chooses to do so. Additionally, consumers can file complaints directly with the TDI for issues related to insurance.

CONSUMER COMPLAINT HANDLING

Most commonly, consumer complaints relate to the handling of claims. Insurance carriers are required to maintain records of all written complaints for either three years or back to the date of the department's last examination, whichever is shorter. If complaints against an insurer suggest a pattern of unfair behavior, the department has the authority to impose regular reporting requirements on the insurer in question. The TDI is also entitled to compare claims information secured from a report or examination to minimum performance standards to determine if such standards are being met.

When a complaint is received by the department regarding an insurer's handling of a claim, the department has the discretion to investigate the insurer's claims handling practices if the complaint history reveals the practices do not meet the department's minimum standards. The TDI may also initiate an investigation when the number or type of complaints is out of proportion compared to similar complaints filed against other insurers who handle the same or similar lines of business. While an investigation is ongoing, the TDI sends quarterly status updates to all involved parties. Once an investigation is completed, the department will review the information obtained and assess if further action is needed. When the department determines that additional action is necessary, a hearing will be scheduled to review the alleged violations of the Act. Violations are defined as:

- Activities prohibited as unfair trade practices or as unfair claims settlement practices
- Activities deemed to be false, misleading, or deceptive under the Texas Business and Commerce Code

A written notice of hearing must be sent to the insurance company or individual no less than 30 days before the date on which it is to be held. The notice will include the hearing schedule as well as a description of the violations alleged. Insurers are permitted to retain legal counsel for these hearings.

MARKET CONDUCT EXAMINATIONS

The TDI also has the authority to perform **market conduct examinations (MCEs)** on insurance companies doing business in the state. Market conduct examinations are designed to detect practices that pose risks to insurance consumers and the overall health of the Texas insurance marketplace. They are not conducted in response to single consumer complaints or employee violation reports. These examinations are focused on how business is conducted as a whole and are not intended to identify sporadic and unintentional errors. MCEs can be holistic in nature, or they can focus on specific types of activity. Information that can be reviewed during an MCE may relate to any of the following:

- Underwriting and rating
- Policy forms and filings
- Tier classifications of insureds
- Licensing compliance
- Complaint handling
- Marketing, sales, and advertising
- Policyholder services
- Claims handling
- Compliance policies and procedures

The department performs MCEs in accordance with the standards set out in the NAIC's *Market Regulation Handbook*. The procedures outlined in the handbook are meant to identify patterns of inappropriate activity by insurers. MCEs can be performed as **desk examinations** in which the department requests documentation from the subject insurer and reviews it away from the insurer's location. They can also be conducted on-site at the insurer's office location or wherever the insurer stores the records needed to complete the MCE. If necessary, the commissioner has the authority to issue subpoenas to insurance carriers demanding they produce the documents and information related to the MCE.

Examinations are not limited only to the material provided by the insurer being examined. The insurance code permits the TDI to utilize data collected or reported to the department, data collected by the NAIC, data from any relevant private or public sources, and even information outside of the insurance industry. The department may also obtain information via interviews with the insurer's employees, reviews of self-evaluations completed by the insurer, interrogatories, and reviews of policy and procedural resources.

When the department deems that an MCE is needed, written notice must be sent to the insurance company in question no later than 60 days before the examination is scheduled to begin. Approximately 30 days prior to the examination, there will be a preexamination conference between the TDI and the insurer's staff that will be involved in the examination. After the examination is complete, there will be an exit conference with the insurer, and then the examiner will author a report about what was found during the examination. A preliminary draft of the report must be provided to the insurer within 60 days of the examination's completion. Once the insurer receives the report, it has 30 days to comment upon the contents of the report. If there is conflict between the TDI and the insurance company, these parties will work together to resolve the disagreements within the following 30 days. After this occurs, the final report is completed including the commentary from the insurer. The final report is then sent to the insurer, and it will have 30 days to accept the report's findings or request a hearing to dispute them. If the insurer is found to have engaged in conduct that violates Texas insurance law, the commissioner has the authority to impose sanctions on the insurer.

REINSURANCE

Texas permits insurance carriers to use **reinsurance** to transfer some or all of their risk to another insurer. Reinsurance can be purchased to cover only the risks of a single insured or policy, or it can be written to cover all qualifying losses for a prescribed time period. Reinsurance policies can pay losses on either a **proportional** or **excess** basis. When using a proportional basis for loss payments, the insurer and the reinsurer agree on a proportional sharing of loss costs, and the premiums collected by the insurer are also shared proportionally with the reinsurer. On policies using an excess basis, the reinsurer only pays if a qualifying loss or losses require payments in excess of the insurer's retention limit or the amount specified in the surplus share treaty.

Because reinsurance is an important risk management tool for insurers, it is subject to some regulation under Texas law. Regulations are in place for reinsurance involving most property insurance and some casualty insurance. Workers' compensation insurance and employer's liability insurance are not subject to the requirements discussed in this section. Reinsurance can only be employed for the risks of a solvent insurer. The insurance code places limitations on the amount of risk that can be assumed by foreign and alien reinsurers. Foreign and alien reinsurers may only assume individual risks that do not exceed 10 percent of the available surplus. This limit may only be exceeded if that insurer purchases reinsurance from another solvent company. For alien insurers, the surplus held for all policyholders in the United States is used in calculating this limit. Alien insurers also have an additional requirement that no single assumed risk can exceed the amount that the alien insurer is statutorily required to deposit with the state. In this context, this is the state through which the alien insurer was granted authority to operate within the United States.

The department also monitors reinsurance reserving. If there is no codified method for calculating the reserves the reinsurer must carry, the department will calculate it. For fire insurers, the insurance code includes a table for calculating required reserves based on the length of the policy term and the amount of unearned premium after accounting for any reinsurance. For example, if a fire insurance company issues a one-year policy with an $1,800 premium, after six months, $900 is considered "earned," and $900 is considered "unearned." If the insurance code table specifies that 60% of the unearned premium must be reserved, the company will set aside $540 as a reserve to cover future claims or a potential policy cancellation. If the insurer has reinsured 50% of the policy, the reserve requirement reduces proportionally to reflect the portion of the risk retained by the primary insurer. In this case, the insurer retains responsibility for 50% of the $540 reserve, amounting to $270. The reinsurer assumes responsibility for the other 50%. While calculations are usually completed annually, the commissioner does have the discretion to make an insurer recalculate the reserve required more frequently if needed. For certain insurers, the department will determine the needed reinsurance reserve for all open risks on December 31 of each calendar year. This provision does not apply to life, fire, marine, inland marine, lightning, or tornado insurance.

CEASE AND DESIST ORDERS

If the department concludes that an insurance carrier or individual has been engaging in prohibited behavior, a formal notification of this finding is sent in the form of a **cease and desist order**. If the alleged behavior is fraudulent, especially egregious, or the violation involves an unauthorized entity engaging in insurance business, the department may issue an **emergency cease and desist order**. These are primarily used in situations where there is the likelihood that public injury could occur at any moment, the prohibited behavior cannot be remediated or rectified using reasonable measures, or the prohibited behavior is likely to have a negative effect on the insurance industry.

A cease and desist order is a legal demand from the TDI that the entity immediately stop committing the actions that are in violation of the Act. Failure to abide by such an order may result in the department placing restrictions on the carrier's business activities or taking disciplinary action against the individual. If the alleged violations of the order are severe enough, suspension or revocation of the insurer's certificate of authority or the individual's insurance license may result. The department has the right to request assistance from the Texas attorney general when enforcing a cease and desist order. If the insurer or individual wishes to appeal a TDI order or ruling, the appeal must be filed within 20 days of the order or ruling.

GENERAL SANCTIONS

Under the Texas Insurance Code, the commissioner is authorized to impose sanctions on any insurer or individual who is granted a license, permit, certificate of authority, certificate of registration, or any other certification within the purview of the commissioner's powers when that party is determined to have violated insurance code or laws. Any sanctions imposed by the commissioner are applied in addition to any other legal consequences imposed by other parts of Texas law. This includes levying penalties and fines, demanding forfeiture of a license or certificate, or ordering the denial, suspension, or revocation of a license or certificate.

Before sanctions are imposed, the party in question is entitled to a hearing. Hearing notices must be sent in writing. The subject of the hearing is required to file a written response to the notice within 20 days of the date it is mailed. The notice must include the following language in capital letters in 12-point boldface type:

> "If you do not file a written response to this notice with the state office of administrative hearings within 20 days of the date this notice was mailed, the scheduled hearing may be cancelled and the commissioner of insurance may grant the relief set out in this notice of hearing, including revocation of your license(s) by default. If you file a written response but then fail to attend the hearing, the commissioner of insurance may grant the relief set out in this notice of hearing, including revocation of your license(s) by default."

If the party fails to appear at the hearing or the hearing concludes with a determination that the insurer or licensee has engaged in wrongdoing in violation of Texas law, the commissioner is permitted to cancel or revoke the certificate or license previously issued to that party.

Aside from invalidating the license or certificate of an insurer or individual, the commissioner has the discretion to impose other types of sanctions including:

- A one-year suspension of a license or certificate
- Issuing a cease and desist order pertaining to the activity that was found to be in violation of the law
- Ordering payment of an administrative penalty
- Ordering payment of restitution
- Any combination of permitted sanctions

When restitution is ordered, the amount to be paid is determined by the commissioner. The commissioner will also dictate the amount of time the party has to pay the restitution required. Restitution can be made to any Texas resident, any Texas insured, or any other entity operating in Texas that suffered hard as a result of the party's violation of or noncompliance with the law. Failure to comply with any imposed sanctions will result in the cancellation of the entity's license or certificate. If the party does not admit to violating the law or the existence of violation is in dispute, the insurer or licensee may agree to accept one or more sanctions in exchange for the commissioner informally disposing of the matter via consent order, agreed settlement, stipulation, or default. Any sanctions that are imposed on an insurer or individual will be reported to the insurance departments or commissioners of all other states.

INSURANCE AGENTS AND ADJUSTERS

Because insurance agents and adjusters are licensed individually, there are some rules specific to them when it comes to violations and disciplinary action. In addition to the general sanctions, the commissioner may take other actions against a licensee who has been found to have committed wrongdoing or engaged in prohibited behavior. If the conduct committed also violated criminal law, the licensee may be subject to criminal penalties including fines, imprisonment, or both.

If an adjuster or agent is found to have engaged in any wrongdoing that violates the law, penalties can include:

- Denial of an initial application for a license or, if applicable, a certificate required to sell certain insurance products
- Suspension or revocation of a license or certificate
- Rejection of a license renewal application
- Imposition of an administrative penalty
- Formal reprimand of the licensee
- Probated license suspension requiring:
  - Regularly reporting to the department on any matter relating to the cause of the probation
  - Limiting business practice only to areas allowed by the department
  - Continuing or retaking professional education until a sufficient degree of skill is attained as determined by the commissioner
- Requiring the licensee to become certified or get recertified in a product line when certification is required for that insurance product

LICENSE REINSTATEMENT

If after a hearing a license application is denied or an existing license is revoked, the individual is not allowed to reapply for a license for five years. The five-year period begins on the effective date of the denial or revocation. In cases where judicial review was completed, it begins on the date the

278

court ordered the denial or revocation. This waiting period does not apply to denials resulting from improperly completed applications, failure to meet continuing education requirements, or not passing the required licensing examination.

Personal Lines Property and Casualty Insurance

INTRODUCTION

In many ways, the regulation of personal lines insurance in Texas aligns with the general content of the standard residential and personal auto insurance policies. While the category of P&C insurance includes a broad range of coverage types, when it comes to personal lines of business, the most commonly purchased policies are those that cover residential and personal auto risks. Residential insurance is normally referred to as "fire insurance" under the Texas Insurance Code, but this term includes homeowner's, renter's, condominium, and dwelling policies. There are some important regulations specific to Texas that will be addressed in this chapter. Additionally, this section will address state government programs designed to assist consumers who have barriers to obtaining sufficient insurance coverage. This chapter will also discuss the process for filing insurance rates and forms in the personal lines residential and automobile insurance space.

DECLINATION, CANCELLATION, AND NONRENEWAL OF INSURANCE POLICIES

Under the Texas Insurance Code, there are restrictions placed on an insurance company's ability to decline applications for insurance and cancel or refuse to renew an insurance policy. These limitations are in place to protect insurance consumers from losing needed coverage.

When a consumer's application for insurance is declined, questions may arise as to the reason or reasons why this occurred. Under Texas law, consumers are entitled to a detailed written explanation of an insurer's decision to decline an application. The consumer must request this information from the insurance company. The explanation provided must include all of the following information:

- The specific characteristics, incidents, or risk factors associated with the customer that violate or do not meet the insurer's underwriting guidelines
- The source from which the insurer obtained this information
- Any other reasons or information deemed necessary by the commissioner

When an insurer opts to cancel a policy during the policy term or decides to not renew the policy on the expected renewal date, the insured is entitled to all of the above information, but he or she does not need to request it from the insurer. When the customer is already insured under a policy, the insurance company is required to send a written notice of cancellation or nonrenewal to the insured. This notice must include all of the explanatory information required by law. If the policy is being cancelled, the notice must be sent at least 10 days before the cancellation goes into effect. For nonrenewal, the correspondence must be sent no later than 60 days prior to the end of the policy period.

Per Texas Insurance Code, cancellation of an insurance policy is defined in one of three ways. In all cases, the change is made without the consent of the insured. An insurance carrier is considered to have cancelled a policy if the coverage provided under the policy is terminated, the insurer declines to provide additional coverage under the policy that the insured would be entitled to, or there is a material change made to the policy that reduces or restricts the coverage the policy provided. The circumstances in which an insurer can cancel a policy vary based on the type of insurance involved and the age of the policy in question. For both personal lines residential and automobile policies, an insurance company can cancel the policy at any time if the insured presents a fraudulent or false claim, the premium is not paid when due, or the department decides that continuing to provide coverage would violate the insurance code or any other law governing the insurance industry.

PERSONAL AUTOMOBILE POLICIES

There are some guidelines specific to auto policies. New policies that have been effective for less than 60 days may be cancelled for any reason. Once a policy has been in effect for more than 60 days, it may only be terminated for a permissible reason. Nonpayment of premiums, violation of insurance law, and fraudulent claim activity are valid reasons for cancellation. A policy may also be terminated if the named insured or any resident of the named insured's household who operates a covered vehicle on a regular basis has his or her driver's license suspended or revoked. If it is not the named insured whose license is suspended or revoked, he or she can avoid cancellation of the entire policy by agreeing to have the policy endorsed to terminate coverage for the unlicensed driver. A policy may also be cancelled if the motor vehicle registration of a covered auto is suspended or revoked. The cancellation cannot go into effect any earlier than 10 days after the written cancellation notice is sent to the insured.

If the insurer wishes to not renew a policy that had already been written, it may cancel the policy on the one-year anniversary of the original effective date. When this happens, written notice must be sent at least 60 days prior to the anniversary date. The insurance code allows an insurance carrier to not renew an auto policy for any reason not prohibited by the law. If the nonrenewal is only due to a named insured not cooperating or complying with a request from the insurance company regarding a covered third-party liability claim, he or she must be given the opportunity to cooperate or comply. Prior to sending a nonrenewal notice, the insurance carrier must have sent written correspondence outlining how the insured has failed to cooperate, which claim requires the insured's cooperation, and a warning that if the insured continues to be noncooperative, the policy will not be renewed. If needed, the automobile coverage can be extended up to 10 additional days to allow time for the named insured to act. An insurance company is not permitted to refuse renewal of an auto policy solely because of an accident or claim for which the insured is not at fault. This includes damage caused by weather events, contact with animals, and contact with falling or flying objects. An insurer can decline policy renewal if there are two or more accidents or claims within a 12-month period. Policy nonrenewal is not allowed when based exclusively on the insured's age or status as an elected official.

HOMEOWNER'S AND PERSONAL RESIDENTIAL POLICIES

Like personal auto policies, homeowner's and residential policies may be cancelled at any time if the insured presents a fraudulent claim or does not pay premiums on time or if the policy is in violation of Texas law. Additionally, a homeowner's or residential policy may be cancelled if the insurance company identifies an increased risk for loss caused by factors that are within the insured's control. For example, an insured who does not fix a damaged roof leaves the property at risk of water damage or roof collapse. If a policy is less than 60 days old, the carrier may cancel the policy if it discovers a condition that increases the risk of loss that was not disclosed on the insurance application and for which there is no prior claim. A new policy may also be cancelled if the insurer does not receive a report of an inspection completed by a qualified property inspector. The inspection must have been completed no more than 90 days prior to the beginning of the insurance policy for the report to be acceptable to the insurer. If such a report is submitted to the insurance company, it is deemed accepted unless the insurance company notifies the insured of its rejection.

There are also situations in which an insurer can decide not to renew a homeowner's or residential policy. If there are multiple claims filed under a policy within a specified time frame, the insurance company may decline renewal of that policy upon its expiration. If the insured makes two claims within a three-year period under the same policy, the carrier is permitted to add a premium surcharge to the policy. The insurer is not allowed to consider claims due to natural disasters or natural causes, claims filed but not paid, or water damage claims occurring after the insured has taken appropriate preventative measures to avoid water damage in its assessment of the policy. The insured must be notified that there is a risk of the policy not being renewed if a third claim is filed within that same three-year period. If this notice is not sent as required, the insurer is not allowed to decline renewal if a third claim is filed. If proper written notice has been sent and a qualifying third claim is filed, the insurance carrier can opt to not renew the policy. As with personal auto policies, notice of nonrenewal must be sent no later than 60 days before the policy expiration date.

RESIDENTIAL INSURANCE

In Texas, insurers have a few options when writing residential insurance. Insurers that are members of the Insurance Services Office (ISO) typically use the homeowner's and dwelling forms available from that organization. Even though these forms are industry standard, insurers must still file them with the state to use them. Alternatively, an insurer may choose to author its own policy forms. These also need to be filed and approved by the state. The last option for insurance companies is to adopt state-level standard policy forms. While not identical, the Texas standard forms are very similar to the ISO policy forms. The chart below shows approximately how the forms align:

ISO Form	Texas Form
HO-1	HO-A
HO-2	HO-A+
HO-3	HO-B
HO-5	HO-C
DP-1	TDP-1
DP-2	TDP-2
DP-3	TDP-3

REQUIRED POLICY PROVISIONS

To ensure that a residential policy is in compliance with Texas law, certain provisions must be included. One such provision relates to mortgaged properties. If the named insured or policyholder violates or fails to comply with his or her duties under the insurance policy, the insurer has the right to deny coverage for a loss. If the property is the subject of a mortgage or is part of a trust, the actions of the insured cannot be used as a justification to deny coverage to the mortgagee or trustee. This applies to losses caused by the insured's neglect or any other factor outside of the mortgagee's or trustee's control that leads to a loss. Insurers are required to honor the mortgagee's or trustee's claim even if coverage is denied to the policyholder.

In situations involving the total loss of real property due to fire, the insurance code treats the policy as a liquidated demand for the full value of the policy. Policies are required to include the exact language of this provision in the body of all fire insurance policies. The personal property coverage of a residential policy is not subject to this mandate.

The insurance code also stipulates that residential property policies must be written in plain language. This can be achieved by conforming to the NAIC model act on policy language or by subjecting the form to the Flesch Reading Ease test or another comparable test. This mandate does not apply to policy language that is included under state or federal law.

PERSONAL AUTOMOBILE INSURANCE

Like any other state, Texas has laws regarding motor vehicle financial responsibility as outlined in the **Motor Vehicle Safety Responsibility Act (the Act)**. This act is part of the Texas Transportation Code, and enforcement is carried out by the **Texas Department of Transportation (TxDOT)**. The most common method of meeting financial responsibility requirements is by purchasing automobile liability insurance. Within the Act, "motor vehicle" is defined as:

> "A self-propelled vehicle designed for use on a highway, a trailer or semitrailer designed for use with a self-propelled vehicle, or a vehicle propelled by electric power from overhead wires and not operated on rails."

This definition does have some very specific exclusions, but generally, if it is a vehicle used or designed to be used on a public roadway, it is required to comply with the Act. For an auto policy to be in compliance with Texas law, it must carry the following minimum liability limits:

- $30,000 per person per accident for bodily injury
- $60,000 per accident for bodily injury
- $25,000 per accident for property damage

Penalties for motorists who fail to comply with financial responsibility requirements are subject to penalty. A noncompliant motorist may be fined up to $1,000. In addition to fines, a motorist's driver's license or vehicle registration may be suspended. Vehicles being driven in violation of the Act may be impounded for up to 180 days at a cost of $15 per day.

POLICY REQUIREMENTS

A Texas personal auto policy must include all of the information that one would expect on an auto policy declarations page: the name of the insured, the insured's address, premium amount, the dates the policy is in effect, and the liability limits. Coverage under the auto policy is triggered when a covered liability loss occurs, and such coverage cannot be terminated via an agreement between the insurance carrier and the insured. When the insurance policy is issued to the owner of a motor vehicle, it must include a provision that losses are covered when the vehicle is operated by someone other than the owner as long as he or she has the owner's permission to do so. For a policy issued for an operator who does not own an automobile, the policy is required to provide coverage for losses involving any vehicle the insured is operating as long as all the policy requirements are met.

Policies are prohibited from requiring an insured to satisfy a judgement for damage prior to making payment. Because of this prohibition, insurance companies are entitled to settle the claims presented to them without undue interference from the insured parties. Texas law also declares that auto liability insurance cannot be used to cover certain liability losses that should legally be covered in another way. Auto liability coverage cannot be used to cover losses for which the insured may be held liable pursuant to workers' compensation laws. Similarly, a personal auto policy cannot be used as an alternative to workers' compensation coverage when an employee of the insured is killed or injured in an auto loss. If the insured was required by law to provide workers' compensation benefits to such an employee, no coverage exists under the auto policy. Finally, auto liability coverage is prohibited from making payment on losses to property that is owned by, rented by, in the possession of, or being transported by an insured.

EVIDENCE OF FINANCIAL RESPONSIBILITY

Generally, drivers who carry suitable auto liability insurance do not need to file proof of coverage with the TxDOT. Motorists who have had their licenses suspended or revoked are typically required

283

to file evidence of financial responsibility with the TxDOT. If a motorist who is required to file evidence of financial responsibility either does not file it or files evidence that does not meet the state's requirements, the motorist's driver's license will be suspended, as will the registration for every motor vehicle registered to that motorist.

While uncommon, drivers can use other methods to fulfill financial responsibility requirements. An insured can own multiple auto policies to comply with the law as long as the combined total of the coverage available meets or exceeds the coverage minimums set by the state. This rarely occurs due to the insurance code requiring that all auto policies issued in Texas meet the minimum policy limit requirements. A driver or operator may also purchase a surety bond and file it with the state as proof of compliance. Funds may also be deposited with the comptroller or a county judge to meet the financial responsibility criteria. These deposits must be for at least $55,000. In situations where a person has more than 25 motor vehicles registered in his or her name, self-insurance is an option. To be self-insured, the individual must file for a certificate of self-insurance. The department of insurance will then review the person's financial records to ensure that the person has and will continue to have the ability to pay for any settlements or judgements resulting from an auto accident. If a self-insured owner fails to pay a judgement, he or she risks having the certificate of self-insurance cancelled.

When the financial responsibility requirements are met using an auto liability insurance policy, the insurance company must provide the insured with a **standard proof of motor vehicle liability insurance form** with the title of **Texas Liability Insurance Card** printed on it. The standard proof of motor vehicle liability insurance form must include:

- The name and address of each insured or covered party
- The make, model, and year of each insured vehicle
- The effective and expiration dates of the policy
- The policy number
- The name of the insurer
- The insurer's toll-free telephone number if the insurer is required by law to have one
- The name and telephone number of the insurance agent, if applicable
- A statement that the coverage provided meets the legal minimum coverage requirements

For digital insurance cards meant to be displayed on a mobile phone or other mobile communication device, the image or document must include:

- The name and address of each insured or covered party
- The make and model of each insured vehicle
- The effective and expiration dates of the policy
- The policy number
- The name of the insurer
- The coverage limits or a statement that the coverage provided meets the legal minimum coverage requirements

Under Texas law, a motorist is mandated to produce evidence of compliance with financial responsibility laws when it is requested by a law enforcement officer. Most commonly, such a request occurs during a traffic stop or following an automobile accident. Only certain documentation will be accepted as proof of financial responsibility. Acceptable documents include:

- A motor vehicle liability policy or a photocopy of a motor vehicle liability policy that meets state requirements
- A standard proof of motor vehicle liability insurance form that is issued by an insurance company
- A digital photo or other electronic document displayed on a portable device that shows all the information that would be on a standard proof of motor vehicle liability insurance form
- An insurance binder showing coverage that complies with legal requirements
- A surety bond certificate
- A certificate of deposit issued by a county judge for the vehicle being operated
- A certificate of deposit issued by the state comptroller for the vehicle being operated
- A certificate of self-insurance or a photocopy of a certificate of self-insurance

When a motorist who was required to file evidence of financial responsibility with the TxDOT substitutes another method of compliance for the one already filed, the department must be notified and approve of the substitution. If a motorist who previously deposited funds with the comptroller chooses to meet financial responsibility requirements by another means, he or she must submit the new evidence to TxDOT. The department will review the information submitted and if approved, will consent to the return of the funds that were deposited. If a motorist desires to cancel, return, or waive evidence previously filed with the TxDOT, he or she must submit a request to the department. A request cannot be made any earlier than two years after the date on which the motorist was mandated to file evidence of financial responsibility. A cancellation, return, or waiver will only be granted under certain circumstances, which include:

- The motorist in question has not been convicted of or forfeited bail for an offense that would result in the revocation or suspension of a driver's license, vehicle registration, or nonresident operating privileges within the two years preceding the request
- The motorist in question is deceased or permanently unable to drive
- The motorist in question surrenders his or her driver's license and vehicle registration(s) to the TxDOT

The TxDOT is prohibited from returning deposited funds to a motorist if any of the following are true:

- There is a pending action for liability damages that would be covered by the filed evidence of financial responsibility
- There is an unsatisfied judgment for liability damages that is owed under the financial responsibility
- The individual for whom the evidence was filed has been involved in an auto accident as an owner or operator, and such accident resulted in damage to another party's property or the bodily injury of another person

REQUIRED AND OPTIONAL COVERAGES

Agents and insurers in Texas are only permitted to write automobile policies that meet the minimum financial responsibility requirements as outlined in the transportation code. For personal auto insurance written in Texas, liability coverage is not the only required element of a policy. There are also coverages that an insurer must make available to customers, but the customer is not required to purchase them.

PERSONAL INJURY PROTECTION COVERAGE

Texas mandates that auto policies include **personal injury protection (PIP) coverage** by default. A policy can only be written without PIP coverage if the insured rejects it in writing. Otherwise, the insurer must provide no less than $2,500 per person per accident for injury expenses. PIP benefits are payable on a no-fault basis and without consideration of other sources of medical coverage. Amounts paid under PIP cannot be recovered from other insurance companies. Insurers may only subrogate for PIP payments if the at-fault driver has not complied with financial responsibility requirements.

PIP provides coverage for reasonable and necessary medical treatment that is rendered within three years following an auto accident. If an insured dies due to an auto accident, PIP will cover funeral expenses. In addition to medical and funeral expenses, PIP also covers an injured insured's lost wages at 80 percent. If the insured is not employed, PIP can cover amounts paid for essential services that the insured would normally provide. Essential services include items such as house cleaning services, lawn care, and childcare.

Insurance companies must pay PIP benefits in a timely manner, which the insurance code defines as no later than the 30th day after suitable proof of loss is received. If an insured is forced to bring legal action against a carrier to collect PIP benefits, the insurer may be ordered to pay attorney's fees, a 12 percent penalty, and interest on the overdue payment. Except when there is a gap in treatment or disability, insurers are obligated to continue paying benefits for six months from the date of the accident based on the initial proof of loss received. Insurers are not obligated to pay PIP benefits if the accident occurred with the intention of causing injury to the insured or if the accident occurred during the commission of a felony. PIP payments may also be denied if the driver was attempting to avoid being arrested by a law enforcement officer.

UNINSURED AND UNDERINSURED MOTORIST COVERAGE

Uninsured (UM) and underinsured (UIM) motorist bodily injury coverage is optional on Texas personal auto policies. Insurers are mandated to offer the coverage on every policy, but the customer is not required to purchase it. Rejection of these coverages must be in writing. If the insured chooses to purchase UM or UIM coverage, he or she cannot purchase policy limits higher than the limit carried for bodily injury liability. This means that if a policyholder has a policy with the minimum limits of 30/60, he or she cannot purchase UM or UIM coverage for more than that amount. Texas law also demands that insurers offer uninsured motorist property damage (UMPD) coverage on every policy. This coverage will pay for damage to the insured's vehicle if he or she is involved in an accident with an uninsured driver. If the insured chooses to buy UMPD, the coverage is subject to a $250 per accident deductible. Unlike PIP benefits, the insurance carrier is allowed to pursue reimbursement of amounts paid under UM, UIM, and UMPD.

MEDICAL PAYMENTS COVERAGE

In Texas, medical payments coverage is fully optional, and insurers are not even required to offer it. Many insurers do offer it to insureds for an additional premium. Because it is not a mandatory coverage, the coverage provided can vary by policy. Generally, only expenses incurred within one year of an auto accident will be covered. Covered costs usually include reasonable medical expenses and funeral expenses. Some policies will only cover the amount the injured person's health insurance does not cover, such as deductibles or copayments. Medical payments coverage does not pay for loss of income or the cost of essential services.

TRANSPORTATION NETWORK DRIVERS

An emerging risk for auto insurers in recent years has been the increasing use of **transportation network companies**. Under the insurance code, transportation network company is defined as follows:

> "a corporation, partnership, sole proprietorship, or other entity operating in this state that uses a digital network to connect a transportation network company rider to a transportation network company driver for a prearranged ride"

The use of transportation networks creates risks related to both drivers and riders who use such services. Under Texas law, transportation network drivers are required to carry automobile insurance or have such insurance provided by the transportation network company on the driver's behalf. If the driver uses his or her own insurance, he or she must ensure that the policy will provide coverage for losses that occur while logged into the transportation network system and while transporting a passenger. Coverage may only be purchased from an insurer authorized to write auto insurance in the state of Texas or a qualified surplus lines insurance carrier.

Because driving for a transportation network exposes the general public to risk, the minimum coverage required is higher than the statutory minimum auto liability coverage. The amount needed varies based on what the driver is doing at the time.

When the driver is logged into the network as available for rides but does not have a passenger, the minimum requirements are:

- $50,000 per person per accident for bodily injury
- $100,000 per accident for bodily injury
- $25,000 per accident for property damage

When the driver is transporting a passenger, the insurance policy must provide at least $1 million in aggregate liability coverage for all bodily injury and property damage resulting from a single accident. If the driver or vehicle is required under law to carry PIP coverage, then there must also be at least $2,500 in PIP coverage on the policy.

If a driver fails to maintain the required insurance coverage or allows it to lapse, the transportation network company (TNC) or its insurer must provide primary liability coverage for any claims. This responsibility applies even if the driver's insurer has not formally denied a claim. With regard to supervising drivers, companies are only responsible to the extent outlined in the transportation network agreement or contract. Before the driver can engage in rides for the transportation network company, the company must provide the driver with a copy of the insurance policy or provide a written statement disclosing the types and amounts of coverage the company provides. Companies must also provide warning that the driver's personal auto policy may not cover losses that occur while the driver is logged in and available for ride services. Texas law permits personal auto insurance policies to exclude coverage for losses related to transportation network services, so this disclaimer is vital to ensuring that the driver understands the risk involved in working with such a network.

Texas Workers' Compensation Act

INTRODUCTION

In Texas, workers' compensation is primarily regulated under the Texas Labor Code, specifically Title 5. This section of the code includes the **Texas Workers' Compensation Act (the Act)**. Most of this regulation is undertaken by the **Texas Division of Workers' Compensation (DWC)**. For most employers in Texas, carrying workers' compensation coverage is optional, making Texas an **elective state** with respect to workers' compensation insurance coverage. Employers who choose to not carry some form of workers' compensation may be exposed to tort liability for employee injuries, while employers who do provide workers' compensation coverage are protected under law because workers' compensation benefits are the exclusive remedy for an injured employee when appropriate coverage is carried. When workers' compensation coverage is the exclusive remedy for an employee, he or she is prohibited from suing his or her employer or any coworkers for negligence. However, even when workers' compensation insurance is the exclusive remedy for employee injuries, employees are permitted to collect exemplary or punitive damages when the employer is found to have been grossly negligent in a way that caused or contributed to the employee's injury.

While uncommon, Texas law does permit an employee to opt out of workers' compensation benefits in exchange for retaining the right to pursue an employer for tort liability even if that employer has workers' compensation coverage. If an employee wishes to opt out, the employer must be notified within five days of the beginning of that person's employment or within five days of the employee being informed that workers' compensation coverage has been obtained by the employer.

If an employer does not have workers' compensation coverage, it can be sued by an injured employee for damages. Texas law limits the defenses an employer can raise when sued by an injured employee. An employer cannot attempt to offset its obligations as an employer by arguing that the employee assumed the risk of injury, was injured due to the negligence of a fellow employee, or that the employee contributed to his or her own injury. The only defenses an employer may raise in this situation are conditions that would disqualify an employee injury from workers' compensation benefits if the coverage did exist. These conditions will be addressed later in this chapter.

The Texas Workers' Compensation Act outlines the specifics of workers' compensation coverage and claims handling. Under the Act, work-related injuries include occupational diseases sustained within the course and scope of employment. Repetitive trauma injuries are treated as an occupational disease under the Act, as are infections that occur due to a work-related injury. The Act defines certain terms that are pertinent to workers' compensation laws and practices. Under this law, an **employer** is a person who contracts with one or more employees and furnishes workers' compensation insurance coverage. This includes self-funded or self-insured employers or governmental entities. The only **compensable injuries** under the Act are those incurred during the **course and scope of employment**. An individual is deemed to be in the course and scope of employment when he or she is performing any duties or activities involving the business or trade of his or her employer and completing those duties in the furtherance of the employer's business or affairs. This definition extends to all locations at which the employee is performing his or her work duties. It includes any time spent traveling on behalf of the employer but does not apply to typical commuting activities.

The Act also defines what constitutes an **employee**. An employee is an individual who provides work or services to another under any contract of hire. Contracts of hire may be express, implied, written, or oral. This definition includes:

- An employee who is temporarily directed by the employer to perform duties outside of his or her usual duties
- A worker who is performing construction, repair, or remodeling work on behalf of an employer at the premises of that employer, except for independent contractors and their employees
- Trainees under the Texans Work program

Under the Act, masters and seamen working on vessels engaged in interstate or international commerce are not considered employees for the purposes of workers' compensation. The Act also excludes those persons performing duties that do not fall within the course and scope of the employer's usual business. A person is treated as an employee when performing legally permissible activities even if the employer is in violation of state law, municipal ordinance, or any laws that restrict working on Sundays.

While the Act broadly defines what constitutes an employee acting in the course of his or her employment, there are circumstances in which an employee may be injured while working but the injury is ineligible for workers' compensation benefits. An employee will not be eligible for benefits when:

- The employee was intoxicated at the time the injury occurred
- The employee was attempting to injure him- or herself on purpose
- The employee was injured while trying to illegally injure another individual
- The injury arose from another individual intentionally injuring an employee for a personal reason unrelated to the employee's work
- The employee was injured while participating in voluntary off-duty social, athletic, or recreational activities, unless there is a reasonable belief that participation was required as part of employment
- The injury arose out of an act of God, unless the employee's usual work exposes him or her to a greater risk of injury from such events
- The employee was injured while engaging in horseplay

In this context, **intoxication** means circumstances in which the employee:

- Has a blood alcohol concentration in excess of the statutory limit
- Is unable to act or think normally due to ingestion of:
  - Alcohol
  - A substance controlled by state or federal law
  - Illicit or dangerous drugs
  - Fumes from glue or spray paint
  - Any other similar substance regulated under law

Testing for intoxicating substances may be done via urinalysis or blood testing. Neither impairment caused by prescription medication legally obtained and taken in accordance with the physician's directions nor any impairment resulting from substances inhaled or absorbed during the course of the employee's work is not considered intoxication.

TYPES OF WORKERS' COMPENSATION COVERAGE

While workers' compensation coverage is generally optional for Texas employers, there are some circumstances in which it is required. For example, companies who contract with the Texas government or other governmental entities are required to carry coverage. Contractors are also permitted to require subcontractors to carry workers' compensation insurance. If an employer chooses to have workers' compensation coverage or is required by law to carry it, there are a few ways that the coverage may be secured.

The most common method of obtaining workers' compensation coverage is to purchase it from a commercial insurer who is authorized to write workers' compensation business in Texas. In these situations, any claims made are handled and paid by the insurer. The employer needs only to make sure that premiums are paid and reporting requirements are met. Commercial insurers are subject to Texas insurance and workers' compensation laws.

The next option for employers is to **self-insure** workers' compensation losses. Qualified employers must apply for and secure a certificate of authority to self-insure from the DWC. Not all employers are qualified to be self-insured. Self-insuring for workers' compensation coverage can be very expensive, and employers who wish to self-insure must provide that they are in a financial position to take on those expenses. Firstly, the employer must have an estimated unmodified manual insurance premium of at least $500,000 held in Texas or a total of at least $10 million nationwide. This amount is calculated by multiplying the applicable classification rate by the total payroll then dividing by 100. If the employer is not large enough to meet these minimum premium requirements, it does not qualify to self-insure. In addition, an employer must produce audited financial statements, meet minimum financial rating requirements, and carry excess insurance with limits of at least $5 million per loss. The employer must also make a security deposit of not less than $300,000. Once the employer is certified to self-insure, it must join the **Texas Certified Self-Insurer Guaranty Association (TCSIGA)**.

Another option for Texas employers is to form a **self-insurance group**. These groups allow employers engaged in similar businesses or industries to pool their resources to self-insure for workers' compensation. For employers to form a self-insurance group, there must be at least five employers in the group, and the group must be sponsored by a trade association recognized by the state. The employers in a self-insurance group are subject to both joint and several liability. Each group member must also be a member of the **Texas Self-Insurance Guaranty Fund (TSIGF)** and contribute money to that fund. A group must apply for and be granted a **certificate of approval** from the insurance commissioner to act as a self-insurer. A statutory deposit must be made, the amount of which is determined by the **Self-Insurance Regulation (SIR)** section of the DWC.

Government and public entities such as school districts, police departments, government agencies, and state colleges and universities are required to carry workers' compensation coverage for their employees. Texas law allows such entities to self-insure individually or as a self-insurance group. When self-insured, government entities are not required to obtain a certificate of approval from the department of insurance. Commercial workers' compensation coverage is also an option.

IMPAIRMENT RATINGS AND MAXIMUM MEDICAL IMPROVEMENT

Since paying workers' compensation benefits relies greatly on an employee's ability to work, **impairment ratings** are extremely important in determining the benefits an employee is entitled to receive. Impairment ratings are typically determined once the employee has reached **maximum medical improvement (MMI)**. MMI is the point at which the employee has recovered as much as possible from his or her injury and further treatment is not anticipated to provide any further improvement. This does not mean that the injured person is healed or cured but rather that he or she has reached what the physician believes to be the best condition that can be attained. The physician must then certify that the employee has achieved MMI. By law, an employee is considered to have reached MMI if he or she has received income benefits for 104 weeks even if the doctor has not provided certification.

Once the employee has reached MMI, he or she will be evaluated for an impairment rating. If the employee has returned to his or her pre-injury condition without any residual issues, the impairment rating would be 0 percent.

MANDATORY BENEFITS

When a workplace injury results in a compensable workers' compensation claim, benefits are to be paid without regard to the employee's liability or contribution to his or her own injuries. Insurance companies and self-insured entities are prohibited from attempting to reduce the amount of benefits paid due to the employee having been fully or partially responsible for his or her own injury.

MEDICAL BENEFITS

When an employee suffers an injury that meets the requirements for workers' compensation benefits, medical expenses must be paid starting from the date the injury occurs. The medical care provided to the injured employee must be reasonable and necessary for the type of injury sustained. More specifically, workers' compensation must pay for care that cures or resolves the employee's condition, alleviates the employee's symptoms that result from the injury, promotes recovery, and increases the employee's ability to return to work duties. Medical care can include, but is not limited to, doctor's visits, hospital services, physical rehabilitation services, surgeries, and diagnostic imaging.

Unless the treatment is being provided in an emergency situation, an injured employee must seek treatment only from doctors approved by the DWC, and all nonemergency treatment must be recommended or approved by a designated doctor—an independent, licensed medical professional chosen by the DWC to evaluate specific aspects of an injured employee's case. This designated doctor collaborates with the treating doctor to ensure treatment aligns with the recovery goals and complies with DWC guidelines. Doctors who provide services for workers' compensation cases are registered with the DWC and are subject to training requirements. Registration and training are required if the doctor does any of the following:

- Furnishes medical services as a treating physician
- Provides medical services authorized by the Texas Workers' Compensation Act
- Completes medical peer reviews related to workers' compensation
- Performs utilization reviews related to workers' compensation
- Sees and treats patients upon referral by a treating physician

If the injured employee wishes to see a different provider, a request must be submitted to the DWC outlining the reasons for the request. Examples of permissible reasons include an impaired doctor-patient relationship, the reputation of the doctor, and concerns about the appropriateness of the treatment. Employees are not allowed to see an alternate provider because of a new medical report or impairment rating. When the employee works for an employer that has at least 10 employees, the doctor may request a job description for the injured employee to help guide decisions about if and when an employee may return to work.

Alternately, workers' compensation-related medical treatment may be provided by a certified workers' compensation health network. A workers' compensation health network is similar to a physician group or multispecialty medical group. Workers' compensation insurers may contract with a workers' compensation health network to provide medical services to injured workers. Such groups must be certified by the state. When a doctor is a member of a certified workers' compensation health network, individual registration with the DWC is not required. When a network is used, injured employees are required to only seek care from in-network providers. Out-of-network care is only payable for emergency care, when there are no in-network providers in the employee's geographic area, or when the employee is referred to the out-of-network provider by the treating physician.

Medical providers are required to submit medical bills no more than 95 days after the date services were rendered. Failure to comply with this requirement will result in the provider forfeiting the right to collect payment for that service. Medical bills must also be paid in a timely manner. From the date of receipt, a workers' compensation insurer has 45 days to pay, adjust, deny, or decide to audit the claim. An audit is performed when there is concern that the injury being treated is not work related, the treatment is not necessary, or if the nature of the injury is unclear. If additional documentation is needed by the insurer, it must be requested during this 45-day period. Once the provider receives a request for additional information, the response must be sent within 15 days.

Another medical benefit under workers' compensation coverage relates to medication. Workers' compensation coverage will pay for prescription and nonprescription medications when needed to facilitate the employee's recovery. Reimbursement is based on a fee schedule adopted by the commissioner of the DWC. Certified workers' compensation health networks are prohibited from dispensing prescription drugs to patients. If an employee's injury necessitates it, workers' compensation will also cover the costs of durable medical equipment, such as wheelchairs, prosthetics, orthotics, or hospital beds. Workers' compensation will cover medically necessary home health care services as well.

WAGE LOSS BENEFITS

The next benefit provided by workers' compensation insurance coverage pertains to loss of income. If the employee is injured to the extent that he or she is unable to work, the Act requires the employee to be paid for the time missed from work. The basis for wage loss reimbursement used most frequently is the **average weekly wage**. The average weekly wage is calculated by taking the average amount earned over the 13 weeks immediately preceding the covered injury. Adjustments may be made to benefits paid due to the **state average weekly wage**. For the purposes of workers' compensation, the state average weekly wage is equal to 88 percent of the average weekly wage and calculated by the Texas Workforce Commission.

Wage loss benefits are paid weekly and may accrue interest if not paid promptly. In most cases, the employee collects a **temporary income benefit** that is payable only for the time in the employee's recovery during which he or she is unable to work. These benefits will be paid until the employee reaches MMI or up to a maximum of 104 weeks. For full-time employees, the weekly benefit paid is usually 70 percent of the employee's average weekly wage. When the employee earns under $10 per hour, the benefit is paid at 75 percent for the first 26 weeks the employee is unable to work. If the employee is able to work at a modified level, such as working fewer hours per week or performing duties for which the pay is lower, then the temporary income benefit is paid at 70 percent of the difference between what the employee is being paid now and his or her pre-injury average weekly wage. The amount paid to an employee under the temporary income benefit is restricted to no more than 100 percent of the state average weekly wage. The smallest amount an employee may be paid under the temporary income benefit is 15 percent of the state average weekly wage. The total of all temporary income benefits paid must not exceed the total amount the employee was paid in the previous calendar year.

Temporary income benefits are not the only reimbursement an injured employee may receive in relation to wage loss. Texas law also allows the following:

- **Impairment income benefits**: benefits payable beginning the day after the employee is certified to be at MMI; this is payable for three weeks per percentage point of impairment or until the employee's death, whichever is earlier.
- **Supplemental income benefits**: benefits payable upon the expiration of the impairment income benefit when:
  - The employee has been unable to return to work.
  - The employee has been able to return to work but is earning less than 80 percent of his or her average weekly wage.
  - The employee has chosen not to commute any remaining impairment income benefits and is actively looking for employment under the work search compliance standards set by the state.

Supplemental income benefits are recalculated quarterly, and payment is issued on a monthly basis. Benefits automatically expire once the employee has been working for 90 days and is making at least 80 percent of his or her pre-injury average weekly wage. The DWC has the authority to refer an employee for vocational rehabilitation or training if such care could improve the employee's likelihood of resuming employment in the same occupation or an occupation similar to the one that the employee had prior to the injury. If a referral is provided and the employee refuses such services, his or her supplemental income benefits will be terminated.

- **Lifetime income benefits**: these benefits are payable for the remainder of an employee's life if the injury sustained resulted in:
  - Total and permanent blindness in both eyes
  - Loss of both hands at or above the wrist
  - Loss of both feet at or above the ankle
  - Loss of one hand and one foot
  - Paralysis in both arms or legs or in one arm and one leg as the result of a spinal injury
  - A permanent traumatic brain injury that affects activities of daily living and renders the employee permanently unable to work
  - Third-degree burns over 40 percent or more of the body that require skin grafting
  - Third-degree burns affecting the majority of both hands, one hand and one foot, or the face and one hand or one foot

Lifetime income benefits are paid at 75 percent of the average weekly wage. A 3 percent increase is applied annually to these benefits.

DEATH BENEFITS

When an employee dies as the result of a work-related injury, workers' compensation coverage provides death benefits to the employee legal beneficiary. The amount paid is 75 percent of the deceased employee's average weekly wage. Death benefit payments are only payable for 104 weeks following the employee's death. A beneficiary can be a surviving spouse, a parent, a child, or a grandchild. A workers' compensation insurer is mandated to pay death benefits even if there are no beneficiaries to collect them. When there are multiple eligible beneficiaries, the benefits are distributed in accordance with Texas law as follows:

- If there is a spouse and no children, the spouse will receive 100 percent of the death benefit.
- If there is a spouse and eligible children or grandchildren, the spouse will receive 50 percent of the death benefit, and the remaining 50 percent will be split equally among the children and/or grandchildren.
- If there are eligible children or grandchildren but no spouse, the death benefit will be split equally among the children and/or grandchildren.
- If there is no spouse and no eligible children or grandchildren, the death benefit will be split equally among any surviving dependents of the employee.
- If there is no spouse, eligible children or grandchildren, or surviving dependents, the death benefit will be split equally among surviving eligible parents of the employee.
- If there are no beneficiaries or eligible parents, the death benefit will be paid into the **Texas Subsequent Injury Fund (SIF)** in an amount equal to 364 weeks of benefits. This fund was established to encourage employers to hire workers with preexisting injuries and is used to offset the costs associated with new work injuries that may be sustained by such employees.

If there is doubt that an employee's death was the result of an occupational disease, the workers' compensation commission has the authority to order an autopsy on the deceased. If the employee's survivors wish to collect death benefits, they must comply with the order but are entitled to have a representative of their own present during the autopsy. The workers' compensation insurer must bear the cost of the autopsy.

Workers' compensation death benefits also include payment for eligible funeral and burial expenses. The amount paid will be either the actual cost of the burial or $10,000, whichever is less. If the employee was killed away from his or her usual workplace, workers' compensation will pay reasonable expenses to transport the body.

Texas Insurance Associations and Funds

INTRODUCTION

As part of insurance regulation, the state of Texas makes use of **guaranty associations** and funds to protect consumers from insurer insolvency. There are also associations devoted to making necessary insurance coverage available to consumers who may not otherwise be able to obtain it. When consumers who wish to purchase insurance are unable to due to limitations imposed by the voluntary insurance marketplace, this creates a **residual market** of consumers in need of insurance protection.

GUARANTY ASSOCIATIONS

With few exceptions, licensed insurance companies in Texas are required to join the guaranty association relevant to the lines of business they write. A guaranty association is made up of insurance companies that operate within the state. Members of the association are required to contribute money to a fund that is managed by the state. When an insurer becomes insolvent or impaired, the money in the fund is used to honor outstanding claims for the insurer in question. Under the Texas Insurance Code, an **impaired insurer** is defined as a member of the association that is subject to a final and non-appealable liquidation order issued by a Texas court or a court in the state where the insurance company is domiciled. Membership in the applicable guaranty association is required for the following lines of business:

- Property and casualty insurance
- Life and health insurance
- Title insurance

TEXAS PROPERTY AND CASUALTY INSURANCE GUARANTY ASSOCIATION

One of the major guaranty associations in Texas is the **Texas Property and Casualty Insurance Guaranty Association (TPCIGA)**. The TPCIGA is a nonprofit association whose membership includes all licensed P&C insurers that do business in Texas. It was established in 1971 to protect policyholders and claimants when insurers become insolvent. It is led by the insurance commissioner and operates under the insurance code. The TPCIGA does not sell or write insurance policies. Its only purpose is to reimburse insureds and claimants for valid claims owed by an insurance company that does not have the funds to pay them. The TPCIGA not only covers property claims, but it will also provide coverage for liability claims, including furnishing a legal defense for the insured when the policy covers it.

Insureds of insolvent insurance companies become eligible for coverage under the TPCIGA when a Texas court issues an order designating the insurer as impaired. Only Texas residents or owners of property permanently located in Texas are eligible for payment under the TPCIGA. Coverage under the TPCIGA is usually limited to $300,000 or the limits of the policy issued by the impaired insurer, whichever is less. If the coverage is for workers' compensation, the TPCIGA will pay up to the amount required by law. In addition to adjudicating and paying claims, the TPCIGA will also refund policyholders up to $25,000 per policy for unearned premiums.

UNAUTHORIZED INSURANCE GUARANTY FUND ACT

The department also maintains a fund for customers who purchased insurance from a company not authorized to do business within the state. This fund was established by the Unauthorized Insurance Guaranty Fund Act. Insureds of unauthorized insurance companies are not eligible for compensation under the applicable guaranty association, so this act was necessary to properly protect such insureds from the financial hardship that can result from purchasing coverage from an unauthorized insurance company. The fund is financed using money obtained through administrative fines imposed by the department, civil penalties collected by the department, and bond forfeitures related to court and administrative proceedings involving unauthorized insurers.

INSURANCE ASSOCIATIONS
TEXAS FAIR PLAN ASSOCIATION (TFPA)

While there are many insurers operating in Texas who sell homeowner's and other residential insurance products, some consumers present risks that a traditional insurer, also referred to as a private or voluntary insurer, does not have the appetite for. An insurer may decline to cover an insured if, for example, there is an extensive loss history or the home is in an area that carries higher risk for loss. In some cases, a community as a whole is underserved by insurance companies. This can present a serious challenge for homeowners because homes purchased using a mortgage are almost always required to carry some degree of insurance coverage.

To accommodate consumers who find themselves in this situation, the department established the **Texas Fair Access to Insurance Requirements (FAIR) Plan Association, or TFPA**. The TFPA performs some operations that you would expect from an insurance company such as issuing insurance contracts, accepting premium payments on the insurance policies sold, and paying for covered claims. Loss and operating expenses are funded using the premiums collected by the TFPA. Any remaining revenue from those policy premiums is held as surplus for payment of future claims.

In addition to these functions, the TFPA works to pool the resources of insurance companies that are licensed to sell residential property insurance in Texas. Membership in the TFPA is mandatory for all such insurers. Member insurers are required to contribute funds to the TFPA in the form of **assessments**. If necessary, the association has the authority to collect additional assessments from members to offset any financial shortfalls that may occur. Insurers are entitled to credits against their assessments for residential policies written in underserved areas. This acts as an incentive for insurers to provide coverage for such areas.

ELIGIBILITY

TFPA policies are only available for one- and two-family homes, townhouses, condominiums, and manufactured homes. There is also a TFPA plan option for rental tenants who cannot obtain renter's insurance through typical means. TFPA plan coverage is not available for commercial properties. To avoid duplication of coverage, TFPA plan policies do not provide coverage for hail or windstorm losses if the property qualifies for coverage under the Texas Windstorm Insurance Association.

The TFPA is considered a market of last resort. This means that it will only provide coverage to consumers who have exhausted efforts to obtain residential insurance through the normal marketplace. To qualify for a TFPA plan policy, an applicant must have been declined by no fewer than two insurance companies authorized to do business in Texas. If the applicant has a current insurance policy, a valid offer of policy renewal, or a valid offer of coverage from an admitted Texas insurer, he or she is not eligible to apply for TFPA plan coverage. The TFPA does not sell insurance to the public directly, and applications may only be submitted using a licensed P&C agent. Once an application is approved, the insured must reapply for traditional insurance coverage every two years. Underwriting criteria can change over time, so reapplication is necessary to ensure that TFPA plan criteria continue to be met.

While the underwriting standards for a TFPA plan policy may not be as stringent as the standards of a traditional insurance company, there are some circumstances in which an application can be rejected. Properties with preexisting damage or that have been condemned cannot be insured under a TFPA plan. The same is true for vacant properties, dwellings that house a business, and farms and ranches with business operations. Mobile homes are only insurable if the wheels are removed and the home is secured to the ground. Property use and condition are not the only factors that can lead to an application being denied. Applicants with criminal convictions involving insurance, such as arson or fraud, are not eligible for coverage. An applicant can also be denied if there is an unusual or excessive liability risk associated with the property, such as a dog of an aggressive breed or a swimming pool without a proper fence. Those with a history of frequent claims may also be excluded from eligibility. This is defined as having more than eight insurance claims paid within a period of three years, excluding glass-only claims.

AVAILABLE POLICY FORMS

There are four policy forms available under the TFPA: **homeowner's**, **dwelling**, **condominium**, and **tenant**. They are structured similarly to the comparable ISO forms and contain sections regarding exclusions, conditions, and coverage extensions, but they are not identical. The dwelling form does not provide personal liability or medical payments coverage, while all the other forms do offer these coverages. The property coverage under the tenant and condominium policy forms is focused mainly on personal property. The homeowner's and dwelling policy forms cover both the dwelling and personal property contained within the dwelling.

Because a TFPA plan policy is intended to insure those who cannot secure the basic minimum coverage needed for a dwelling, coverage is provided on a named perils basis. The perils covered by all TFPA plan policy forms are:

- Fire and lightning
- Sudden and accidental smoke damage
- Explosion
- Aircraft and vehicles
- Riot and civil commotion

Vandalism and malicious mischief are included in the homeowner's, condominium, and tenant policies but are only available for a dwelling policy via endorsement. Theft of personal property is covered by all policy forms except for the dwelling form.

There are various endorsements available to modify the coverage provided under a TFPA plan policy such as replacement cost coverage endorsements, hail and windstorm exclusion endorsements, and exclusions pertaining to specified animals or buildings. Replacement cost coverage for a residence cannot be added to the dwelling policy form. Under the homeowner's form, the home must be insured for 100 percent of its replacement value to add the replacement cost endorsement.

COVERAGE LIMITS AND DEDUCTIBLES

Like most other property policies, TFPA plan policies also impose a per loss deductible for covered losses. The available options are 1 percent or 2 percent of the total loss amount. This means that if a loss occurs that is valued at $50,000, the insured would be obliged to pay either $500 or $1,000 of the loss depending upon the deductible selected. The deductible percentage is listed on the policy declarations page.

By default, TFPA plan policies reimburse property claims at **actual cash value (ACV)** up to the applicable policy limit. The policies have maximum coverage limits for each type of coverage offered. The maximum coverage available for each coverage part is as follows:

- Coverage A—Dwelling: $1 million
- Other Structures: 10 percent of the dwelling coverage amount
- Coverage B—Personal Property
  - Dwelling form: up to 50 percent of the dwelling coverage amount
  - Homeowner's form: up to 70 percent of the dwelling coverage amount
  - Condominium and tenant forms: $500,000
- Coverage C—Personal Liability: $300,000
- Coverage D—Medical Payments to Others: $5,000 per person and $25,000 per occurrence

TEXAS WINDSTORM INSURANCE ASSOCIATION (TWIA)

The southeastern coast of Texas is frequently affected by hurricanes and tropical storms. Because these types of natural disasters result in significant loss payments, it is not unusual for insurers in the voluntary insurance market to decline hail and windstorm coverage for residents of this area. In many cases, an insurance company is willing to write a homeowner's or other residential policy but require the policy to be amended with an endorsement excluding coverage for windstorm and hail losses. The **Texas Windstorm Insurance Association (TWIA)** was created to fill the gap in available coverage for coastal areas. Like TFPA plan policies, TWIA policies are only used as a last resort when an insured cannot obtain necessary coverage for hail and wind losses. TWIA policies only cover wind and hail, so coverage for any other perils would need to be purchased under a separate policy.

ELIGIBILITY

Applications for TWIA coverage may only be submitted via insurance agents licensed to do business in Texas. To qualify for a TWIA policy, the property must be located in an area designated as a catastrophe area by TWIA. The catastrophe area consists of counties that are located on the coast, called "first-tier coastal counties."

First-tier coastal counties include:

- Aransas County
- Brazoria County
- Calhoun County
- Cameron County
- Chambers County
- Galveston County
- Harris County (limited to the area east of State Highway 146)
- Jefferson County
- Kenedy County
- Kleberg County
- Matagorda County
- Nueces County
- Refugio County
- San Patricio County
- Willacy County

In addition to geographical requirements, the property for which the applicant is seeking coverage must be of a type that TWIA will cover. This includes residential structures and the personal property housed within. Manufactured homes are also eligible. In contrast to TFPA plans, commercial buildings are eligible for TWIA coverage. This includes commercial townhomes, condominiums, and business personal property. Certain outdoor property such as fences and swimming pools can also be covered by a TWIA policy.

To be eligible for TWIA coverage, the applicant must have been declined for hail and windstorm coverage by a traditional insurer that writes hail and windstorm coverage in his or her geographic area. TWIA rules allow properties to be inspected as part of the application process. The building to be covered must meet building code requirements, and this must be certified by either the Texas Department of Insurance or the TWIA. The building must also be in insurable condition, meaning that it must not be in disrepair or be in a hazardous condition. If the property is located in a flood plain rated V or VE under the current **Flood Insurance Rate Map** and the location is eligible for flood insurance under the **National Flood Insurance Program (NFIP)**, then the applicant must provide proof of valid flood insurance for the property to be eligible for TWIA coverage.

AVAILABLE POLICY FORMS

The two basic policy forms available under the TWIA are the dwelling form and the commercial form. Since TWIA policies are designed only to cover property, the dwelling form is used for all residential insureds. For both policy types, endorsements are available to tailor coverage to meet the customer's needs. As previously discussed, TWIA policies only cover losses resulting from windstorm and hail. Both dwelling and commercial policies include coverage for specified incidental expenses such as reasonable repairs to protect the property from further damage, removal of personal property to a safe location before an impending loss, and debris removal costs. The dwelling form includes an additional coverage extension for improvements, alterations, and additions made to covered properties. This extension only applies when the insured is a rental tenant or condominium owner.

POLICY CONDITIONS

The conditions contained in TWIA policies mostly mirror those found in ISO property policies. There are a few important differences relating to the insured's and insurer's duties under the policy. Under TWIA policies, the policyholder must report any covered loss to the TWIA claims department no more than one year after the date of loss. The commissioner may, on a case-by-case basis, extend this period by up to 180 days if good cause is shown. If the TWIA requires any additional information to adjust the claim, a notice must be sent to the policyholder no later than 30 days after the claim is reported. Once the needed information is received, the insured must be notified of the TWIA's coverage position on the claim. If the coverage position is that some or all of the claim will be paid, the TWIA has 10 days to issue payment. If there is action required of the insured before the claim payment can be made, the TWIA has 10 days to issue the payment after the insured has completed the action. To determine the amount payable for a loss, the TWIA will pay the lowest of the property's ACV, the cost to repair or replace the property, or the applicable policy limit.

The conditions relating to legal action being taken against the TWIA are quite different from those found in retail property policies. Policyholders are not permitted to file a lawsuit against the TWIA, its agents, or its representatives, neither privately nor under a class action suit. If coverage is afforded in full or in part and the dispute in question relates to the valuation of a claim, the insured's only remedy allowed under the policy is to demand an appraisal. The appraisal process under the TWIA dwelling policy is essentially the same as that found in the ISO policies.

If the dispute concerns a full or partial denial of coverage, the policyholder must notify the TWIA in writing of his or her intent to file a suit. This must be done within two years of the TWIA notifying the insured of the total or partial denial of coverage. The TWIA policy also reserves the TWIA's right to demand alternative dispute resolution (ADR) prior to the insured filing the suit. The TWIA must send a demand for ADR within 60 days of receiving the insured's notice of intent. After that request is made, ADR must be completed within the next 60 days. This deadline can be extended by agreement of all parties or by rule of the commissioner. The only bases upon which an insured can bring a suit related to a coverage dispute are if the coverage denial was correct and the amount of damages the insured is entitled to recover.

COVERAGE LIMITS AND DEDUCTIBLES

The maximum coverage limits available under TWIA policies are reviewed annually and adjusted as needed to keep up with inflation. As of January 1, 2024, the maximum limits available are as follows:

- Dwellings: $1,773,000
- Contents of apartments, townhouses, or condominiums: $374,000
- Commercial properties and public buildings: $4,424,000
- Manufactured homes: $115,800

Policyholders have multiple deductible options to choose from. Under dwelling policies, the standard deductibles are $100, $250, or 1 percent of the loss value. Some consumers qualify for larger deductibles, which would result in a lower premium. Large deductible options are available at 1.5, 2, 2.5, 3, 4, or 5 percent. For commercial policies, the standard deductible is 1 percent with large deductible options of 2 or 5 percent.

TEXAS AUTOMOBILE INSURANCE PLAN ASSOCIATION

As with residential insurance, some consumers may also have difficulty securing the auto insurance needed to lawfully own and/or operate a motor vehicle in Texas. Most states use an assigned-risk program to insure these consumers. The **Texas Automobile Insurance Plan Association (TAIPA)** is an assigned-risk program and was established to assist motorists that encounter such difficulty. All insurers authorized to write auto insurance in the state are required to be members of TAIPA. TAIPA operates as a nonprofit organization and funds its operations using assessment payments from member companies.

ELIGIBILITY AND COVERAGE

TAIPA policies only provide state minimum coverage for liability and PIP. UM and UIM coverage is also available. No medical payments coverage or first-party property damage coverage is available. TAIPA policies are also available for businesses who are unable to obtain state minimum auto coverage. TAIPA coverage may only be purchased by eligible parties through a licensed agent who is certified to handle TAIPA policies. To be eligible for a TAIPA policy, the applicant must:

- Have a valid driver's license or be pursuing an SR-22 document in order to obtain a valid license; an SR-22 is a document certifying that the person to whom it is issued carries legally mandated automobile insurance coverage and is usually needed to reinstate a revoked driver's license
- Reside in Texas or possess a motor vehicle registered in Texas
- Certify that he or she has been rejected for auto insurance by at least two insurance carriers within the past 60 days

PLAN INSURERS

Once an application is approved, the insured will be assigned to an eligible insurance company. To qualify, the insurer must have written auto liability coverage in the state for at least five years and act as a serving carrier for an assigned-risk program in at least one other state. Participating companies have the option of issuing TAIPA policies themselves or contracting with a servicing carrier to act on their behalf. Insureds under TAIPA policies must reapply every three years.

Another goal of TAIPA is to incentivize authorized insurers to voluntarily write policies in underserved geographic areas. Designation of underserved areas is done by the commissioner and takes the following into consideration:

- Overall availability of auto insurance
- How many uninsured drivers are in the area
- How many TAIPA insureds are in the area
- Any other factor the commissioner deems relevant

Encouraging insurance companies to write policies in these locations helps reduce the need for TAIPA policies. It also serves to promote competition in the auto insurance marketplace.

TEXAS MEDICAL LIABILITY INSURANCE UNDERWRITING ASSOCIATION

The **Texas Medical Liability Insurance Underwriting Association (TMLIUA)** is a **joint underwriting association** created under the Texas Insurance Code to ensure that medical professionals have access to needed professional liability insurance coverage. It is often called simply the **JUA (Joint Underwriting Association)** in publications and other materials issued by the association. During the 1970s, many private medical liability insurers exited the Texas market, leaving a coverage gap for Texas medical providers. Any Texas-licensed insurer who writes liability coverage in the state is required to be a member of the JUA. This applies regardless of if the insurer does business in the medical liability or medical malpractice insurance space.

The JUA is funded using the premiums paid by health care providers who carry policies under the JUA. If there is a deficit in funding, the JUA may collect additional funds from the **policyholder stabilization reserve fund**, assessments charged to policyholders, and assessments charged to member insurers, in that order. The JUA maintains two separate policyholder stabilization reserve funds. One is only for nursing homes and assisted living facilities, and the other is for all other eligible medical providers. Policyholders under the JUA pay policyholder stabilization reserve fund charges annually alongside the annual premium due for the policy. These funds are the first source of recoupment for the JUA when its operations result in a deficit. If the policyholder stabilization reserve fund is not sufficient to offset the deficit, the next step is to levy a special assessment on the medical providers who are covered by JUA policies. If this still does not provide the funding needed to overcome the operational deficit, then the member insurers will be charged a special assessment as well.

ELIGIBILITY AND COVERAGE

Like the insurance associations discussed previously in this chapter, the JUA is an insurer of last resort. To qualify for a policy under the JUA, the insured must be a licensed medical provider or facility and have been rejected by at least two insurers operating in the voluntary insurance market. Partnerships, professional associations, and professional corporations may also obtain insurance via the JUA, but only if coverage is available individually to all owning members of the group. An application can be submitted directly to the JUA by a medical provider, or a licensed insurance agent can submit the application on the customer's behalf.

Medical providers can obtain primary or excess medical professional liability coverage through the JUA. If an individual is a member of a professional organization and wants separate limits for his or her own professional liability coverage, then he or she will need to obtain a separate policy from the one that covers the organization. The JUA requires that policies carry a minimum of $100,000 per occurrence and $300,000 aggregate per annual policy period. The most coverage available under a single policy is $1 million per occurrence with a $3 million annual aggregate limit. Defense and legal costs are paid in addition to the applicable policy limit. Texas law prohibits JUA policies from covering punitive or exemplary damages.

P&C General Knowledge Practice Test

Want to take this practice test in an online interactive format? Check out the bonus page, which includes interactive practice questions and much more: **mometrix.com/bonus948/propertycasual**

1. Brian is driving a new Ford F-250 with a current actual cash value (ACV) of $68,000. He carries 25/50/25 in liability, uninsured, and underinsured on all three of his household vehicles as well as full coverage with $1,000 deductibles. Another driver, also carrying 25/50/25, totals Brian's F-250. When all is said and done, how much of the cost of replacement will fall on Brian?

   a. $0
   b. $1,000
   c. $18,000
   d. $43,000

2. Tracey was laid off eight years ago. She experienced a severe sequence of financial hardships and has spent several years picking up the pieces. According to the rules contained within the Fair Credit Reporting Act (FCRA), which of the following can still be taken into account from her consumer report?

   a. Tax liens from eight years ago
   b. Bankruptcy from eight years ago
   c. Outstanding collections from eight years ago
   d. Civil judgments from eight years ago

3. Matt is the proud owner of a 1980s Fox body mustang. He restored the engine in its entirety, and he customized every detail, from the interior to the wheels. He hardly drives it, as he prefers instead to use it as a show car. In addition, Matt has saved the receipts of every purchase he has made relating to his prized possession. Which type of policy would serve Matt best?

   a. Market value
   b. Replacement cost value (RCV)
   c. Actual cash value (ACV)
   d. Stated value

4. Clint files a hail claim on his mobile home after a terrible storm sweeps through the area. He has an actual cash value policy, under which his home is insured for $87,000. He has a two percent deductible and needs a replacement on a roof valued at $8,000. The roof is five years old and is estimated to depreciate at a rate of $400 per year. How much will Clint's insurer pay towards his roof?

   a. $6,260
   b. $6,000
   c. $4,260
   d. $4,000

303

5. Under which type of business policy will one NOT find products and completed operations coverage?

    a. Commercial auto

    b. General liability

    c. Businessowners policy (BOP)

    d. Small business

6. Which of the following would NOT be considered *general* damages?

    a. Disfigurement

    b. Loss of companionship

    c. Lost wages

    d. Mental anguish

7. John is a mechanic at a small shop. When repairing a machine during a breakdown, he slips on a splotch of oil and bangs his knee into the concrete floor. Not until a few years later does a doctor identify that fall as the source of his problems. At the time of the injury, the shop's liability policy was covered by ABC Insurance Co., but now the shop's coverage is through AAA Insurance Co. When the claim is filed, neither insurer covers the loss. Which type of policy does the auto shop most likely have with AAA Insurance Co.?

    a. Occurrence

    b. Claims-made

    c. Retroactive

    d. Concurrent

8. Norton gets into an accident at an intersection in front of his church. He swears the other driver is at fault, whereas the other driver swears right back that it was Norton's fault. Norton calls the other driver's insurance company and provides his side of the story, but the company takes the side of their driver and denies liability. Norton then calls his own insurer to ask what to do. Because he has full coverage, he can file the claim on his own policy *as though* the accident were his fault. He will be responsible for his own deductible for now, but his vehicle will be repaired, and his insurer will take the claim to court if necessary to defend him. When that process is completed, Norton will get his deductible refunded. This process is known as:

    a. Concealment

    b. Arbitration

    c. Mediation

    d. Subrogation

9. John notices that his workers' compensation premium nearly doubled from his previous bill. He phones his agent, furious at this drastic and sudden change. Upon review, the agent tells John that the new premium is a symptom of his success in the previous year. John's revenue drastically overshot the projections based on his own historical trends. This change in cost was prompted by his:

    a. Premium audit

    b. Refractory revenue

    c. Annual tax filing

    d. Year-in-review

10. If Jane and James collide on the road and both are found to be partially at fault, the finding of negligence can be split, even down to a percentage of fault for loss determination. Which of the following describes this situation?

a. Contributory negligence
b. Mutual negligence
c. Comparative negligence
d. Allocated negligence

11. Which of the following CANNOT be subject to a coinsurance penalty in the event of a total loss?

a. Agreed value
b. Market value
c. Replacement cost
d. Actual cash value

12. In the past, pollution (now generally excluded) as claimed against a business liability policy was covered by:

a. Coverage A
b. Coverage B
c. Coverage C
d. Coverage M

13. Janie's state passes legislation raising the minimum auto coverage requirements from $20,000 to $25,000. Her insurer raises her limits, as well as all other drivers in her position, without charging extra premium through the next renewal. What is the name for this blanket change in coverage?

a. Accommodation
b. Liberalization
c. Specification
d. Satisfaction

14. Bradley has a full-coverage auto policy with $500 deductibles on both collision and comprehensive. He strikes a tire in the road that thrashes his front bumper and cracks his windshield. What is the total deductible Bradley will pay to fix the entirety of the damage?

a. $0
b. $200
c. $500
d. $1,000

15. Liz runs a small computer repair and installation business. Currently, she has a small liability policy as well as a business-use auto policy on her work van. Her insurance agent tells her that she can bundle these into a single policy called a:

a. Commercial package policy
b. Businessowners policy
c. Business income policy
d. Commercial integrated policy

16. Kevin and his wife, Mary, are coming back from vacation when Kevin becomes drowsy during the long drive. He accidentally veers into the other lane and strikes another driver's vehicle head-on. Kevin carries medical payments coverage on his policy. Whose medical bills will be paid by this coverage?

   a. Kevin's only
   b. Kevin's and Mary's
   c. The other driver's
   d. Kevin's, Mary's, and the other driver's

17. If an organization—not a partnership, LLC, or sole proprietorship—owns a policy, who is NOT considered an insured?

   a. Executive officers
   b. Spouses of executive officers
   c. Directors
   d. Stockholders

18. Which of the following is NOT covered under earthquake insurance?

   a. Damage to vehicle(s)
   b. Damage to personal property
   c. Building code upgrades
   d. Debris removal

19. Which is NOT true of windstorm policies?

   a. They can only be purchased as riders on homeowners policies.
   b. Insurers are allowed to place a moratorium on new policies prior to a major storm.
   c. Many insurers in low-risk states incorporate them automatically.
   d. Without this coverage, deductibles may run as high as 10 percent of the total insured value.

20. Karen has the following auto policy:

   A: 50/100/50
   D: $500
   G: $500
   U: 50/100/50
   W: 50/100/50

She has been shopping around for a better rate and signs up for the exact same policy at another insurer. She was told that she should wait to terminate her first policy until the second officially issues. During the brief window when both policies are active, Karen is struck in a hit-and-run and sustains $150,000 in injuries. Between both policies, how much will her insurance pay towards these expenses?

   a. $50,000
   b. $100,000
   c. $150,000
   d. $200,000

21. Before Jalyn can begin auto coverage, a driving record must be run. This helps assess the risk involved as well as protect the insurer against:

    a. Concealment
    b. Fraud
    c. Misrepresentation
    d. Indirect loss

22. Jason will be moving into a new apartment next month, and the apartment complex requires that he carry renter's insurance. Which homeowners form will be used?

    a. HO-3
    b. HO-4
    c. HO-5
    d. HO-6

23. Donna and Gregory are going through a nasty divorce. When Gregory drops off their son Luke, he bumps into the back of Donna's car. He doesn't mention it and drives away. Donna believes he did it on purpose, so she calls the authorities and then reports it to Gregory's insurance company. Assuming Donna is correct, under which coverage will her vehicle be repaired?

    a. Liability
    b. Property damage
    c. Collision
    d. Uninsured

24. Which is NOT a standard building block of a businessowners policy (BOP)?

    a. General liability
    b. Workers' compensation
    c. Business income
    d. Business property

25. Sandra asks her father, Albert, to move closer to home because he is getting older and has recently been diagnosed with early-stage dementia. Albert does not want to be a burden to his daughter, so he asks if she could help him get set up with a condo near where she lives. Sandra realizes that her father is going to need insurance for the condo. Where might Sandra and Albert run into a hurdle in getting the condo insured?

    a. Offer and acceptance
    b. Consideration
    c. Legal purpose
    d. Competent parties

26. Fabio's Pizza Parlor recently suffered a fire that destroyed much of the kitchen. During the restoration period, insurance paid for various things, from the rent to employee wages. Which policy was responsible for these payments?

    a. Equipment breakdown
    b. Business income
    c. Extra expense
    d. Loss of revenue

27. After being hit by an oncoming vehicle, Susie not only received damages from the incident itself, but she also received an additional payment to cover damages between the time of the incident and the date upon which the claim was settled. What is the term for this additional amount?

    a. Prejudgment interest
    b. Interim interest
    c. Retroactive interest
    d. Fiduciary interest

28. While at the car dealership, Karlee calls in for an auto quote and signs up for coverage on the same call. She does not have access to her email, so she has not had the chance to receive a proof of coverage. However, she feels confident that she can drive the vehicle because the agent gave her verbal confirmation that she is covered. His verbal confirmation, legally, would be considered a:

    a. Binder
    b. Warranty
    c. Representation
    d. Certificate of insurance

29. Within the confines of personal auto insurance, which of the following does NOT require an endorsement in order to be covered?

    a. Having a vehicle stolen
    b. Hitting a deer
    c. Vehicle damage from falling limbs
    d. Striking a mailbox

30. Commercial crime insurance policies offer coverage for losses that:

    a. Occur throughout the policy term as well as up to one calendar year prior
    b. Occur throughout the policy term and are claimed therein
    c. Occur throughout the policy term but are reported up to one year after expiration
    d. Occur throughout the policy term, regardless of the date of claim

31. Which of the following is NOT an obligation of the insurer?

    a. To defend
    b. To indemnify
    c. To mitigate
    d. To settle

32. In order for coverage A to kick in and pay for damages, the bodily injury or property damage covered must be caused by a(n):

    a. Accident
    b. Event
    c. Peril
    d. Occurrence

33. After discovering a leak in her roof, Debbie calls a professional, who tells her that the roof needs to be replaced. It is 15 years old and devalues at an estimated $450 per year. Debbie has a one percent deductible replacement cost value (RCV) policy on her home, covered at $277,000. A new roof will cost $17,500. How much will Debbie's insurer pay?

- a. $17,500
- b. $14,730
- c. $10,750
- d. $7,980

34. Dave's loss is covered by two different insurance policies. Policy A has a limit of $25,000, and Policy B has a limit of $100,000. Dave experiences a loss of $60,000. Policy A maxes out at $25,000, and Policy B pays the other $35,000. Which provision makes this outcome happen?

- a. Apportionment
- b. Equal shares
- c. Fiduciary responsibility
- d. Stewardship

35. Bob runs a body shop, and a runaway fire destroyed much of the equipment in his shop. His insurance covered the damage and even paid his rent while the restoration was underway. During the delay, Bob rented several lifts and other pneumatic tools to get him by while he waited on the replacements. Insurance did not cover these charges, but it could have if Bob had also carried:

- a. Business income
- b. Loss of use
- c. Equipment breakdown
- d. Extra expense

36. Danielle carries an actual cash value (ACV) policy on a modular home. After a formidable hailstorm sweeps through her area, her windows are damaged, and she is at risk of a leaking roof. She has ABC Roof & Restoration inspect her property, and they tell her that not only does she have roof damage, but her home's siding and outbuildings have taken a beating, and a few of her gutters are dented. When all the damage is filed and Danielle has paid her deductible, the payout is large enough to cover the roof and gutters so that any mishaps over the next two years will be repaired by the installer. Although depreciation prevents Danielle from affordably re-siding her house, her positive experience was made possible by having access to a high-quality:

- a. Warranty
- b. Appraisal
- c. Representation
- d. Adjuster

37. If Dave's roof is leaking after a hailstorm but he is not around or able to report it, his mortgage lender must do so. This is due to a provision called:

- a. Vicarious responsibility
- b. Adverse impact
- c. Loss payable
- d. Care of lien

38. Jared carries a policy on a Toyota Camry he is still paying off. Jared lives with his mother, Cara. The loan for the vehicle was co-signed at the credit union by his grandmother, Margaret. His brother, Derrick, sometimes operates the vehicle. In this scenario, who would be considered an additional insured?

    a. Margaret
    b. Cara
    c. Derrick
    d. The credit union

39. Which of the following is NOT typically covered under a cyber first-party policy?

    a. Ransom payments for data held by intruder
    b. Legal fees if customer sues over breach of information
    c. Equipment damages resulting from a breach
    d. Public relations campaign to restore brand image

40. Aaron is an auto glass installer who does onsite replacements. While traveling to a customer's home for an installation, he causes an accident in which he is injured. Which coverage steps in to cover the costs associated with his injuries?

    a. Liability
    b. Collision
    c. Medical payments
    d. Workers' compensation

41. Tony has several rental properties, which are not registered under an LLC or listed as an asset for a business. When he looks over his auto policies, which factor should he scrutinize?

    a. Under-insured
    b. Uninsured
    c. Liability
    d. Loss of use

42. Greta is refinancing her home, and the lender is unable to proceed without information regarding her current insurance. Which of the following will be needed in order to process the loan?

    a. Binder
    b. Warranty
    c. Whole contract
    d. Certificate of insurance

43. Kevin owns a home in the mountains that he visits a couple of times a year but only during colder months for hunting season. He doesn't keep much of his own property there, but he wants a policy that can cover weather-related losses, especially ice. Which policy best suits his needs?

    a. HO-6
    b. DP-1
    c. HO-8
    d. DP-2

44. Which is NOT an obligation of the insurer?

   a. The insurer must provide a detailed denial letter, when applicable.
   b. The insurer must respond promptly when a claim is filed.
   c. The insurer must refer the insured to a qualified attorney.
   d. The insurer must investigate claims as thoroughly as possible.

45. Which of the following would NOT be considered a catastrophic loss?

   a. Earthquake
   b. War
   c. Terrorism
   d. Nuclear disaster

46. Ronald just purchased a property near the beach in an at-risk area as it pertains to flooding. The home needs an extensive renovation before Ronald can move in, but he wants to be sure he has coverage before beginning any work on the property. Which policy would he need to purchase in order to ensure he has flood protection in addition to dwelling-under-construction coverage?

   a. HO-3
   b. HO-5
   c. DP-3
   d. None of the above

47. Shelley slips and falls while shopping at ABC Retail. If she is to be covered under their coverage C: medical payments, how long does she have to file the claim?

   a. 30 days
   b. 90 days
   c. One year
   d. Indefinitely

48. Helen is in the market for a home. She finds one she likes, but it is at the top of her budget, and her debt-to-income (DTI) ratio could become an issue. Helen's buyer's agent asks her to shop around for insurance, specifically making sure which of the following figures is high enough to accommodate the situation?

   a. Cash value
   b. Deductible
   c. Estimated replacement cost
   d. Dwelling coverage

49. Calvin applies for a businessowners policy (BOP). In order to initiate coverage, he must provide both historical revenue and employee costs as well as a slew of other figures. He must also anticipate the growing revenue for the upcoming year, and the insurer will in turn determine how much insurance will be required based on those figures. When submitting the application, the agent will collect which of the following from Calvin?

   a. Deposit premium
   b. Initial premium
   c. Subjective premium
   d. Annotated premium

50. Bobby is the pre-owned sales manager at a local car dealership. One of the perks of his job is being able to use the dealership's vehicles rather than having to own his own vehicle or carry his own insurance policy. One morning, the vehicle in use will not start, so Bobby borrows his neighbor's car to get to work. When an accident occurs, the dealership's insurance covers the claim. Which endorsement must have been present for this outcome to occur?

   a. BIPD
   b. Underinsured
   c. DOC
   d. Business Comprehensive

51. Jeff purchased his Dodge RAM when the market was high. Two years later, he totals his vehicle when he slams into another driver. With the car market having slumped, the amount that his insurer is willing to pay for his loss is far below the amount needed to pay off the vehicle. How will this be settled?

   a. GAP insurance
   b. Arbitration
   c. ACV reevaluation
   d. Underinsured coverage

52. Johnny went out with his friends last night and, after several drinks, asked one of them to drive him home. When he woke up, he realized his car was still back at the bar. The only real risk he could imagine is if the car were to be stolen, but since he has full coverage and the car is fairly old at this point, he decides to wait until later in the day to go back and get it. What sort of hazard is at play here?

   a. Negligence
   b. Moral
   c. Physical
   d. Morale

53. Which mathematical law is based on the idea of increased predictability as the number of exposure units increases?

   a. Zipf's law
   b. Law of averages
   c. Law of large numbers
   d. Law of margins

54. Jerry has a small bass boat and doesn't want to purchase a watercraft policy. He already has a home and auto bundle, with boat coverage listed under his homeowners. Which of the following events will NOT be covered by his current setup?

   a. His boat is stolen while he is at the lake.
   b. His daughter trips and falls while they are fishing.
   c. His boat and trailer are damaged in an accident between home and the lake.
   d. His boat is destroyed in a garage fire.

55. Barbara purchased a home from Clayton Homes, and it was delivered, blocked, leveled, and skirted. Which type of homeowners policy will she need?

a. HO-5
b. HO-6
c. HO-7
d. HO-8

56. After an auto accident occurs, Athena calls her insurance company. In the beginning of the conversation, they ask her to describe the damage to her vehicle. They ask if she has been injured as well as if the vehicle is drivable. These questions are asked in lieu of a paper:

a. Declaration
b. Notice of claim
c. Subrogation
d. Proof of loss

57. Which of the following conditions involves valuing a property by its actual cash value (ACV) while not allowing a payout to be higher than the cost to repair or replace it?

a. Aggregate limit
b. Recovered property
c. Loss settlement
d. Our option

58. If looking to save on homeowners premiums, one may opt for a policy that only covers a predetermined list of perils. What is the name for such coverage?

a. Select
b. Slated
c. Broad
d. Traditional

59. Which of the following represents a physical hazard?

a. Leaving the front door unlocked
b. Intermittent hail
c. Dense ice on a roof
d. Vandalism

60. Gerry purchases an auto policy on his Toyota Camry. Which of the following is he unlikely to find on his insuring agreement?

a. Lawsuit liability
b. Covered perils
c. Vehicle to be covered
d. Policy exclusions

61. Kenneth is closing on a condo next Friday. Before he can move in, he'll have to provide his buyer's agent with a proof of homeowners coverage. Which homeowners form will be used?

a. HO-3
b. HO-4
c. HO-5
d. HO-6

62. Insurance policies tend to exclude coverage when property is in the possession of another party, such as a storage facility or an auto shop. In the verbiage of the policy, this exclusion is stated as having no benefit to:

    a. Possessors
    b. Arbiters
    c. Bailees
    d. Consumers

63. Which is NOT a common exclusion in a homeowners insurance policy?

    a. Vermin
    b. Firearms
    c. Home-based business
    d. Terrorism

64. Which of the following would NOT be considered an insurance condition?

    a. A proof of loss must be provided.
    b. Protective measures must be taken to avoid future loss.
    c. Changes in the contract must be provided by mail.
    d. Cooperation is required during an investigation.

65. Rebekah initiates a fire policy on a property she owns. The agent tells her that, as a general rule, anything not specifically excluded in the contract's language is covered. What type of policy is Rebekah initiating?

    a. Open
    b. Named
    c. Comprehensive
    d. Diminutive

66. Auto accident-related lawsuits, when filed, typically revolve around an accusation of negligence. Negligence is not typically considered criminal, but it does cause damage, whether physical, bodily, or emotional. Which term describes the legal affiliation with such negligence?

    a. Tort
    b. Liable
    c. Indirect
    d. Consequential

67. Frankie paid off her full homeowners term as soon as she received the bill. She passed away soon after, and when her family terminated the policy, the year was not up. The insurer sent out a refund check to cover the:

    a. Cash surrender value
    b. Unearned premium
    c. Pro rata payment
    d. Escrow fund

68. Paul is a wealthy investor. His best friend, John, is an inventor who believes his next big project is destined to succeed, but he needs financial support as soon as possible to get the project underway. Paul believes in John, but he knows supporting this endeavor is risky, so he calls his insurance agent to see if there is any way to get insured against this high risk. His agent says they cannot help Paul with mitigating the risk. Which of the following best explains why the insurance company cannot help Paul in this instance?

    a. The insurance company does not have a policy with John, so they cannot provide coverage to Paul regarding any potential investments between the two.

    b. The nature of investment is considered too risky to cover because the insurance company is more likely to lose money than make it—i.e., a pure risk.

    c. Insuring against the investment risk would require an additional rider which would incur a probationary period of 90 days. This would prevent Paul from being able to invest with a safeguard in place as quickly as John needs.

    d. Investment risks are inherently speculative and thus uninsurable.

69. Which is NOT a typical exclusion on a builder's risk policy?

    a. Off-premises theft
    b. Faulty design
    c. Mechanical breakdown
    d. Terrorism

70. If Jake is looking to purchase a mobile home, which is NOT a determining factor in the type of coverage he will receive?

    a. Location (state) of the home
    b. Manufacturer of the home
    c. Age of the home
    d. Whether the home is in a mobile home park

71. Alvin has a long driveway. At the end closest to his house, there is a huge oak tree. He never parks below the tree because he is worried about falling limbs. When he trades his old car in for a new vehicle, the loan mandates that he carry full coverage. He decides he might as well park under the tree because his comprehensive coverage grants him the ability to file for a new windshield. Which sort of hazard is at play when Alvin decides to park under the tree?

    a. Physical
    b. Moral
    c. Environmental
    d. Morale

72. Kenny wants to buy a homeowners policy that will protect against as much as possible while covering as much as possible, from the structure to his stuff. Which type of policy will he buy?

    a. HO-2
    b. HO-3
    c. HO-5
    d. HO-8

73. Shelley's wedding ring set cost three months' salary, and she wants it protected. She purchases a policy to cover the ring set, which is ultimately classified under:

a. Inland marine
b. Homeowners
c. Extra expense
d. Indemnity

74. Tommy, already insured with ABC Insurance Co., calls in and changes his auto policy from liability to full coverage. Later that day, he calls in a claim. He caused a head-on collision, and he will need the full coverage to repair or replace his own vehicle. ABC asks to see the incident report in order to verify the timing discrepancy. Naturally, there will be a red flag as pertains to the:

a. Proof of loss
b. Obligations of the insurance company
c. Notice of claim
d. Liability exclusions

75. Nico is looking to minimize risk and is willing to pay to avoid unexpected costs. She wants to choose a policy that covers every type of peril that is not specifically excluded. What is the name for this type of policy?

a. Broad
b. Comprehensive
c. Umbrella
d. Special

76. AAA Insurance Co. decides to corner the homeowners insurance market by writing fewer exclusions, such as earthquakes, into their insurance contracts. While this strategy helps them gain market shares, it also opens them up to problems of:

a. Speculative risk
b. The law of large numbers
c. Adverse selection
d. FCRA violations

77. Greg owns a landscape and grading company that utilizes several large pieces of machinery in various locations. To ensure coverage and avoid headaches, Greg should boost his commercial property policy with a(n):

a. Addendum
b. Waiver
c. Floater
d. Amendment

78. All of the following are considered nonaccidental losses EXCEPT:

a. Lightning strike
b. Corrosion
c. Mechanical breakdown
d. Deterioration

79. An insurer's profit model is predicated on the idea that the total value of premiums paid by the aggregate of customers and the investments made with that money is greater than the payouts potentially required. What is the name for this concept?

a. Risk-based pricing
b. Pure risk
c. Insurable interest
d. Annual aggregate

80. ABC Building Supplies purchases a concrete manufacturer, and ABC's liability coverage extends to the purchased organization. Under the terms of the insurance policy, which of the following is NOT true?

a. Coverage will be automatically provided for the concrete manufacturer for 90 days or until the end of the policy term, whichever comes first.
b. Coverages A and B will be extended to the concrete manufacturer for losses that occurred no more than one calendar year prior to the acquisition.
c. In order for coverage to apply, ABC must either control a strict majority interest in the concrete manufacturer or own it entirely.
d. In order for coverage to apply, the concrete manufacturer must be unable to obtain any comparable insurance otherwise.

81. Which of these limits sets the total amount of liability for a particular insured's renewal period?

a. Per person
b. Aggregate
c. Per annum
d. Term limit

82. While she was driving, Jackie was hit by an oncoming car, and her vehicle is no longer operable. Her policy includes a rental reimbursement provision which pays up to $54 per day, with a maximum of $1,000. The rental vehicle secured by the oncoming driver's insurer costs $81 per day, and Jackie needs the vehicle for a total of 14 days. When all is complete, how much will Jackie have spent out-of-pocket for the rental?

a. $0
b. $378
c. $756
d. $1,000

83. Johnny, a business owner, is being sued by an aggrieved client. Johnny's liability policy gets put into use, but costs of the legal dispute continue to grow. Which of the following is least likely to be covered by the insurer's supplementary payments?

a. Johnny travels to another city and stays in a hotel in order to testify.
b. Johnny hires an investigator to gather information for the insurer's lawyers.
c. As the case drags on, the lawyer fees exceed Johnny's coverage limits.
d. As the case heats up, bail bonds for Johnny have to be paid.

84. Greg owns a roofing company. From 2000–2010, he had his general liability insurance with AAA Insurance. From 2010 to the present, he has used ABC, Inc. Eric, one of Greg's employees, fell from a ladder in 2008 but did not believe he was injured. In 2015, he visited a doctor for chronic pain in his side, and it was determined that his fall seven years prior was the most likely cause. When the claim was filed, ABC paid. Which type of policy does Greg most likely carry?

    a. Occurrence
    b. Claims-made
    c. Retroactive
    d. Concurrent

85. ABC Farms is a large, commercial farm that generates $10 million in revenue each year. ABC's operations include raising cows and pigs for later sale of their meat to local restaurants, a commercial store open to the public daily, as well as seasonal events. Would ABC Farms be eligible for farm owners insurance?

    a. Yes, it fits the requirements for farm owners insurance.
    b. No, farm owners insurance is for family-operated farms with minimal commercial exposure.
    c. No, ABC does not generate enough revenue to qualify for farm owners insurance.
    d. Yes, it is eligible due to the sale of meat to local restaurants and not worldwide sales.

86. Which is NOT a duty of the insured?

    a. The insured must provide all pertinent information to a claim investigation.
    b. The insured must pay the deductible at the time the repairs are completed.
    c. The insured must report all damage to the proper authorities.
    d. The insured must give the insurer both a proof of loss and notice of claim.

87. Garvis carries full coverage on two vehicles, with deductibles of $250 per comprehensive or collision incident. He purchases a new sedan and causes an accident on the way home. When the damages are repaired, how much will Garvis owe the body shop who does the work?

    a. $0
    b. $250
    c. $500
    d. $1,000

88. Sometimes, increases in auto insurance have to do with the auto market as a whole, especially the used auto market. In recent times, popular trucks and SUVs—even when several years old—are seeing spikes in premiums, due to their inflating:

    a. Cash value
    b. Replacement cost
    c. Stated value
    d. Salvage value

89. Dave buys a car from Jim. He does not have the cash to pay for it outright, so he will be making payments directly to Jim. The only way Jim agrees to this is if Dave can prove in his insurance policy that if the car is totaled, the insurance company will pay Jim the amount owed before any proceeds are given to Dave. This makes Jim:

    a. A named insured
    b. The first named insured
    c. An additional insured
    d. A fiduciary insured

90. Evan is a delivery driver for Paul's Pizza and Wings. He causes an accident on the way to a customer's home. The other driver is injured and goes on to sue not just Evan but also Paul's Pizza and Wings. Why might Paul's have to payout?

    a. Employment liability
    b. Captive liability
    c. Commissioned liability
    d. Vicarious liability

91. Which is NOT a typical source of underwriting as it pertains to auto insurance?

    a. Occupation
    b. Location
    c. Credit report
    d. Telematics

92. Insurance companies offer insureds peace of mind by promising to compensate them for the losses they sustain. This allows people to go about their daily lives, or businesses to go about their daily operations, with the assurance of knowing that they will not be held liable for the losses they encounter. What is the term for this promise to cover a loss?

    a. Assumption
    b. Indemnity
    c. Subrogation
    d. Warranty

93. Terry purchases a car from a local dealer. He calls and gets insurance on it before he ever leaves the lot. A week later, he begins having engine troubles, and the dealership agrees to take back his vehicle. When Terry calls to cancel his auto insurance, the agent processes his request in such a way that it is as though Terry never initiated the policy at all. Which term refers to this type of cancellation?

    a. Flat
    b. Total
    c. Retroactive
    d. Short rate

94. Henry is looking to buy a historic home. They don't make homes like this anymore, so repairing or replacing the structure could be cost-prohibitive. Which type of policy was designed for precisely such residences?

    a. HO-5
    b. HO-6
    c. HO-7
    d. HO-8

95. Which is most UNLIKELY to be covered by a farm owner's policy?

 a. Outbuildings
 b. Side-by-sides
 c. Livestock
 d. Irrigation equipment

96. Which acronym within the mortgagee clause allows a lender to transfer rights to another lender?

 a. LIRB
 b. ISAOA
 c. ATIMA
 d. FCRA

97. Which of the following falls outside the purview of employer's liability insurance?

 a. Loss of consortium lawsuits
 b. Judgements
 c. Lost wages
 d. Ongoing care

98. Bob loses control of his car and ultimately causes a four-car pileup. There are several injuries as well as two totaled vehicles. There is only so much insurance liability to go around, so before long, lawyers are involved. Which of the following are these lawyers unlikely to pursue?

 a. Compensatory damages
 b. Exemplary damages
 c. Special damages
 d. General damages

99. Calvin works in outside sales for a window installer. On his way back from quoting a home for replacement windows, he causes an auto accident. The claimant files a lawsuit both against Calvin and the window installation company because Calvin was operating on their behalf at the time of the incident. Whose insurance will make the payout?

 a. Calvin's insurance will pay.
 b. The window installation company's insurance will pay.
 c. Each will pay 50 percent.
 d. Neither; personal vehicles are not covered when in use for business.

100. Kathy purchases a new home and moves in, then lists her former residence for sale. She knows it could take a few months before she lands a buyer, so she needs to keep her old residence insured in cases of fire or basic perils, which could happen while she's away. Which type of policy would she be looking for?

 a. HO-2
 b. HO-3
 c. DP-1
 d. DP-2

101. Garrett owns a small general contractor business and wants to apply for coverage with ABC Insurance Co. ABC tells him that to apply for such coverage, he will need tax documents and proof of business coverage dating back two years. Unaware this was coming, Garrett asks why ABC needs the documentation, and they explain that it is to reduce:

    a. Moral hazard
    b. Morale hazard
    c. Exposure
    d. Indirect loss

102. The sun is in John's eyes, and he doesn't see Susan breaking. John's truck knocks Susan's SUV into Jason's sedan. From the perspective of Jason's insurer, Susan represents the:

    a. Proximate cause
    b. Cause in fact
    c. Actual cause
    d. Intermediate cause

103. Robert leaves the dealership with a brand-new truck and causes an accident on his way home. He forgot to call his insurance company to inform them of the purchase, so he worries that he will have no coverage for the incident. Fortunately for Robert, additional vehicles are automatically covered without notification for up to:

    a. 48 hours
    b. 7 days
    c. 14 days
    d. 30 days

104. Which would NOT qualify for coverage under an equipment breakdown policy?

    a. A sump pump
    b. A refrigerator
    c. A forklift
    d. A transformer

105. John has auto insurance, so he knows that whether he is hit by another driver, strikes a vehicle or object, or has his vehicle stolen, he will not shoulder the bulk of the financial burden. In exchange, he pays premiums monthly, which are calculated by a slew of factors. This transaction amounts to John selling his:

    a. Exposure
    b. Liability
    c. Risk
    d. Insurable interest

106. Karen is throwing her daughter a pool party. Several children from her daughter's class show up, along with their parents. One of the parents slips and falls down. The parent sues Karen, whose insurer steps in. From the insurer's perspective, this parent's injury is a:

    a. First-party loss
    b. Second-party loss
    c. Third-party loss
    d. Liability consideration

107. Allen causes a car accident, and an injury attorney gets involved. The attorney seeks the maximum payout under Allen's policy, intending to compensate both himself and the defendant in the case. Which section of Allen's policy will the attorney target?

a. Liability
b. Medical payments
c. Comprehensive
d. Collision

108. Which of the following is NOT typically found on a declarations page?

a. Options
b. Endorsements
c. Exclusions
d. Additional interests

109. Greg and Mindy purchase a new home, but they keep their old one and decide to rent it out to their son. The property remains in their name, and they are not concerned with the contents, as they'll have their son take out his own renter's policy for that. If Greg and Mindy are looking to minimize the chances of paying out of pocket for losses, which type policy should they use?

a. DP-2
b. HO-5
c. DP-3
d. HO-7

110. Which would be an example of an insurer's indirect loss?

a. Smoke from a covered fire did additional damage to property in the attic.
b. A rental vehicle becomes necessary when a suitable replacement vehicle cannot be located.
c. An earthquake occurs three miles away, and its tremors cause structural issues to a property.
d. An aggrieved employee breaks into a business and torches its equipment.

P&C General Knowledge Answer Key and Explanations

1. A: Underinsured coverage is considered a stacking coverage, meaning it can be pulled from multiple household vehicles, not just the one involved in the incident. If Brian had no underinsured coverage, he could have been looking at a $43,000 cost after the other driver's $25,000 was exhausted. If Brian had underinsured at 25/50/25 only on a single vehicle, he would have been responsible for $18,000. Fortunately for Brian, having this coverage on multiple vehicles means he has enough coverage for the entire loss.

2. B: Bankruptcies on a consumer report count for 10 years, whereas other civil and tax liabilities are cut off at seven years. Arrests, convictions, etc. are not counted by the same timing and may remain.

3. D: Also known as agreed value, stated value policies allow the insurer and the insured to come to an agreement at the beginning of the policy. These are often used for antique, unique, or customized vehicles. Both parties must agree on the vehicle's value in order for this type of policy to work. With vehicles or other similar highly valuable and/or antique possessions, a stated value policy would serve best.

4. C: As an actual cash value (ACV) policy, both the deductible (two percent, or $1,740) and depreciation ($400 per year over five years, or $2,000) must be taken into account. Answer A does not take depreciation into account. Answer B does not factor in the deductible.

5. A: Commercial auto policies cover drivers and vehicles, and they can also cover trailers and equipment. Products and completed operations coverage deals with liability during the process of working. Because anyone operating a vehicle cannot be in the process of completing a product or operation at that moment, this type of policy would not be compatible with commercial auto.

6. C: Special damages are awarded for costs relating directly to a loss. Lost wages would fall under that umbrella. General damages are awarded for residual or ongoing problems, which may have stemmed from the same cause but are not direct costs. Options A, B, and D are all considered general damages.

7. C: Under an occurrence policy, ABC would have paid. Under a typical claims-made policy, AAA would have paid. Under a retroactive policy, however, a stipulation could be made limiting the dates under which the new insurer would be liable. This type of policy would be the most likely reason for coverage not being provided.

8. D: Subrogation takes place when an insurer fronts the cost of a claim in an at-fault status because they intend to pursue payment for the damages from another party. This happens when the insurer of an at-fault party refuses liability, but it can also happen when an insurer attempts to direct a customer to a repair facility they do not trust. In either case, it can result in an extended process, but it is usually to the benefit of the insured.

9. A: Premiums are already anticipated to climb steadily, but when a business grows rapidly rather than steadily, premiums must be adjusted. For this reason, premium audits are typically issued annually to keep premiums from leaping tremendously all at once. Sometimes an employer has to

323

bring on more employees than expected in order to keep up with demand. When business booms, expenses rise—workers' compensation is one of those expenses.

10. C: Situations of comparative negligence can be tricky—having both insurers agree on a percentage of fault can extend an investigation, with both sides hoping to bolster their end of the arrangement. Even still, many auto accidents are not the fault of a single driver involved; rather, they occur from several factors.

11. A: Coinsurance applies when a policyholder wants to insure a property for a portion of its value, rather than at 100 percent. For instance, if Debra owns a brick home she does not foresee ever burning down, and she is on a fixed income, she may want to insure the property at a lower amount than full replacement. If her mortgage requires that she insure the home for at least 80 percent of the value, she might purchase a policy at 80 percent. However, over time, the insured amount could rise more slowly than inflation or cost of materials. By the time of a loss, this could mean that Debra carries *less* than 80 percent, in which case she might face a penalty. Initiating an agreed value policy from the beginning means that the figure will never change and cannot therefore become out of sync with any coinsurance requirement.

12. B: While coverage B is most commonly associated with advertising and injury, due to the "wrongful entry" verbiage, contaminated products formerly fell under personal injury. While producers tend not to release contaminated products on purpose, insurers were sure to hedge future bets by creating such an exclusion. Now, the coverage must be purchased as an option/extension.

13. B: Liberalization refers to changes made not to a single policy but to all policies of a given type, so long as this is done with no additional premium payments being required. Liberalization is not something that happens often, as it can contribute to added risk on the part of the insurer.

14. C: Even though both the bumper and the windshield took damage, these would not count as separate claims because they were both caused by the same event. Had Bradley hit a tire during a hailstorm, he might have seen two separate deductibles, but as it stands, he faces a single collision claim, which results in a single deductible.

15. A: The commercial package policy (CPP) serves as a means of simplification. Typically based around a general liability policy, CPPs allow a small business owner the ability to tie the policies—and pay them—together. If an insurer already owns one aspect of the business risk, it works in their favor to go ahead and acquire the rest. A businessowners policy (BOP) takes the process one step further. A BOP offers less customizability on a small scale, instead automatically bundling general liability, commercial property, and business income. Given that Liz doesn't already have these three, the commercial package makes the most sense without requiring an upcharge.

16. B: Medical payment coverage is a separate line item which applies to insured drivers through the policy. This can mean the named insured, spouses, children, or people permitted to borrow the vehicle. Injuries done to other parties will fall under liability—bodily injury rather than medical payments.

17. B: Spouses of named insureds are covered when the named insured falls under an individual (sole proprietor) or a joint enterprise. If the commercial interest is larger (LLC, organization, or trust), then spouses no longer fall under that direct coverage.

18. A: While all of the above are results of the covered event, vehicle damage is excluded because it is eligible for coverage under comprehensive coverage on the vehicle itself. Earthquake insurance follows many of the strictures of a homeowners policy, covering structures and belongings while excluding vehicles.

19. A: Windstorm policies can be added to a homeowners policy or purchased separately. The option chosen typically has to do with where one lives. Insurers are allowed to place a temporary suspension on new policies onboarded within a day or two before a major event such as a hurricane. Wind coverage is included in many homeowners policies outside of the major hurricane and hail areas, but, in those states, special events such as hurricanes can incur much higher deductibles.

20. A: The first number under U coverage is key here: one cannot "double dip" on insurance, so the figure would be split based on the coverage at hand. With Karen's policy having a limit of $50,000 per person and $100,000 total, and with her being a single person, the limit is $50,000 in total.

21. A: Insurance contracts are said to be based on good faith, meaning all parties are operating under the presumption that each side is being both fair and honest, regardless of the potential outcome. This driving record is used to uncover any potentially relevant information the insured may have forgotten or intentionally neglected to mention.

22. B: The HO-4 is also known as the tenant's form because it is a specific policy in which nothing to do with the physical structure itself is covered, as the structure is not owned by the tenant. The tenant is instead granted coverage on personal property and personal liability. These tend to be the least expensive fire policies due to the limited risk.

23. D: If Gregory indeed bumped into Donna's vehicle on purpose, then (pending an investigation by his insurance company) his insurer will refuse to pay. Intentional damage or harm is not covered. At this point, if Donna wants her vehicle fixed, she will likely have to file a police report to prove damages, and then file an uninsured claim. Her claim will then be treated as a hit-and-run.

24. B: Workers' compensation can be added onto a businessowners policy (BOP), but it is not a standard inclusion. There are several types of policies that can augment a BOP—flood, data breach, commercial auto, and more.

25. D: Because of Albert's mental state, there is a good chance that a power of attorney will be needed in order to provide competent parties to the equation. When powers of attorney are involved, this is usually because the policy owner has had either a temporary or permanent lapse in cognitive judgment. Powers of attorney would also be needed in the case of death or probate, but these situations would not be components in a new contract.

26. B: If Fabio had a businessowners policy (BOP), then business income would fall within that umbrella. However, it is also possible to purchase such a policy separately. In the event of damage to business property, rendering it unable to make revenue, business income steps in for a brief period to help cover expenses.

27. A: The settling of the claim is the date of judgment. Prejudgment, therefore, is an additional or supplemental payment made to cover the expenses prior to that date. These can be supplemental, included in liability, or distributed in any other way, as dictated by the policy at hand.

28. A: While binders are a legal document and must be provided to a customer as soon as possible, verbal binders are every bit as legally binding. Unlike many documents, such as car titles, ID cards, etc., binders are valid upon verbal receipt. For example, if a teen buys his first car at a car lot and receives verbal confirmation that he is covered, the dealer is legally allowed to let that teen leave with the full assurance that they have done their job. Still, a paper or electronic copy must soon follow.

29. D: Striking a mailbox is covered under liability – property damage. The others are covered by collision or comprehensive (other-than-collision), both of which require endorsements on the policy as well as deductible amounts to be covered by the insured due to the incident.

30. C: Commercial crime policies only cover losses that occur within the policy's dates. However, because losses due to crime are not immediately apparent, ample time must be given for these losses to be discovered and, in turn, reported. This window spans the course of a single year. In theory, if one does not notice that a crime has caused a loss within a year, the loss cannot have been consequential to the functioning of one's business.

31. C: Each of the above is a duty of the insurer (defend—litigate, indemnify—protect the insured against financial burden, settle—finalize the claim financially) except for mitigation, which is a duty of the insured to keep the damage from spreading. For instance, if there is active water damage, it is the insured's responsibility to mitigate that damage by taking precautions to stop the leak and have it addressed.

32. D: While these words might be considered synonyms, the term *occurrence* as it pertains to liability coverage refers to an accident or to exposure to an outside event which causes the covered damage. Falling trees, theft, and other covered perils—when they come to fruition—are considered occurrences.

33. B: With a replacement cost value (RCV) policy, the total payout will follow the estimate done by the roofing company. Were this the only figure in the equation, option A would be correct. However, a deductible must be taken into account, making option B correct. Option C factored in depreciation but no deductible, and option D factored in both (which would be accurate in an actual cash value (ACV) policy).

34. B: While the amount paid was not equal, equal shares states that policies pay the same amount until the liability limit of the smaller of the two policies has been reached. Had the loss been $20,000 instead of $60,000, both policies would have paid $10,000.

35. D: In this case, what Bob needed was for extra expenses sustained by the loss to be covered. The business income policy was responsible for paying the rent. Loss of use is common on homeowners policies—among others—and it involves paying to temporarily relocate an insured while their dwelling is being restored.

36. B: If a roofer had inspected the damage on the roof alone and then advised Danielle to file for only the roofing, she would have been able to repair far less of the damages because of the smaller payout, and she never would have known that more was available. Especially on ACV policies where all damage is subject to depreciation, a thorough inspection for everything that might go wrong can make the difference between a favorable and an awful claim experience.

37. C: Because the mortgage lender has rights to be paid on a policy, the loss payable clause stipulates a certain level of default responsibility on the part of the lender. While rare, this is a case of ensuring that the insurer remains an insurable interest in the property as well as ensuring that the lender takes care of their investment.

38. D: By default, an insured is the party who might expect to suffer a covered loss. Jared, who carries the policy, is the insured. As the technical owner of the vehicle, his credit union must be listed on his policy as an additional insured. Because Jared is still paying off the car, it is the credit union's money on the line in the event of a total loss. Therefore, the credit union's name will be listed as a means of ensuring they receive payment in the event of such an outcome.

39. C: The coverages within this type of policy are immense, but they generally do not extend to property damages or injuries that occur as a result of a breach. These damages or injuries would be covered under other associated policies, depending on the extent, from liability to property insurance.

40. D: The key information here is that Aaron is on the job. As a general rule, auto insurance never adopts responsibility for injuries that fall under the purview of workers' compensation. Had Aaron been injured in his off hours, the correct answer would have been option C, medical payments.

41. C: When it comes to liability coverage, the most important aspect is accounting for the financial protections of the insured. If the insured does not own any property and suing this insured would not yield hefty rewards, then carrying state minimum coverage will likely suffice. If the insured does have assets, these need to be factored in when determining the insured's liability limits, as lawsuits can result in judgments, liens, or even asset seizures.

42. D: A binder and a certificate of insurance are almost identical. However, a certificate of insurance has a bit more description, showing line-item coverage without getting into the minutiae involved in a full contract. Certificates of insurance provided to lenders can also include invoices when the insurance is set to fall into escrow.

43. D: A DP-2 still operates on named—as opposed to open—perils, but a DP-1 is severely limited. A DP-1 does not cover many weather-related losses, such as the weight of ice or snow. A DP-2 allows for a little more coverage without extending to open peril and further increasing the price.

44. C: An insurer is not allowed to sway an insured against retaining an attorney, nor are they allowed to obscure the process to suit their own interests at the cost (or to the detriment) of the insured. Openness, thoroughness, and promptness can be used as measures in determining the insurer's obligations.

45. A: Earthquakes are considered extra-hazardous, meaning that they are often excluded without a specific endorsement to grant the coverage, usually at a higher cost. Catastrophic losses are excluded because when the damage occurs, it is widespread and would be unaffordable for any given insurer to cover.

46. D: None of the given options would suit Ronald's needs, as flood insurance is not available under any home policy. Flood insurance is a FEMA-controlled program and must be purchased separately.

47. C: While medical payment coverage is robust in its offerings, it does come with a window in which a claim must be filed. In order to provide for a reasonable time period, unless otherwise specified, claims must be filed within one year of the date of loss—in this case, Shelley's injury.

48. B: A lender will ensure that any purchase is sufficiently covered in terms of cash value, replacement cost, and dwelling coverage. In fact, they will not issue the loan without it. When customers run into debt-to-income (DTI) issues, the lender will suggest taking a policy with a high deductible in order to reduce the cost of the policy. This in turn lowers the escrow payment and therefore the mortgage payment. It is not ideal in the event that a claim needs to be filed, but sometimes it is the only way a loan can be processed.

49. A: The deposit premium is called such because the ultimate figure is subject to (and quite likely to) change. While the agent can successfully estimate Calvin's premium with the information at hand, it is ultimately up to the underwriters to scrutinize the details and return with a fixed amount of coverage by which the correct premium will be calculated. The payment made with the application will then apply towards the final figure.

50. C: The Drive Other Car (DOC) endorsement is added onto business policies—typically in the auto industry, where vehicles are constantly in-and-out. This endorsement allows employees or other insureds covered under the business auto policy to operate non-owned vehicles as well, while coverage extends to the driver.

51. B: If Jeff and his insurer are unable to come to an agreement on a settlement figure, arbitration is the next step. Ideally, if Jeff has guaranteed asset protection (GAP) insurance, the problem goes away. GAP pays for the difference between a total loss value and the loan amount. However, as a financial product, GAP is either purchased at the dealer at the time of sale or purchased separately; it is not part of auto insurance. Underinsured coverage can kick in to help replace a vehicle when the other driver is at fault, but it does not have sufficient coverage to pay for the loss. (Ex: a driver with 25/50/25 totals Jeff's brand-new Mercedes Benz.)

52. D: This scenario would be considered a morale hazard. When it comes to insurance, as far as the insurer is concerned, there is only insurable interest if the insured believes their product (home, auto, life) is worth taking care of. The main difference between moral and morale hazards is determined by the intention of the covered party. A moral hazard is indicated by a deliberate intent to perform riskier behavior, whereas a morale hazard is more of an unconscious indifference to risk as an item becomes less and less valuable over time.

53. C: The law of large numbers is a statistical axiom employed by insurance companies as a foundational basis for their operational predictions in terms of forecasted payouts—the larger the amount of incidences and customers a company can gather data on, the more accurate their predictions can be. Zipf's law has to do with distribution trends, and the law of averages is used primarily in a sales context, where it predicts outcomes based on probabilities.

54. B: While a homeowners policy covers personal liability and medical payments, the injuries must occur on the home premises. Damage and injuries caused while boating make up the bulk of a watercraft policy. The scenarios in options A and D can be covered by a homeowners policy, but they are subject to the full homeowners deductible. It may not be beneficial for Jerry to file such claims, but the coverage is there. Option C would be covered under Jerry's auto policy, as coverage tends to extend to trailers and what is being hauled. Again, coverage would be limited but present.

55. C: The HO-7 specifically covers mobile homes. Certain modular homes can fall under this policy type as well, depending on the state in which the policy is written.

56. D: The questions referring specifically to the damages done are a verbal means of providing a proof of loss. A notice of claim comes into play when Athena provides the date, time, and location of the incident, at which point the loss is allocated into a claim.

57. C: The loss settlement provision can acknowledge the value of a property based on actual cash value (ACV) while opting not to pay out that figure in the amount of a total loss. For instance, a Fox Body Mustang could be worth $20,000, but if the insurer can find one similar for $10,000, then, by a loss settlement condition, they still recognize that the value of the car is $20,000, but they only have to cover the cost of replacement, which would be $10,000.

58. C: A broad form policy (HO-2) only covers named perils. This means that if the peril (whether weather, arson, etc.) does not appear on the contract, it will not be covered. This saves on cost, as the homeowner assumes all risk that is not specifically listed.

59. C: Ice on a roof presents a physical hazard because it is a circumstance that threatens to cause a loss. While the ice itself is not an issue, it could become one if heavy enough, making it a physical hazard. Leaving the front door unlocked could be an example of either moral or morale hazard, depending on the scenario. Hail and vandalism are perils (outside events that cause loss).

60. C: Insuring agreements are blanket forms that lay out how a given insurer's coverage works. These agreements specify the coverages being granted and how they apply as well as illumination on the legal process during lawsuits. Because insuring agreements apply to all insureds being covered, it is unnecessary to specify a given vehicle or customer.

61. D: The HO-6 is condo-specific. Owners of condominium units require special forms since what they are purchasing has more to do with the contents and liability within the unit. Another party has power over most decisions and liability regarding the structure of the building itself.

62. C: A bailee is someone in possession of another's property. Insurance excludes damages done under these circumstances. For example, if Terrence has roadside assistance on his auto policy, his insurer will not agree to pay if damage occurs between when the vehicle is picked up by a tow company and dropped off at its destination.

63. B: Firearms often come equipped with low limits. Insureds have the option to raise these limits or to opt for an articles policy to specifically protect their firearms. However, firearms are not typically excluded for coverage under a policy.

64. C: Options A, B, and D are all examples of conditions that must be met in order for an insurance company to pay a claim. Changes in the contract must be provided to the insured by mail, but this is a rule for endorsements rather than conditions. Conditions, from the insurer's perspective, refers to if-then statements.

65. A: An open peril policy is broad. There is a list of what *is not* covered, but coverage kicks in when perils fall outside the scope of that list. A named peril policy, by contrast, tells what *is* covered, and anything that does not fit neatly into that box is not covered.

66. A: There are two forms of courts: criminal and civil. Tort law has to do with one party filing non-civil damages against another, as it still claims violations or damages done. Specifically, auto accident legal suits are considered unintentional torts.

67. B: From the standpoint of the insurer, unearned premium means that the insured has paid for insurance which has not yet been provided. This refund would be calculated pro rata, but it is to refund unearned premium. Cash surrender refers to life insurance rather than fire.

68. D: Regardless of the severity of the risk, speculative risk is any risk that has the potential for gain rather than loss, which violates the principle of indemnity. As such, investments and any other sort of gambles that have the potential to earn the insured money, rather than lose it, are considered speculative risks and are uninsurable.

69. A: While option C—mechanical breakdown—might seem most reasonable here, the answer is off-premises theft. The amount of coverage involved may be reduced for off-site theft or damage to the property, but it is not excluded. Construction can involve property being transported between various locations, so the coverage follows.

70. B: Laws vary by state as to what is and is not covered under a manufactured home policy. Stipulations can vary drastically. Typically, mobile/manufactured homes under 10 years of age are granted preferential treatment, as the risk is at its lowest. Homes older than 10 years may not be eligible for replacement cost coverage whatsoever, depending on the state. Having a home in a qualified mobile home park can also grant significant savings on the premium. The manufacturer will factor into the replacement cost (or actual cash value) in the event of a claim, but the manufacturer has little or nothing to do with initial coverage offerings.

71. B: Moral hazards involve intentionally taking on risks you would normally avoid *due to* the knowledge that it's now somebody else's problem—namely, the insurer's. This is considered a moral dilemma because Alvin's insurer calculated his premiums based on his previous risk profile. They have no way of assessing a sudden change in his "moral" character that could lead to a higher risk profile.

72. C: An HO-5 is an HO-3 (special form) policy with the added bonus of personal property being covered as stringently as the structure itself. With an HO-3, Kenny would be maximizing peril benefits for his home itself (anything not excluded is covered), but with an HO-5, his belongings will be granted that same level of coverage.

73. A: Shelley will purchase a personal articles policy. Though unintuitive, this technically falls under the purview of inland marine, which serves as a catch-all for fire policies that don't fit neatly under homeowners policies.

74. C: The proof of loss is in the incident report: Tommy wrecked his vehicle, meaning there was a loss. The obligations of the insurer do not change—ABC pays for at-fault accidents when collision coverage is present, and they do not pay when it is not. Liability exclusions would not apply here, barring extreme circumstances. The question at hand is whether the notice of claim precedes the request for coverage. If so, Tommy is potentially committing fraud.

75. D: "Special" is a bit of a misnomer, as special form policies make up a significant amount of all fire policies. The contract in such policies revolves around exclusions. The insurer tells the insured up-front what *will not* be covered while agreeing to cover anything outside of those parameters.

76. C: Adverse selection refers to the tendency to acquire at-risk exposures that are not necessary. As a general rule, exclusions form due to industry experience. Opening oneself up to adverse selection means that, by taking on excessive risks, one can be almost certain of increased expenditures down the road.

77. C: In fire policies, floaters are the term used to specify policy riders. In a case such as this, frequently used off-site machinery could present a real headache if a policy hasn't been revised to include such coverage. This is because the majority of the risk takes place away from the address on the insurance policy. A commercial property floater is what Greg would need to buy.

78. A: While a lightning strike is not exactly an accident (though it is unintended), "nonaccidental" in this context refers to losses which occur due to regular use and are not covered by insurance policies. Rust and wear and tear also fall into this category. While some of these losses may be covered by warranties, they are excluded from insurance coverage.

79. C: Insurable interest is the goal in an insurance application. If there is a way to invest in an individual, a business, a home, etc. for future profit, an insurer intends to find it. To determine whether the investment is worthwhile, the insurer will perform inspections, review claim history, and research several other factors. Premiums are based on the risk determined by this research (risk-based pricing).

80. B: Such an acquisition, when coverage is extended, operates on an occurrence basis. Any claims with loss dates prior to the acquisition and effective dates of the policy will not apply, and those claims shall not be covered.

81. B: Aggregate limits set a per term/per period limit, above which payouts do not have to be issued. Limits also have per person, per occurrence, and/or per accident figures. These limits are disclosed at the beginning of a policy.

82. A: The trick to this question is noting that the oncoming driver was at fault. With this being the case, the other insurer is responsible for 100 percent of the rental charges so long as liability is not contested. In the event that the other insurer disagreed with liability, Jackie could have been required to file under her own policy first, then wait for arbitration to resolve the issue.

83. B: One might think option D is the correct answer, due to the criminal nature involved in bail bonds. However, the determining factor in supplemental payments as pertains to liability revolves around permission. The insurer must elect what it will pay for, typically in advance. If Johnny hires an investigator on his own, he would be operating outside the agreed parameters. If an investigator is to be hired, that would be a decision to be made by the insurer, rather than by Johnny.

84. B: Under a claims-made policy, the insurer is responsible for paying for the loss at the time of the claim's filing. A retroactive stipulation limits the dates with which a claims-made policy is applicable. An occurrence policy is one where the insurer covers the loss at the time of the incident, regardless of when the claim is filed.

85. B: No, farm owners insurance is for family-operated farms with minimal commercial exposure. ABC's exposure is too large to have adequate coverage under a farm owners policy and should look to obtain a commercial farming policy that would be better suited to cover the meat operation as well as the unique exposure customers bring when they visit a property.

86. B: While paying the deductible must be done during the claims process, it is not considered a duty of the insured. These duties instead revolve around what is necessary to file the claim—typically statements and documentation that allow the insurer to understand exactly what has happened.

87. C: Failing to report a new purchase immediately will, in this case, cost Garvis a little more than had he given his insurer a call. Regardless of coverage otherwise, new purchases with liens default to $500 until otherwise requested. This is the most popular deductible amount by far and has been chosen as the insurance default.

88. A: Unless otherwise specified (such as when purchasing new car replacement insurance), vehicle values are determined by the value of the vehicle at the point of loss. The rarity of early-2000s model trucks and SUVs increases their actual cash value because the amount people are willing to pay for them is staying steady or even, in some cases, increasing over time. This prevents the vehicle from depreciating at the rate which simple age would suggest it should. Replacement cost is used in homeowners insurance, and stated value tends to be used for antique policies or others in which an amount is agreed at the beginning of the contract. The salvage value has to do with total loss determination, but it is not the basis for what an insurer will pay the insured.

89. C: While the word additional sounds like an afterthought, additional insureds can be mortgage lenders, auto finance companies, or anyone else who has a financial stake in the product being insured. In this case, Dave is both named insured and first insured, but he also needs to make sure Jim is listed.

90. D: Vicarious liability comes into play when one party is acting vicariously on the behalf of another. Evan would have never been delivering pizzas on his own time or for the fun of it. He was only there because he was working on behalf of another—namely, Paul's Pizza and Wings. If Paul's is responsible for Evan's very presence where the accident took place, then Paul's could be seen as liable for the accident, at least in some measure or degree.

91. A: Unless one is specifically applying for business-use auto insurance, occupation will not be a factor in determining rate or eligibility. Location and telematics (driving habit monitoring) factor heavily into price determinations, while one's credit report factors into whether one is eligible for coverage and, if so, at which risk tier.

92. B: Indemnity refers to the act of shielding another party (the insured) from loss, liability, or burden. While more specific policies can be purchased which list various perils to be avoided, the concept of indemnity is at play whenever there is an agreement to shield one party financially.

93. A: A flat cancel is a cancellation processed as of the original effective date. This can happen for a few reasons. Maybe the vehicle purchase never went through. Maybe the policy issues at a higher rate than initially quoted, so the insured wishes to stay with their original insurer. Either way, in these instances, back-dating to the original inception helps to avoid confusion.

94. D: The HO-8 is for homes that can't be feasibly covered under an HO-3 or an HO-5. Most home policies treat repairs and replacements by the replacement cost. With most homes taking the same materials, this keeps things simple. For older homes, however, where different materials were used than are available today, that coverage becomes actual cash value (ACV) in order to accommodate the difference.

95. B: While side-by-sides are almost universal on farm properties as a means of getting around, due to their status as ATVs, they require separate policies. Tractors, being classified as machinery rather than vehicles, face no such scrutiny and are covered in addition to livestock, virtually all forms of farm equipment, and nearly everything else that keeps the farm up and running.

96. B: Most mortgagee clauses are equipped with both ISAOA and ATIMA, which stand for "its successors and/or assigns" and "as their interests may appear," respectively. Should one lender purchase another or simply decide to sell a chunk of its mortgagees, the "successor" comes into play. The new owner of the loan (new mortgagee) carries the right to maintain an additional interest in the insurance policy at hand.

97. D: Employer's liability insurance can be brought within the umbrella of workers' compensation, or it can be purchased as a separate coverage. While workers' compensation covers medical costs (including ongoing care), employer's liability covers legal costs as well as those associated in a legal capacity. Wrongful termination, for instance, would also fall under employer's liability.

98. B: Special and general damages are the two types of compensatory damages. As such, they are quite likely to arise. However, exemplary damages (also known as punitive damages) are reserved for cases of recklessness. If Bob were drinking and driving or if he were traveling severely over the speed limit, then Bob might be pursued with such a suit. However, punitive/exemplary damages do not apply in a regular car accident.

99. A: The insurance payout follows the concept of named insured in owned autos. Because Calvin was driving his own vehicle, his insurance policy will cover the loss, and the damages will not be split. Had he been driving a company vehicle, he would be an insured operator of that vehicle, and the damages would be covered under the business's policy. This is why pizza restaurants tend to have delivery drivers use their own vehicles. It reduces overhead costs for the businesses.

100. C: The DP-1 is the most basic dwelling policy available. This excludes content coverage, which would suit Kathy now that her belongings aren't at her old house. The DP-1 offers a means of avoiding risk of a total loss, depending on the peril at hand.

101. C: General contractors run a high risk of liability claims. Customers can be unsatisfied due to faulty work, damage from helpers, dissatisfaction with the final product, or any other number of factors. In order to control exposure, many insurers require extra documentation from higher-risk industries in order to prove a clean history. This does not guarantee that the contractor won't face a claim in the future, but it is the only real safeguard for the insurer when accepting such a risk.

102. A: Susan's SUV was the cause of the damage to Jason's sedan, making her the proximate cause. Actual cause and cause are, in fact, synonymous and are represented by John in this case, as the entire accident was caused by him.

103. C: A ruling of 14 days is considered ample time to return a defunct vehicle if needed, arrange selling a swapped vehicle, etc. Surpassing that period means running the risk of having no coverage on a new vehicle, but until that time, a valid ID card and a proof of purchase/bill of sale can serve as a proof of insurance.

104. C: While forklifts can be—and are—essential to the operations of many businesses, a breakdown policy revolves around systems, rather than operable equipment. Breakdown policies cover breakdowns due to a particular outside cause. Wear and tear, negligence, and lack of maintenance can void coverage, especially as it pertains to air conditioning units.

105. C: Insurance, in its most simplistic terms, is the transfer of risk. If John had no insurance, he would assume responsibility for every risk associated with operating his vehicle. By making premium payments, John is effectively selling his risk to a third party (the insurer) at a rate determined by his present and historical exposure.

106. C: The insured (Karen) is the first party. Karen's insurer is the second party. Anyone else to whom damage or injury occurs is a third party. Had a tree fallen on Karen's home, for instance, this would have been a first-party loss.

107. A: The presence of an injury lawyer may suggest that the answer is option B—medical payments. However, medical payments is a coverage that follows the insured rather than the injured third party. Bodily injury coverage is part of coverage A—liability, and it is what the injury lawyer will target.

108. C: Exclusions are included in the copy of the contract/policy itself. Declarations pages are commonly provided as a means of proving coverage, so they include premiums, limits, deductibles, interests, provisions, etc. They do not, however, include any language stipulating how the policy operates.

109. C: A DP-3 provides the most comprehensive policy for anyone who owns a home, doesn't live in it, and doesn't want the headache of worrying about all the things that could happen to the building and its contents. A DP-3 presents the largest suite available for these coverages, offering an open peril coverage for the dwelling. Any peril that is not listed as excluded will be covered.

110. B: An indirect loss is a loss that is caused by a wholly separate loss. In the scenario in option B, the insurer has to pay rental expenses due to an accident that caused the separate need for a rental. In each of the other occurrences, the damage is singular, rather than ongoing, and is treated as a single occurrence—even the smoke damage.

P&C Texas-Specific Practice Test

1. ABC Insurance is incorporated in Massachusetts. The company wants to expand its business into Texas. In the state of Texas, what type of insurer would ABC be categorized as?

    a. Domestic
    b. Alien
    c. Nonresident
    d. Foreign

2. Which of the following best describes a formal demand from the insurance department that an insurance company immediately discontinue engaging in activity that violates Texas insurance law?

    a. Notice of hearing
    b. Cease and desist order
    c. Injunction
    d. Certificate of authority

3. Miranda resides in Texas. She is contracted with a local insurance company to perform an array of business tasks including appointing sales agents, adjusting claims, and providing reporting to the insurance company. What type of license does Miranda need to perform her duties?

    a. Public adjuster
    b. Staff agent
    c. Managing general agent
    d. Risk manager

4. In Texas, which entity is authorized to declare a geographical area underserved for the purposes of residential insurance availability?

    a. The insurance commissioner
    b. The governor
    c. The department of insurance
    d. The Texas FAIR Plan Association

5. Carey owns a single-family home in Galveston County, Texas. It is about a mile off the coast of the Gulf of Mexico. He is able to obtain a homeowner's policy, but the insurance company will not write it unless the policy is endorsed to exclude damages from wind and hail. Which of the following programs would be able to assist Carey with this gap in coverage?

    a. NFIP
    b. TFPA
    c. TWIA
    d. NAIC

6. For an insurer that is organized as a Texas Lloyd's plan, which entity must be granted a certificate of authority by the Texas Department of Insurance?

    a. The insurance company formed by the plan
    b. The chief executive officer
    c. The managing underwriter
    d. The attorney-in-fact

7. Curtis works for an insurance agency in Texas. He is tasked with several different duties as part of his daily work. Of his duties listed below, which one by itself would NOT require Curtis to be licensed as an agent?

    a. Reviewing insurance applications with clients to ensure that all relevant information is provided

    b. Taking new claims reports from insureds and entering them into the agency's claims management system

    c. Providing information on auto insurance rates to clients who inquire

    d. Accepting deposit premiums from commercial insureds

8. Daniel recently graduated from college and purchased his first car. He bought auto insurance from ABC Insurance Inc., which went into effect about three months ago. If ABC wanted to cancel Daniel's policy, which of the following reasons would permit it to do so under Texas insurance law?

    a. Daniel forgets to send in the check for his premium payment.

    b. Daniel and his girlfriend move in together, and he does not add her to his policy.

    c. Daniel is involved in a fender bender in a parking lot and does not report the claim because there was no damage to either car.

    d. Daniel receives tickets for two moving violations within 60 days.

9. Which of the following unfair trade practices involves multiple parties working together to force a competitor out of the insurance market in order to stifle competition?

    a. Intimidation

    b. Discrimination

    c. Boycott

    d. Misrepresentation

10. Under Texas law, insurers are required to keep records of written claims complaints on file for three years or _____, whichever is shorter.

    a. until the policyholder signs a release to settle the claim in question

    b. going back to the date of the insurer's last department examination

    c. until any litigation concerning the claim is dismissed

    d. going back to the handling adjuster's first day of employment with the insurer

11. Amanda was recently hired by a small property and casualty insurance company as a claims adjuster trainee. Due to a staffing shortage, she will begin adjusting straightforward claims as soon as her trainer, who is a licensed claims adjuster, is comfortable with her doing so. How long will the Texas Insurance Code allow Amanda to adjust claims as an unlicensed trainee?

    a. Up to 90 days

    b. Up to 45 days

    c. Up to 6 months

    d. Up to 12 months

12. Molly lives in Texas. She just turned 18 and bought her first car. She speaks to an agent who tells her that he can get her a great deal on a personal auto policy that carries liability limits of 25/50/25, collision coverage with a $500 deductible, and $2,500 in personal injury protection (PIP) coverage. Why would the agent be unable to legally sell this policy to Molly?

   a. It is against the Texas Insurance Code to offer clients the cheapest policy available.
   b. Auto insurance cannot be sold to anyone under the age of 21.
   c. The limits on the policy are less than the minimum amount the state requires.
   d. The policy does not include comprehensive coverage, which is required on all Texas auto policies.

13. If a Texas insurance agent plans to discontinue working in the insurance business, why is it preferable to voluntarily terminate the license rather than just letting it expire?

   a. Expired licenses are subject to fines for incomplete continuing education hours.
   b. Licensees who allow their licenses to expire will not be eligible for a new license in the future.
   c. It is against the law to let a license expire intentionally.
   d. If a license is not renewed before it expires, it is considered revoked under Texas law.

14. Which of the following is NOT required to obtain a certificate of authority from the Texas Department of Insurance to write policies within the state?

   a. Commercial property insurers
   b. Texas Lloyd's plans
   c. Surplus lines insurers
   d. Health maintenance organizations

15. Anna was involved in two at-fault auto accidents and got three tickets for moving violations in a single year. Her current auto insurer refused to renew her policy, and she has been rejected by three other carriers as well. She applies for a policy under the Texas Automobile Insurance Plan Association (TAIPA) and is approved for a policy. For auto liability coverage, what are the limits under Anna's new policy?

   a. 50/100/25
   b. 30/60/25
   c. 25/50/25
   d. 30/60/30

16. Jack owns a single-family home that is insured under an HO-3 policy issued by XYZ Insurance. It is worth $435,000, so Jack had it insured for that amount. Unfortunately, a sudden tornado strikes Jack's city and destroys his home. Due to the magnitude of the damage caused by the tornado, XYZ Insurance is unable to pay its insureds' valid claims and becomes insolvent. A judge issues an order stating that XYZ is an impaired insurer, so Jack must resolve his claim with the Texas Property and Casualty Insurance Guaranty Association (TPCIGA). What is the most Jack will be able to collect from the TPCIGA for the loss of his home?

   a. $435,000
   b. The actual cash value of the home
   c. The full replacement cost of the home
   d. $300,000

17. Taran is an appointed insurance agent for ABC Insurance in Texas. He was appointed by ABC on June 28, 2019. When will his appointment expire?

    a. It does not expire and only ends when Taran requests termination of the appointment.
    b. June 28, 2021
    c. It does not expire and only ends when ABC terminates or withdraws the appointment.
    d. June 28, 2024

18. The Texas Department of Insurance is led by the Commissioner of Insurance. How is the Commissioner of Insurance selected?

    a. He or she is appointed by the governor and confirmed by the Texas State Senate.
    b. He or she is elected by a vote of department of insurance employees.
    c. He or she is elected by a statewide vote.
    d. He or she is appointed and confirmed by the Texas State Senate.

19. For Texas insurance agents and adjusters, how many hours of continuing education must be devoted to ethics to renew a license?

    a. Three
    b. One
    c. Four
    d. Five

20. Under Texas law, which of the following is an agent NOT allowed to collect directly from an insured?

    a. Service fees
    b. Finder's fees
    c. Inspection fees
    d. Application fees

21. ABC Insurance is domiciled in Texas. Its financial health is currently being assessed by the Texas Department of Insurance. Which of the following factors is the department permitted to consider in its evaluation of ABC?

    a. Number of full-time employees
    b. Credit agency ratings
    c. Frequency of bad faith litigation
    d. Loss experience

22. General Insurance Company is expanding into the Texas market. After reviewing the company's application for a certificate of authority, the Texas Department of Insurance determines that General will need to deposit $1.7 million with the comptroller as a condition of issuing the certificate. Under the insurance code, how must General deposit the required funds?

    a. Certified check
    b. Cash via an armored carrier
    c. Electronic funds transfer
    d. Company check

23. Under Texas law, what is the minimum liability coverage required for a transportation network driver when there is a paying passenger in his or her vehicle?

  a. $500,000 per loss for all injury and property damage
  b. $1 million per loss for all injury and property damage
  c. $50,000 per loss per person for injury, $100,000 per loss for injury, $50,000 per loss for property damage
  d. $30,000 per loss per person for injury, $60,000 per loss for injury, and $25,000 per loss for property damage

24. Corey works at a Texas restaurant as a fry cook. While working one day, he thinks he smells gas but does not think anything of it since all of the cooking appliances in the kitchen run on gas. An hour or so later, he passes out and hits his head on the side of the deep fryer. He suffers a concussion as well as a first-degree burn to his forehead. The next day, his manager discovers that the smell was coming from a punctured gas hose. A claim is submitted to his employer's workers' compensation insurance. How will the insurer respond to Corey's claim?

  a. It will accept his claim because his exposure to the gas fumes occurred during the normal course of his employment.
  b. It will deny the claim because Corey did not report the gas smell to management immediately, which could have prevented his injury.
  c. It will deny the claim because Corey was intoxicated by the gas fumes when he was injured.
  d. It will only pay benefits at 50 percent since Corey was partly at fault for his injuries because he did not attempt to locate the source of the gas fumes.

25. Which cause of loss is NOT covered in any version of the Texas Dwelling Policy (TDP)?

  a. Windstorm
  b. Vandalism
  c. Theft of personal property
  d. Smoke damage

26. Dana works as an auto adjuster for an insurance company in Texas. The company only writes insurance for people who reside in Texas. She recently received a claim for a rear-end accident in which her insured was at fault. Despite Dana trying to contact the insured multiple times over the span of 60 days, he never responded to her calls, emails, or letters. She then notified underwriting of the insured's lack of cooperation. What must happen before the insured's policy can be flagged for nonrenewal?

  a. Dana must continue making attempts to contact the insured for at least 30 more days.
  b. The other driver must file a lawsuit against Dana's insured.
  c. Dana must try to make contact with the insured at his residence either personally or via a private investigator.
  d. Dana must send him a letter explaining that his continued refusal to cooperate could cause the policy to not be renewed.

27. Which personal auto coverage are Texas insurers NOT required to offer a policyholder when selling a policy?

  a. Underinsured motorist coverage
  b. Medical payments coverage
  c. Personal injury protection coverage
  d. Uninsured motorist coverage

28. Patrick was killed in a work accident, and his death is covered under Texas workers' compensation law. He is unmarried, has no children, and both of his parents are deceased. How will his workers' compensation death benefits be handled?

    a. The amount paid will be deposited into the Texas Subsequent Injury Fund.
    b. Nothing will be paid because benefits are only owed when there are eligible survivors.
    c. The amount will be deposited with the state and held in case an eligible beneficiary should be discovered.
    d. The amount will be deposited with the Texas Property and Casualty Insurance Guaranty Association.

29. Which of the following scenarios is most likely to result in the issuance of an emergency cease and desist order by the Texas Department of Insurance (TDI)?

    a. An insurance company that routinely makes settlement offers on liability claims that are unreasonably low
    b. An insurance agent selling personal lines property insurance written by an insurance company that does not have a Texas certificate of authority
    c. An unlicensed agency employee typing up and mailing notices of renewal to insureds
    d. An insurance agency advertising policies promising high claims payouts

30. Maura holds a Texas nonresident insurance agent license. She currently lives in California and has a resident insurance agent license there. She is planning to move to Texas to be closer to family and already has a new job lined up with a Texas insurance agency. What will Maura need to do to receive a Texas resident insurance agent license?

    a. Nothing, because a nonresident license automatically converts to a resident license when the licensee changes his or her legal address.
    b. She will have to complete the Texas licensing process as if she were a completely new applicant.
    c. She will need to wait for her California license to expire before applying for a Texas resident agent license.
    d. She will need to surrender her California resident agent license.

31. In Texas, insurers who write residential insurance are entitled to inspect the property being insured. When an insurer requires a property to be inspected, when is the earliest the inspection may occur?

    a. The effective date of the policy
    b. 30 days before the date the insurance application is submitted
    c. 90 days before the effective date of the policy
    d. 60 days before the agent binds coverage

32. Which of the following parties would NOT be eligible for coverage under the Texas Medical Liability Insurance Underwriting Association?

    a. Nurse practitioners
    b. Medical equipment manufacturers
    c. Skilled nursing facilities
    d. Hospital employees

33. Under Texas workers' compensation law, when will an injured employee be determined to have reached maximum medical improvement (MMI)?

a. 104 weeks from the date the employee started receiving income benefits
b. 6 months from the date of the employee's first visit with the treating physician
c. 3 years from the date of injury
d. 52 weeks from the date of injury

34. Which of the following would be considered a violation of the Texas Unfair Claim Settlement Practices Act?

a. Requesting income tax documents from a claimant who is claiming loss of income
b. Delaying an offer of settlement to an insured for auto property damage because another driver is at fault for the accident
c. Requiring a third-party claimant to sign a release before issuing payment for a settlement
d. Requesting an insured submit to an independent medical examination as part of an uninsured motorist bodily injury claim

35. In Texas, how often are insurers subject to examination of financial records by the Texas Department of Insurance (TDI)?

a. Annually
b. At least once every ten years
c. Every other year
d. At least once every five years

P&C Texas-Specific Answer Key and Explanations

1. D: If an insurer is domiciled in one state and doing business in a different state, the insurer is considered a foreign insurer in the latter state. In this case, ABC would be considered a domestic insurer in Massachusetts and a foreign insurer in Texas. Alien insurers are those incorporated outside of the United States. Nonresident refers to licensed insurance personnel who live outside of Texas but handle insurance matters in Texas.

2. B: If the Texas Department of Insurance determines that an insurer has been conducting activities that violate the insurance code or Texas law, the commissioner will issue a cease and desist order. This order demands that the insurer cease such activities immediately. Failure to comply with this order can result in penalties up to and including revocation of the insurance company's certificate of authority to transact insurance in Texas.

3. C: The description of Miranda's duties aligns with those of a managing general agent under Texas law. Managing general agents can perform essentially all of the work a licensed agent can do, but they also have tasks that go beyond the scope of a regular insurance agent.

4. A: A community is designated as underserved by rule of the insurance commissioner. This declaration makes residents of that community eligible for coverage under the Texas FAIR Plan Association program.

5. C: Carey would likely be able to secure wind and hail insurance coverage through the TWIA or the Texas Windstorm Insurance Association. This program was designed to provide insurance coverage to property owners located in coastal areas. Such areas are prone to hurricanes and tropical storms, so many consumers cannot secure wind or hail damage coverage in the voluntary insurance marker. NFIP is the National Flood Insurance Program, TFPA is the Texas FAIR Plan Association, and NAIC is the National Association of Insurance Commissioners.

6. D: Texas Lloyd's plans are unique in that they are formed by an individual or group of individuals with the intention of selling and writing insurance coverage. The members of a Lloyd's plan are referred to as underwriters. Because the membership of a Lloyd's plan is made up of underwriters, an attorney-in-fact is appointed to represent the underwriters, and part of this representation involves obtaining a certificate of authority.

7. B: This task on its own would not require Curtis to have an insurance license in Texas. Unlicensed staff are authorized to obtain information about claims for the purpose of logging claims into a claims management system. They can also provide claims information and status updates to a limited extent.

8. A: Once a new auto policy has been in effect for more than 60 days, an insurer may only cancel it for a reason permitted under the Texas Insurance Code. One such reason is failure to pay premiums on time.

9. C: Boycotting occurs when multiple parties collude to push a competitor out of the market. For example, a group of agents would be boycotting an insurer if they all agree to not do business with that insurer or only refer undesirable applications to that insurer.

10. B: For written complaints, insurers are mandated to keep records for three years after the complaint is filed or going back to the date the department last examined the insurer, whichever is shorter.

11. D: Unlicensed claims adjuster trainees are permitted to adjust claims under the supervision of a licensed adjuster for up to 12 months. Trainees must also be registered with the department of insurance.

12. C: Auto liability policies sold in Texas must meet the minimum liability requirements established by law. Currently, Texas mandates coverage of at least 30/60/25. On the policy Molly is offered, both the per person and per accident coverage for bodily injury liability are too low to meet the state requirements.

13. A: Texas insurance licensees are subject to continuing education (CE) requirements that must be met every two years. If a licensee allows his or her license to expire instead of terminating it voluntarily, he or she will be charged with a fine of $50 per unfinished CE hour.

14. C: In Texas, surplus lines insurers are permitted to write business without a certificate of authority as long as capital and/or surplus requirements are met.

15. B: TAIPA policies provide only statutorily required auto coverage. In Texas, the minimum liability limits are 30/60/25, so that would be the liability coverage a TAIPA policy would carry.

16. D: In most cases, recovery under a claim that is taken over by the TPCIGA follows the limits carried on the policy in question or $300,000, whichever is less. Because Jack's home and policy limits are more than $300,000, that would be the most he could recover from the TPCIGA.

17. C: Once an insurer appoints an agent, the appointment lasts until the insurer withdraws or terminates the appointment. If the appointment is ended for improper behavior, the insurer must report the behavior to the Texas Department of Insurance.

18. A: For the Commissioner of Insurance position in Texas, the governor appoints a candidate. The candidate must then be approved by the state senate before he or she becomes the commissioner.

19. A: For each renewal period, at least three hours of the required continuing education hours must be focused on ethics. The remaining required hours may be on any insurance topic as long as any course taken is approved by the Texas Department of Insurance.

20. B: Because insurance agents are usually paid in the form of commissions by the insurers they sell insurance for, there are limited circumstances in which an agent can accept direct payment from a client. An agent may charge clients service, inspection, and application fees but only to offset the costs associated with obtaining coverage for the client.

21. D: When evaluating the financial condition of an insurance company, the Texas Department of Insurance and the insurance commissioner may consider many factors—one of which is loss experience. Some other factors that can be considered include investment operations, the existence of contingent liability contracts, and the types of risks being insured.

22. C: Per the Texas Insurance Code, all deposits of more than $500,000 must be processed using an electronic funds transfer (EFT). Because General's required deposit is more than $500,000, the only option to deposit the money with the state is an EFT.

23. B: Texas law requires that when a transportation network driver is actively transporting a rider, there must be liability coverage of at least $1 million aggregately for bodily injury and property damage. When a driver is logged in but not transporting a passenger, the required limits are 50/100/25.

24. A: While Texas law generally excludes workers from collecting workers' compensation benefits for injuries that occur while an employee is intoxicated, there is an exception for intoxication that occurs unintentionally due to a condition present during the course of the employee's usual work.

25. C: None of the base TDP policies provide coverage for theft of personal property. In terms of perils covered, the TDP forms align closely with the ISO dwelling policy forms.

26. D: Before a Texas personal auto policy can be not renewed due to the insured's noncooperation with a claim investigation, correspondence must be sent to the insured warning of this possibility. Once the letter is sent, the insured must be given reasonable time to respond.

27. B: In Texas, medical payments coverage is an entirely optional coverage on auto policies. While many insurers do offer it to customers, it is not required. Personal injury protection coverage is part of Texas auto policies by default but may be rejected by the policyholder in writing. Uninsured and underinsured motorist coverage must be offered to the policyholder, who may then accept or reject it.

28. A: When there are no eligible beneficiaries or surviving parents, workers' compensation insurers are still required to pay death benefits. These benefits are paid into the Texas Subsequent Injury Fund.

29. B: One situation that can trigger the TDI to issue an emergency cease and desist order is insurance being written or sold by an unauthorized entity. If the line of business in question, in this case personal lines property, is one that requires insurers to obtain a certificate of authority, it is in the best interest of the public for the TDI to stop these unauthorized sales immediately.

30. D: Under Texas law, a licensed insurance agent is not permitted to have resident agent licenses in other states if he or she holds a resident agent license in Texas. Maura will need to surrender or terminate her California resident license before she can be granted a Texas resident license.

31. C: When an insurer requests an inspection on a residential property as a condition of providing coverage, the inspection must be completed no more than 90 days prior to the effective date of the policy. If the inspection is completed earlier than that, the insurer has the right to reject the inspection report.

32. B: The Texas Medical Liability Insurance Underwriting Association, also known as the JUA or TMLIUA, was established to allow medical professionals and facilities in Texas to obtain medical liability insurance from the association if they are unable to obtain coverage in the voluntary market. Because manufacturers of medical equipment are not medical providers, they do not qualify for coverage by the JUA.

33. A: An injured worker is deemed to have reached MMI when the treating physician certifies that MMI has been achieved or at 104 weeks from the date income benefits started being paid—whichever comes first.

34. B: Under the Texas Unfair Claim Settlement Practices Act, an insurer is prohibited from unreasonably delaying making a settlement offer to an insured on the basis that another party or policy is responsible for paying for the damages claimed.

35. D: Examinations of financial records of insurers must be completed by the TDI at least once every five years. These examinations are performed by an examiner employed or appointed by the TDI. These examinations are in addition to the annual financial reporting requirements.

Bonus Practice Tests:
P&C General Knowledge Tests #2 and #3

To take these additional Property and Casualty practice tests, visit our bonus page: **mometrix.com/bonus948/propertycasual**

How to Overcome Test Anxiety

Just the thought of taking a test is enough to make most people a little nervous. A test is an important event that can have a long-term impact on your future, so it's important to take it seriously and it's natural to feel anxious about performing well. But just because anxiety is normal, that doesn't mean that it's helpful in test taking, or that you should simply accept it as part of your life. Anxiety can have a variety of effects. These effects can be mild, like making you feel slightly nervous, or severe, like blocking your ability to focus or remember even a simple detail.

If you experience test anxiety—whether severe or mild—it's important to know how to beat it. To discover this, first you need to understand what causes test anxiety.

Causes of Test Anxiety

While we often think of anxiety as an uncontrollable emotional state, it can actually be caused by simple, practical things. One of the most common causes of test anxiety is that a person does not feel adequately prepared for their test. This feeling can be the result of many different issues such as poor study habits or lack of organization, but the most common culprit is time management. Starting to study too late, failing to organize your study time to cover all of the material, or being distracted while you study will mean that you're not well prepared for the test. This may lead to cramming the night before, which will cause you to be physically and mentally exhausted for the test. Poor time management also contributes to feelings of stress, fear, and hopelessness as you realize you are not well prepared but don't know what to do about it.

Other times, test anxiety is not related to your preparation for the test but comes from unresolved fear. This may be a past failure on a test, or poor performance on tests in general. It may come from comparing yourself to others who seem to be performing better or from the stress of living up to expectations. Anxiety may be driven by fears of the future—how failure on this test would affect your educational and career goals. These fears are often completely irrational, but they can still negatively impact your test performance.

Elements of Test Anxiety

As mentioned earlier, test anxiety is considered to be an emotional state, but it has physical and mental components as well. Sometimes you may not even realize that you are suffering from test anxiety until you notice the physical symptoms. These can include trembling hands, rapid heartbeat, sweating, nausea, and tense muscles. Extreme anxiety may lead to fainting or vomiting. Obviously, any of these symptoms can have a negative impact on testing. It is important to recognize them as soon as they begin to occur so that you can address the problem before it damages your performance.

The mental components of test anxiety include trouble focusing and inability to remember learned information. During a test, your mind is on high alert, which can help you recall information and stay focused for an extended period of time. However, anxiety interferes with your mind's natural processes, causing you to blank out, even on the questions you know well. The strain of testing during anxiety makes it difficult to stay focused, especially on a test that may take several hours. Extreme anxiety can take a huge mental toll, making it difficult not only to recall test information but even to understand the test questions or pull your thoughts together.

Effects of Test Anxiety

Test anxiety is like a disease—if left untreated, it will get progressively worse. Anxiety leads to poor performance, and this reinforces the feelings of fear and failure, which in turn lead to poor performances on subsequent tests. It can grow from a mild nervousness to a crippling condition. If allowed to progress, test anxiety can have a big impact on your schooling, and consequently on your future.

Test anxiety can spread to other parts of your life. Anxiety on tests can become anxiety in any stressful situation, and blanking on a test can turn into panicking in a job situation. But fortunately, you don't have to let anxiety rule your testing and determine your grades. There are a number of relatively simple steps you can take to move past anxiety and function normally on a test and in the rest of life.

Physical Steps for Beating Test Anxiety

While test anxiety is a serious problem, the good news is that it can be overcome. It doesn't have to control your ability to think and remember information. While it may take time, you can begin taking steps today to beat anxiety.

Just as your first hint that you may be struggling with anxiety comes from the physical symptoms, the first step to treating it is also physical. Rest is crucial for having a clear, strong mind. If you are tired, it is much easier to give in to anxiety. But if you establish good sleep habits, your body and mind will be ready to perform optimally, without the strain of exhaustion. Additionally, sleeping well helps you to retain information better, so you're more likely to recall the answers when you see the test questions.

Getting good sleep means more than going to bed on time. It's important to allow your brain time to relax. Take study breaks from time to time so it doesn't get overworked, and don't study right before bed. Take time to rest your mind before trying to rest your body, or you may find it difficult to fall asleep.

Along with sleep, other aspects of physical health are important in preparing for a test. Good nutrition is vital for good brain function. Sugary foods and drinks may give a burst of energy but this burst is followed by a crash, both physically and emotionally. Instead, fuel your body with protein and vitamin-rich foods.

Also, drink plenty of water. Dehydration can lead to headaches and exhaustion, especially if your brain is already under stress from the rigors of the test. Particularly if your test is a long one, drink water during the breaks. And if possible, take an energy-boosting snack to eat between sections.

Along with sleep and diet, a third important part of physical health is exercise. Maintaining a steady workout schedule is helpful, but even taking 5-minute study breaks to walk can help get your blood pumping faster and clear your head. Exercise also releases endorphins, which contribute to a positive feeling and can help combat test anxiety.

When you nurture your physical health, you are also contributing to your mental health. If your body is healthy, your mind is much more likely to be healthy as well. So take time to rest, nourish your body with healthy food and water, and get moving as much as possible. Taking these physical steps will make you stronger and more able to take the mental steps necessary to overcome test anxiety.

Mental Steps for Beating Test Anxiety

Working on the mental side of test anxiety can be more challenging, but as with the physical side, there are clear steps you can take to overcome it. As mentioned earlier, test anxiety often stems from lack of preparation, so the obvious solution is to prepare for the test. Effective studying may be the most important weapon you have for beating test anxiety, but you can and should employ several other mental tools to combat fear.

First, boost your confidence by reminding yourself of past success—tests or projects that you aced. If you're putting as much effort into preparing for this test as you did for those, there's no reason you should expect to fail here. Work hard to prepare; then trust your preparation.

Second, surround yourself with encouraging people. It can be helpful to find a study group, but be sure that the people you're around will encourage a positive attitude. If you spend time with others who are anxious or cynical, this will only contribute to your own anxiety. Look for others who are motivated to study hard from a desire to succeed, not from a fear of failure.

Third, reward yourself. A test is physically and mentally tiring, even without anxiety, and it can be helpful to have something to look forward to. Plan an activity following the test, regardless of the outcome, such as going to a movie or getting ice cream.

When you are taking the test, if you find yourself beginning to feel anxious, remind yourself that you know the material. Visualize successfully completing the test. Then take a few deep, relaxing breaths and return to it. Work through the questions carefully but with confidence, knowing that you are capable of succeeding.

Developing a healthy mental approach to test taking will also aid in other areas of life. Test anxiety affects more than just the actual test—it can be damaging to your mental health and even contribute to depression. It's important to beat test anxiety before it becomes a problem for more than testing.

Study Strategy

Being prepared for the test is necessary to combat anxiety, but what does being prepared look like? You may study for hours on end and still not feel prepared. What you need is a strategy for test prep. The next few pages outline our recommended steps to help you plan out and conquer the challenge of preparation.

STEP 1: SCOPE OUT THE TEST

Learn everything you can about the format (multiple choice, essay, etc.) and what will be on the test. Gather any study materials, course outlines, or sample exams that may be available. Not only will this help you to prepare, but knowing what to expect can help to alleviate test anxiety.

STEP 2: MAP OUT THE MATERIAL

Look through the textbook or study guide and make note of how many chapters or sections it has. Then divide these over the time you have. For example, if a book has 15 chapters and you have five days to study, you need to cover three chapters each day. Even better, if you have the time, leave an extra day at the end for overall review after you have gone through the material in depth.

If time is limited, you may need to prioritize the material. Look through it and make note of which sections you think you already have a good grasp on, and which need review. While you are studying, skim quickly through the familiar sections and take more time on the challenging parts.

Write out your plan so you don't get lost as you go. Having a written plan also helps you feel more in control of the study, so anxiety is less likely to arise from feeling overwhelmed at the amount to cover.

STEP 3: GATHER YOUR TOOLS

Decide what study method works best for you. Do you prefer to highlight in the book as you study and then go back over the highlighted portions? Or do you type out notes of the important information? Or is it helpful to make flashcards that you can carry with you? Assemble the pens, index cards, highlighters, post-it notes, and any other materials you may need so you won't be distracted by getting up to find things while you study.

If you're having a hard time retaining the information or organizing your notes, experiment with different methods. For example, try color-coding by subject with colored pens, highlighters, or post-it notes. If you learn better by hearing, try recording yourself reading your notes so you can listen while in the car, working out, or simply sitting at your desk. Ask a friend to quiz you from your flashcards, or try teaching someone the material to solidify it in your mind.

STEP 4: CREATE YOUR ENVIRONMENT

It's important to avoid distractions while you study. This includes both the obvious distractions like visitors and the subtle distractions like an uncomfortable chair (or a too-comfortable couch that makes you want to fall asleep). Set up the best study environment possible: good lighting and a comfortable work area. If background music helps you focus, you may want to turn it on, but otherwise keep the room quiet. If you are using a computer to take notes, be sure you don't have any other windows open, especially applications like social media, games, or anything else that could distract you. Silence your phone and turn off notifications. Be sure to keep water close by so you stay hydrated while you study (but avoid unhealthy drinks and snacks).

Also, take into account the best time of day to study. Are you freshest first thing in the morning? Try to set aside some time then to work through the material. Is your mind clearer in the afternoon or evening? Schedule your study session then. Another method is to study at the same time of day that you will take the test, so that your brain gets used to working on the material at that time and will be ready to focus at test time.

STEP 5: STUDY!

Once you have done all the study preparation, it's time to settle into the actual studying. Sit down, take a few moments to settle your mind so you can focus, and begin to follow your study plan. Don't give in to distractions or let yourself procrastinate. This is your time to prepare so you'll be ready to fearlessly approach the test. Make the most of the time and stay focused.

Of course, you don't want to burn out. If you study too long you may find that you're not retaining the information very well. Take regular study breaks. For example, taking five minutes out of every hour to walk briskly, breathing deeply and swinging your arms, can help your mind stay fresh.

As you get to the end of each chapter or section, it's a good idea to do a quick review. Remind yourself of what you learned and work on any difficult parts. When you feel that you've mastered the material, move on to the next part. At the end of your study session, briefly skim through your notes again.

But while review is helpful, cramming last minute is NOT. If at all possible, work ahead so that you won't need to fit all your study into the last day. Cramming overloads your brain with more information than it can process and retain, and your tired mind may struggle to recall even previously learned information when it is overwhelmed with last-minute study. Also, the urgent nature of cramming and the stress placed on your brain contribute to anxiety. You'll be more likely to go to the test feeling unprepared and having trouble thinking clearly.

So don't cram, and don't stay up late before the test, even just to review your notes at a leisurely pace. Your brain needs rest more than it needs to go over the information again. In fact, plan to finish your studies by noon or early afternoon the day before the test. Give your brain the rest of the day to relax or focus on other things, and get a good night's sleep. Then you will be fresh for the test and better able to recall what you've studied.

STEP 6: TAKE A PRACTICE TEST

Many courses offer sample tests, either online or in the study materials. This is an excellent resource to check whether you have mastered the material, as well as to prepare for the test format and environment.

Check the test format ahead of time: the number of questions, the type (multiple choice, free response, etc.), and the time limit. Then create a plan for working through them. For example, if you have 30 minutes to take a 60-question test, your limit is 30 seconds per question. Spend less time on the questions you know well so that you can take more time on the difficult ones.

If you have time to take several practice tests, take the first one open book, with no time limit. Work through the questions at your own pace and make sure you fully understand them. Gradually work up to taking a test under test conditions: sit at a desk with all study materials put away and set a timer. Pace yourself to make sure you finish the test with time to spare and go back to check your answers if you have time.

After each test, check your answers. On the questions you missed, be sure you understand why you missed them. Did you misread the question (tests can use tricky wording)? Did you forget the information? Or was it something you hadn't learned? Go back and study any shaky areas that the practice tests reveal.

Taking these tests not only helps with your grade, but also aids in combating test anxiety. If you're already used to the test conditions, you're less likely to worry about it, and working through tests until you're scoring well gives you a confidence boost. Go through the practice tests until you feel comfortable, and then you can go into the test knowing that you're ready for it.

Test Tips

On test day, you should be confident, knowing that you've prepared well and are ready to answer the questions. But aside from preparation, there are several test day strategies you can employ to maximize your performance.

First, as stated before, get a good night's sleep the night before the test (and for several nights before that, if possible). Go into the test with a fresh, alert mind rather than staying up late to study.

Try not to change too much about your normal routine on the day of the test. It's important to eat a nutritious breakfast, but if you normally don't eat breakfast at all, consider eating just a protein bar. If you're a coffee drinker, go ahead and have your normal coffee. Just make sure you time it so that the caffeine doesn't wear off right in the middle of your test. Avoid sugary beverages, and drink enough water to stay hydrated but not so much that you need a restroom break 10 minutes into the test. If your test isn't first thing in the morning, consider going for a walk or doing a light workout before the test to get your blood flowing.

Allow yourself enough time to get ready, and leave for the test with plenty of time to spare so you won't have the anxiety of scrambling to arrive in time. Another reason to be early is to select a good seat. It's helpful to sit away from doors and windows, which can be distracting. Find a good seat, get out your supplies, and settle your mind before the test begins.

When the test begins, start by going over the instructions carefully, even if you already know what to expect. Make sure you avoid any careless mistakes by following the directions.

Then begin working through the questions, pacing yourself as you've practiced. If you're not sure on an answer, don't spend too much time on it, and don't let it shake your confidence. Either skip it and come back later, or eliminate as many wrong answers as possible and guess among the remaining ones. Don't dwell on these questions as you continue—put them out of your mind and focus on what lies ahead.

Be sure to read all of the answer choices, even if you're sure the first one is the right answer. Sometimes you'll find a better one if you keep reading. But don't second-guess yourself if you do immediately know the answer. Your gut instinct is usually right. Don't let test anxiety rob you of the information you know.

If you have time at the end of the test (and if the test format allows), go back and review your answers. Be cautious about changing any, since your first instinct tends to be correct, but make sure you didn't misread any of the questions or accidentally mark the wrong answer choice. Look over any you skipped and make an educated guess.

At the end, leave the test feeling confident. You've done your best, so don't waste time worrying about your performance or wishing you could change anything. Instead, celebrate the successful completion of this test. And finally, use this test to learn how to deal with anxiety even better next time.

> **Review Video: Test Anxiety**
> Visit mometrix.com/academy and enter code: 100340

Important Qualification

Not all anxiety is created equal. If your test anxiety is causing major issues in your life beyond the classroom or testing center, or if you are experiencing troubling physical symptoms related to your anxiety, it may be a sign of a serious physiological or psychological condition. If this sounds like your situation, we strongly encourage you to seek professional help.

Additional Bonus Material

Due to our efforts to try to keep this book to a manageable length, we've created a link that will give you access to all of your additional bonus material:

mometrix.com/bonus948/propertycasual

Made in the USA
Coppell, TX
18 January 2025